New Perspectives on Delarivier Manley and Eighteenth-Century Literature

This first critical collection on Delarivier Manley revisits the most heated discussions, adds new perspectives in light of growing awareness of Manley's multifaceted contributions to eighteenth-century literature, and demonstrates the wide range of thinking about her literary production and significance. While contributors reconsider some well-known texts through her generic intertextuality or unresolved political moments, the volume focuses more on those works that have had less attention: dramas, correspondence, journalistic endeavors, and late prose fiction. The methodological approaches incorporate traditional investigations of Manley, such as historical research, gender theory, and comparative close readings, as well as some recently influential theories, like geocriticism and affect studies. This book forges new paths in the many underdeveloped directions in Manley scholarship, including her work's exploration of foreign locales, the power dynamics between individuals and in relation to states, sexuality beyond heteronormativity, and the shifting operations and influences of genre. While it draws on previous writing about Manley's engagement with Whig/Tory politics, gender, and queerness, it also argues for Manley's contributions as a writer with wide-ranging knowledge of both the inner sanctums of London and the outer developing British Empire, an astute reader of politics, a sophisticated explorer of emotional and gender dynamics, and a flexible and clever stylist. In contrast to the many ways Manley has been too easily dismissed, this collection carefully considers many points of view and opens the way for new analyses of Manley's life, work, and vital contributions to the full range of forms in which she wrote.

Aleksondra Hultquist is an Honorary Researcher at the Centre of Excellence for the History of Emotion, 1100–1800, and a Managing Editor of *ABO: Interactive Journal for Women in the Arts, 1640–1830*. She has published articles on Eliza Haywood and Aphra Behn and is currently finishing her monograph, *The Amatory Mode*.

Elizabeth J. Mathews is a PhD candidate at the University of California, Irvine. She has published an essay on Aphra Behn's rhetoric of emotion in *ABO* and is currently working on a study called "Bad Writing: Responses to Early Gothic Fiction and the Cultivation of Emotional Taste."

Routledge Studies in Eighteenth-Century Literature

For a full list of titles in this series, please visit www.routledge.com.

3 The Rise of Literary Journalism in the Eighteenth Century
Anxious Employment
Iona Italia

4 Gender and the Fictions of the Public Sphere, 1690–1755
Anthony Pollock

5 The Female Reader in the English Novel
From Burney to Austen
Joe Bray

6 Originality and Intellectual Property in the French and English Enlightenment
Edited by Reginald McGinnis

7 Eighteenth-Century Authorship and the Play of Fiction
Novels and the Theater, Haywood to Austen
Emily Hodgson Anderson

8 Visuality, Print, and the Body in Eighteenth-Century Satire
"The Scope in Ev'ry Page"
Katherine Mannheimer

9 Mary Wollstonecraft, Pedagogy, and the Practice of Feminism
Kristin Collins Hanley

10 Sex and Death in Eighteenth-Century Literature
Edited by Jolene Zigarovich

11 Women and Gift Exchange in Eighteenth-Century Fiction
Richardson, Burney, Austen
Linda Zionkowski

12 New Perspectives on Delarivier Manley and Eighteenth-Century Literature
Power, Sex, and Text
Edited by Aleksondra Hultquist and Elizabeth J. Mathews

New Perspectives on Delarivier Manley and Eighteenth-Century Literature

Power, Sex, and Text

Edited by Aleksondra Hultquist and Elizabeth J. Mathews

 Routledge
Taylor & Francis Group

NEW YORK AND LONDON

First published 2017
by Routledge
711 Third Avenue, New York, NY 10017

and by Routledge
2 Park Square, Milton Park, Abingdon, Oxon OX14 4RN

Routledge is an imprint of the Taylor & Francis Group, an informa business

© 2017 Taylor & Francis

Library of Congress Cataloging-in-Publication Data

Names: Hultquist, Aleksondra, editor, author. | Mathews, Elizabeth J., editor.
Title: New perspectives on Delarivier Manley and eighteenth-century
literature: power, sex, and text / edited by Aleksondra Hultquist and
Elizabeth J. Mathews.
Description: First edition. | New York; London: Routledge, 2016. |
Series: Routledge studies in eighteenth-century literature; 12 | Includes
bibliographical references and index.
Identifiers: LCCN 2016008111
Subjects: LCSH: Manley, Mrs. (Mary de la Rivière), 1663–1724—Criticism
and interpretation. | Manley, Mrs. (Mary de la Rivière), 1663–1724—
Political and social views. | English literature—18th century—History
and criticism | Power (Social Sciences) in literature. | Sex in literature. |
Literary form. | Women and literature—England—History—18th century.
Classification: LCC PR3545.M8 Z75 2016 | DDC 823/.5—dc23
LC record available at https://lccn.loc.gov/2016008111

ISBN: 978-1-138-67660-2 (hbk)
ISBN: 978-1-315-55999-5 (ebk)

Typeset in Sabon
by codeMantra

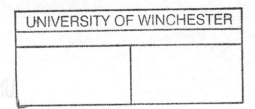

MIX
Paper from
responsible sources
FSC
www.fsc.org   FSC® C013056

Printed and bound in Great Britain by
TJ International Ltd, Padstow, Cornwall

Contents

Foreword   ix
KIRSTEN T. SAXTON

Delarivier Manley Chronology of Works   xiii
Primary Works in Modern or Facsimile Editions   xv
Acknowledgments   xvii

Introduction: Breaking Open the Conversation
on Delarivier Manley   1
ALEKSONDRA HULTQUIST AND ELIZABETH J. MATHEWS

PART I
Power

1 *The Adventures of Rivella* as Political Secret History   15
   RACHEL CARNELL

2 The Politics of Servitude: *The Husband's Resentment.*
   In Two Examples in Delarivier Manley's
   The Power of Love   30
   EARLA WILPUTTE

3 Vengeance, Vows, and "Heroick Vertue": Reforming
   the Revenger in Delarivier Manley's *Almyna:*
   or, The Arabian Vow   43
   MISTY KRUEGER

4 "Through the Black Sea and the Country of Colchis":
   A Geocentric Approach to Delarivier Manley's
   The Royal Mischief (1696)   57
   BERNADETTE ANDREA

PART II
Sex

5 Interrupting Pleasure: Ideology and Affect in Delarivier
   Manley's *The New Atalantis*   75
   ERIN M. KEATING

6 Manley's Single Ladies   92
   JENNIFER FRANGOS

7 Manley's Queer Forms: Repetition, Techno-performativity,
   and the Body   106
   KIM SIMPSON

8 From Pleasure to Power: The Passion of Love in
   The Fair Hypocrite   122
   ALEKSONDRA HULTQUIST

PART III
Text

9 Manley's "Sentimental" Deserted Mistress, Women Writers
   in Literary History, and *The Lost Lover*   137
   VICTORIA JOULE

10 Delarivier Manley Understands the Ladies Better Than You:
   The Female Wits, Genre, and Feminocentric Satire   153
   KATHARINE BEUTNER

11 A Manifesto for a Woman Writer: *Letters Writen* as
   Varronian Satire   171
   CHRIS MOUNSEY

12 Examined in Manley Style: Epistolary Modes in the
   Periodical Writings of Delarivier Manley   188
   JEAN McBAIN

13 The Miscellaneous *New Atalantis*   201
   NICOLA PARSONS

   Afterword   215
   TONI BOWERS

   Selected Bibliography   219
   Contributors   233
   Index   237

Foreword

Kirsten T. Saxton

The genesis of this collection was a special session panel entitled, "'The Lady's Pacquet Broke Open': Narrative Transgression in the Fiction of Behn, Manley, and Haywood," which I organized and chaired at the 1995 Modern Language Association Convention in Chicago as a fifth-year graduate student. At that time, I was advised that the best bet for getting the session approved was to include all three authors. I was over the moon: first to be accepted and then to share the panel with feminist literary critical rock stars Ros Ballaster and Toni Bowers. Ballaster's and Bowers's work was part of a groundswell of 1990s feminist literary scholarship that built on the trailblazing work begun a generation before. Behn, Manley, and Haywood began to be part of larger conversations regarding eighteenth-century studies. In 1993, Heidi Hutner edited the first critical collection on Behn, *Rereading Aphra Behn: History, Theory, and Criticism*,[1] and in 2000, my graduate school colleague Rebecca Bocchicchio and I coedited *The Passionate Fictions of Eliza Haywood: Essays on Her Life and Work*.[2] The critical legacies of these three early British women have since become richly nuanced, and yet in the two decades since that first panel, we have had no critical collection on Manley until now. Some years ago, unsuccessful at getting someone else to take it up, I decided to do it myself. However, my energies were elsewhere, and the collection languished. Over one of those wonderful mentor-y lunches, Rachel Carnell and Catherine Ingrassia gave me "permission" to pass the project on, and it was with delight that I offered the collection to Aleksondra Hultquist and Elizabeth Mathews, members of a newer generation of feminist scholars whose focus and attention beautifully serve both Manley and the essayists and who quickly brought the project to fruition. I am grateful for their excellent work.

Some two decades ago, inspired by the new literary criticism by newly minted professors such as Bowers and Ballaster, my generational cohort (across the country, a whole slew of us) were transfixed by Behn, Manley, and Haywood. We became champions of these texts' messy refusal to be placed easily in histories of the novel or what we indulgently viewed as the liberal history of the previous generation of feminist scholars; we pushed for the addition of *Fantomina* in the *Norton Anthology of Women's Literature*, and we celebrated edited collections and new editions of primary texts.

Those years marked the changing boundaries of eighteenth-century studies: Felicity Nussbaum and Laura Brown's 1987 collection *The New Eighteenth Century* reimagined the field with its inclusion of women writers, non-novelistic prose, and theory. Judith Butler's *Gender Trouble* was hot off the presses, and it seemed that after decades of struggle, the moment of critical truth had arrived. Never again would gender be ignored as a crucial topic, nor would women writers ever again receive less than their fair share of critical attention. At our best, we saw ourselves as appreciative of the previous generation's wisdom, glad for our opportunity to extend their wisdom righteously for the greater critical good. We could broaden their horizons, push their envelopes, and complicate what we deemed their essentialist notions with increasingly nuanced and theoretically informed readings of social positionality and textual complexity.

Of course we too would become the critical generation against whom the next generation could and should push back. Twenty years later, I welcome the expansion of our field and its new critical methodologies, its shifts of attention to new objects of inquiry and new layers of knowledge. Current scholarship, for example, recognizes the complex social connections between male and female writers and usefully traces the results of a variety of claims and impacts on, and in, women's writing. In this collection, for example, contributors read Manley's work in terms of geocriticism, periodical epistolarity, and performative technical narration, approaching her writing in ways that earlier criticism (including my own) left unexamined in our focus on gender politics.

Despite my generally genial vision toward more and new levels of critical awareness and the consistent shaking up of our comfort zones, I do worry about some trends in eighteenth-century studies, particularly in light of current political arguments that we are beyond gender (or race, or other "identity" categories). For example, we need to be diligent regarding the work it takes to keep good critical editions of early women writers in print. As Toni Bowers noted in *Eighteenth Century: Theory & Interpretation*, despite the fact that Janet Todd and Ballaster produced editions of Behn's *Love-letters between a Nobleman and his Sister* (1684–87) and Manley's *The New Atalantis* (1709) for Penguin in the 1990s, both are out of print.[3] Editions, of course, must exist for good scholarship as well as teaching (noncritical editions do not provide adequate substitutes). And, as Alison Conway noted in her 2012 essay "Accessing Liberal Education," "comparing the 2011 ASECS conference program to that of the Austin meeting of 1996, I calculate roughly that session titles naming women and women authors have dropped by almost 50%, from about 15% to 8% of the program."[4] While this may suggest that women writers were simply included without note, an overview of the program suggests this was not the case. I am unsurprised but sad that this wonderful collection has only one male contributor. This gendered disparity suggests to me that women's writing is still not quite central, not entirely, as does a recent inquiry from a colleague asking if my college would consider a candidate whose dissertation was "only on women."

I think that in our own work, with graduate students and colleagues, we can usefully separate out the braided strands of the idea that literary studies have "moved on" from women's writing and feminist theory—a movement that is typical of the cyclical nature of literary critical trends—and the *separate* idea that the realities shaping women's everyday lives have not "moved on" but require attention and action. I wonder about the ways in which my generation might best respond in our own historical moment. How can we map the critical conversation in new directions without ceding old ground? We need simultaneously to push our critical and theoretical work in new directions and to recall the material conditions that underlie that work—conditions in which gender still plays a formidable role. These days particularly we must take a page from Manley, always brave and trenchant in her critiques of the abuse of power, and work collectively to use the power that we have, and that she did not, to address and to work to change the material conditions in which the next generation of scholars and students labor. This collection represents the best sort of labor, the critical conversation, a conversation that is capacious in scope; it is collegial, critical, curious, and groundbreaking. Our task now is to be sure the conversation continues.

Notes

1. Heidi Hutner, ed., *Rereading Aphra Behn: History, Theory, and Criticism* (Charlottesville: UP of Virginia, 1993).
2. Kirsten T. Saxton and Rebecca Bocchicchio, eds., *The Passionate Fictions of Eliza Haywood: Essays on Her Life and Work* (Lexington: UP of Kentucky, 2000).
3. Toni Bowers, "The Achievement of Scholarly Authority for Women: Trends in the Interpretation of Eighteenth-Century Fiction," *Eighteenth Century: Theory and Interpretation* 50.1 (2009): 57. *The New Atalantis*, edited by Ros Ballaster and Alan Freeman, is available from NYU Press (1992).
4. Alison Conway, "Accessing Liberal Education," *ABO: Interactive Journal for Women in the Arts, 1640–1830* 2.1 (March 2012): Open Access, accessed March 5, 2015, http://scholarcommons.usf.edu/cgi/viewcontent.cgi?article=1033&context=abo.

Delarivier Manley Chronology of Works

1695 "To the author of *Agnes de Castro*"
1696 *Letters Writen by Mrs Manley*
The Lost Lover: or, The Jealous Husband, a comedy (staged and published)
The Royal Mischief, a tragedy (staged and published)
1700 *The Nine Muses, or, Poems Written by Nine several Ladies Upon the Death of the late Famous John Dryden esq.*: "Melpomene: The Tragick Muse" and "Thalia: The Comick Muse" (collection was possibly organized and edited by Manley)
1705 **Queen Zara and the Zarazines, Wherein the Amours, Intrigues, and Gallantries of the Court of Albigion, During her Reign, are most Pleasantly Exposed; and as Surprising a Scene of Love and Politics Represented as Perhaps This, or any Other Age or Country has hitherto Produced. Supposed to be Translated from the Italian Copy. Now Lodged in the Vatican at Rome*
1707 *Almyna: or, The Arabian Vow, a tragedy* (staged 1706)
The Lady's Pacquet of Letters, taken from her by a French privateer in her passage to Holland, or, The Lady's Pacquet Broke Open (Part 1)
1708 *The Lady's Pacquet of Letters, taken from her by a French privateer in her passage to Holland, or, The Lady's Pacquet Broke Open (Part 2)*
1709 *Secret Memoirs and Manners of Several Persons of Quality of Both Sexes. From the New Atalantis, an Island in the Mediterranean. Written originally in Italian*
* An Heroick Essay upon the Unequal'd Victory Obtain'd by Major-General Webb over the Count dela Motte at Wynendale
1710 *Memoirs of Europe towards the Close of the Eighth Century. Written by Eginardu, Secretary and Favorite to Charlemange, and Done into English by the Translator of the New Atalantis*
The New Atalantis (reissued)
1711 editor *Examiner* (replacing Jonathan Swift) issues 46–52
Court Intrigues as a Collection of Original Letters from the Island of the New Atalantis, &c. (Previously published as *The Lady's Pacquet of Letters*)
The Duke of M[arlborough]'s Vindication, in Answer to a pamphlet lately published called Bouchain; or a Dialogue between the Medley and the Examiner.

A Learned Comment on Dr. Hare's Sermon

A True Narrative of What Passed at the Examination of the Marquis de Guiscard at the Cock-pit the 8th of March 1710/1711. His Stabbing Mr. Harley and Other Precedent and Subsequent Facts Relating to the Life of the Said Guiscard.

A True Relation of the Several Facts and Circumstances of the Intended Riot and Tumult on Queen Elizabeth's Birthday, Gathered from Authentick Accounts; and Published for the Information of All True Lovers of Our Constitution in Church and State

1713 *The Honour and Prerogative of the Queen's Majesty Vindicated and Defended against the Unexampled Insolences of the Author of the Guardian, in a Letter from a Country Whig to Mr. Steele*

1714 *The Adventures of Rivella, or the History of the Author of the Atalantis, with secret memoirs and characters of several considerable persons, her own contemporaries*

A Modest Inquiry into the Reason of the Joy Expressed by a Certain Sett of people upon the Spreading of a Report on her Majesty's Death

1716 *The New Atalantis* (reissued)

1717 *Lucius, the First Christian King of Britain, A Tragedy* (staged and published)

Memoirs of the Life of Mrs. Manley (a reissue of *Rivella*)

1720 *The Power of Love in Seven Novels: The Fair Hypocrite; The Physician's Stratagem; The Wife's Resentment; The Husband's Resentment. In Two Examples; The Happy Fugitives; The Perjur'd Beauty.*

Lucius, the First Christian King of Britain (reissued)

The New Atalantis (reissued)

1724 *Mrs. Manley's History of Her Own Life and Times* (a reissue of *Rivella*)

1725 *A Stagecoach Journey into Exeter, describing the humour of the road, with the characters and adventures of the company. In eight letters to a friend.* (posthumously published; a reissue of *Letters Writen*)

1736 *The New Atalantis* (reissued)

1741 *The Power of Love* (reissued)

*question of attribution

Primary Works in Modern or Facsimile Editions

Andrea, Bernadette, ed. and intro. *English Women Staging Islam, 1696–1707: Delarivier Manley and Mary Pix*. Toronto: Iter/Centre for Reformation and Renaissance Studies, 2012.

Ballaster, Ros, ed. *The New Atalantis*. New York: Penguin, 1992.

Ballaster, Ros, and Alan Freeman, eds. *The New Atalantis*. New York: NYU Press, 1992.

Carnell, Rachel, and Ruth Herman, eds. *The Selected Works of Delarivier Manley*. 5 vols. London: Pickering and Chatto, 2005.

Hodgson-Wright, Stephanie, Anne Lake Prescott, and Betty S. Travitsky, eds. *Delarivier Manley*. Aldershot: Ashgate, 2006.

Stevenson, Jane, and Peter Davidson. *Early Modern Women Poets (1520–1700): An Anthology*. Oxford: Oxford University Press, 2001.

Zelinsky, Katherine, ed. *The Adventures of Rivella*. Peterbourough, ONT: Broadview, 1999.

Acknowledgments

The editors would like to thank Kirsten T. Saxton, whose panel at the 1995 Modern Language Association Convention was the impetus for this collection. We have been honored to move the project from her idea to final product, and her confidence in our abilities and her supportive mentoring have been invaluable. Our contributors have been by turns patient, supportive, intellectually challenging, and responsive. Their ideas and research are, of course, at the core of this book, and all have been a pleasure to work with. We especially appreciate their willingness to read and engage with each other's essays, which made this collection truly a conversation. This project has had two excellent editors: the first, Ann Donahue of Ashgate, who was enthusiastic about the project from the beginning, and whose gracious introduction of Elizabeth Levine at Routledge allowed the book to come to fruition when it was uncertain that it would.

Aleksondra Hultquist would like to thank the Australian Research Council's Centre of Excellence for the History of Emotion, 1100–1800, and the University of Melbourne, which provided funding for research and travel for this project. Several colleagues from Australia have provided emotional and intellectual support, including Katherine Firth and Andreas Loewe (who provided valuable feedback and, most importantly, a room of my own), Jean McBain, Grace Moore, Bronwyn Reddan, Jessica Scott, and Stephanie Trigg. Very early research for this work occurred at the Chawton House Library in 2010, when Jacqueline Granger was the librarian; her ability to find nuggets of gold is unsurpassed. Untiring professional encouragement came from Ros Ballaster, Toni Bowers, Jennie Batchelor, Karen Gevirtz, Robert Markley, and Kirsten T. Saxton. Jim Hultquist, Carmela and Thomas Pogranicy, Amy Scholes (and all the Ballet Mums), Lesley Sieger-Walls, and Ana Torres have provided the things an academic needs most: sympathetic ears, time, financial support, and childcare. And finally, special thanks to Al Coppola, best reader and fiercest ally, who unconditionally sustains all that I do; for you my thanks is more than I can express and a sliver of what you deserve.

Elizabeth Mathews is grateful to The Huntington Library, San Marino, California, for its imaging services, and to the University of California, Irvine, for its excellent research access. Nick Tamburro encouraged me through all the twists and turns of this project and gave me the hours I needed to complete it—without him, my professional life would not be possible.

Introduction

Breaking Open the Conversation on Delarivier Manley

Aleksondra Hultquist and Elizabeth J. Mathews

Delarivier Manley (c. 1667/72–1724) was the foremost woman writer in the age of Queen Anne, a master of exposing private information, as she did in her *Lady's Pacquet Broke Open* (1707) or the more famous *New Atalantis* (1709). Eighteenth-century scholars unfamiliar with Manley's corpus may still have heard of her, perhaps as the sensationalist who penned a character who murders and chops up her bigamous husband to obtain justice, or the woman who contracted her own (possibly accidental) bigamous marriage, or the peer of contemporaries who have a bit more cultural cachet, like Richard Steele and Jonathan Swift, or the target of satires like *The Female Wits* (staged 1696) and *The Dunciad* (1728). Despite or because of her reputation, her writing earned her extreme popularity in her time and critical condemnation in the centuries after her death.

Recovery work has enabled the critical moment in which we find ourselves, where Manley is increasingly known and studied; however, she has yet to receive the attention devoted to Aphra Behn and Eliza Haywood, her fellow members of the "triumvirate of wit." Early work from feminist critics, especially Ros Ballaster's *Seductive Forms* (1992), has done much to place Manley on the radar of scholarship and encourage the recuperation of her works. But much of that early work can be expanded upon. Twenty-first-century Manley scholarship, especially the work of Rachel Carnell and Ruth Herman, has established Manley as a writer who merits analysis in conjunction with subjects like party politics, imperialism, sexuality, violence, and genre. Yet, while the critical conversation grows, not enough voices have joined.

The attention of respected scholars over the last several decades has not yet erased the stigma of previous critics' dismissal. In English departments otherwise inclusive of women writers and popular texts, some professors still discourage young scholars from working on such a marginal author, and though the most recent Norton anthology references Manley in its introduction, it does not feature her writing.[1] Nevertheless, the study of Manley has burgeoned in recent years, with scholars exploring her life and work through conference papers, articles, and monographs. This book, the first multiauthor collection on Manley, aims to give the author a firm push toward canonicity with the many rich and varied conversations contained herein.

Biography

In addition to the longstanding trend of critical dismissal of Manley's work, the lack of reliable sources on Manley's life has posed a challenge to scholars who wish to situate this scholar in her milieu. Her life is a swarm of rumors, lies, and exaggerations surrounding a carefully crafted public personality. The actual documentary record of her life contains (to date) some letters to Robert Harley, Earl of Oxford; a debt transfer and notice of imprisonment in 1705; and her arrest for libel in 1709. Other than these, we have her published works and other people's letters in which she is mentioned, and what Herman has called her scraps of correspondence.[2] She requested that her personal papers be destroyed after her death. From various communications about her, we can gather she was witty, extremely charming, a very capable writer, and a poor speller.[3]

Carnell has drawn attention to Manley's sophisticated textual flexibility through the author's creation of her own distinctive narrative style, which is quasi-autobiographical, quasi-political, and quasi-fictional.[4] Manley spent much of her career creating herself rhetorically as a character; clearly her self-crafted emblematic image, that of Rivella in *The Adventures of Rivella* (1714) and of Delia in *The New Atalantis*, was the one she wanted to leave as her biographical legacy.[5] As such, everything she states about herself (much of it through the voices of others, or through a third-person description) must be taken critically; the actual biography of Manley, once edited for self-aggrandizement, prejudices, and rumors, is rather scarce.

We know for certain that she was the daughter of Sir Roger Manley (c. 1621–1687) and Marie-Catherine (c. 1643–1675). Her father was a royalist who spent years in exile during the Commonwealth government as a military officer and historian; he was unexceptionally successful at both. Her mother was a French-speaking noblewoman from the Spanish Netherlands and died when Manley was quite young, maybe as early as her infancy or as late as when she was five years old. Because there is no surviving record of her birth, we cannot substantiate her birth place or year, but Manley was likely born on the Isle of Jersey, where her father was lieutenant governor, between 1667 and 1672. We have little information on her early childhood. Her father's will notes that she was one of five children at the time of his death. She seems to have been educated at home, and though her specific education is unclear (scholars disagree about whether it was a typically feminine education or the "liberal" education of a young man, as she claims), she was obviously widely read and proud of her ability to be conversant on many topics.

By her father's death in 1687 Manley was of a marriageable age, and she claimed in her works that she had been hoping for an appointment to the court of Mary of Modena prior to James II's 1688 abdication. Her father's modest career success and fortune provided little dowry, and her face was severely scarred from a childhood bout of smallpox. Neither wealth nor beauty would have secured her a suitable marriage, but it seems that her charming personality, quick wit, and pleasing manners almost made up for these deficiencies. From what we can tell, she would have made a charismatic courtier.

In *The New Atalantis*, Manley claims to have been seduced, married, possessed, and ruined by her cousin (and possibly one of her legal guardians), John Manley, about fifteen years her senior, whose wife was alive at the time. Scholars and biographers often see this incident as the pivotal point in her life—this social "ruin" led to her needing to financially support herself with a career in writing.[6] There are several ways of interpreting this marriage: John as bored enough to seduce his cousin, or anxious enough to need ready cash (Manley's moderate inheritance was quickly run through); Delarivier as anxious to leave a quiet life in the country for a residence in London; their need to hide an illegitimate pregnancy; her possible delusions about the viability and legality of polygamy. We, of course, do not know if she was aware that his wife was still living, if they had been sexually involved before the marriage, or even by whom the ceremony was performed (though it was likely a dissenting minister). Regardless, they had a son christened in Westminster in 1691. Manley seems to have discovered about this time (if she didn't know before) that the marriage was bigamous and therefore illegal. By 1694 she was living with Barbara Palmer (nee Villiers), Duchess of Cleveland, and she left the household soon after, having been accused of trying to seduce Cleveland's son, an illegitimate child of Charles II. Manley seems to have left London and lived in Exeter or somewhere else in the "West Country" until about 1696, when two plays were produced in London and she had composed a draft (at least) of *Letters Writen*. This, along with her published poems in *The Nine Muses*[7] in London in 1700, marks (for the modern scholar) the beginning of her professional writing career.

She was the mistress of John Tilly, governor of Fleet prison, between 1697 and 1702. There are hints of risks and schemes—this is the time when she was involved with the infamous and (so she hoped) profitable Bath-Albemarle trial, recounted in *Rivella* (her involvement yielded no financial benefit). The years between 1702 and 1709 were likely tumultuous ones for her. Tilly married a wealthy widow; Manley was very ill; she was in Fleet prison in 1705 (for debt?); she may have had up to three children to provide (or arrange) for and worry about;[8] she met and fell out with Richard Steele. J. A. Downie has suggested (and Carnell's work deeply supports) that she was not yet writing political propaganda.[9] (In this collection, however, Chris Mounsey argues that her political writing strategies may have started as early as 1696.) In 1706 her play *The Royal Mischief* (written 1696) was rather unsuccessfully produced, and in 1707 came the publication of *The Lady's Pacquet of Letters ..., Or, The Lady's Pacquet Broke Open*, which documents her friendship with Richard Steele.[10] By 1709 *The New Atalantis* was published, and this text inaugurated the main interpretation of Manley as a political satirist. She was arrested and interrogated as its author in 1709, though the charges were dropped. We are unsure what portion of the text, exactly, caused the arrest.

Between 1711 and 1713 she was known as a leading figure for Tory propaganda, distinguished by publications of the second part of *The New Atalantis* and *Memoirs of Europe* in 1710. In 1711, she became editor of the *Examiner* (issue numbers 46–52), replacing Jonathan Swift, a friend whom she seems to have met through her printer (and likely lover) John Barber. She wrote several pamphlets for Swift, including *The D. of M——h's Vindication* and *Learned Comment*, in 1711. By 1712, her health was not good; Barber feared her death by dropsy, and though she lived another twelve years, she was severely affected by ill health for the rest of her life.

The Adventures of Rivella was published in 1714, and she seems to have been enjoying a run of fame and perhaps fortune from the reprints of *New Atalantis*. Her final play, *Lucius, the First Christian King of Britain*, was produced in Theatre Royal in Drury Lane in 1717 and ran for fifteen successive nights to crowded houses.[11] So despite the Hanoverian succession, a political change that might have ended her career as a Tory satirist, Manley appears to have been clever and flexible enough to write, publish, produce, and get paid. She was living independently near Oxford by 1717, gaining respectability and reputation through her talent, political acumen, and literary friendships.

By 1719 she had written *The Power of Love in Seven Novels*, a collection of adapted novellas published in 1720. It was her final recognized published work, though Herman claims that she was writing and publishing poetry at the time.[12] Manley died in 1724 after prolonged illness. Her reputation as a witty conversationalist, clever writer, and attentive mentor lasted for several decades after her death, but as soon as 1785 Clara Reeve in *The Progress of Romance* declared Manley to be scandalous, exceptionable, and gradually sinking into oblivion.[13] As Carnell has argued, various revisionist perspectives—the ascension of Whig politics, increasingly restrictive Victorian morality, personal grudges (like Winston Churchill's biography of his ancestor the Duke of Marlborough), and the "rise" of the novel—had a great amount of power in diminishing her latterly acquired reputation for respectability.

Breaking Open Bibliography and Criticism

Along with the slippage of biography is the slippage of bibliography. We still have no extensive bibliography, as Mary Ann O'Donnell and Patrick Spedding have provided for us for Aphra Behn and Eliza Haywood.[14] Scholars have been questioning the bibliographical lists to be sure that what we are reading is in fact attributable to Manley, such as J. A. Downie's above-mentioned casting of well-considered doubt on the authorship of *Queen Zarah*, and Herman's recent poetic attributions.[15] While her outright plagiarism is not entirely confirmed by Carnell, the "flexibility" of Manley's borrowings is certainly clear.[16] But scholars also wonder what more might belong to Manley's oeuvre. Just as the information about Manley is piecemeal and scattered, so are the modern publications of her works. Most eighteenth-century scholars are familiar only with *The Adventures of Rivella* and *The New Atalantis*, in part because of twentieth-century reprints. Today, only Katherine Zelinsky's Broadview edition of *Rivella* (1999) is still available in an affordable edition.[17] Meanwhile, the rest of her works have few easily accessible modern editions. While facsimile editions of her work can be ordered and electronic editions can be accessed, they are difficult for new scholars to read, and sometimes illegible due to errors in scanning.[18] The only scholarly collection of works by Carnell and Herman is "Selected," and its price makes it out of reach in terms of an edition for teaching or studying for most young scholars. (Many contributors to this collection found it difficult to get hold of Carnell and Herman's edition.) While numerous eighteenth-century writers' works have become available online in recent years, Manley's have lagged behind this trend. We hope that this edition inspires accessible editions of her works so that future students and scholars have the chance to break open the critical conversation as has happened in Aphra Behn and Eliza Haywood studies.

Scholarship on Delarivier Manley has provided an excellent solid foundation on which the literary scholar can draw.[19] Ros Ballaster, Rachel Carnell, and Ruth Herman have especially ensured that Manley is properly positioned in terms of her historical trail, not just her historical reputation.[20] Last century's energetic scholarship revolving around the rise of the novel suggests her important contributions to early prose fiction, but recent criticism points out that this association may have done her more harm than good by depicting her as a "bad" novelist, as Toni Bowers's Afterword in this collection emphasizes.[21] Manley's central place as a writer of secret histories has been firmly established.[22] Important discussions concentrate on gendered aspects of Manley's writing and its connection to social and political realms, especially as she contributes to party politics.[23] Even so, much remains to be done, and the existing scholarship is ripe for reconsideration in light of growing awareness of Manley's multifaceted contributions to eighteenth-century literature. This, the first critical collection on Manley, begins that vital work by revisiting the most heated critical discussions and adding new perspectives that will change the conversation.

Breaking Open Power, Sex, and Text

We organize the chapters in three distinct but interconnecting sections where Manley scholarship currently is being broken open: "Power," "Sex," and "Text." Individually, each essay distinguishes itself by its particular engagement with an aspect of Manley studies that many have considered closed for discussion or that has never been opened in the first place. As a compilation, the essays demonstrate the wide range of thinking about Manley's literary production and the significance of this influential author. While authors reconsider some of her well-known texts through her generic intertextuality or unresolved political moments, the collection focuses more on those works that have been less studied: her dramas, her correspondence, her journalistic endeavors, and her late prose fiction. The methodological approaches in this collection incorporate traditional approaches to Manley, such as historical research, gender theory, and comparative close readings, as well as some of the recently influential approaches such as geocriticism and affect studies.

We begin the collection with the section "Power," which reexamines an area of particular energy in Manley studies thus far. One of the most fruitful discussions of Manley to date has to do with her relationship to the Tory Ministry and her complicated association to the propaganda machines of both Whig and Tory governments, especially in conversations begun by Ros Ballaster, Toni Bowers, Rachel Carnell, and Ruth Herman. Such readings have situated Manley's work in terms of "new-Tory" writing, political vows, and the close relationship between imaginative writing and law.[24] Additionally, scholars like Bernadette Andrea have addressed Manley's presentation of imperial issues.[25] The section on "Power" in this collection builds on these political perspectives on Manley's work. In this section, scholars use historical, political, and geographical contexts to reconsider the power dynamics that play out in Manley's literature—particularly the political dimensions of personal matters. This section demonstrates that never far from Manley's texts is the insistence that the power the privileged wield can be countered by the more furtive, and very disruptive power, available to the disenfranchised, the secretive, and the subtle.

Rachel Carnell, the initiator of many vital conversations on Manley, opens the section with her contribution, "*The Adventures of Rivella* as Political Secret History." In this essay, Carnell demonstrates that recontextualizing *Rivella* as a political secret history rather than a generically unstable autobiography illuminates the political nature of Manley's maneuverings within and around this work. By refocusing attention from her own scandals, which could have been exploited by political opponents, to the scandals of others, Manley announced herself to be a continuing threat to whoever was unwise enough to make an enemy of her. In this way, Carnell shows that Manley's deft use of information for personal and political gain creates surprising commonality with Sarah, Duchess of Marlborough, her political opponent. Carnell looks past the history of reframing *Rivella* as personal to assert the text's, and Manley's, political context and influence.

Earla Wilputte also clarifies the political nature of what appears to be Manley's apolitical work. In contrast to scholars who have dismissed *The Power of Love* (1720) as overly didactic and disengaged from current affairs, Wilputte reads the *Husband's Resentment* novels from the collection as equivocal, and thus critical of established social and political norms. In her essay "The Politics of Servitude: *The Husband's Resentment. In Two Examples*," Wilputte delineates Manley's subtle depiction of abuses of power. While carefully considering the distinctive power dynamics of different relationships, Wilputte draws parallels among servants, wives, subjects, and authors to reveal the complexity of servitude.

In "Vengeance, Vows, and 'Heroick Vertue': Reforming the Revenger in Delarivier Manley's *Almyna: or, The Arabian Vow*," Misty Krueger analyzes another understudied work in the Manley corpus. She shows how *Almyna* (staged 1706) was at the forefront of a nationalistic trend in theater toward reason and bloodless resolution. Focusing on Manley's portrayal of revenge, Krueger evaluates the way in which Manley's heroine uses persuasive speeches to embody masculine civic virtue while countering vengeful men's dangerous effeminacy, establishing the importance of women's peacekeeping role.

Bernadette Andrea's essay "'Through the Black Sea and the Country of Colchis': A Geocentric Approach to Delarivier Manley's *The Royal Mischief* (1696)" expands the section's consideration of power to a global scale, situating Manley's play within its setting's multilayered imperial investments. Andrea maps Colchis's long history of depiction as a space of cultural interaction, which resonates in *The Royal Mischief* to create a work that destabilizes the prevalent binary of East/West and centers feminine capability. Using geocriticism, Andrea delves deeply into the sometimes misidentified setting of Colchis, drawing on sources that Manley could have been aware of. The tradition of the region as a borderland and its role in early modern Europe's imperial narrative highlight Manley's participation in a larger discourse on gender, place, and power.

The "Sex" section extends work on gender and sexuality in Manley. Previous scholarship has engaged in feminist readings of her texts, and Terry Castle, Ruth Herman, David Michael Robinson, and Jane Spencer have begun the work of queering Manley, especially in the scenes of the Ladies of the New Cabal of *The New Atalantis*.[26] "Sex" demonstrates the ways in which Manley's corpus investigates the subtleties of the political and emotional aspects of sex, sexuality, and gender. While overt sexuality, adultery, and violence have been explored in Manley's works, the nuances of queerness, asexuality, emotionality, and affective perspectives have not. The scholarship in this section reexamines the reiteration of sex and love in her works, exploring the generative possibilities her portrayals suggest.

Erin M. Keating examines an old favorite in a new light in her essay, "Interrupting Pleasure: Ideology and Affect in Delarivier Manley's *The New Atalantis*." Keating describes the affective dynamics of Manley's treatments of virtue, sex, and physicality in general, showing how Manley draws attention to the construction, aesthetics, and destructiveness of ideas of feminine virtue and contrasts their artificiality and eroticized distress with the fully material body. Keating complicates the accepted views on Manley's signature text and her approach to feminine virtue by revealing a critique of the erotic spectacle of female suffering. However, she argues that Manley cannot present a satisfying alternative to this spectacle, given the strictures of genre and society.

Jennifer Frangos picks up the thread of Manley's alternatives but views these possibilities as more promising for women. In "Manley's Single Ladies,"

Frangos focuses on the hitherto neglected subject of asexuality. Through the lens of the new asexuality movement, Frangos sees coherence between the choices of some of Manley's single characters and the presentation of her fictionalized self. This reading extends Manley's critique of the sexual double standard to the decision of some of her characters to opt out of heterosexual exchange altogether. Frangos's essay adds to a body of work that challenges a heteronormative approach to eighteenth-century studies.

Kim Simpson also presents a nonheteronormative reading of Manley's work in "Manley's Queer Forms: Repetition, Techno-performativity, and the Body," which asserts that her maligned use of formula can be read as proto-queer. Simpson considers the citationality and materiality in Manley's work and the relationship between the two. She argues that Manley's repetitions in relation to gender and sexuality establish a world of oppressive necessity and constructed identities, while also creating openings for productive disruption. Like Keating, Simpson reads Manley's fictional pregnant bodies as not just warnings against sex, but textual opportunities with transformative potential.

Aleksondra Hultquist concludes the section by demonstrating how Manley's portrayal of desire in *The Power of Love* was in conversation with her source material and a body of work on the passions in "From Pleasure to Power: The Passion of Love in *The Fair Hypocrite*." Taking seriously the creative work of Manley's adaptation (as her contemporaries would have), Hultquist reveals that Manley's alterations to Painter's tale qualify his message about the destructive nature of desire and saving grace of virtue. Manley's *Fair Hypocrite* instead emphasizes the virtuous quality of desire itself, both for the state and for individuals. This essay asserts the importance of one of Manley's most dismissed literary productions as a significant player in the discourse of the passions that permeated eighteenth-century philosophical conversations.

Finally, the section "Text" demonstrates how Manley has made vital contributions to the full range of forms in which she wrote, synthesizing existing genres and creating new ones that resonate in literature for generations. For decades, Manley has carried the stigma of being a "bad" writer, both morally and aesthetically. The critical tendency to read her secret histories as novels caused her to be perceived as a weak novelist rather than a clever political stylist. Her repetition of seduction scenes, violent betrayals, and powerful and sometimes violent women became a practice readers could not see past, much less see an inherent value in. These essays reconceive the ways in which Manley plays with genre and texts, writing and thinking, and argue that Manley influenced her own and others' approaches to satire, periodical writing, and drama. Her textual forays created the satiric prose author that we know. The essays in this section explain how that occurred.

Recognizing Manley's contribution to the creation of sentimental comedy, Victoria Joule argues that the often-dismissed play *The Lost Lover* (1696) deserves serious consideration. In "Manley's 'Sentimental' Deserted Mistress,

Women Writers in Literary History, and *The Lost Lover*," Joule shows how Manley's play departs definitively from previous comedic tradition, claiming sympathy for the deserted mistress type and punishing rather than reforming the rake. Her analysis of the play's performance history explains the play's lack of success and the resonance Manley likely intended it to have. Finally, Joule touches on Manley's treatment of models for women writers and the investment of sympathy for women more broadly.

Like Joule, Katharine Beutner addresses Manley's treatment of women writers, as well as her treatment as a woman writer. In "Delarivier Manley Understands the Ladies Better Than You: *The Female Wits*, Genre, and Feminocentric Satire," Beutner presents the possibility that the depiction of Manley in *The Female Wits* reveals a truer portrait of the author (or at least a facet of her) than Manley scholarship currently acknowledges. She suggests a broadening of the term *feminocentric* to include not only positivist, proto-feminist agendas, but also reciprocal female-authored satire, regardless of its cruelty. Linking the attacks on Manley and her own attacks on female writers to Manley's literary ambition, Beutner argues that a clear view of Manley's career is only possible when looking at her work holistically, across the many genres in which she wrote.

Chris Mounsey, in "A Manifesto for a Woman Writer: *Letters Writen* as Varronian Satire" approaches the beginning of Manley's career with a similarly transgeneric perspective. Mounsey suggests that the first three of Manley's known published works form a previously unrecognized strategy, the key to which lies in *Letters Writen* (1696), which he reads as an early experiment with Varronian satire. Mounsey finds Varronian techniques and political attacks in the preface and epistolary narrative of *Letters Writen*, which could shed light on Manley's political allegiances and career hiatus and forge a connection to Manley's work in the later *Atalantis*. By reframing Manley's initial dabbling in different genres as the canny work of a satirist, he makes a case for Manley's early importance as a stylist.

Jean McBain also addresses Manley's epistolary technique in her essay, "Examined in Manley Style: Epistolary Modes in the Periodical Writings of Delarivier Manley." Focusing on the neglected aspects of form and style in Manley's *Examiner* writing (1711), McBain reads Manley's *Examiner* work in the context of the epistolary tradition within periodicals, which entails a different relationship to authenticity, authority, impartiality, and publicity than the epistolary secret history. By attending to the rhetorical functions of letters within periodicals, McBain contributes to an understanding of Manley's stylistic range and to the study of eighteenth-century periodicals in general.

In the final chapter of the collection, "The Miscellaneous *New Atalantis*," Nicola Parsons revisits Manley's most famous work from a previously overlooked formal perspective. Parsons directs attention to the structure of the text, arguing that its fragmentary, digressive features engage deliberately with a literary tradition. By detailing this tradition and exploring the effects of Manley's own miscellaneity, Parsons complicates our received under-standing of the text's political intent and furthers the work of attending to the textual details that have long been neglected in Manley studies.

Though we have grouped these essays under the larger rubrics of the themes of power, sex, and text, many of them could move fluidly between such organizational themes. Most of the essays in this collection address genre in some way, which reflects the extent of Manley's abilities as a writer, the tendency of her work to blur formal boundaries, and the way that criti-cal readings and misreadings of generic categories shape perceptions of the works themselves. Connections among the personal, social, and political appear often in these essays, illuminating Manley's interest in power dynam-ics. Reputation also figures heavily, as Manley's fictional concern as well as the object of careful and skilled negotiation in her real life. More than one essay addresses the affective dimensions of Manley's texts, which are ripe for this approach. It is a strength that arguments about genre, gender, politics, perception, and emotion cross in work on Manley. In addition to making these essays rich, this complexity also indicates that we have arrived at a generative critical moment in Manley studies.

The current Manley scholarship is invested in contradiction. Contradiction not just in the sense of contesting previous claims or correcting ahistorical readings, but also in reconciling what appear to be contradictory interpre-tations. Manley invites many such contradictory interpretations: she can be read as a genius or a hack, proto-feminist or antifeminist, Orientalist or counter-Orientalist, classist or not, a staunch Tory or a political oppor-tunist, canny or vicious. In contrast to the many ways Manley has been too easily dismissed, this collection carefully considers many points of view, and opens the way for new ones on the subjects in this volume as well as the many aspects of Manley's work and life that remain to be addressed. The "breaking" this collection performs is neither violent nor divisive; it is the work of scholars who are ready to crack the seal on critical conversations old and new, and to let the discussion unfold.

Notes

1. *The Norton Anthology of English Literature: The Restoration and the Eighteenth Century*, 9th ed. (New York: Norton, 2012), 2,192. The Longman anthology does not mention her at all.
2. Ruth Herman, *The Business of a Woman: Political Writings of Delarivier Manley* (Newark, DE: University of Delaware Press, 2003), 30.
3. Both catalogs of the British Library and the United States Library of Congress have her listed as "Mrs. (Mary de la Rivière) Manley." There is no evidence that she was christened as a "Mary" nor that she ever referred to herself as such. She used the name "Dela" in her correspondence and publications.
4. Rachel Carnell, *A Political Biography of Delarivier Manley* (London: Pickering and Chatto, 2008), 13. See also Ruth Herman, "An Exercise in Early Modern Branding," *Journal of Marketing Management* 19, no. 7–8 (2003).

5. Carnell, 51–2.
6. Carnell, 71. Ballaster suggests that the break with John Manley may have taken several years, viii–xi.
7. This was a collection of elegies in honor of John Dryden; all four contributors to the collection—Sarah Fyge Egerton, Mary Pix, Catharine Trotter, and Susanna Centlivre—were later satitrized as disloyal friends and Whig loyalists in *The New Atalantis*. Ballaster xiii.
8. Rachel Carnell, "Delarivier Manley's Possible Children by John Tilly," *Notes and Queries* (2007): 446–48.
9. J. A. Downie, "What If Manley Did Not Write *The Secret History of Queen Zarah?*" *Library: The Transactions of the Bibliographical Society* 5 (2004): 247–64. Ros Ballaster suggests that *The Royal Mischeif*, produced in 1696, was overtly political. Ballaster, xi–xii. Herman reads her work in specific political contexts; see especially Ch. 1, *Business*, for political leanings in Manley's early work.
10. Part 2 of the *Lady's Pacquet* was published one year later (1708) as *The Unknown Lady's Pacquet*. Manley's works are published along with Marie Catherine La Motte, Baronne d'Aulnoy's *Memoirs of the Court of England* and *The History of the Earl of Warwick*.
11. Carnell, *Political Biography*, 220.
12. Herman, *Business of a Woman*, 32–33. Herman also has found evidence of a possible additional volume of *The New Atalantis*, though such a text, if it exists, has never been found. It may simply have been an advertising ploy.
13. Clara Reeve, *The Progress of Romance* (London 1785), 118–20.
14. Mary Ann O'Donnell, *Aphra Behn: An Annotated Bibliography of Primary and Secondary Sources* (New York: Garland, 1986). Patrick Spedding, *A Bibliography of Eliza Haywood* (London: Pickering and Chatto, 2004).
15. Ruth Herman "A New Attribution to Delarivier Manley?" *Notes and Queries* 48 no. 4. (2001): 401–03.
16. Rachel Carnell, "More Borrowing from Bellegarde in Delarivier Manley's *Queen Zarah and the Zarazains*," *Notes and Queries* 51 (2004): 377–79.
17. Ros Ballaster and Alan Freeman's *Atalantis* edition from NYU Press (1992) is available but rather expensive, and the affordable Penguin edition (1992/3) is out of print.
18. Published facsimiles include Mary Delarivier Manley and Patricia Köster, *The Novels of Mary Delariviere Manley, Vol. 2* (Gainseville, FL: Scholars' Facsimiles and Reprints, 1971) and Stephanie Hodgson-Wright, *Delarivier Manley* (Aldershot: Ashgate, 2006).
19. Ballaster's 1992 Penguin edition of *The New Atalantis* contains a bibliographic list of her works, though some attributions are currently in doubt and others may be missing.
20. See Carnell's *Political Biography* and Herman's *Business*, and Ballaster's introduction to *The New Atalantis* and *Seductive Forms: Women's Amatory Fiction 1684–1740* (Oxford: Clarendon Press, 1992).
21. See especially J. Paul Hunter, *Before Novels* (New York: Norton, 1990); Micheal McKeon, *Origins of the English Novel* (Baltimore: Johns Hopkins University Press, 1989); and John J. Richetti, *Popular Fiction before Richardson: Narrative Patterns 1700–1739* (Oxford: Clarendon Press, 1969).
22. See especially Ballaster, *Seductive Forms*; Eve Tavor Bannet, "'Secret History': Or, Talebearing inside and Outside the Secretoire," *Huntington Library Quarterly* 68,

no. 1/2 (2005): 375–96; Rebecca Bullard, *The Politics of Disclosure 1674–1725: Secret History Narratives* (London: Pickering & Chatto, 2009); and Nicola Parsons, *Reading Gossip in Early Eighteenth-Century England* (Basingstoke: Palgrave Macmillan, 2009).

23. For gender and society see especially Catherine Gallagher, *Nobody's Story: The Vanishing Acts of Women Writers in the Marketplace, 1670–1820* (Berkeley: University of California Press, 1994); Paula McDowell, *The Women of Grub Street: Press, Politics, and Gender in the London Literary Marketplace* (Oxford: Clarendon Press, 1998); and Janet Todd, *The Sign of Angellica: Women, Writing and Fiction, 1660–1800* (New York: Columbia University Press, 1989). For Manley's contributions to political writing, see especially Herman; Melinda Alliker Rabb, *Satire and Secrecy in English Literature from 1650 to 1750* (New York: Palgrave Macmillan, 2007); and Carole Fungaroli Sargent, "How a Pie Fight Satirizes Whig-Tory Conflict in Delarivier Manley's *The New Atalantis*," *Eighteenth-Century Studies* 44.4 (2011): 515–33.

24. See especially Toni Bowers, *Force or Fraud* (Oxford: Oxford University Press, 2012) and Kathryn Temple "Manley's 'Feigned Scene': The Fictions of Law at Westminster Hall," *Eighteenth-Century Fiction* 22 (2010).

25. See Bernadette Andrea, *English Women Staging Islam, 1696–1707: Delarivier Manley and Mary Pix* (Toronto: Iter/Centre for Reformation and Renaissance Studies, 2012). Also *Women and Islam in Early Modern English Literature* (Cambridge: Cambridge University Press, 2007).

26. Terry Castle (ed and intro), *The Literature of Lesbianism: A Historical Anthology from Ariosto to Stonewall* (New York: Columbia University Press, 2003). See also Ruth Herman's reading of gender and sexuality in "Enigmatic Gender in Delarivier Manley's *New Atalantis*," in Chris Mounsey, ed. *Presenting Gender: Changing Sex in Early-modern Culture*. Lewisburg, PA: Bucknell University Press, 2001, 202–24; David Michael Robinson, "'For How can they be guilty?' Lesbian and Bisexual Women in Manley's *New Atalantis*," *Nineteenth-century Contexts* 23 (2001): 187–220; Jane Spencer, *Rise of the Woman Novelist: From Aphra Behn to Jane Austen* (Oxford and New York: Basil Blackwell, 1986).

Part I
Power

1　*The Adventures of Rivella* as Political Secret History

Rachel Carnell

Delarivier Manley's *The Adventures of Rivella* (1714) has long fascinated modern scholars, because of its complicated narrative frame, its coy expression of a public female voice, and its complex relationship to other literary genres.[1] Critics describe Manley's textual mix of fact and fiction as a "quasi-fictional autobiography" or a "pseudo-autobiography."[2] Some scholars have found that the work gives them insights into eighteenth-century conceptions of law.[3] Toni Bowers has recently argued that we should view the work neither as fictionalized autobiography nor as political scandal novel, but as a "precursor to the late twentieth-century literary form that has come to be known … as 'faction'—a deliberately destabilizing mixture of fact and fiction."[4] However, viewing *Rivella* as almost postmodern in its generic instability detaches the work from the primary genre Manley was working in: the political secret history. In recognizing the markers of secret history within this work, we may see how the work functioned as both an autobiography and a political power play when it first appeared in the last month of Queen Anne's reign.

Manley's best-selling *Secret Memoirs and Manners of several Persons of Quality of both sexes, From … the New Atalantis* (1709) and *Memoirs of Europe* (1710) often appeared to twentieth-century readers as poorly organized novels.[5] However, in Manley's own era, they would have been legible as anecdotal political secret histories, a genre popular in the late seventeenth century for opposition political propagandists who strung together *petites histoires*, anecdotal "little histories," to counteract the grand narratives of the party in power.[6] This genre was deployed by Whigs critical of Charles II's ties to France, following the model of Procopius's *Anekdota*, which had appeared in popular English translations in 1674 and 1682. As Annabel Patterson and Rebecca Bullard have shown, these Whig secret histories from the 1670s and 1680s often described Charles's extramarital affairs, emphasizing the control his mistresses held over him and so casting doubt on his ability to stand up for himself or his nation against the French monarch Louis XIV. The popularity of this largely Whig political genre continued during the Exclusion crises and into the reign of James II, as concern about that monarch's Catholicism intensified.[7] In William and Mary's reign, Whig secret histories helped reinforce Whig ideology, but with the accession of

Queen Anne in 1702, Tory secret histories, such as *The Secret History of Queen Zarah and the Zarazians* (1705, previously believed to be written by Manley but now attributed to Joseph Browne), mocked court figures including Sarah Churchill, Duchess of Marlborough, a staunch lobbyist for the Whigs.

Manley followed the new trend of adapting the Whiggish genre of secret history to Tory ends in her *Secret Memoirs and Manners ... From the New Atalantis*, which includes anecdotes from the reign of Charles II, the backdrop to previous Whig secret histories.[8] Once the Whig ministry had been dismissed in 1710, Manley did not write another full-length political secret history, although she continued to write pamphlets, alongside Jonathan Swift, promoting Tory policies, particularly the Tory desire for a swift end to the War of Spanish Succession. By June 1714, however, when Manley's *The Adventures of Rivella* appeared, Queen Anne was dying, and the Tories were anticipating a change to a Whig ministry with the arrival of the House of Hanover.

The title page of Manley's *Rivella* announces it as a biography that incorporated some secret memoirs of several public figures: *The Adventures of Rivella; or, the History of the Author of the Atalantis. With Secret* Memoirs *and* Characters *of several considerable Persons her* Contemporaries. The initial advertisements for it also emphasized its inclusion of anecdotes of the type that would be found in a secret history by emphasizing that it was "interspersed with Memoirs and Characters of several persons Cotemporary with the said Author."[9] By including diverting gossip about public figures (particularly those involved in the Bath-Albemarle lawsuit), Manley avoided discussing certain details of her own life that she would prefer not to have publicized. However, there may also have been another reason why she chose to narrate her own life story in the format of a political secret history: she may have been signaling to Robert Harley, Earl of Oxford, that she had not been adequately compensated for her Tory publications.

Manley's narrator points out that in the matter of "Gratitude or Generosity" in their patronage, "the *Tories* did not come up to the *Whigs*, who never suffer'd any Man to want Incouragement and Rewards if he were never so dull, vicious or insignificant."[10] The Earl of Oxford, who was drinking heavily and losing favor with the queen in the spring of 1714, was engaging in behavior that could easily have been mocked by court satirists of either party, including Manley. Although readers today tend not to pay attention to the clues on the title page of *Rivella* identifying the work as a secret history, Oxford certainly would have noticed that Manley was once again brandishing the political power of her celebrity pen. On June 14, 1714, less than two weeks after the publication of *Rivella*, Oxford sent her a bank draft for £50. I have suggested elsewhere that his motivation for sending the payment was the letter Manley wrote him on June 3, in which she pointedly observed that other Tories felt she had been inadequately rewarded for her efforts on behalf of the Tories in writing *The New Atalantis* and inadequately compensated for the expenses and humiliation she incurred in the lawsuit for libel that ensued.[11] In hindsight, I would qualify this observation. Manley's letter, sent two days after *Rivella* was published, might have had, by itself, little effect on Oxford. However, linked to the publication of a work that signaled Manley's readiness to return to the genre of the political secret history, the letter would have been much more persuasive.

Delarivier Manley died in July 1724, and a posthumous fourth edition of *Rivella* (entitled *Mrs. Manley's History of Her Own Life and Times*) appeared in October.[12] In his preface to this fourth edition, dated September 29, 1724, Edmund Curll offers an explanation of the work's provenance that may be at least partially true. He suggests that the writer Charles Gildon, "upon a Pique, the Cause of which I cannot assign" wrote an account of Mrs. Manley's life, which Curll was bringing to press under the title *The History of Rivella*. Both Gildon and Curll were opportunists, and Curll himself may well have seen the opportunity in publishing such an account (and may even have commissioned the work), which would have offered a "severe Invective upon some Part of her Conduct."[13] He suggests that when only two pages of the work had been printed, Mrs. Manley heard that such a work was in press and wrote to him asking him not to print any more of it until she met with him. Curll claims that he informed Manley that he would be "proud" to meet with her and told her that she should call on him that very afternoon. He then explains that he arranged for Manley to meet Charles Gildon and that they struck up an arrangement: Gildon would "order a Total Suppression of all his Papers and Mrs. *Manley*, as generously resolved to write *The History of her own Life, and Times*, under the same title which Mr. *Gildon* had made Choice of."[14]

The reconciliation that Curll describes likely involved Manley paying Gildon for agreeing not to publish what he had written. In a follow-up letter ostensibly written by Manley, which Curll includes in this preface, she enthusiastically thanks him for his intervention to keep Gildon's manuscript from seeing the light of day: "your Services are such to me, that can never be enough valued. My pen, my Purse, my Interest, are all at your Service: I shall never be easy, 'till I am grateful."[15] We do not know whether Manley paid Curll for his hand in suppressing Gildon's version of her life, or whether he felt himself sufficiently well paid by being allowed to publish a work by a best-selling author, whose works were usually published by the well-connected and successful Tory printer John Barber, with whom Manley was living at that time.

In his 1724 preface, Curll offers no explanation for why Gildon would have wanted to write "severe Invective" upon some parts of Manley's life. Curll's preface suggests that he felt there must have been some particular "Pique," the origins of which he could not explain, but in fact, Gildon, as a Whig hack writer, would have needed no particular or personal resentment to write a life of Manley, whose own political secret histories had offered severe invectives upon the lives of the most prominent Whig courtiers active during the reigns of Charles, James, William and Mary, and Anne. One of Gildon's patrons was the Whig MP and pamphleteer, Arthur Maynwaring, himself confidant and political secretary to Sarah, Duchess of Marlborough, one of the Whigs' staunchest lobbyists during Anne's reign and one of Manley's most visible targets in *The New Atalantis* and *Memoirs of Europe*.

Before his death in 1712, Maynwaring had been active in the partisan pamphlet wars between Whigs and Tories. At the request of the Duchess of Marlborough, he had read Manley's *New Atalantis* for her and summarized its contents, recounting in detail the scene in which she is attacked by an angry mob resentful of her influence at court and her accumulated wealth.[16] Maynwaring had also helped edit drafts of some of the duchess's insinuating and disrespectful letters to Queen Anne, and he may have authored some verses and pamphlets insinuating that Queen Anne harbored a lesbian passion for her new court favorite, Abigail Masham, pamphlets to which the duchess sometimes alluded in her letters to the queen.[17] In the summer of 1711, Arthur Maynwaring was the lead author of the satirical Whig periodical *The Medley*, which was published in response to the satirical Tory periodical *The Examiner*, originally penned by Jonathan Swift but written by Manley in the summer of 1711. In other words, Gildon's political patron had been sparring with Manley for several years; it would require no special pique for Gildon to continue the political duel.

In the late spring of 1714, a year and a half after Maynwaring's death, Queen Anne was ill enough that court watchers would have been preparing for the Hanoverian succession and the predicted shift from a Tory to Whig ministry. Charles Gildon may have felt that the time was ripe to take on Manley, hoping that the incoming Whig ministry would be sympathetic to a mocking treatment of a well-known Tory satirist. Gildon would have understood the Whig side of these propaganda wars and might have decided that he could make a profit by spreading some personal gossip about Manley, best-selling author of so much sexual and political gossip about court Whigs. In choosing the name *Rivella* for his protagonist, Gildon was giving Manley a transparent pseudonym just as she had designated by pseudonym so many court and society figures in her secret histories. Gildon presumably planned to tell Manley's life in the style of a political secret history.

What sort of personal gossip might Gildon have made public? Manley's seduction by and irregular marriage to her bigamous first cousin, John Manley, a Tory MP, would have served as scandalous fodder in a Whig secret history designed to tarnish her reputation. In *The New Atalantis*, however, Manley had already offered a sympathetic version of that portion of her life in the story of "Delia," an innocent adolescent who is seduced and betrayed into bigamy by an older cousin after her father's death. The five years in which Manley lived openly with John Tilly, Governor of the Fleet Prison, would not have been a secret, but she was probably relieved to seize control of how those years were narrated. In *The Adventures of Rivella*, she presents her years living with Tilly as an intellectually and emotionally satisfying partnership. Tilly, as Cleander, appears to take an initial interest in Manley because she is reading a copy of la Rochefoucauld's *Moral Reflections* when he first meets her. The narrator sums up their five-year relationship: "RIVELLA tasted some Years the Pleasure of Retirement, in the Conversation of the Person beloved."[18]

However, Manley offers little information in *Rivella* about her relationship with Tilly other than the beginning and the end of the romance. Her admiring narrator, Lovemore, describes her first encounter with Tilly, in which he picks up her copy of la Rochefoucauld. In this account, Tilly is first drawn to Manley as a reader and then as a conversationalist:

> He form'd an Idea from that Book of the Genius of the Lady, who chose it for her Entertainment, and tho' he had but an indifferent Opinion hitherto of Woman's Conversation, ... He found an Opportunity of confirming himself before he parted, in *Rivella*'s Sense, and Capacity for Business as well as Pleasure; which were agreeably mingled at Supper.[19]

As the relationship draws to an end five years later, following the death of Tilly's legal wife (from whom he was separated during his years living with Manley), Manley's narrator frames Tilly's decision to marry a wealthy heiress as an act of generosity on Manley's part:

> she conjur'd him to make his Addresses to the Lady, for tho' he might be so far influenced by his Bride as afterwards to become ingrateful, she would much rather that should happen, than to see him Poor and Miserable, an Object of perpetual Reproach to her Heart and Eyes; for having preferr'd the Reparation of her own Honour, to the Preservation of his.[20]

This version of events, underscoring the selflessness of Rivella's love for Cleander, is at odds with archival evidence that suggests that at the end of their relationship, there may have been legal wrangles between Manley and Tilly.

A torn and partly illegible document in the London Metropolitan archive refers to a debt of £30 owed by Manley to George Haynes, for which John Tilly had apparently promised some security. The document suggests that in 1705 Manley made a legal agreement to repay Tilly, although there is no indication of the provenance of this debt or whether or not Manley ever repaid Tilly her share of it.[21] Some light may be shed on this puzzle by another document in the Hertfordshire archives: an undated note in Mary, Lady Cowper's papers in which she offers an explanation, based on gossip about Manley recounted by a clergyman, for why Manley may have been so harsh on the Cowper family in her *New Atalantis*.

This note provides an example of the sort of "secret history" about the author of *The New Atalantis* that Gildon might have written before Manley negotiated to rewrite the manuscript:

> A Clergy man told me this
> De la riviere manley authoress of ye Atalantis was the Daughter of an apple woman in St. Andrews Holbourn[.] She gave herself ye name for the beauty. Shee married John Manley Esq. at ye time his first wife was alive in Cornwall (tho the first was an old woman). She had a son by him.[22]

Thus far, aside from the false assertion that Manley was the daughter of an apple woman rather than of the Royalist military officer Sir Roger Manley and his wife, a gentlewoman from the Spanish Netherlands, the clergyman does not reveal anything about Manley that she herself had not already revealed through the brief story of Delia that she included in *The New Atalantis*: her irregular marriage to her cousin and the birth of their son, illegitimate because of his father's bigamy.

Lady Cowper's source, however, refers to three more illegitimate children to whom Manley herself never alluded in the story of Delia nor mentioned in her account in *Rivella* of her years of quiet pleasure "in the Conversation of the Person beloved":[23]

> She had 3 bastards by Tilly wch he put out to Nurse to a Fellow had outlived all his Creditors & got out of ye fleet & they now are all 3 alive in a Cellar in fetter lane, they are 3 red haired boys & ye man begs wth y^m. After Tilly she was kept by the Cook y^t Tilly had given her credit upon for when [?] she wanted to eat. The Cook sued Tilly in the Ct. of Ch: for her board after he had left her & had forbid the Cook to trust her. Mr. Francis Cowper was Tillys Council & the Cook and Mrs. Manley were cast. W^{ch} was the reason of her spight to the family of the Cowpers.[24]

This account of Manley's relationship with Tilly may well have elements of truth in it. Certainly it seems likely that she bore children to Tilly. Moreover, it is conceivable that these former lovers, who initially were drawn together, according to the account in *Rivella*, during their attempt to mediate in the famous Bath-Albemarle lawsuit (contesting the estate of the wealthy Duke of Albemarle), might have ended their own relationship in a legal wrangle. There was, in other words, ample material in Manley's life for the maligning secret history that Charles Gildon had planned. When Manley took over the authorship of *Rivella*, she not surprisingly chose to focus on the risible behavior of those involved in the Bath-Albemarle lawsuit rather than on the lawsuits she had faced herself.

Manley devotes a full third of *The Adventures of Rivella* to the Bath-Albemarle lawsuit. The admiring male narrator of *Rivella* actually refers to this extended digression as a "secret history" when he observes to his correspondent: "I have finish'd the Secret History of that tedious Law Suit, which I justly fear has likewise tir'd your Patience."[25] In this mini secret history, Manley mocks, under easily recognizable pseudonyms, the well-known figures in that protracted inheritance case, including Lord Bath, Lord Albemarle, Christopher Monck, and Ralph, Duke of Montagu. Montagu, a remarkably unscrupulous and opportunistic courtier, had been until his death in 1709 one of the most powerful Whig politicians at court since the reign of Charles II.[26] More relevant to court watchers in the reign of Queen Anne was that in 1705 Montagu had finally gained the dukedom he had long sought by marrying his son, John, to Lady Mary Churchill, daughter of the Duke and Duchess of Marlborough, whose influence with Queen Anne secured the dukedom for Montagu.

Lord Crafty (Ralph Montagu) appears in *Rivella* as someone who used all his charm to try to persuade Manley to help mediate the lawsuit to his advantage: "he did all that was in his Power to shake her Fidelity to the *Baron* [Lord Bath]," which included telling her that "all his good Fortune had come by Ladies, but he had never found any of so great Ability as her self."[27] Manley's narrator, however, shows that Crafty's flattery toward her ultimately led Baron Meanwell to distrust the mediation process, and Crafty and Meanwell (Montagu and Bath) finally "clapt up an hasty Agreement."[28] Their agreement left Rivella (Manley) and Cleander (Tilly) without any reward and in debt for the expenses they incurred in humoring one of the claimants to the disputed estate, Timothy Double (Christopher Monck, son of Colonel Thomas Monck). During the negotiation process, they plied him with expensive clothes and fine food and wine; the debt incurred during this failed mediation is one of the reasons Manley's narrator gives for Cleander's (Tilly's) decision to abandon Rivella and marry a woman with a fortune. The pseudonym of *Crafty* reminds readers of Ralph Montagu's willingness to ignore those to whom he had previously pledged allegiance. In other words, as Lord Crafty, Montagu is endowed with all the worst traits that Tories could pin on Whigs: self-serving ambition, dissimulation, and disloyalty, exactly the political qualities Manley assigns to the Duke and Duchess of Marlborough in her previous secret histories.

One of the reasons that modern readers may not immediately think of *Rivella* as a political secret history is that the title for the posthumous fourth edition, published shortly after Manley's death in 1724, presents the work as *Mrs. Manley's History of her Own Life and Times*, a much less political presentation than suggested by the original title, *The Adventures of Rivella; or, the History of the Author of the Atalantis. With Secret* Memoirs *and* Characters *of several considerable Persons her* Contemporaries. However, the title pages for the first two editions omit the printer's name, an omission that hints at the publisher's perception of the work as politically risky. The first edition was printed for Edmund Curll by the trade publisher John

Roberts; the use of a trade publisher (who was paid in advance for printing and materials by the actual publisher) further suggests that Curll saw the work as possibly libelous. The second edition (1715), advertised as being published for "J. Roberts" (although his name was not on the title page) rewords the subtitle, but does not change its emphasis: *The History of the Author of the Four Volumes of the New Atalantis.*[29]

The third edition openly lists both Curll and Roberts as publishers, thus suggesting that neither was worried about prosecution for libel in 1717. At this point, their main concern was probably profit (rather than avoiding prosecution for libel), and the new title and subtitle market the work both to those interested in Mrs. Manley's life and in the genre of secret history: *Memoirs of the Life of Mrs. Manley (Author of the Atalantis), Containing Not only the History of Her Adventures, but Likewise an Account of the most considerable Amours in the Court of King Charles II'd.* By replacing the name "Rivella" with "Mrs. Manley," the new title leaves no doubt that this is a work about the well-known Mrs. Manley's life and adventures. The reference to the "Amours in the Court of King Charles II'd" aligns the work with Whig political secret histories popular during King Charles's reign. It may seem odd that *Memoirs of the Life of Mrs. Manley (Author of the Atalantis)* would be marketed as a Whig secret history, since *The New Atalantis* and its sequel, *Memoirs of Europe*, were such ideologically Tory works. However, Curll and Roberts, in revising the title page in 1717, were probably thinking about how to market a new edition of *Rivella* three years after the peaceful Hanoverian succession. The court and ministry were securely Whig under George I; hence a title page alluding to Whiggish treatments of Charles II's reign might have helped sell copy.

Curll's prefatory material to the fourth edition, *Mrs. Manley's History of Her Own Life and Times*, further detaches the work from its political context. The new title markets the work as specifically autobiographical in the autumn of 1724 and aims at a new readership following Manley's death a few months earlier. Curll's detailed account of Manley's negotiation with Charles Gildon also personalizes an initially political work. Curll cites an ostensible letter from Manley at the start of their negotiations in which she suggests that her usual printer, John Barber, with whom she lived from about 1709 until her death in 1724, might be jealous (for reasons either professional or romantic): "I will come to your House; for if you come upon this Hill [i.e. Lambeth Hill, where Barber's printing house was located], *B.* will find it out; for God's sake let us try if this Affair can be kept a Secret."[30] In fact, Barber was a savvy enough publisher and businessman that he would have perfectly understood Manley's need to make the arrangements she made with Curll and Gildon. Manley's letter—if Curll did not invent it— encouraged Curll to keep the negotiations quiet, an arrangement that would have suited Manley both professionally and personally. When incorporated into the preface for the posthumous 1724 edition, the letter, however, would have guided readers to look for personal rather than political intrigue.

Ten years earlier, when the first edition appeared with a title page suggesting that it was a secret history, the political import of Manley's *The Adventures of Rivella* would have been unmistakable to its contemporaries. Manley's narrator's comment about the Tories not providing the same level of patronage that the Whigs offered their writers was clearly a political jab. In particular, Manley was probably thinking of her former friend Richard Steele when she suggested that the Whigs "never suffer'd any Man to want Incouragement and Rewards if he were never so dull, vicious or insignificant."[31] Manley had mocked Steele mercilessly in *The New Atalantis*, partly for personal reasons and partly because he represented the voice of the partisan opposition as editor of the Whig-controlled *London Gazette*, a position that paid him £300 per year.

Manley coyly suggests in *Rivella* that she may have approached the Whigs about writing for them, but "the *Whigs* were so unforgiving they would not advance one Step towards a *Coalition* with any Muse that had once been so indiscreet to declare against them."[32] Whether or not Manley actually intended to switch sides in the pamphlet wars, this comment, in a work published without author or publisher listed on the title page, would have drawn attention to the fact that whatever she wrote, the power of her name alone would have ensured that many copies would be sold.

This sort of comment in *Rivella* would have made an impression on Robert Harley, Earl of Oxford, whom Manley seems to have visited in mid-May, just at the point when the first edition of *Rivella* would have been going to press. On June 3, 1714, two days after the first advertisements announcing the work's publication appeared, Manley wrote to Oxford.[33] She refers to having waited on him "three weeks agoe" and to writing "in Obedience to yr Lordships Commands." Rather than offering Manley any immediate cash reward for her work for the Tories when she waited on him, Oxford seems to have suggested that she explain her reasons in writing. She mentions the "Fears and the Hardships" she suffered when she was arrested for libel in October 1709, following the publication of *The New Atalantis*. She also refers to John Barber's connection to the "Society for Rewarding of merit" and the assurances by Lord Masham and Sir William Windham that they had recommended that Oxford "send me an hundred pound." Lord Masham was the husband of Lady Abigail Masham (bedchamber woman to Queen Anne, who had replaced her cousin the Duchess of Marlborough as favorite to the queen), whom Manley had depicted in glowing terms in the second volume of *The New Atalantis*. The Earl of Oxford, meanwhile, in the spring of 1714, was finding himself outmaneuvered by Henry St. John, Viscount Bolingbroke, who was gaining Lady Masham's favor in preference to himself. Manley's allusion to Lord Masham, then, would have struck a chord with Oxford, as he attempted to regain favor with the Mashams. Manley ends her begging letter to Oxford with a reference to her failing "Health and Circumstances" brought on by the "persecutions" she suffered "by endeavouring to serve the Cause."[34]

Manley's plea to Oxford for payment acquired some urgency by the spring of 1714, because it was clear that he had lost favor with Queen Anne and would not hold on to power much longer. Manley was savvy to approach Oxford before he was dismissed from office, as he would be in late July. She was also astute to time her letter to coincide with the appearance of *The Adventures of Rivella*, a work that put Manley's celebrated name front and center again on the bookstalls under the transparent guise of a biographical secret history including other mini memoirs of several persons her "cotemporaries."

Oxford seems to have decided that it was prudent to reward Manley as she had hinted, and she wrote him a gracious letter on June 14, thanking him for the "Bill of fifty pounds."[35] Whatever hints of blackmail Manley may have been offering in her *Adventures of Rivella*, Oxford's payment seems to have secured her allegiance to him: she wrote again to Oxford later that summer, following his dismissal, suggesting that she write a pamphlet in his defense that would offer "a true account of the Changes made just Before the Death of the Queen."[36]

By framing her personal memoir as a political secret history in 1714, Manley demonstrated a willingness to use her celebrity as a form of potential political blackmail to secure the monetary reward she thought her due. This maneuver aligns her with Sarah, Duchess of Marlborough, who had engaged in a similar attempt at political blackmail, a few years earlier, when she refused the queen's request to return her intimate letters. In her biography of the Duchess of Marlborough, Ophelia Field draws our attention to the similarities between Marlborough and Manley: "Both had a healthy cynicism about politics and an indifference to the respect usually shown to their superiors; both were defamers and self-vindicators; both played with the lethal power of half-truths; and both betrayed their friends' secrets."[37]

Manley and Marlborough were engaging on opposite sides of the partisan battle, but their strategies overlapped and intersected at the height of partisan conflicts of 1709 and 1710. In the fall of 1709, Marlborough was trying desperately to nudge the queen back toward a Whig foreign policy of continuing the War of Spanish Succession. Marlborough was resentful of her cousin Abigail Masham's having replaced her as the queen's court favorite and worried about Masham's collusion with another cousin of the latter, Robert Harley, who was working with the Tories to bring about a separate peace that would undermine the Whigs' and the Allies' foreign policy goal of "No Peace Without Spain." By spreading reports about the scandalous "intimacy" between Lady Masham and the queen (an "intimacy" asserted and descried by the Whigs troubled by the political influence that Lady Masham was exerting with the queen in favor of Harley's Tory policies), Marlborough hoped to pressure Anne to dismiss her new court favorite.

In a letter to Queen Anne written in late October or early November 1709, the Duchess of Marlborough refers to Manley's just published *New Atalantis* as evidence that the world was talking about Lady Masham and the queen's relationship. Marlborough refers to a "new book that is come out," describing Manley's *New Atalantis*: "the subject is ridiculous, and the book not well written, but that looks so much the worse, for it shews that the notion [of Abigail's favoritism] is extensively spread among all sorts of people." Disingenuously, the Duchess of Marlborough refers to Manley's work as "a dialogue between Madame Maintenon and Madam Masham," which is the subtitle to *The Rival Dutchess*, a satire about lesbian relationships possibly written by Marlborough's friend Arthur Maynwaring, which the duchess had already mentioned to the queen in a disrespectful letter she had written in the summer of 1708 in which she referred to so "great a passion for such a woman" as "strange & unaccountable." She had added in that 1708 letter that she hoped, "*the having noe inclination for any, but of one's own sex is enough to maintain such a character as I wish may still bee yours.*"[38] In alluding a year later to *The New Atalantis* as if it were similar to these earlier Whig verses and pamphlets, Marlborough misrepresents Manley's Tory work. She is also directly disobeying the queen's request in July 1708 that Sarah never mention again "that person ... who you are pleased to call the object of my favour."[39]

The Duchess of Marlborough had not read *The New Atalantis* herself, but Arthur Maynwaring had summarized several portions of the book for her, including the scene in which Hilaria (Abigail Masham) saves the duchess from a mob of rabble. In other words, Marlborough knew perfectly well that Manley's work was written to compliment Lady Masham and therefore was not *The Rival Dutchess*, the Whiggish pamphlet about lesbian friendship that is designed to mock Masham's relationship with the queen. In eliding Manley's best-selling *New Atalantis* with an earlier pamphlet that had not gone into multiple editions, Marlborough is able to suggest misleadingly that "the notion" of the queen's passion for Lady Masham "is spread among all sorts of people."[40]

After this bitter epistolary attack, the duchess saw very little of the queen for the next six months, although in April 1710 she arranged what would be their final meeting. During this conversation, the queen refused to respond to any of the duchess's concerns about Lady Masham, and the duchess collapsed into tears. Shortly after this final interview, the queen requested that the duchess return all of her letters. Not only did the duchess refuse, but she alluded to the power she knew those early love letters could produce if published, in light of the allegations about the queen's current intimate relationship with Lady Masham. Marlborough suggested in fact that she would "take a little better care of the rest [of those letters]"; she also reminded the queen that she had many of them in her arsenal: "I have drawers full of the same in every place where I have lived."[41] In response to the suggestion that the Duchess of Marlborough may have been embezzling funds from the Privy Purse, Queen Anne replied, "Everybody knows, cheating is not the Duchess of Marlborough's crime," implicitly confirming that the more serious charge was blackmail,[42] because of her awareness of "what Sarah might do with the other letters in her possession."[43] Eventually Marlborough appears to have agreed not to publish these letters in return for keeping £22,000 that she had borrowed from the Privy Purse. Manley and other court watchers were probably aware of this power struggle, given Jonathan Swift's allusion to it in the *Examiner*.[44]

The Duchess of Marlborough had not yet been dismissed from her court office: the queen knew that if she dismissed the duchess that the Duke of Marlborough would immediately resign as captain-general of the allied forces fighting in the War of Spanish Succession. Even though the queen was considering a separate peace with Spain and the possibility of Marlborough's eventual dismissal, she was not yet ready to pursue this course. The Duchess of Marlborough may have felt that she could retain some power over the queen by refusing to return her letters, but it was clear that her power was fading quickly. Queen Anne had lost patience with Whigs like the Earl of Sunderland, a secretary of state and son-in-law to the Marlboroughs, who had overreached not only by arresting Manley for opposition satire but by prosecuting the Tory divine, Henry Sacheverell, for a sermon in defense of passive obedience. The queen abruptly dismissed Sunderland in June 1710, with no cause given. The Duchess of Marlborough herself would be asked to return her own keys of office in January 1711.

Ultimately the Duchess of Marlborough, not yet a published author, did not have the power over Queen Anne in 1710 that Manley would have over the Earl of Oxford in 1714. Marlborough, however, did eventually exercise the posthumous power of describing Queen Anne in her memoirs, *An Account of the Conduct of the Duchess of Marlborough* (1742), a narrative that would help shape history's view of Anne as neither very bright nor very politically astute. In fact, Anne was bright enough to outmaneuver the duchess and the Whigs and sign treaties to end the War of Spanish Succession when she felt it was appropriate to do so. Marlborough's depiction of the queen in her memoirs, however, secured Anne's position in history as lacking wit and political skill, a view that has only recently begun to be challenged.[45]

Both Manley and Marlborough understood the power of the personal letter (Manley's to Oxford, Marlborough's to the queen) accompanied by a publication (*Rivella*) or threat of publication (the queen's letters to the duchess). When Marlborough turned to writing her memoir (a project she labored over for decades), which would so influence subsequent perception of Anne's reign, she, unknowingly (since she apparently never read Manley's works), was following Manley's example of crafting her memoir as a form of quasi-secret history. Marlborough does not use pseudonyms but offers an eyewitness insider account of many of the events of Anne's reign, including Whig versions of many of the same events that Manley described in her political secret histories through Tory anecdotes.[46] By reading Manley's 1714 memoir as a political secret history, we may begin to understand the counter-narrative of Anne's reign, told through the voice of a Tory blackmailer rather than a Whig one.[47]

Notes

1. Ros Ballaster argues that while the male narrator "appears to have 'authored' the perfect female object[,] she is, in reality, elsewhere 'authoring' him": *Seductive Forms: Women's Amatory Fiction from 1684–1740* (Oxford: Clarendon, 1992), 150. In *Nobody's Story: The Vanishing Acts of Women Writers in the Marketplace, 1670–1820* (Berkeley and Los Angeles: University of California Press, 1994), Catherine Gallagher examines how in *Rivella*, which she defines as an *"histoire scandaleuse"* (137), Manley "opposes the truth of a political crime to the fictionality of a fictional alibi" (90). In *The Women of Grub Street: Press, Politics, and Gender in the London Literary Marketplace* (Oxford: Clarendon Press, 1998), Paula McDowell refers to *Rivella* as a "literary autobiography" with a "high degree of self-consciousness not only as political participant but as *author*" (220).
2. Ruth Herman describes *Rivella* as an "unreliable" biographical source: *The Business of a Woman: the Political Writings of Delarivier Manley* (Newark: University of Delaware Press, 2003), 17. In *A Political Biography of Delarivier Manley* (London: Pickering and Chatto, 2008), I refer to the work as a "quasi-fictional autobiography" (3). Donna Kuizenga describes *Rivella* as a "pseudo-autobiography," in which "truth is clothed in fiction, but we cannot tell where the one ends and the other begins; see "Villedieu and Manley: Teaching Early Modern Pseudo-Autobiographies," in ed. Faith E. Beasley, *Teaching Seventeenth- and Eighteenth-Century French Women Writers* (New York: The Modern Language Association of America, 2011), 250–7: 255.
3. Kathryn Temple has aligned the work with legal discourses of the time, emphasizing how Manley maps "romance onto law" revealing "law's inner emotional life, its fictions, and in the end, its desire for fiction." See "Manley's 'Feigned Scene': The Fictions of Law at Westminster Hall" *Eighteenth-Century Fiction* 22 no. 4 (Summer 2010): 573–98, 598. Susan Sage Heinzelman points out that the heroine of *Rivella* "embodies the historically specific and gendered affiliation between the literary and the legal." See "Teaching Eighteenth-Century Law and Literature: *The Adventures of Rivella*," in ed. Austin Sarah, Cathrine O. Frank, and Matthew Anderson, *Teaching Law and Literature* (New York: The Modern Language Association of America, 2011), 345–53: 345.
4. Toni Bowers, *Force or Fraud: British Seduction Stories and the Problem of Resistance, 1660–1760* (Oxford: Oxford University Press, 2011), 195.
5. The title of Patricia Köster's facsimile edition of Manley's secret histories encourages readers to view them as novels: *The Novels of Mary Delariviere* [sic] *Manley 1705–1714*, 2 vols. (Gainesville: Scholars' Facsimiles and Reprints, 1971). This tendency to view these secret histories as novels began as early as a decade after Manley's death, when her *New Atalantis* was reprinted in 1735 in *The Weekly Novellist*; see Carnell, *Political Biography*, 237, and Carnell, "Slipping from Secret History to Novel," *Eighteenth Century Fiction* 28, no. 1 (fall 2015): 1–24.
6. See Lionel Gossman, "Anecdote and History," *History and Theory* 42 (May 2003): 143–68 and Carnell, *Political Biography*, 175–6.
7. See Annabel Patterson, *Early Modern Liberalism* (Cambridge: Cambridge University Press, 1997), 183–98, and Rebecca Bullard, *The Politics of Disclosure 1674–1725: Secret History Narratives* (London: Pickering & Chatto, 2009), 45–62. See also Eve Tavor Bannet, "'Secret history': Or, Talebearing Inside and

Outside the Secretorie," in *The Uses of History in Early Modern England*, ed. Paulina Kewes (San Marino: Huntington Library, 2006), 367–88.

8. As Rebecca Bullard suggests, Manley not only mocked the Whigs but mocked some of the very features of the genre of secret history by having her trio of narrators (Intelligence, Fame, and Virtue) relate merely "open secrets, common gossip or just historical fact, not previously undiscovered intelligence"; these narrators appear as "*ingénues*". … who form the narrative frame of *The New Atalantis*"; this frame functions as "a kind of archetype of Whig secret history" (*Politics of Disclosure* 93), which Manley is satirizing.

9. See Carnell, *Political Biography*, 15–16.

10. Manley, *The Adventures of Rivella* in *Selected Works of Delarivier Manley*, 5 vols., eds. Rachel Carnell and Ruth Herman (London: Pickering & Chatto, 2005), 4: 54. References are to this edition.

11. Carnell, *Political Biography*, 160–61.

12. The date on the title page is 1725.

13. Preface to the Fourth Edition of *Rivella* in *Selected Works of Delarivier Manley*, 4: 235.

14. *Rivella*, 4: 236.

15. Ibid., 4: 236.

16. See Carnell, *Political Biography*, 187.

17. See Ophelia Field, *The Favourite: Sarah, Duchess of Marlborough* (London: Hodder and Stoughton, 2012), 202.

18. *Rivella*, 4: 51.

19. *Ibid.*, 4: 35–6.

20. Ibid., 4: 52.

21. London Metropolitan Archives MJ/SP/1705; see also Carnell, *Political Biography*, 133.

22. Hertfordshire Archives, DE/P/F211; see also Carnell, *Political Biography*, 132.

23. *Rivella*, 4: 51.

24. *Ibid.*, 4: 51.

25. Ibid., 4: 49.

26. In *Queen Anne* (London: Routledge & Kegan Paul, 1980), Edward Gregg asserts, "In a corrupt age … [he] … had acquired a singular reputation of profitable dishonor" (195).

27. *Rivella*, 4: 48–9.

28. Ibid., 4: 49.

29. For details about the publication history, see Carnell, *Political Biography*, 15–16.

30. *Rivella*, 4: 236.

31. *Ibid.*, 4: 54.

32. Ibid., 4: 56.

33. The *Daily Courant* for June 1, 1714, announces the publication "This Day" by John Roberts (the trade publisher); see Carnell, *Political Biography*, 242 n23.

34. BL Add. MS 70032, June 3, 1714; this letter is reprinted in Ruth Herman's *The Business of a Woman*, 257.

35. BL Add. MS 70032, June 14, 1714, reprinted in Herman, *Business of a Woman*, 259.

36. BL Add. MS 70033, August 30, 1714, reprinted in Herman, *Business of a Woman*, 260.

37. Ophelia Field, *The Favourite: Sarah, Duchess of Marlborough* (London: Hodder and Stoughton, 2003), 233.

38. Sarah Marlborough to Queen Anne, 26 July 1708, cited in David Green, *Queen Anne* (London: Collins, 1970), 275–6.
39. BL Add. MS61417 fo. 145; Anne to Sarah Marlborough [July 6, 1708], cited in Frances Harris, *A Passion for Government: the Life of Sarah, Duchess of Marlborough* (Oxford: Clarendon Press, 1991), 146.
40. Sarah Marlborough to Queen Anne, [late October or early November] 1709, cited in *Private Correspondence of Sarah, Duchess of Marlborough* (London: H. Colburn, 1838), 2 vols, 1:235.
41. Cited in Field, *The Favourite*, 262–3 and Frances Harris, *A Passion for Government*, 172.
42. Ophelia Field offers this interpretation of the queen's comment, cited from Add MS 61430, Duke of Marlborough to the Duchess of Marlborough 12/23 July 1708 (*The Favourite*, 213).
43. Francis Harris, *A Passion for Government*, 179. See also Ophelia Field, *The Favourite*, 212–13.
44. In *The Examiner*, 16 (November 23, 1710), Swift describes a certain "Woman" [i.e. the Duchess of Marlborough] responsible for the "Allowance" of "a Lady of my own Acquaintance" [i.e. Queen Anne] who appropriated £22 of the Lady's allowance of £26, referring, as Francis Harris points out, to Queen Anne's annual household allowance of £26,000 and the £22,000 which the Duchess of Marlborough appropriated from the privy purse to help pay for the construction of Marlborough House, a sum she did not repay, presumably in exchange for agreeing not to make public the many letters of love and devotion the queen had sent her over their several decades of friendship. See Harris, *A Passion for Government*, 175, and Jonathan Swift, *The Examiner and Other Pieces Written in 1710–11*, ed. Herbert Davis (Oxford: Basil Blackwell, 1966), 24. For a discussion of how Manley further develops this gossipy style of political satire when she takes over *The Examiner* in July 1711, see Jean McBain "Examined in Manley Style: Epistolary Modes in the Periodical Writings of Delarivier Manley," in this collection.
45. See, for example, Edward Gregg, *Queen Anne* (London: Routledge & Kegan, Paul, 1980) and Anne Somerset, *Queen Anne: the Politics of Passion* (New York: Knopf, 2013).
46. See Carnell, "Reading Austen's *Lady Susan* as Tory Secret History," *Lumen* 32 (2013): 1–16.
47. Recent research on Manley and Marlborough was supported by a Faculty Scholarship Initiative, funded by Cleveland State University in 2015.

2 The Politics of Servitude

The Husband's Resentment. In Two Examples in Delarivier Manley's The Power of Love

Earla Wilputte

The Power of Love: In Seven Novels (1720) opens with Delarivier Manley performing the role, "*with all Submission*," of the "*most Devoted, most Obedient Humble Servant*" to Mary Granville, Lady Lansdowne.[1] In her Dedication, Manley praises Lady Lansdowne's "Fortitude, Heroick Vertue, and Conjugal Love" that led her "to support a voluntary Eighteen Months Imprisonment with [her] Lord," George, Baron Lansdowne in the Tower of London when he was charged with high treason.[2] Although critics concede that in writing *The Power of Love* Manley was more interested in commercial success than political purpose,[3] by dedicating the book to Lady Lansdowne, Manley cannot help but provide it with a political veneer. While not explicitly endorsing Jacobitism, Manley's *The Husband's Resentment. In Two Examples* (Novels IV and V) question what honorable behavior is—in love, marriage, and politics. The answer would appear to be closely associated with one's socialized role: wife or husband, servant, subject of the king. Manley's deliberate expansions of the servants' roles in the two *Husband's Resentment* novellas, as contrasted with their roles in her source William Painter's *Palace of Pleasure* (1566) novels 43 and 58, lead readers to question the social ideologies of servitude as she reveals the complexity of power dynamics in domestic politics.

Signing herself "*Your Ladyship's most Devoted, most Obedient Humble Servant*," Manley positions herself subserviently to her Jacobite patron, though she is obliged to show allegiance to her Hanoverian king, George I. Torn between two relationships—one with her patron and one with her king—Manley is not unlike the women in her resentment tales: emotionally involved with one man but legally bound to another. Her role as author also embodies an element of servitude as she must carefully balance her duties of instructing and delighting her readers. She writes that her tales have been written "with the same Design as Mr. *Dryden* had" in his *Fables Ancient and Modern* (1700);[4] that is, she offers stories with, as Dryden wrote, "some instructive moral ... [that] leap[s] foremost into sight without the reader's trouble of looking after them."[5] But Manley's seven novels are not as transparent as Dryden's fables. In fact, the "divers new Incidents" she adds to

Painter's translations demand that her readers do apply some "trouble of looking" if they are to glean from them any patently "instructive" lesson.[6]

That looking begins with the connection Manley offers upon concluding her story of *The Wife's Resentment* (Novel III) and introducing two novels of husband's resentment to offset the horror of the former—"That we may not leave upon the Minds of our Readers too great an Impression of the Cruelty of Woman-kind."[7] Painter does not include any such editorial comment. Manley is explicit in her desire that readers receive a fair and accurate representation of domestic violence, noting that "out of ten thousand Histories, where even a Million might be produced, [she] bring[s] two Examples, that a Husband dishonoured is a no less terrible Animal, than a Wife jealous, injur'd, and betray'd."[8] Apparently there may be more vengeful husbands than wives, but Manley does not unequivocally draw that conclusion. In her refashioning of Painter's two translated *Husband's Resentment* novels, she deliberately problematizes who is actually to blame for the adulteries and their consequences.[9]

Manley's role of authorial servant to her readers entails teaching them without appearing to be impertinent. This involves some subterfuge or misdirection in her storytelling. Catherine Gallagher has noted that in many satires of the period "smitten women, pining for a man who is not their legal master, serve as a figure for the fickleness of the nation as a whole, which had become rather quickly disenchanted with George I. Desire for the Stuart Pretenders was represented as a kind of adulterous attraction throughout the first half of the eighteenth century."[10] Though probably not really pining for the Stuart Pretender, Manley uses the infidelity trope to explore the consequences of unequal relationships within marriage, and to gesture toward those of a mismatched king and his people. The inferior social and political status of servants and wives in the two resentment tales under examination here, as well as the role of servants within their plots, are key to understanding Manley's point. Despite the morals drawn at the end of each of the *Husband's Resentment* novels about how imperative it is for wives to be faithful, readers are led to question the legitimacy of the husbands' acts of vengeance. This moral uncertainty is strengthened when one notes how some servants in each tale, despite their loyalty, are not treated equally to each other.

In stark contrast to the exemplary marriage of the Lansdownes, in which the good wife voluntarily incarcerated herself with her husband in the Tower, Manley's first Example of *The Husband's Resentment* (Novel IV) relates a tale of marital vengeance in which an adulterous wife is immured against her will with the corpse of her lover. The climax is a macabre echo of George I's long-term imprisonment of his wife, Sophia Dorothea, whom he had confined in Ahlden castle since 1694 and would keep there until her death in 1726, and his suspected involvement in the murder of her lover, Philip Königsmarck. The contemporaneous parallel politicizes the novel by implicating the king, as well as what Kirsten Saxton calls the "sexist social and juridical systems," in the disproportionate oppression of wives.[11] The Jacobite Lansdownes, in comparison to George I, appear civilized and meritorious. In the second Example of *The Husband's Resentment* (Novel V), the husband deliberately treats his adulterous wife lovingly to deter suspicion when she suddenly dies after eating a salad. The tale ends with the observation that husbands must comply with the "received Maxims of the World," suggesting that he was compelled both to avenge his dishonor and to hide his murderous revenge. "A Man, though perhaps not vindictive, nor cruel in his Nature, is reduced … either to punish the Infamy of his Wife, or by tolerating Hers, to live in greater Contempt and Infamy himself."[12] His duty to society comes first, and Manley's conclusion reads as a satiric apology for what men must do to maintain honor.

Rachel Carnell reads Manley's closing remarks to Novels IV and V as "cautionary dogmatism" and "monolithic didacticism"[13]; however, we cannot trust that these conclusions are heartfelt. Manley's equivocal tone throughout the resentment novels does not suggest that she supports the decisive morality dealt out to the offending parties by the righteous, aristocratic authorities. The resentment novels are not moral fables like Dryden's and Painter's: they imitate life, with all of its unfairness and, as one servant character observes, "the Baseness and Ingratitude of the World."[14] The *Husband's Resentment* tales and the author's interjections blur the boundaries between right and wrong behavior by destabilizing accepted social codes of propriety, and questioning the relationship between husbands and wives, masters and servants, and implicitly, between author and reader.

The social consequences of the upper class stepping out of its sphere to demean itself with the lower classes are insidious in these novels.[15] Domestic and social instability result when Amadeus, a Marquis (Novel IV), and a President of Grenoble (Novel V) wed lower-class women whom their societies believe are of easy virtue and could have been possessed as mistresses; and again when each wife takes a lover of lower class than her husband. The household servants in each case are aware that the marital rights of their master are usurped by a lesser man. Desideria's promiscuous behavior with her lover Horatio "gave such umbrage to her People" that they began "making Reflections disadvantageous to her Honour;" "[t]hey lov'd and honour'd [Amadeus]; but neither respected nor esteem'd their Lady, because they doubted [i.e., suspected] she was unfaithful to his Bed."[16] They lose respect for her because she disrespects her husband. But though their dislike for their mistress may seem like loyalty to their master, it actually erodes his authority because, according to marital law, "the husband and wife are one person in law: that is, the very being or legal existence of the woman is suspended during the marriage, or at least is incorporated and consolidated into that of the husband: under whose wing, protection, and *cover*, she performs everything; and is therefore called in our law-french a *feme-covert*."[17] Disrespect for the wife is also disrespect for the husband, her lord and their master. Manley exhibits how this works when Amadeus's Groom of the Chamber, cognizant of his Lady's affair, must carefully negotiate the delicate relationship in which he is subservient to one master in two bodies:

> That faithful Servant, ... related to him [Amadeus], That, with great Grief, not only himself, but the other Servants, had beheld their Lady's intimacy with that young Fellow [Horatio]; .... That he had often thought to reveal to him his Suspicions, but was still with-held by the Reflection he made to himself of the great Power the Marchioness had over his Lordship, which might end in his [the Groom's] Ruin, if he were not able to bring something more than Suspicion towards her Conviction.[18]

The Groom recognizes the politics of duty and gratitude that Desideria, Amadeus's wife, does not, even though both servant and wife are bound by them. Servants are not permitted to reveal their suspicions about their Lady because it would cast aspersions on their master's character. The Groom knows that, because Amadeus is enthralled by Desideria, her power threatens his own employment and he must therefore tread carefully. This threat is realized in Novel V when the adulterous Madam la Presidente regards the servant, Ursula, who suspects her affair with Peter the clerk, as "her evil Genius," and she "perpetually teiz[es] her Husband" to dismiss her from the house.[19] But the President heeds neither his wife's teasing nor his servant's complaints, for "[h]e was a wise Man, and always examined the Cause, by which he was better able to judge of the Effects."[20] Unfortunately for both his wife and Ursula, the President's wisdom is self-serving and he willingly sacrifices his wife's life and his servant's employment for his and his daughters' reputations. Though the Groom and Ursula receive different treatments from their masters, it is not immediately clear why. Both are long-time, faithful domestics to their masters; in fact, both are troubled to find that their masters do not reciprocate their fidelity. The Groom, upon discovering that he is not among those servants being taken to France with his master, "gently complain'd of a Distinction so much to his Disadvantage,"[21] feeling that his service has not been properly appreciated. But, as Amadeus explains, it is because he especially depends upon the Groom that he desires him to stay behind to help him with his plan of surprising his wife and her lover together. Upon hearing this, the Groom divulges that he has suspected Desideria's adultery, and swears that, now encouraged by his master, he will "succeed or die in the Attempt" of proving her affair.[22]

The Groom in Novel IV acts in complete opposition to Novel V's servant, Ursula, who, also suspicious of her Lady's fidelity, reports it to her master before he introduces the subject to her. Manley's narrator acknowledges that though Ursula is an "honest plain Creature" and her love for her master is "as strong, and almost as natural, as for her own Child," the servant is still "impertinent" in speaking her mind.[23] The President demands to witness his wife's infidelity with his own eyes so that he can know that Ursula isn't designing to make a quarrel between him and his wife. As Paddy Lyons has pointed out, "Records show the legal system heard and weighed evidence from servants at best with caginess and scruples and with little readiness to rely on the observations or understanding of a subaltern class."[24] When Ursula "came to complain to her Master, in good earnest, of what Indecencies she had discovered, the *President* thought her ill Will had misled her, and had occasioned Mistakes."[25] But Ursula, believing that her years of dedicated service should merit some respect from the President, especially when she has his best interests in mind, responds not as a servant but as an individual, or an intimate family member.

> This Distrust put the poor old Nurse into a dreadful Case, and [she] exposed his Honour to a World of Reproaches, and a deluge of Tears! That she should have suckled him, and brought him up, nay, and loved him better than his own Mother, to meet such Returns! She had rather die a Thousand times over than have her Truth suspected! Of all Men living he ought not to question her Veracity![26]

This outburst sounds very similar to what a wife might express to a husband who suspects her marital fidelity. The tiers of relationships in these novels—husbands and wives, masters and servants—reflect upon each other, demonstrating the layers of mastery and servitude and the shifting and interdependent roles within the domestic hierarchy. Ursula's reproach of her master is completely antithetical to the gentle complaining of the Groom who knows his place. Significantly, unlike the female servants who are each given names—Alicia in Novel IV and Ursula in Novel V—the Groom is identified only in terms of his household duty. His personality and desires do not encroach on his master's business, nor does he expect anything more than appropriate recognition of his service. Born of "old faithful Domesticks in the Family" and "bred, from his Infancy, with the Marquis,"[27] the Groom is confided in and trusted to assist Amadeus, though only within his capacity of servant. Ursula, on the other hand, expects that her longtime intimacy with the President's family earns her the right to speak to her master as an equal. But much to her chagrin, Ursula's social subjectivity, like the Groom's and Alicia's in Novel IV, is entirely dependent upon her social position and the whims of her employer.

Manley adds a passage in her Novel V that is not in Painter in which she philosophizes on the value of good, loyal servants and how they are unappreciated. Writing of Ursula, she observes,

> Such old Servants, when they happen to be faithful, are inestimable Treasures; but never valued by the young People, their Honesty and their Care are lost upon an unexperienced, thoughtless Generation, who in the Pride of Youth, look with an evil Eye upon all those who

have more Discretion than themselves, or presumes to give them good Advice! And yet old Servants will go on in their own way, their Love descends to their Master's Children, and so must their Concern; though they are so little thank'd, or rather hated for it.[28]

Just as the husbands meet with disaster for marrying younger women who are beneath their class and who do not respect them, we witness a similar generational difference between "old Servants" and the "thoughtless Generation" that disrespects "Discretion." Both husbands resent their wives' adultery because it manifests their scorn of their husbands' age, social standing, and honor, as well as the honor the men have extended in elevating their lower-class wives. The husbands then are permitted to avenge their mistreatment. But the husband/masters rarely extend any sympathetic understanding to their servants when they are similarly scorned by their employers, who do not appreciate their efforts to save their masters' honor. Refusing or unable to see the parallels in their cases, the husbands treat their servants as insensible.

Ursula, though completely loyal to her master, is berated by him as "a base, malicious old Creature," "an Inventer of Lies," and dismissed from employment and the country (though the President admits that he will pay her an annual pension for the rest of her life if she does not spread her "Lies").[29] The President's cruel treatment of Ursula may be interpreted in part as his displaced anger with his unfaithful wife. Manley's change of Painter's nameless "trustie seruant" who has "scrued [his Maister] the space of xxx. yeres"[30] into the female Ursula (a name meaning bear, a notoriously maternal creature) suggests an affinity between the roles of servant and wife/mother; however, Manley's added observation that old and truly loyal servants' "Love [and Concern] descends to their Master's Children" is more important than any surface parallel. Loyal servants seemingly bind themselves voluntarily to their masters through their exercise of duty and their very real affection for them much more than wives dedicate themselves to their husbands. This imbalance in fidelity suggests that the relationship between master and servant, though "founded in convenience, whereby a man is directed to call in the assistance of others,"[31] can be more enduring and caring than a marriage, but it is still vulnerable to the master's or husband's will.

The President sacrifices a loyal servant in order to save his own reputation and that of his two daughters. No one must know that his wife has had an affair with Peter, the man whom he "had charitably bred ... up from a young Lad" to be his Foot-boy, and then his Clerk; therefore, Ursula must be let go even as his guilty wife must be secretly punished.[32] (The lover, like Ursula, is commanded to leave Grenoble; however, his punishment is regarded even by him as light, as the President could have killed him.) Without overtly calling attention to the apparent sexism here, Manley makes it evident that the women servants are treated more harshly than the men, just as her two examples of husbands' cruel resentment outweigh her one example of a wife's resentment (Violenta's revenge against her bigamist husband in Novel III). Manley's back-to-back positioning of Novels IV and V (where Painter separates them with 14 tales) also encourages readers to draw comparisons between the Groom and Ursula. Their unequal treatment, seemingly based upon their sex though also grounded in their levels of professional discretion, in turn raises suspicions in readers about the objectivity of each husband's judgment against his wife.

In Example I of *The Husband's Resentment*, a female servant overtly functions to reflect upon the wife's behavior. Painter's nameless "old woman,"[33] who is little more than plot machinery in his novel, becomes Manley's Alicia, furnished with her own backstory. First employed by Amadeus "in the Nature of a *Spanish duenna*" to read Desideria lectures on virtue and to spy on her so that he can be assured of his young wife's fidelity while he is away, Alicia is described as a "doating Beldame" having a clandestine affair with a younger man who passes for her nephew.[34] Alicia requires a greater salary to keep her lover in gifts, and, although she is soon corrupted by her mistress's kindness and liberality, her relationship with Desideria stems from her "Heart and Soul" being "charmed" by her, and she "wished for nothing more than to pay her Ladies good offices in Kind."[35] Believing herself treated as an individual by her mistress, Alicia is motivated to serve Desideria more fervently than her master. In both Manley and Painter's versions, Alicia is treated barbarously when Amadeus discovers her betrayal. Forcing his way into the bedroom to discover the lovers, Amadeus delivers Alicia "a great Kick on the Stomach that threw her backwards, where she lay half an Hour without Power to stir or speak."[36] Identified as "a wicked Assistant to their infamous Love" and a "cursed Confidant," Alicia is forced to participate with her mistress in Horatio's execution, and is "severely scourg'd, and thrust forth of the Castle almost naked."[37] The punishments visited on Alicia and Ursula for their corruption or impertinence are regarded by readers as harsh but perhaps necessary to deter insubordination. In comparison with the punishment that each wayward wife receives, they are humane. Contemporaneous women's writing often describes wives and servants as equivalent roles—Mary Chudleigh claims, "Wife and servant are the same / But only differ in the name,"[38] and Mary Astell states that "she has no reason to be fond of being a Wife, or to reckon it a peice of Preferment when she is taken to be a Man's Upper-Servant."[39] But Manley's two *Husband's Resentment* novels clearly depict the wife's role as even more restricted than a servant's: wives "must forego their Delights ... to preserve their Lives from Death."[40]

Yet insubordination—in wives and servants, as well as citizens—must be punished for the sake of maintaining social stability. The two husbands, though at fault for making bad marriages in the first place, are responsible, as figures of authority and government, for correcting domestic and social wrongs and so are compelled to punish their adulterous wives as an example to their subalterns. But Manley's narrator makes a point of describing each

husband's resentment and revenge as personally rather than socially motivated, and each uses a dissembling show of love to trick his wife and society
into a false sense of security. Amadeus thinks that Desideria should "fall
an unexceptionable Oblation to his great Revenge;" that is, she should be
offered up as a sacrifice to his religious devotion to honor. In both Manley
and Painter's versions, Amadeus "bestow[s] upon her a *Judas* Kiss" before
putting into action his plot to catch her with her lover.[41] Betraying her with
a kiss, the same sign that Judas uses to identify Jesus to the soldiers who
come to arrest him, villainizes Amadeus while emphasizing that Desideria
is deliberately set up. Further, both Manley and Painter's comparison of
the Marquis' behavior to the "Tears of a false Crocodile, who rejoices at
deceiving them whom he designs immediately to destroy" suggest that neither author condones the Marquis' duplicity or his glee in his entrapment
of his wife.[42] In Novel V, the President takes duplicity even farther, duping
the whole town into believing that he "was passionately fond of his Wife"
even as he schemes to poison her.[43] The cold-blooded secrecy with which
the President executes his plan does not lead readers to regard his revenge
as an impartial act of justice.[44]

Both wives, however, are definitely in the wrong and in need of strict
supervision and correction. Desideria is vain and ambitious. She is pleased
when Amadeus tells her they are being transferred to the French court
because she plans to have "the Consolation of having her Lover [Hora
tio] with her, 'till Time and good Fortune might present her with another;
perhaps the King himself ... Her Head was immediately running upon the
Figure she should make, and the Design she had of concerning her self in
all Affairs of State, which she reckon'd to have the sole Management of, by
the Doatage of her Lord."[45] Where Amadeus has looked down the social
ladder and wedded an inferior, Desideria looks up and intends to govern the
State through her manipulation of her husband and the French King. Her
worldly values in pursuit of power persist, in conflict with Amadeus's more
transcendent values of love and honor. In Novel V, Madam la Presidente,
unhappy with only one man, also restlessly desires "Variety" and chooses a
clerk, "preferr'd only for living in the same House with her," as her lover.[46]
The narrator slyly wonders whether the President's daughters "were his, or
his Man's," concluding it "is not much Matter" as he is "excessively fond of
his Wife and Daughters."[47] Amadeus's "Doatage" and the President's excessive fondness render them vulnerable to their wives and more easily duped
by them. In both cases, the husbands are partly responsible for their wives'
infidelity because they are not manly enough to control them or themselves.
Amadeus "lost much of the Esteem of the World by playing so foolish a part
[as wedding Desideria]. Some ridiculed him, some stared, others reproached
him, but all condemned, in every Particular, a Match so unequal."[48]

It is a given in Novel IV that Desideria will commit adultery because, as
the narrator explains, it is innate in her very upbringing: "no better could
be expected from her. She was an Enemy to Regularity, had no Notion of

Honour, very little of Vertue, and had neither Birth nor Education sufficient to set a Value upon the Dignity she was rais'd to."[49] In Novel V, the narrator remarks that though the President's wife is resolved that "Variety could contribute to her Satisfaction" in marriage, "one would have better forgiven her if she had singled out a Man of Merit, or Quality, or Fortune!"[50] The men that Desideria and Madam la Presidente take as lovers are both of lower social status than their husbands: Horatio, a "plain-meaning Country Squire," and Peter, a former footman, now clerk. Peter beats his mistress when she tries to teach him discretion; spends her money on "private Lodgings, ... Horse and *Valet*"; bad-mouths his master; and, when caught in bed with the President's wife, behaves pusillanimously: "he threw himself at [the President's] Feet upon his Knees in his Shirt, implored his Pardon, and begged him to save his Life; with the naughty Children, he cry'd, *pray, pray, he would never do so no more.*"[51] Later, alone with his mistress, he calls the President "a Testy Prig" and brags that he could have beaten him had he not been "naked, without Cloaths and Weapons."[52] Readers hope that Peter will get his comeuppance for his insolence, vanity, and two-facedness; however, he escapes scot-free except for having to leave Grenoble when the President commands it.

Horatio, on the other hand, is portrayed sympathetically, especially as he is executed for his crime of passion. Horatio is a likeable young man who loves and respects his mistress. (Her feelings for him are more doubtful.) He dares not make advances to Desideria because she is a lady and outranks him; she initiates the affair. Later, Alicia secrets Horatio into Amadeus's castle to meet Desideria by disguising him in her own "Gown and Petticoat ... with some Head-gear ... that he might very well pass for a Female of Mrs. *Alicia*'s Acquaintance."[53] While "[m]uch of the print hysteria about women servants wearing their mistress's castoff clothing reflects a concern that sartorial shape-shifting enables a kind of sexual class-climbing," Manley complicates matters further with Horatio's cross-dressing.[54] Horatio in drag is doubly demeaned, literally appearing as a woman, and a servant—doubly inferior in social status to Amadeus, even though he is cuckolding him. The narrator describes Horatio after his execution as "that once innocent Person, who had been so sillily allur'd by the dazzling Vanity, and proffer'd Embraces of a great Lady, to his destruction."[55] He is a victim both of Desideria's seduction and her husband's wrath, and readers pity him for being a pawn to each of them.

Horatio's feminization, in conjunction with his status, especially in relation to his mistress, and in his death, reminds readers of the page Van Brune in Aphra Behn's *The Fair Jilt* (1688). In Behn's novella, Miranda treats her handsome young page "more like a lover, than a servant" to coerce him to murder her sister.[56] The "ravished youth" does poison the girl (though not fatally) but is caught and sentenced to hang.[57] Despite his guilt, "all the beholders [are moved] with ... much pity" for his youth and beauty, and how he was influenced by his wicked mistress.[58] Miranda is forced "to stand under the gibbet, with a rope about her neck, the other end ... fastened to the gibbet where the page was hanging; ... an inscription in large characters upon her back and breast, of the cause why."[59] In Manley's first *Resentment* novel, the public spectacle of justice extends further. Amadeus, the wronged husband, orders his wife to hang Horatio, to be witnessed by everyone in the castle. "[B]ecause she alone was not able to perform that fatal and detestable Work, he commanded, That since that old Hag [Alicia] had been a wicked Assistant to their infamous Love, she should also be an Instrument to help her Lady to dispatch him."[60] Together they hang Horatio from the bedchamber's ceiling beam "in the Sight of many Spectators," and then Desideria is condemned to be closed up in the chamber "in utter Darkness" with Horatio's "putrid Carcase."[61] Rather than the pageant-like spectacle of Miranda's punishment under Van Brune's scaffold, Desideria suffers "Enclosure," "Darkness," and "the Stench of that loathsome Dungeon" until she dies in "Silence, and without Sobs or Tears."[62] Painter remarks that she was "ouercome with sorrow and extreme paine," but Manley is more speculative: "being, as was supposed, wounded with Self-conviction, for that shameful Misery which she had brought upon her self!"[63] She sounds doubtful of Desideria's "supposed" frame of mind, making it seem much more likely that she starved or died of shock.

Both husbands—Amadeus and the President of Grenoble—are regarded as just in their revenge on their adulterous wives even though the narrators ambivalently describe their actions. In his *Commentaries on the Laws of England* William Blackstone notes that, by "the old law," a husband "might give his wife moderate correction. For as he is to answer for her misbehaviour, the law thought it reasonable to intrust him with this power of restraining her, by domestic chastisement, in the same moderation that a man is allowed to correct his servants or children. ... the courts of law will still permit a husband to restrain a wife of her liberty, in case of any gross misbehaviour."[64] Manley's two *Husband's Resentment* novels, offering two murdered wives, one "severely scourged" maid, another driven out of her country as a liar, and one hanged lover, suggest a husband's power can be grossly abused.

Both *Husband's Resentment* novels end with a tidy moral by the narrators—Novel IV warning wives to keep on the "Path of Vertue, so to preserve their Lives from Death," and Novel V commending the "wise Husband" for avenging "himself upon his Enemies, and yet preserv[ing] the Honour of his Family."[65] But Novel V concludes with remarks by a speaker (not the narrator) on the tale's outcome. The single quotation marks running down the text of the last paragraph indicate that someone unknown is speaking. In Painter's translation he includes part of the conversation among Emarsuitte (who told the story), Parlamente, and Hircan, picking up where Emarsuitte points out "the light behauior of a woman and the great pacience and prudence of a man." Parlamente adds that cheating wives would rip up their gardens to avoid their husbands' revenge; and her husband, Hircan, cryptically declares that "If sallades be so costly … and so daungerous … I will prouoke appetite with other sawces, or els hunger shall be my chiefest."[66] Manley's conclusion retains Hircan's threatening tone and Emarsuitte's praise of husbands as the speaker warns that adultery is an "immortal" "Offence" that can never be expiated except with one's life. The speaker goes on to say that a wronged husband must "punish the Infamy of his Wife, or by tolerating hers, … live in greater Contempt and Infamy himself," thus indicating how a husband must also observe a kind of social servitude.[67]

What Carnell identifies as "cautionary dogmatism" may be Manley's own servitude to social maxims. As a woman author at the end of her career she may have chosen to appear conventional even as she impertinently challenges social ideologies and George I's cruel treatment of his wife. The layers of mastery and servitude explored in these two novels manifest the interdependent roles within a domestic as well as a national hierarchy. While wives, servants, and subjects owe obedience and respect to husbands, masters, and king, such servitude is contingent upon their superiors maintaining a personal equilibrium. Should masters fall prey to the power of love, they are subject to hatred and revenge, all of which overrule reason and justice and risk the stability of the state. For the politics of servitude to function successfully, the primal passions must be subservient to the rational powers of the mind.

Notes

1. Delarivier Manley, *The Power of Love: In Seven Novels* (London: 1720), xvi, *Eighteenth-Century Collections Online*, Gale, Dalhousie University, http://galenet.galegroup.com/servlet/ecco.
2. Ibid., ix.
3. Rachel Carnell, *A Political Biography of Delarivier Manley* (London: Pickering and Chatto, 2008), 234; Debbie Welham, "The Political Afterlife of Resentment in Penelope Aubin's *The Life and Amorous Adventures of Lucinda* (1720)," *Women's Writing* 20, 2 (2013): 55, accessed June 24, 2014, doi:10.1080/09699 082.2013.754257.
4. Manley, xv.
5. John Dryden, "Preface to *Fables Ancient and Modern*," in *Of Dramatic Poesy and Other Critical Essays*, 2 vols. (London: Dent, 1962), 2:273.
6. Manley, xv.
7. Ibid., Novel IV, 229.
8. Ibid., Novel IV, 229.
9. Painter's Nouelle 43 "The Ladie of Thurin" is translated from Matteo Bandello, and Nouelle 58 "President of Grenoble" from the 36th tale of Marguerite de Navarre's *Heptaméron*.
10. Catherine Gallagher, *Nobody's Story: The Vanishing Acts of Women Writers in the Marketplace 1670–1820* (Berkeley: University of California Press, 1994), 112.
11. Kirsten T. Saxton, *Narratives of Women and Murder in England, 1680–1760: Deadly Plots* (Aldershot: Ashgate, 2009), 128.
12. Manley, Novel V, 290.

13. Carnell, 230.
14. Manley, Novel V, 286.
15. See Aleksondra Hultquist's essay in this collection for more on the political effects of unequal marriages.
16. Manley, Novel IV, 245; 259.
17. Sir William Blackstone, *Commentaries on the Laws of England* [1765–69], 4 vols. (Chicago: University of Chicago Press, 1979), 1:430.
18. Manley, Novel IV, 261.
19. Ibid., Novel V, 276.
20. Ibid., Novel V, 277.
21. Ibid., Novel IV, 260.
22. Ibid., Novel IV, 262.
23. Ibid., Novel V, 275.
24. Paddy Lyons, "What do the Servants Know?" in *Theatre and Culture in Early Modern England, 1650–1737: From Leviathan to Licensing Act*, ed. Catie Gill (Surrey: Ashgate, 2010), 11.
25. Manley, Novel V, 277.
26. Ibid., Novel V, 278.
27. Ibid., Novel IV, 259–60.
28. Ibid., Novel V, 276.
29. Ibid., Novel V, 283.
30. Painter, William. *The Palace of Pleasure* [1566], 2nd ed., ed. Joseph Jacobs, 3 vols. (London: Ballantyne Press, 1890), 2:101, accessed July 16, 2014, www.gutenberg.org/ebooks/34053.
31. Blackstone, 1:410.
32. Manley, Novel V, 273.
33. Painter, 1:244.
34. Manley, Novel IV, 238; 240; 239.
35. Ibid., Novel IV, 240.
36. Ibid., Novel IV, 267; see also Painter, 1:247.
37. Ibid., Novel IV, 269; 270.
38. Lady Mary Chudleigh, "To the Ladies," ed. Jack Lynch, accessed Oct. 16, 2014, http://andromeda.rutgers.edu/~jlynch/Texts/ladies.html.
39. Mary Astell, *Some Reflections on Marriage*, in *A Celebration of Women Writers*, ed. Mary Mark Ockerbloom, 94, accessed Oct. 16, 2014, http://digital.library.upenn.edu/women/astell/marriage/marriage.html.
40. Manley, Novel IV, 271.
41. Ibid., Novel IV, 256; [2]63, mistakenly printed 163.
42. Ibid., Novel IV, 259.
43. Ibid., Novel V, 288.
44. See Misty Krueger's essay on *Almyna* in this collection for a similar "critique of unchecked power."
45. Manley, Novel IV, 258.
46. Ibid., Novel V, 273.
47. Ibid., Novel V, 274.
48. Ibid., Novel IV, 236–7.
49. Ibid., Novel IV, 243.
50. Ibid., Novel V, 273.
51. Ibid., Novel IV, 239; V, 275; 281.

52. Ibid., Novel V, 285.
53. Ibid., Novel IV, 265.
54. Kristina Straub, *Domestic Affairs: Intimacy, Eroticism, and Violence between Servants and Masters in Eighteenth-Century Britain* (Baltimore: The Johns Hopkins University Press, 2009), 37.
55. Manley, Novel IV, 269.
56. Aphra Behn, "The Fair Jilt," in *Oroonoko, The Rover and Other Works*, ed. Janet Todd (Toronto: Penguin, 1992), 55.
57. Ibid., 55.
58. Ibid., 59.
59. Ibid., 58.
60. Manley, Novel IV, 269.
61. Ibid., Novel IV, 269; 270.
62. Ibid., Novel IV, 271.
63. Painter, 1:248 accessed July 16, 2014, www.gutenberg.org/ebooks/20241; Manley, Novel IV, 271.
64. Blackstone, 1:432–3.
65. Manley, Novel IV, 271; Novel V, 289.
66. Painter, 2:103.
67. Manley, Novel V, 289–90.

3 Vengeance, Vows, and "Heroick Vertue"

Reforming the Revenger in Delarivier Manley's *Almyna: or, The Arabian Vow*

Misty Krueger

After *The Royal Mischief*'s run in April 1696 and *The Female Wits*' parody of the tragedy later that year, Delarivier Manley abstained from writing drama for a decade.[1] In late 1706, she returned to the stage with *Almyna: or, The Arabian Vow*,[2] a drama remarkably different from *The Royal Mischief*. Manley shifted from celebrating a femme fatale's desires to promoting a chaste woman's reform of men's passions. Rather than focusing on licentiousness and hyperbolic violence, *Almyna* privileges reason and restraint over mad ravings and retribution. These modifications align Manley's work with transformations in theatrical taste.[3] While scholars have examined *Almyna* in terms of Orientalism, adaptation, politics, and feminism, they have not explored fully how the play represents Manley's development as a dramatist writing on trend.[4] After the turn of the century, playwrights favored repentance over the Restoration-era trope of blood-as-spectacle, and unlike heroic tragedies, civic tragedies[5] show that "the word" holds greater value than "the sword." Manley realizes this change through her new presentation of vengeance. In part, this essay identifies revenge as the linchpin in Manley's turn from heroic tragedy to civic drama.

In *The Royal Mischief*, Manley reproduces a Restoration-era model of revenge that depicts how revengers threaten an authority figure's rule and endanger the social and political stability.[6] As such, the play chronicles the intrigues of characters driven by lust, hatred, and ambition to commit crimes of passion.[7] Even the Prince of Libardian is motivated by revenge to murder, thus revealing vengeance's power to jeopardize a ruler's ability to be a good sovereign. By the end of *The Royal Mischief* almost every character dies as a result of vengeance. Manley explores revenge again in *Almyna*, but to a different effect. In *Almyna*, Manley's titular female protagonist's carefully articulated logic thwarts successive violence and surprisingly provides the would-be victim and the revenger with a happy ending. Contrary to *The Royal Mischief*'s Homais, *Almyna* shows that a strong female character must not instigate revenge. She must dissuade it. She must become, in the words of Manley's contemporary, playwright John Dennis, "the preserver of Nations,"[8] not the cause of their downfalls. By their good examples, women must help men reject their impulses for vengeance and violence so that they can rule with compassion. As I argue in this essay, in *Almyna* Manley demonstrates that a woman's heroic virtue is the antidote for vengeance, thus allowing the playwright to rehabilitate rather than punish the revenger.[9] Manley's revision of revenge ultimately offers repentance as a method for securing public good.

Prefacing Revenge and "Heroick Vertue"

While most of *Almyna*'s 1707 preface apologizes for the extenuating circumstances affecting the play's December 1706 run at the Queen's Theater,[10] the preface also provides clues for the play's connections to revenge tales, heroic virtue, and civic duty. Manley states that her "fable is taken from the Life of that great Monarch, *Caliph Valid Almanzor*, who Conquer'd *Spain*, with something of a Hint from the *Arabian* Nights Entertainments."[11] The references to Caliph Almanzor and *The Arabian Nights' Entertainments* provide evidence for Manley's return to revenge. Although the first citation might seem to refer merely to Manley's sultan, it recalls protagonists of the same name from seventeenth-century revenge plays. Examples include George Chapman's *Revenge for Honour*, a revenge tragedy with a plot involving the caliph's directive to punish adultery, and John Dryden's *The Conquest of Granada*, a heroic tragedy that includes also an "Abdalla"—the name Manley gives to the sultan's rebellious brother.[12]

Manley's reference to *The Arabian Nights' Entertainments* further points to revenge. Manley takes more than a "hint" from the *Entertainments*, as she adapts the Scheherazade framing narrative and its revenge plot to form her own: a sultan who has been spurned by an adulterous wife habitually marries young women only to order their executions after the nuptials, and a woman uses language to save her own life and end a vicious cycle of vengeance. In comparing the *Entertainments'* full title with Manley's subtitle, *The Arabian Vow*, we find a second revenge correlation. A look at the 1706 English edition's long title—*Arabian Nights Entertainments Consisting of One Thousand and One STORIES, TOLD BY the Sultaness of the* Indies, *to divert the Sultan from the Execution of a Bloody Vow he had made to Marry a Lady every Day, and have her head cut off next Morning, to avenge himself for the Disloyalty of his first Sultaness, &c.*[13]—suggests that Manley specifically appropriates the sultan's "Bloody Vow ... to avenge himself." Manley interprets this vow as a repetitive act of vengeance, one that she repurposes theatrically in order to highlight virtue's triumph over vengeance.

According to the preface, John Dennis is the source for Manley's turn to virtue. After all, she claims that Dennis's "excellent Pen" and "View of what Heroick Vertue ought to attempt" in his 1706 *Essay upon Opera's* inspired her to create Almyna. In his essay, Dennis argues that "Virtue" has "been the preserver of Nations" and that the English must continue to "teach publick Virtue and publick Spirit."[14] A consideration of the timing of Manley's play contra an opera at a rival theater, as well as the nationalistic language of

Dennis's essay, further suggests that Manley picks up Dennis's charge for playwrights to "defend the English stage" against its "Mortal Foes": foreign entertainment, namely operas, and effeminacy.[15] Dennis calls for a "British Muse" to save the stage (i.e., England), and Manley answers with Almyna's voice.[16] *Almyna*'s prologue, spoken by actor Colley Cibber, echoes this sentiment as it labels *Almyna* "an English PLAY" and criticizes a "high-tasted Age" that prefers operas over home-grown tragedies.

As in Dennis's prose, *Almyna*'s prologue associates foreignness with effeminacy. Cibber labels operas "Strumpet[s]" and "Wantons" who deceive, while English tragedies are cast as "Chast Wives" who represent "Truth." Cibber urges "Patrons" to use their "Manlier Judgments" (possibly a pun on Manley's name, which interestingly doubles as an anagram of Almyna). Cibber calls for playgoers to delight in what "informs the Mind" rather than what "vainly charms the Ear." In essence, the prologue encourages audiences to man up and support edifying English drama, rather than enchanting Italian operas. In a time when opera threatened to displace English tragedy, Manley does her part to bolster the British cause. She gives audiences an English-language play that depicts exotic images while exploring a crisis of male effeminacy. An examination of the play's discourse counters these problems with Almyna's characteristically Christian, civic speeches and invectives against revenge and irrational impulses. At the same time, this analysis allows for a greater understanding of the vastly understudied male characters in the play.

Vows of Vengeance

Manley's handling of this theatrical and even national quandary can be seen in her portrayal of male characters that either physically seek or speak of seeking revenge, namely, Sultan Almanzor, the Vizier (Almyna's father), and Prince Abdalla. Manley opens the play in familiar territory as she depicts prominent images from seventeenth-century drama: vengeance on behalf of injured honor and a vendetta against women. To begin, exposition sheds light on Almanzor's vengeful vow. In a detail taken directly from the *Arabian Nights' Entertainment*, the vizier explains that Almanzor responds to his first wife's adultery (committed with a base "moorish Slave"[17]) by ordering all sultanesses' deaths; to avoid being made a cuckold again, subsequently all of his wives will die the mornings after the nuptials.

Almanzor's vow signals a recurring act of vengeance, one that Rene Girard calls "an interminable, infinitely repetitive process."[18] We know that this process began before the dramatic present of the play with the sultan's brother, the King of Tartary, who discovered his own wife's infidelity, and we learn that a desire for vengeance is passed on to Almanzor, who experiences the same dilemma. Almanzor hails revenge as a necessary path when he explains his brother's history to Abdalla: "Well did he [Tartary] execute, his instant Veng'ance on 'em, / And by his Scymiter unite their Fates."[19] Almanzor's vow affirms and regenerates this act every time the scimitar strikes or Almanzor's mutes strangle a new bride. As Almanzor understands it, his vow is justified: his first wife dishonored him by defiling the marriage bed and threatening legitimate succession with an illegitimate heir, so he has the right to redeem his honor.[20] Almanzor adapts the language of the Koran to validate his command: if women have no souls, then their deaths bear no moral, social, or religious consequences. The sultan's vow is law not only because of his own juridical power, but also it is a religious rite that excuses him from wrongdoing. According to everyone other than the sultan, this law is an abuse of his authority and their religion, for it punishes innocent people rather than perpetrators of a real crime.

While the community might be willing to validate the sultan's *original* revenge against an adulterous wife, it does not excuse his crimes against women. As the grand vizier explains, Almanzor garners no approval from his subjects for his cruel vow against women who have not proven themselves to be false. The vizier criminalizes the decree in asking, "What is it else but Murther? horrid Murther!" and in calling the vow "Rash," "Cruel," and "most prodigious."[21] He openly associates the mandate with revenge as he ponders:

> For cou'd Youth, Innocence, and Beauty, plead
> Against Revenge, and [Almanzor's] rigid sense of Honour,
> The Sultaness, who but this Morning dy'd,
> Might well have hop'd, to shine her length of Years.[22]

Likewise, the sultan's brother states that "Revenge and Hate" motivate Almanzor, and in a vocalization of his vendetta, Almanzor suggests that men succumb to their passions, including "Jealousy, Revenge, or Treachery," because of "female Falsehood."[23] As the vizier argues that Almanzor's vow epitomizes jealousy and projects a single man's fears onto the entirety of the female sex, the sultan's own words show much of the same. Personal honor, hatred, and dread characterize his leadership.

Because the sultan is motivated personally by revenge, but officially uses his power to enforce his vendetta, *Almyna* situates revenge in terms of a private/public impasse. Almyna confirms that revenge jeopardizes the sultan's ability to rule well when she explains how his vow tarnishes the public image of an otherwise noble and sensible ruler. When she says that Almanzor appears "wise, and good in all things else; / Brave, Generous, and Just,"[24] she paints a picture of a man whose good qualities are clouded by revenge.

Almanzor is not the only figure in the play to struggle with retaliation, for the vizier and prince vow to seek vengeance, too. If we accept that revenge is a repetitive act, we see that their desire for retribution is linked to the sultan's vow, which was inspired by his elder brother's vow, and so forth. As Girard notes:

> Every time [revenge] turns up in some part of the community, it threatens to involve the whole social body. There is the risk that the act

of vengeance will initiate a chain reaction whose consequences will quickly prove fatal to any society of modest size. The multiplication of reprisals instantaneously puts the very existence of a society in jeopardy, and that is why it is universally proscribed.[25]

In Act III we witness this "chain reaction" when the vizier offers to retaliate against Abdalla because he intends to wed the vizier's daughter Almyna instead of her sister. The vizier aims "To make [his] Vengeance sure"[26] by killing Abdalla for breaking Zoradia's heart. Unlike the sultan, who creates a law to inflict his payback, the vizier has no legal recourse. Instead, he fantasizes that he can climb to the Heavens "for [his] Revenge" and "Ransack the Stores of Lightning, Storms and Thunder! / Pluck the Bolts hissing, from the Forger's hand! / And hurl them glowing, on the Traytor's [Abdalla's] head."[27] The vizier's enthusiasm for vengeance reiterates the play's message that men are unable to control their passions and that this effeminacy produces violence.

The same *might* be said of Abdalla's actions near the end of the play. In Act IV he warns Almanzor, "Dare not, for thy own, to touch her [Almyna's] sacred Life, / Whilst I have Breath, Revenge shall be my cry!"[28] Although Abdalla *seems* to offer up another image of an honorific revenger, the reasons behind this revenge cry are questionable. The vizier implies that usurpation rather than Almyna's liberation motivate Abdalla and the mob to storm the castle; thus, Abdalla might not actually be seeking revenge, but political advancement.[29] After all, the vizier defines the "ambitious Prince['s]" quest to save Almyna as "pretence, what ever the Design."[30] If we trust the vizier's opinion, we are forced to recognize Abdalla's manipulation of the language of revenge.

Although scholars of the play have noted that Manley shies away from making overt political gestures in the work, when we consider these characters' charges for revenge, we should remember that "revenge drama," as John Kerrigan claims, is "an opportunistic vehicle for current affairs."[31] Even if Abdalla acts on behalf of Almyna's life, his revenge threatens his ruler's sovereignty and royal succession. Some scholars read hints of James II or the Jacobite pretender in Abdalla, thus drawing a connection between the play and real-life politics, and a handful of scholars have explained that eighteenth-century audience members and readers were concerned about the oaths of allegiance depicted in Act I, as well as the discussion of the crisis of inherited rulership that results from the sultan's inability to produce a legitimate heir.[32] This crisis of bloodline resembles England's own succession problem as Queen Anne, like her uncle, lacked a natural-born legitimate heir to the throne.[33] Unlike the Stuarts, of course, the sultan chooses revenge over progeny. In paying allegiance to vengeance, he dwells too much on the past and intervenes in succession rather than securing a future of royal offspring. It is up to Almyna to convince Almanzor that he must abolish his Arabian vow for his own sake and for his subjects.

"Heroick Vertue" Reforms the Revenger

Through Almyna's magnificent speeches, Manley establishes the kind of civic tragedy promoted by Dennis. Almyna is a forward-thinking (female) hero who brandishes words rather than weapons to restore glory to the ruler and nation. In examining Almyna's language, we find an Arabian character's strikingly English promulgation of a Christian understanding of vengeance, which indicates that final judgment and punishment of crimes belongs to Heaven, not to man. When Almyna first considers sacrificing herself to the sultan's vow in order to show him the error of his ways, her father explains that they must "Leave ... the work to Heav'n, ... / (For Heav'n in its own time, redresses Wrongs)."[34] Here we should recall Bible verses such as Romans 12:19 ("Vengeance is mine") that teach Christians that God will judge men and redress wrongs. Manley shows us, nonetheless, that men do not easily learn this lesson, for moments after having this conversation with Almyna the vizier offers to seek revenge against Abdalla. Almyna, however, takes this proclamation to heart and extends a Christian notion of reforming man's passion for revenge.

In a sense, Manley allows Almyna a practice run in reforming the play's principal revenger; her first attempt comes with Almyna's cooling her father's flames by showing him a reasonable path: "Dry up your Tears, and smooth that furrow'd Brow. / Passions, my Lord, but seldom mend a Wrong; / Where Anger ends, Repentance still begins!"[35] This anti-revenge oratory foreshadows the ultimate outcome for the sultan: repentance. Whereas the vizier's aforementioned tirade imitates the language of seventeenth-century heroic tragedy, Almyna's expressions resemble eighteenth-century sentiments in civic drama and pathos-driven she-tragedies. Almyna represents an early form of what Brett D. Wilson calls a "race of female patriots" in the "civic mode of drama" that comes to govern early eighteenth-century tragedies; she symbolizes "public-spirited women" and "patriotic sentiment" that is popular in plays such as Dennis's *Liberty Asserted*, Catharine Trotter's *Revolution of Sweden*, and Nicholas Rowe's *Jane Shore*.[36] As Wilson remarks, early eighteenth-century tragedies were "recognizing that women can have 'heroick Virtue' in their own right" and that such "civic passion" makes possible a "new regime."[37] In supporting this "new regime"—a new heroic model—for tragic drama, Manley shows the potential for language to combat men's destructive tendencies and for women to champion civil rights. The vizier's rant allows Almyna, in fitting pathetic territory, to offer herself up as a scapegoat for all women, her father's desire for vengeance, and eventually for the sultan's. The play does not stage this sacrifice as mere passive resignation, for Almyna's kind of virtue does not register as submission, as we find in many seventeenth-century tragic heroines.

On the contrary, Almyna's self-sacrifice reads as a new kind of masculine female heroic that draws on a rhetoric of reason and virtue. Almyna first attempts to change her father's vengeful state-of-mind by appealing to logic: "You have already been in part reveng'd, / Just at the Altar, dashing all his hopes; / He suffers more from Grief, than you from Rage."[38] If his rationale holds up, the vizier already achieved retribution through his satisfying knowledge of Abdalla's grief; therefore, he need not commit a reckless act of violence. While he recognizes her good judgment in saying, "Wisdom is in thy heart, but Rage in mine," the vizier's mind is not easily changed, for he concedes, "I am not fit to hear, tho' thou to speak; / Unless to Vengeance, thou coud'st tune thy Voice."[39] Of course, Almyna does not alter her tune; the vizier's resistance encourages her all the more to break down his rage. Dennis's *Essay* comes to mind as Almyna explains in the voice of a "British Muse":

> We that want Reason's force, to check the Passions.
> Expecting all things, from their Vows, and flat'ry
> In nothing answer'd, but in Disappointment.
> But I to Glory have resign'd my Life,
> That Spiritual Pride of Noble hearts!
> And not to be as Love, Cloy'd with Possession.
> Glory the strongest passion of great Minds![40]

Rather than accept defeat, Almyna rejoices with her father in "the Heroick Deeds" that they can "perform" in stopping the vizier's vengeance.[41] In her first victory over vice, Almyna truly embodies the part of a virtuous hero. Her father admits, "Glory shines around [her] lovely Face"; to him she is "Something Divine"; and she "gives [his] Soul an awe."[42] At last, we know that the vizier has been converted when he says, "Speak on Prophetick Maid, thy Father hears."[43] More evidence of this realization comes at the end of the play when the vizier criticizes that initial desire for revenge that led Almyna to sacrifice herself:

> Curse on the fury that did lead me on.
> Curse on my Ill tim'd Vengeance on the Prince;
> Revenge stills turns on the Avenger's head,
> Oh! better were it much to suffer Wrong,
> Leaving to Heav'n, the time and means of Vengeance.[44]

In echo of his own statement in Act II, the vizier's words in Act V confirm the cyclic nature of vengeance and reiterate that it is better left to God's judgment. The vizier can only articulate this problem now because Almyna suppressed his desire for vengeance.

With one revenger down, Almyna's true test comes in trying to assuage another to replace his vow of vengeance with her own vow of glory. This task is both civic and religious, selfless and self-righteous. Almyna behaves as a "female Christ figure," as Jean I. Marsden notes, who has been summoned by a higher power to die for her country, and a pseudo-missionary looking to convert the sultan.[45] According to statesman Alhador, Almyna's self-ascribed "noble Work" receives divine endorsement: "Fate ordain'd

[Almyna] to do its work, / And make a Convert, of our mighty *Sultan*."[46] If we follow the analogy, the sultan is a heathen that needs deliverance, and Almyna seeks to bring this to him by reforming his barbaric, or read here as *foreign*, passion for revenge. Alhador's prophecy that Almyna's "Vertue" will lead the sultan to cry, "Here ends our Vow! for here *Almyna*'s Reign begins!"[47] suggests that he will be redeemed and that she will one day rule over (or with) him. Certainly Alhador indicates that Almyna can usher in political stability and a future free from Almanzor's revenge. Before this can happen, however, the Scrooge-like sultan has to face the ghosts of his past and his future; he has to learn how to listen to reason in order to save his soul.

Almanzor's nightmare in Act IV solidifies the play's warnings against revenge first by confirming a higher power's opposition to his actions, and then by preemptively strengthening Almyna's argument for redemption. In the dream-vision, Almanzor passes a lake "laden with all [his] sins," sees his prophet on the other side judging him for his actions, and faces the dead queens who point at him "with revengeful Rage."[48] Almanzor recognizes that he murdered these women "in the fear of Jealousy," that he is "Charg'd with the Blood of Innocents," and that he must atone for his "rash Vow."[49] He witnesses the punishment for his crimes in saying: "Deep in the horrid River I was plung'd, / My strugling Soul, already tasting Torments. / Our Queen's aloud, shouting revengeful Joy!"[50] Manley not only paints a picture of the sultan's future if he does not repent and repeal his vow, but also uses his dream to lay the foundation for Almyna's great debate with Almanzor.

While Almyna has no knowledge of Almanzor's dream, she clairvoyantly evokes images from the dream in her argument. She capitalizes on the sultan's fear of his murdered wives' revenge against him and reinforces the providential nature of her goal to reform him. As examples, she questions the sultan's vow by invoking his fear of God's judgment, and she refers to the "Queens, [who] shall urge him, to revenge 'em," and the "horrid River" that he will "never! never! … cross."[51] In her discourse, Almyna not only taps into the sultan's fear of a vengeful God who denies him passage, but also exposes the dangers of Almanzor's perversion of sacred texts. She argues that Almanzor's jealousy and revenge motivated his misreading of the Koran, and in acknowledging this fallacy Almyna exposes the sultan's use of religious authority to sustain an impious revenge:

> Suppose I take an Oath to slay the Innocent,
> The Crime were less, much less to break the Vow,
> Than by performing it, to run on Murder.
> But thou securest thy self, from thoughts of Sin:
> For that our Prophet, in his *Alcoran*,
> As thou explain'st says Women have no Souls,
> But mighty Sultan, tell thy heart but this;
> Had not thy beautious, faulty Queen done Ill?

> Woudst thou the Letter, e're have so expounded?
> Revenge, and Jealousy, arrests the Text:
> Thus taught to speak, to put a gloss on Murder.
> Oh, horrid Crime! Murder of Innocents![52]

Here Manley highlights an example of male "irreligious" speech, to quote Marguerite Corporaal, where there is a "contrast between men's deceitful, dishonourable speeches, on the one hand, and the female character's honest, virtuous words, on the other."[53] Like a cross-examiner in a courtroom, Almyna links revenge to eternal damnation, revealing that the sultan's afterlife appears grim if he continues to uphold his irreverent Arabian vow: "Dost thou not tremble; Sultan, but to think? / How fatal to thee, the Mistake may prove? / What will our Prophet say, at thy last day?"[54] Again, Manley draws upon the sultan's dream and familiar Christian rhetoric about God's final judgment against revengers.

As with the vizier, Almyna draws on multiple logical approaches to convince Almanzor to change. Beyond inducing the fear of an angry god, Almyna appeals to Almanzor's sense of justice. She acknowledges that he had the right to "dispise" the "inconstancy of a weak Woman" and "punish" his first wife for her crime, but she also urges him to "forget" the past and "so end Revenge; / Not hold a trembling innocent World in awe, / For Crimes that are not theirs."[55] Yet she asks him to stop thinking about himself as an injured man and to start thinking of himself as a respectable leader. This transition is difficult for Almanzor, and he questions if he has "become so monstrous to [his] People" or if they believe that his "Revenge was just."[56] Clearly he identifies his vow as one of vengeance, yet he considers it just *because* he made it. Only through debating with Almyna can Almanzor see that he has been a monstrous rather than a fair monarch. Almyna opens his eyes to what his vow represents—a recurring act of revenge that is a crime against women *and* all of his subjects. Ultimately, Almanzor changes his view because Almyna frames the argument about his corrupt rule in sensible terms: his people *do* see the murders of innocent victims as unlawful acts against women and their families, not as a justified reprisal for a monarch's injury. The original murder of a guilty wife satisfied that injury to the sultan's honor, but the successive murders are interpreted as tyranny. Even if the play does not make overt partisan claims, this passage imparts a dramatic critique of unchecked power.

As it turns out, the debate on revenge and rulership addresses the problem as much as the solution: even unyielding monarchs are capable of change when good subjects guide them. We see the beginning of this transformation when Almanzor claims that he will stop marrying and murdering women. First he states that after Almyna dies "the remainder of [his] Life will waste, / In Penitence for [his] rash Vow, and [her] fair Loss."[57] Luckily, Almanzor demonstrates the full realization of his conversation and saves Almyna when "the Mutes are going to strangle her," according to the stage directions.[58] If Almanzor's logic is to be believed, he designed her death scene as a "Tryal" to test "How far [her] bravery of Soul cou'd reach."[59] Regardless, we should notice that Almanzor recognizes that Almyna has a soul and that he claims to have been "vanquish'd, by [Almyna's] heroick Deeds."[60] Finally, we see rewards of "Heroick Virtue": no more women will fall victim to the sultan's vow, and Almyna gains glory and a long marriage to the sultan.

While the audience is surely happy with this outcome, the play has one more thing to accomplish. It must illustrate how the sultan has become that wise, good ruler that Almyna described in Act II. The final act transfers its anxieties from Almanzor to Abdalla, who represents a foil to a ruler who has learned from his mistakes and is finally capable of maintaining justice. In contrasting the sultan's repentance with Abdalla's death, Manley uses Almanzor as a mouthpiece to give his subjects, and the English audience, two lessons about repentance and recklessness: first, "Thus are we punish'd for our rash Resolves. / Our cruel Vow, be expiated here," and second, *"For Heav'n no Hopes, but Penitence allows. / Either for cruel, rash, or perjur'd Vows."*[61] In the play's final message about rebellion and vengeful vows, Manley demonstrates that penitence is the best method for ensuring a rehabilitated, secure state. If we read tragic drama as a sign of the political sphere, as Lisa Freeman claims we should,[62] we find in *Almyna: or, The Arabian Vow* a happier forecast for the nation, one endowed with natural succession and responsible leadership.

From Royal Mischief to Rewriting Revenge

By weaving a series of plots that address the ramifications of revenge, *Almyna: or, The Arabian Vow* at first evokes conventional revenge elements from seventeenth-century drama but finds a way to provide a revenge tale's morals without murdering the revenger. While revengers in heroic tragedies typically refuse to convert from being an avenger to a penitent, Manley's Almyna—like a theatrical messiah—shows Sultan Almanzor the way to redeem himself through repentance, trust, and true love. By the end of *Almyna*, the protagonist's "noble Work" corresponds with that of the playwright's. As Almyna reforms the revenger, Manley re-forms revenge. Manley's new staging of revenge-conquered-by-virtue reflects the tenets of Dennis's *Essay* as *Almyna* develops a dramatic, civic project that anticipates plays' focus on reform and revenge later in the century, such as Edward Young's 1721 *The Revenge* and John Brown's 1755 *Barbarossa*.[63] Manley's play, a precursor for such dramatic hits, demonstrates the potential for a revision of the bloody seventeenth-century revenge tale, the type Manley first imitated in *The Royal Mischief*. In the end, "Reason rein[s] the Passions," as Almyna puts it, and Manley's play provides the lesson required by Dennis as it both "teach[es] publick Virtue and publick Spirit," and purges effeminacy and corruption.[64] In this eighteenth-century manifestation of the vengeance tale, audiences learn that reason trumps revenge, masculine wisdom must reign over effeminate passion, reform is possible, and the nation can be governed by sensible leaders who rule with the people's best interests in mind. These lessons reflect not only a new, happy ending for the revenge tale, but also a transformation in Manley's drama, which now uses powerful words rather than hyperbolic stage spectacle to entertain audiences.

Notes

1. Delarivier Manley, *The Royal Mischief. A Tragedy. As it is Acted by His Majesties Servants*. London: R. Bentley, F. Saunders, and J. Knapton, 1696. Fidelis Morgan, *The Female Wits: Women Playwrights of the Restoration*. London: Virago, 1981. Beyond a theory that Manley abandoned drama because of negative reactions to *The Royal Mischief*, it is uncertain why Manley left off writing for the stage. Perhaps she was absorbed in her personal life, including amatory liaisons with John Manley and John Tilly. Perhaps her friendships with other writers, such as Sarah Egerton or Richard Steele, diverted her attention; maybe her profitable assistance in legal cases kept her from the stage. Possibly she was making her first foray into scandal writing and composed *Queen Zarah*, although Rachel Carnell argues in *A Political Biography of Delarivier Manley* (London: Pickering and Chatto, 2008) that Manley did not write the work. For more information on Manley's biographical details and political secret history, readers will find Carnell's essay in this current collection very useful. For additional studies on *The Royal Mischief* and *The Female Wits*, see Bernadette Andrea's, Katharine Beutner's, and Chris Mounsey's essays, which are published also in this book collection.
2. Delarivier Manley, *Almyna: or, The Arabian Vow. A Tragedy. As It Is Acted at The Theatre Royal in the Hay-Market, by Her Majesty's Servants*. London: William Turner, 1707.
3. Studies of John Dennis's and Nicholas Rowe's tragedies mark this change in theatrical taste. See Lisa Freeman, *Character's Theater: Genre and Identity on the Eighteenth-Century English Stage*. Philadelphia: University of Pennsylvania Press, 2002; Jean I. Marsden, *Fatal Desire: Women, Sexuality, and the English Stage, 1660–1720*. Ithaca, NY: Cornell University Press, 2006; Alfred Schwartz, "An Example of Eighteenth-Century Pathetic Tragedy: Rowe's *Jane Shore*," *Modern Language Quarterly* 22, no. 3 (1961): 236–47; and Brett D. Wilson, *A Race of Female Patriots: Women and Public Spirit on the British Stage, 1688–1745*. Lewisburg, PA: Bucknell UP, 2012.
4. In many of the following examples *Almyna* is briefly mentioned, while in a few cases the play receives significant attention. See Rachel Carnell's *A Political Biography of Delarivier Manley*; Jean I. Marsden's *Fatal Desire*; Ruth Herman's *The Business of a Woman: The Political Writings of Delarivier Manley*. Newark: University of Delaware Press, 2003; Pilar Cuder-Domínguez's *Stuart Women Playwrights, 1613–1713*. Burlington, VT: Ashgate, 2010; Bridget Orr's "Galland, Georgian Theatre, and the Creation of Popular Orientalism," in *The Arabian Nights in Historical Context Between East and West*, Saree Makdisi and Felicity Nussbaum, ed. (Oxford: Oxford UP, 2008), 103–130, and *Empire on the English Stage, 1660–1714*. Cambridge: Cambridge UP, 2001; Su Fang Nu's "Delariviere Manley's *Almyna* and Dating the First Edition of the *English Arabian Nights' Entertainments*," *English Language Notes* 40, no. 3 (2003): 19–26; Margarete Rubik's *Early Women Dramatists 1550–1800*. New York: St. Martin's, 1998; Jacqueline Pearson's *The Prostituted Muse: Images of Women & Women Dramatists 1642–1737*. New

York: St. Martin's, 1988; Constance Clark's *Three Augustan Women Playwrights* (New York: P. Lang, 1986); and Patricia Köster's "Humanism, Feminism, Sensationalism: Mrs. Manley vs. Society," *Translations of the Samuel Johnson Society of the Northwest* 4 (1972): 42–53.

5. Brett D. Wilson discusses this subgenre at length in *A Race of Female Patriots*.

6. For a discussion of revenge as a theatrical phenomenon, see Misty Krueger, "'The Last Dear Drop of Blood': Revenge in Restoration Tragic Drama." PhD Diss, University of Tennessee, 2010, and Misty Krueger, "Revenge in Early Restoration England and Sir William Davenant's *Hamlet*," *New Perspectives on the Eighteenth Century* 8 no.1 (2011): 31–50.

7. For a discussion of *The Royal Mischief* in terms of empire, place, and other Restoration writings, see Bernadette Andrea's essay included in this book collection.

8. John Dennis, *Essay upon the Opera's After the Italian Manner, Which are about to be Establish'd on the English Stage: With some Reflections on the Damage which they may bring to the Publick* (London: John Nutt, 1706), 8.

9. We might consider Manley's choice in *Almyna* to save her revenger a contrast to her decision to punish her rake in *The Lost Lovers*, as Victoria Joule explains in her essay in this collection.

10. Certain issues prevented the play's success—namely, Anne Bracegirdle's retirement three days into the play, Robert Wilkes's illness, the high price of admission (to account for costume expenses), and the competition from the popular opera, *Camilla*, which was staged simultaneously at Drury Lane. While the preface claims that the Queen's Company intended to stage the drama again in the following season, the play did not enjoy return performances. The preface claims that Manley was not in London when the play was staged. Rachel Carnell, *Political Biography*, 146, argues that Manley's finances and desire to avoid creditors is likely a cause for her absence. Also, see Constance Clark, *Three Augustan Women Playwrights*, 172, for information on the play's staging.

11. Delarivier Manley, *Almyna*, n.p. The preface and prologue are on unnumbered pages.

12. George Chapman, *Revenge for Honour. A Tragedie*. London: Richard Marriot, 1654. John Dryden, *The Conquest of Granada by the Spaniards in Two Parts: Acted at the Theatre Royall*, London: Henry Herringman, 1672. Manley also composed poems for *The Nine Muses*, a collection published in honor of the late Dryden; thus, his work might have been on her mind when she considered writing a drama again. Delarivier Manley, *The Nine Muses, Or, Poems Written by Nine Severall Ladies Upon the Death of the Late Famous John Dryden, Esq.* London: Richard Basset, 1700.

13. The oldest copy in the *Eighteenth-Century Collections Online* database is the 4th edition: *Arabian Nights Entertainments: Consisting of One Thousand and One Stories, Told by the Sultaness of the Indies, to Divert the Sultan from the Execution of a Bloody Vow He Had Made to Marry a Lady Every Day, and Have Her Cut off Next Morning, to Avenge Himself for the Disloyalty of His First Sultaness, &c. Containing A Better Account of the Customs, Manners, and Religion of the Eastern Nations, viz. Tartars, Persians, and Indians, than is to be Met with in any Author hitherto Publish'd. Translated into French from the Arabian Mss. by M. Galland, of the Royal Academy; and Now Done into English* Vol. 1. 4th ed. London: Printed for Andrew Bell, 1713. Su Fang Nu argues that Manley probably draws upon the 1706 English translation instead of the 1704 French one. Nu, 24, points out that

the play's vocabulary for "exotic" items, such as "dervish" or "Alcoran" shows "the French influence." Nu further suggests that Manley's fascination with exotic tales might derive from the work of her father, Sir Roger Manley, a translator and publisher. For scholarly work on eighteenth-century translations of *The Arabian Nights*, see Saree Makdisi and Felicity Nussbaum, ed., *The Arabian Nights in Historical Context Between East and West*. Oxford: Oxford UP, 2008, and Yuriko Yamanaka and Tetsuo Nishio, ed. *The Arabian Nights and Orientalism: Perspectives from East and West*. New York: I.B. Tauris, 2006.

14. Dennis, *Essay upon Opera's*, 8 and 7.
15. Ibid., 2.
16. Ibid., 3.
17. Delarivier Manley, *Almyna*, 1.i, 3. Because the original play text's lines are unnumbered, citations to this text will refer to act, scene, and page numbers.
18. Rene Girard, *Violence and the Sacred*, Trans. Patrick Gregory. (Baltimore: Johns Hopkins UP, 1977), 14.
19. Delarivier Manley, *Almyna*, 1.i, 11.
20. Earla Wilputte's essay, also included in this book collection, addresses a similar plot point found in Manley's later fiction, the *Husband's Resentment* novels from *The Power of Love: In Seven Novels* (1720). As in *Almyna*, a *Husband's Resentment* tale (Novel IV) depicts a wife's infidelity and a husband's revenge. According to Wilputte, Manley's *Husband* tales shows that there is a fine line between what society considers just and unjust behavior, i.e., revenge, when a husband's honor is concerned.
21. Ibid., 1.i, 1, and 1.i, 3.
22. Ibid., 1.i, 4.
23. Ibid., 1.i, 4, and 1.i, 9.
24. Ibid., 2.i, 20.
25. Girard, *Violence and the Sacred*, 14–15.
26. Delarivier Manley, *Almyna*, 3.i, 26.
27. Ibid., 3.i, 27.
28. Ibid., 4.i, 51.
29. This reading aligns with Bridget Orr's assertion in "Galland, Georgian Theatre, and the Creation of Popular Orientalism," 108, that the play "mount[s] a high-Tory critique of disloyalty."
30. Delarivier Manley, *Almyna*, 5.ii, 64.
31. John Kerrigan, *On Shakespeare and Early Modern Literature: Essays* (Oxford: Oxford University Press, 2001), 242. Most critics tend to read Manley's work as Tory propaganda, but Rachel Carnell, 150, argues that the play contains "multiple and conflicting ideologies." Ruth Herman makes a similar argument in *The Business of a Woman: The Political Writings of Delarivier Manley*, 179.
32. For more on this allegorical reading, see Rachel Carnell's and Bridget Orr's work on the play. Ruth Herman's and Rachel Carnell's biographies provide ample context for interpreting the sensitive issue of oath taking in 1706. It is well known that the extended ceremony and staging of oaths offended the play's Whig dedicatee, Elizabeth Montagu, Countess of Sandwich (the Earl of Rochester's daughter).
33. For additional context, see Rachel Carnell, *A Political Biography*, and Pilar Cuder-Domínguez, *Stuart Women Playwrights, 1613–1713*.

34. Delarivier Manley, *Almyna*, 2.i, 21.
35. Ibid., 3.i, 26.
36. Wilson, *A Race of Female Patriots*, vii–viii. See John Dennis, *Liberty Asserted. A Tragedy. As it is acted at the New Theatre in Little Lincoln's-Inn-Fields.* London: George Strahan and Bernard Lintott, 1704; Catharine Trotter, *Revolution of Sweden. A Tragedy. As it is acted at the Queens Theatre in the Hay-Market.* London: James Knapton and George Strahan, 1706; and Nicholas Rowe, *The Tragedy of Jane Shore. Written in Imitation of Shakespear's Style.* London: Bernard Lintott, 1714.
37. Wilson, *A Race of Female Patriots*, 94.
38. Delarivier Manley, *Almyna*, 3.i., 27.
39. Ibid.
40. Ibid.
41. Ibid., 3.i, 28.
42. Ibid.
43. Ibid.
44. Ibid., 5.ii, 60.
45. Marsden, *Fatal Desire*, 128.
46. Delarivier Manley, *Almyna*, 2.i, 21, and 3.i, 29.
47. Ibid., 3.i, 29.
48. Ibid., 4.i, 39. Because this scene asks the audience to gaze upon Almanzor's body in his bedchamber, Marsden, *Fatal Desire*, 127, reminds us that the opening of Act IV provides a reversal of discovery scenes from she-tragedies.
49. Delarivier Manley, *Almyna*, 4.i, 39.
50. Ibid.
51. Ibid., 4.i, 45.
52. Ibid., 4.i, 44.
53. Marguerite Corporaal, "'Will You to My Discourse Vouchsafe an Eare?': Women Dramatists' Negotiation of Gender and Genre on the Public Stage around 1700," *Journal of English Studies* 4 (2003–2004): 45.
54. Delarivier Manley, *Almyna*, 4.i, 44.
55. Ibid., 4.i, 46.
56. Ibid., 4.i, 46, and 4.i, 47.
57. Delarivier Manley, *Almyna*, 4.i, 47.
58. Ibid., 5.i, 63.
59. Ibid., 5.ii, 64.
60. Ibid.
61. Ibid., 5.ii. 68.
62. Lisa Freeman, *Character's Theater*.
63. Edward Young, *The Revenge A Tragedy. As It Is Acted at The Theatre-Royal in Drury-Lane.* London: W. Chetwood, 1721. John Brown, *An Account of Barbarossa, The Usurper of Algiers. Being the Story on Which the New Tragedy, Now in Rehearsal at The Theatre Royal in Drury-Lane.* London: W. Reeve, 1755.
64. Delarivier Manley, *Almyna*, 5.ii, 62, and Dennis, *Essay upon Opera's*, 7.

4 "Through the Black Sea and the Country of Colchis"

A Geocentric Approach to Delarivier Manley's *The Royal Mischief* (1696)

Bernadette Andrea

During the second half of the seventeenth century, both the suppression of the public stage and its "restoration" along with the monarchy were represented through shifting signifiers of Islam, most of them distorted by English ignorance and prejudice.[1] Such signifiers range from Oliver Cromwell's depiction as a "Turkish tyrant" to Charles II's portrayal as the polygamous "Grand Signior."[2] The first production to test the ban on public performances—William Davenant's *The Siege of Rhodes* in 1656—featured a Muslim character as its protagonist. John Dryden's *The Conquest of Granada*, which launched the genre of Restoration heroic drama in 1670, followed Davenant's lead. Within this ideological framework, English women found new opportunities for public expression as actresses, patrons, and playwrights. While other women penned and even performed plays during the Restoration, the sustained professional career of Aphra Behn, who bore the orientalist epithet "Loves great *Sultana*," set the stage for the groundbreaking season of 1695/96 that debuted a cluster of female playwrights dubbed "the female wits."[3] Their plays include Catharine Trotter's *Agnes de Castro*, Manley's *The Lost Lover; or, The Jealous Husband* and *The Royal Mischief*, and Mary Pix's *Ibrahim, The Thirteenth Emperor of the Turks* and *The Spanish Wives*. The pseudonymous "Adriane" also staged a play, *She Ventures and He Wins*, and a posthumous production of Aphra Behn's *The Younger Brother: or, The Amorous Jilt* appeared.[4] By this count, "[o]ver one-third of all the new plays that season were by women or adapted from women's work," which in Paula Backscheider's assessment made it "unique—absolutely unique—in British theatrical history."[5]

Equally significant, two of these plays contain explicitly Islamicate themes, whereas none of the male playwrights for this season followed suit.[6] Launched in April 1696, Delarivier Manley's *The Royal Mischief* drew on *The Travels of Sir John Chardin into Persia and the East Indies*, a French Huguenot's eyewitness account from the 1660s and 1670s of the Persian Safavid dynasty and its client states. Staged in June 1696, Mary Pix's *Ibrahim, the Thirteenth Emperor of the Turks*, relied on the British consul Paul Rycaut's *History of the Turkish Empire, From the Year 1623 to the Year 1677*, another eyewitness account. Additional plays by "the

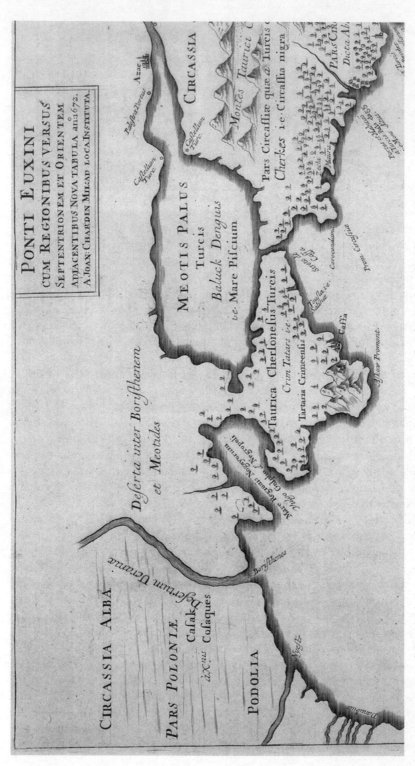

Figure 4.1 Map of the Black Sea region, from Sir John Chardin, *The Travels of Sir John Chardin into Persia and the East Indies* (London: Printed for Moses Pitt, 1686). RB 114374, The Huntington Library, San Marino, California.

female wits" deal with cross-cultural encounters in medieval Spain, which bore traces of its Islamic past.[7] Western fantasies about Muslim rulers' harems, wrongly dubbed "the seraglio," accordingly informed the theatrical debut of this group of playwrights by providing themes and shaping their reception as women challenging patriarchal limits.[8] Despite evidence that the "female wits" and the "first feminists" predominantly endorsed the orientalism of male travel writers, some English women during the early eighteenth century did articulate a counter-orientalist stance—or "dissent within the tradition"—in their literary productions.[9] Mary Wortley Montagu's *Turkish Embassy Letters* offers a famous, if often problematic, example of seeking to engage Ottoman Muslim women on their own terms; in Manley's case a generation prior, this counter-orientalist stance involved turning the tradition on itself by locating the source of gender despotism in England rather than displacing it onto exoticized cultural others.[10]

In this context, one approach to Manley's play is through the model of "transculturation" that Mary Louise Pratt recast for literary and cultural studies in her influential investigation of how travel narratives constituted Eurocentric imperialist discourses in the "contact zones" of Africa, the Caribbean, and South America from 1750 to 1850. As Pratt explains in *Imperial Eyes: Travel Writing and Transculturation*, her titular term describes "a phenomenon of the contact zone," which consists of "social spaces where disparate cultures meet, clash, and grapple with each other, often in highly asymmetrical relations of domination and subordination."[11] As Ania Loomba elaborates in *Colonialism/Postcolonialism*, this term productively "underscores the interaction, the borrowings and lendings, the appropriations in both directions which trouble any binary opposition between Europe and its 'others.'"[12] In addition to postcolonial approaches to the eighteenth century, Pratt's model has informed important studies of eighteenth-century women and empire, such as Kathleen Wilson's *The Island Race*, Felicity Nussbaum's *Torrid Zones*, and Laura Brown's *Ends of Empire*, to name only a few.[13] Yet, applying the model of transculturation *tout court*, which presumes the colonial mastery of "the West" (and particularly England) over "the Rest," to the proto-imperial era prior to the eighteenth century seems premature, particularly with respect to the still powerful Islamicate regions featured in Manley's *The Royal Mischief*.[14] While their colonial efforts in the Caribbean and North America were gaining traction, in no sense could the "marginal English" be seen as hegemonic in relation to the Islamic empires of the Ottoman Turks and Safavid Persians.[15]

More apt, in my view, is Mita Choudhury's model in *Interculturalism and Resistance in the London Theater, 1660–1800*, which follows postcolonial theorist Homi Bhabha in emphasizing "the 'inscription and articulation of culture's hybridity' in the written and unwritten, voiced and silenced, visible and invisible dimensions of theatrical culture."[16] In stressing hybridity *within* England's emerging imperialist project during the long eighteenth century, Choudhury attends to "tendentious interactions between different cultures" as represented on the London stage through the projections

Edward Said defines as Orientalism.[17] While Choudhury examines the later eighteenth-century playwrights Elizabeth Inchbald and Hannah Cowley under the heading "Female Orientalism," which relied on a "seemingly uncomplicated East/West binary opposition," she does not address the earlier "female wits" and their relationship to emerging "feminist orientalism" at the turn of the eighteenth century.[18] As I propose, Manley in *The Royal Mischief* challenges the gendered binary opposition of East and West that subtends Said's influential formulation through characters such as Homais, a Colchian princess associated with the land of the Amazons.[19] Positioned in the liminal space between East and West, as I shall elaborate below, Homais deconstructs such oppositions when she challenges the patriarchal blackening of her reputation by proclaiming, "[t]here's none can say their lives were ever fair."[20] Other characters, such as the apparently heroic Levan Dadian and the apparently virtuous Bassima, also function to undermine these oppositions.

Adding to this focus on key characters, I submit that Manley's counterorientalist challenge extends to the multilayered or palimpsestic setting of *The Royal Mischief*, which has been mistaken for "Turkey" and/or "Persia" in criticism on the play. In fact, the primary action occurs in the Black Sea region around Colchis, which was a liminal zone between the two major Islamic empires of the era: the Ottomans and the Safavids. The list of competing empires impinging on Colchis also includes the expansionist Russian empire and the prospective British empire. More broadly, Colchis resonated for Renaissance audiences as the goal of the classical Greek hero Jason and his Argonauts, whose adventures remained archetypal for the Western European discourse of empire.[21] It was also the home of Medea, the powerful and forlorn native woman who assisted him. Specifically, Medea was the daughter of the King of Colchis, who betrayed her natal family by facilitating Jason's theft of the Golden Fleece, which became a celebrated emblem for early modern imperialists.[22] When Jason, who brought her to Corinth as his wife, betrayed her because she was a "barbarian" woman, she wreaked her revenge by killing their children, which has become a troubling icon for modern feminists.[23] Following the methodology of "geocriticism," which pursues the "*multifocalization* of views on a given referential space" rather than privileges a close reading of a particular scene, I therefore adduce a wide range of English-language texts from the early sixteenth century through the end of the seventeenth century to situate the setting of *The Royal Mischief* within a larger debate about gender and empire in the early modern period.[24]

Mapping the Imperial Imaginary of Manley's *The Royal Mischief*

The main plot of *The Royal Mischief*, Manley's second play for the public stage and her first tragedy, involves Homais, the young wife of the elderly prince of Libardian and the eventual lover of his nephew, Levan, who is the prince of Colchis. Their relationship was considered incestuous by early modern English standards. Intersecting plots involve Osman, the grand vizier, who is in love with Bassima, a captured princess who becomes Levan's wife as part of a peace treaty. She is from Abcas, a country adjacent to Colchis. Selima is sister to the prince of Libardian and wife of Osman; she discovers his attraction for Bassima with disastrous results. Ismael, who previously took Homais's virginity, now seeks to take Osman's viziership. And Acmat is a eunuch who facilitates Homais's "royal mischief," which Elizabeth Hollis-Berry insightfully connects to "emergent individualism and imperialism."[25] The plot concludes with Bassima poisoned, Osman blown out of a cannon, Selima gathering his burning body parts, Homais murdered by her husband, Levan committing suicide, and the prince of Libardian crying, "O horror, horror, horror!"[26]

In line with Choudhury's intercultural analysis of the "tendentious inter-actions between different cultures," the Islamicate setting of Manley's first tragedy is at the same time geographically precise *and* posited as a gener-alized space onto which an English audience can project its proto-imperial desires and anxieties.[27] As such, the first stage direction of *The Royal Mischief* reads: "Scene of the castle of Phasia in Libardian and the prince of Colchis's camp before it."[28] According to John (Jean) Chardin (Manley's primary source), Libardian refers to "a country that extends itself a great way into Mount Caucasus."[29] He continues his textual mapping:

> Colchis is situated at the end of the Black Sea. To the east it is enclosed with a little kingdom, which makes part of Georgia ...; to the south, by the Black Sea; to the west, by the Abcas; and to the north, by Mount Caucasus.... All the oriental people call Colchis Odische, and the Colchians Mingrelians.[30]

As the visual map that Chardin includes with his travelogue shows, due north of Colchis was the land of the Amazons. (See Figure 4.1.) Although Homais is immured in the royal apartments throughout the play, she asserts her independent agency by manipulating characters and events to achieve her ends, which include sexual fulfillment and political power. Indeed, by the last act, she has assumed the role of *de facto* general, issuing orders to enable a palace coup.[31] She may therefore be seen as "Amazonian" in a cultural and geographical sense.

To comprehend the imperial imaginary of *The Royal Mischief* neverthe-less requires broader attention to the body of English printed texts that fash-ion a composite image of Colchis and the Caucasus region from the middle of the sixteenth century, when a stabilized English nation began to advance its imperialist ambitions, through the end of the seventeenth century, when these ambitions began to manifest themselves in the consolidation of col-onies in the Caribbean and North America and in the increasing power of English shipping in the Mediterranean, long considered an "Ottoman lake."[32] While Manley does not explicitly acknowledge these additional texts, she may have been aware of them directly or indirectly. As evidence of her familiarity with this tradition, she repeatedly emphasized her "Liberal Education," which centered on the Greek and Latin classics, even if in translation.[33] She was conversant with scholarly histories of the Ottomans, including her father's *History of the Turkish Empire Continued, From the Year of Our Lord, 1676, to the Year 1686*, as well as the popular *Letters Writ by a Turkish Spy*, which she claimed was part of his *oeuvre*.[34] We also have evidence, albeit more circumstantial, that she read Alexander Ross's 1649 English version of the Qur'an and histories of the Muslim conquest of Spain.[35] Hence, Colchis as a multilayered setting for early modern English discourses of empire, and one with a specifically gendered valence in the figure of Medea, could not but impinge on Manley's engagement with the proliferation of Islamicate themes that characterized the late seventeenth-century London stage.

In general, the early modern textual tradition referencing Colchis consists of two threads, which ultimately intersect. First are the works that subtend the humanist tradition in England, starting with *The Dictionary of Syr Thomas Eliot* (1538) and *Bibliotheca Eliotae* (1542). Both draw on classical sources to define Colchis historically as "an Ile in Asia, where Medea was borne" and geographically with respect to "the ryver callyd Phasis."[36] This humanist project resulted in subsequent translations of Herodotus, Seneca, Lucan, Virgil, Pliny, and Ovid that reinforced the palimpsestic view of Colchis via ancient history and contemporary geography. The universal histories and cosmographies that proliferated during the sixteenth and seventeenth centuries similarly staked their humanist credentials on references to Colchis.[37] More broadly, as early as the 1560s Colchis became a metonym for the furthermost border of the "civilized" world in a wide range of books, including those focusing on theology and medicine. For an example from theology, Roger Edgeworth in "An expositio[n] of the first epistle of Saynt Peter the Apostle, set fourth in traictises or Sermons, preached in the Cathedral Churche of Bristow" (1557) foregrounds Colchis as a geographical and historical touchstone for the spread of Christianity to the farthest reaches of Asia:

> There is *Colchis*, where *Jason* hadde the Golden fleice, as Poetes faine ["to relate or represent in fiction; to fable" (*OED*)]. *Mithridates* that noble kinge, that kepte open warre with the Romaynes by the space of sixe and fortye yeares, was kinge there in *Ponto* fyrste, and afterwarde of *Armenia, Capadotia*, and of the mooste parte of all maygne, and great *Asia*: And I thincke verelye it is twoo thousande myle aboute by lande frome Jerusalem, where Sayncte Peter begonne to preache.[38]

For an example from medicine, John Hall's *A most excellent and Learned Woorke of Chirurgerie* (1565) mentions the deadly root "Hermodactylus" as "of the contrey Colchis, where it did plentifully growe," along with the herb "Sanguis draconis" or "dragons bloud."[39] That the flora of Colchis is both deadly and associated with monstrous creatures such as dragons reinforces the region's position as a barbaric borderland due to its northern and eastern location vis-à-vis the classical *œcumene*. Again, Manley was conversant with this humanist tradition, at least in translation, and she elaborates this sense of Colchis as "the outer limits of civilization," which makes it both familiar and extreme.[40]

Related to this discourse of civility and barbarity, Colchis, and particularly the story of Jason and Medea, transmuted into a trope overdetermined by race, religion, and gender for what William Kerrigan and Gordon Braden identify as "the Western ideal of imperialism."[41] During the 1570s, a second thread consequently emerged with the publication of Richard Eden's 1577 translation of early Spanish accounts of the Americas in *The History of Travayle in the West and East Indies*, which includes works by Pietro Martire (Peter Martyr), Sebastian Münster, and Sebastian Cabot.[42] This foundational text for the early modern discourse of empire links the Old and New Worlds through the myth of the fountain of youth associated with Medea, who is said to have, in classicist Charles Anthon's words, restored Aeson, the father of Jason, "from the decrepitude of age to the bloom of early youth" by having "drawn off all the blood from his veins, and then to have filled them with the juices of certain herbs."[43] Peter Martyr's assessment is more cynical: "I wyll not attribute so great power to nature, but that God hath no lesse reserved this prerogative to hym selfe, then to search the hartes of men, or to geve substaunce to privation, (that is) beyng, to no beyng, except we shall beleeve the fable of *Colchis* of *Eson* renovate, to be as true as the wrytynges of *Sibylla Erythrea*."[44] As Martyr's *De Orbe Novo* [On the New World] (first published in 1530) constitutes the bulk of Eden's collection of the first books on the Americas translated into the English language, its inclusion of Colchis within a debunking of a feminized indigenous lore is significant. As we have seen, Manley's recourse to the Colchian setting reinforces her gendered critique of empire through the character of Homais, whom she does not completely condemn, by means of the subversive power of women's "cunning" in the root sense of "[k]nowledge; learning, [and] *erudition*."[45]

This humanist-inflected discourse of empire focusing on the Americas, which referenced Colchis through the geographically inflected story of Jason and Medea, also informed contemporaneous renditions of Ottoman and Safavid history, which encompassed the Islamicate regions of Central and West Asia. Specifically, by 1595, fifteen years after England had initiated formal trading ties with the Ottoman Empire, Abraham Hartwell translated Giovanni Tommaso Minadoi's *The History of the Warres between the Turks and the Persians* during the 1570s and 1580s. Significantly, Minadoi shifts from the classical view of Colchis to its present situation as a contested border zone. In a further departure from humanist practice, he emphasizes current names for the region, its more recent history, and its contemporary ethnic groups.[46] Colchis, as a locale on the margins of the "civilized" world, thus starts to function in a new way "to exorcize the fears created by all these foreign dangers," which, as Jésus López-Peláez Casellas shows, ranged from Catholic Spain to the Islamic empire of the Ottomans. In these cases, "othering" instantiates a progressive darkening as central to this racialization, with religion another constitutive aspect. The Colchis case nevertheless complicates Casellas's emphasis on "a repository of non-white others that help to define a white Early Modern (English and/or European) self."[47] To start, the racialization of the Colchians evokes the barbaric northerner rather than the southerner (European or African), and hence an extreme whiteness. As Mary Floyd-Wilson asserts in her influential study of *English Ethnicity and Race in Early Modern Drama*, "We cannot underestimate the importance of the fact that our earliest theory of a somatically based concept of ethnicity accounted for the strange habits, temperament, and excessively white appearance of the tribe of northerners," which included the British.[48] In contemporary descriptions of Colchis such as Minadoi's, "the *Tartar Nomades*...the *Mengrellians*...the *Georgians*...[and] the *Moscovites*" are also associated with sorcery and other "dark arts," which relates to earlier theological and medical references to Colchis as deadly and dangerous.[49] As both excessively white and dangerously dark, these northerners on the border of Europe and Asia accordingly function as another, albeit often neglected, foil for the early modern English and/or European self. As gendered subalterns, Medea and the Amazons, both linked to Colchis, combine with this racialized otherness to shore up the core definition of early modern Europe and its emerging global discourse of empire. That Homais, whose "royal mischief" unsettles the "dual, hierarchical" oppositions that support western patriarchy and its imperialist discourses, is a *Colchian* princess is therefore crucial.[50]

This trend toward layering classical and contemporary Colchis, with its gendered imperial referents, similarly characterizes Richard Knolles's *The Generall Historie of the Turkes, from The first beginning of that Nation to the rising of the Othoman Familie* (1603), which Manley certainly read, as her father contributed to later editions.[51] It is also informed by the spate of eyewitness accounts by Englishmen traveling in the Ottoman and Safavid empires from the late sixteenth century onwards. These popular works, such as William Lithgow's *A Most Delectable and True Discourse, of an admired and painefull peregrination, to the most famous kingdomes in Europe, Asia and Affricke* (1616) and Fynes Moryson's related *Itinerary* (1617), reinforce Colchis as a palimpsestic space signifying the double-edged power of Medea, who both facilitates and undermines the early modern western, and increasingly anglocentric, discourse of empire. As Lithgow writes, "As we sailed betweene *Thracia* and *Bithinia*, a learned *Grecian* that was in my company shewed mee *Colchis*, whence *Jason* with the assistance of the *Argonautes*, and the aid of *Medeas* skill, did fetch the golden fleece."[52] Moryson, on the other hand, merely lists Colchis as one "of the adjacent Province of *Asia* the lesse, named *Pontus*" in the course of his descriptive geography of the Black Sea, having really traveled only as far as the island of Tenedos in the Aegean.[53] While Lithgow appears merely to have glanced at Colchis on a tour of the Black Sea, and Moryson's itinerary did not take him to Colchis at all, their references, however passing, chart an extended genealogy that informs both Chardin's eyewitness account of his travels through this region and Manley's subsequent play.

In summary, this *"multifocalization* of views on a given referential space"—in this case drawing on literary, theological, medical, geographical, and historical texts—underscores the specificity of Colchis as a liminal zone between Europe and Asia, Christendom and *Dar al-Islam* (roughly translated as "the Islamic world").[54] Furthermore, the story of Jason and Medea, which begins in Colchis, became increasingly vital for "the Western ideal of imperialism" and its gendering.[55] A comprehensive understanding of the importance of this locale for the imperial imaginary of Manley's *The Royal Mischief* thus enables us to extend our assessment of her protagonist, Homais, beyond the generic "femme forte" model of heroic drama into a "transcultural" historical and an "intercultural" dramatic space.[56] In the conclusion to this essay, I assess how this geocritical approach to Manley's play more specifically nuances a literary critical view of her counter-orientalist challenge, which is far more complex than a misreading of her setting as "Turkey" or "Persia" allows.

Locating Manley's Colchis as a Palimpsestic Space

Colchis, then, constitutes the palimpsestic space *par excellence*: its Greco-Roman and Christian genealogy made it assimilable to the Western European "Self"; yet, it was deemed "Oriental" and increasingly Muslim, hence "Other." Louis Wann, in his groundbreaking dissertation, "The Oriental in the English Drama of the Sixteenth and Seventeenth Centuries," assumes the characters in Manley's *The Royal Mischief* are Christian because the play is set in greater Georgia, to which Christianity was introduced as early as the fourth century CE.[57] However, Chardin, whom Wann cites for support, shows that the region was shifting religious allegiances during the early modern period. Indeed, many Georgians converted to Islam to serve the Safavid shah, who placed some of them on the thrones of its client kings. Moreover, the Safavid shah married prominent Georgian women, which linked many Safavid princes to Georgia genealogically and politically.[58] Wann therefore erroneously concludes that "[t]he characters themselves are practically all in Chardin's narrative, though some names are changed to make them sound more 'Oriental'. For example, the Prince of Libardian is simply George, Osman is Papona. The English audience would not realize that Eastern Christians might have names different from Turks or Persians and still be genuine Orientals."[59] Rather, as the evidence of Manley's reading of Knolles and Chardin indicates, an English audience may well have understood that in this liminal zone, religious, racial, and cultural identities were fluid. I contend, as a result, that Manley's use of Islamicate names—which Ruth Herman has shown come from the proto-novel *The Rival Princesses; or, The Colchian Court* (1689)[60]—is symptomatic of her strategic mapping of the palimpsest that is Colchis, with its multilayered and shifting identities.

Perhaps the proximity of "self" and "other" in this historically layered locale, or perhaps the transition between these designations in Chardin and Manley's era, has obscured the specificity of this setting even more thoroughly for some of the most astute critics of the play. For instance, Cynthia Lowenthal in her foundational study of *Performing Identities on the Restoration Stage* incorrectly identifies the setting of *The Royal Mischief* as "the exotic realm of Turkey."[61] More recently, Pilar Cuder-Domínguez in her indispensable treatment of *Stuart Women Playwrights* states that the play is "set in contemporary Persia."[62] As we have seen, Chardin and Manley precisely identify the setting of the play as Colchis and Abcas in the Caucasus region bordering the Black Sea. This region, as Chardin indicates, was under Persian control during Levan Dadian's reign. The Ottomans are mentioned as a possible counterweight to the Safavids in Manley's play, but are not rulers over Colchis.[63] More to the point, Colchis and the surrounding regions were hotly contested border zones throughout the seventeenth century, with the Ottoman and Safavid empires asserting their claims over a mixed Christian and Muslim region where religious allegiances, which would harden in subsequent centuries, were still in flux.

This setting, I ultimately maintain, is less reminiscent of the hegemonic Islamic empires represented on the English stage by Dryden and others— such as the Mughals, Ottomans, and Safavids—and more related to Restoration representations of Islamic Spain, which privileged the liminal moments of the initial conquest by the "Moors" (Arabs and Berbers) in 711 and the final conquest by the Catholic sovereigns in 1492. Like Spain, the borderland regions of Colchis and Abcas feature "[t]emporary foreigners and explicitly tolerated enemies," to recall Casellas's formulation. As such, they can be assimilated into a potentially "whitened" identity, unlike anti-Christian "perpetual enemies" and "absolute outsiders," about whom the leading Elizabethan and Jacobean jurist, Sir Edward Coke, pronounced, "*Infidelis sunt Christi et Christianorum inimici*" [infidels are the enemies of Christ and of Christians]. Yet, as we have seen, even with "temporary foreigners," a residue of otherness persists to trouble England's proto-imperial construction of self.[64] In particular, Colchis, as a region deemed barbaric as much for its northern as for its "Oriental" location, comes disturbingly close to the classical geo-humoral conception of the English as "excessively white" and therefore less civilized and even less intelligent than those of more "temperate clime[s]," for which seventeenth-century England's premier poets, John Milton and John Dryden, continued to apologize.[65] Yet,

Colchians were also potentially darkened for their association with Central Asian and Islamic cultures and histories. In addition to this "racial trouble," the Western European discourse of empire, which evoked Colchis through the story of Jason and the Golden Fleece into the early modern era, hinged on the "gender trouble" associated with the figure of Medea, the "Oriental" woman who wreaks havoc (at least momentarily) on western patriarchy.[66] Manley's dramatic addition to the layered representation of Colchis, by collapsing "self" and "other" on a geographical as well as a characterological register, thus reinforces the repetition with a difference that defines her counter-orientalist challenge to the gendered discourse of empire.

Notes

1. See Bernadette Andrea, General Introduction to *English Women Staging Islam, 1696–1707: Delarivier Manley and Mary Pix* (Toronto: Iter/Centre for Reformation and Renaissance Studies, 2012), 11, 13–14. The title quote comes from the *Travels of Sir John Chardin into Persia and the East Indies* (1686); see Appendix A in Andrea, *English Women Staging Islam*, 133–38.
2. For details, see Matthew Birchwood, *Staging Islam in England: Drama and Culture, 1640–1685* (Cambridge: D. S. Brewer, 2007), 52–68.
3. Janet Todd, *The Secret Life of Aphra Behn* (New Brunswick, NJ: Rutgers University Press, 1996), 320 (emphasis in original), citing Thomas Creech. For more on "the female wits," see Katharine Beutner's essay in this collection.
4. For an "Overview of the London Season of 1695–96," see Constance Clark, *Three Augustan Women Playwrights* (New York: Peter Lang, 1986), 26–34.
5. Paula R. Backscheider, *Spectacular Politics: Theatrical Power and Mass Culture in Early Modern England* (Baltimore: Johns Hopkins University Press, 1993), 71.
6. On terminology, see Marshall G. S. Hodgson, "Usage in Islamic Studies," in *The Venture of Islam: Conscience and History in a World Civilization*, 3 vols. (Chicago: University of Chicago Press, 1974), 1.56–67. As he specifies, "'Islamicate' would refer not directly to the religion, Islam, itself, but to the social and cultural complex historically associated with Islam and the Muslims, both among the Muslims themselves and even when found among non-Muslims" (59).
7. Manley and Pix wrote other plays focusing on Islamicate themes after their debut, including Manley's *Almyna: or, The Arabian Vow* (performed in 1706 and published in 1707) and Pix's *The Conquest of Spain* (1705), both included in Andrea, *English Women Staging Islam*. For details, see Yolanda Caballero, "Patterns of Female Exploration in Delarivier Manley's Oriental Plays," in *Strangers in Early Modern English Texts* (*Anglo American Studies*, vol. 41), ed. Jesús López-Peláez (Frankfurt am Main: Peter Lang, 2011), 227–56.
8. On these terms, see N. M. Penzer, *The Harem: An Account of the Institution as It Existed in the Palace of the Turkish Sultans with a History of the Grand Seraglio from Its Foundation to the Present Time* (Philadelphia: J. P. Lippincott, 1937) and Leslie P. Peirce, *The Imperial Harem: Women and Sovereignty in the Ottoman Empire* (New York: Oxford University Press, 1993).
9. Bernadette Andrea, *Women and Islam in Early Modern English Literature* (Cambridge: Cambridge University Press, 2007), 94. For more, see Bernadette Andrea, "Islam, Women, and Western Responses: The Contemporary Relevance

68   *Bernadette Andrea*

of Early Modern Investigations," *Women's Studies: An Interdisciplinary Journal* 38 (2009): 273–92.

10. Kim Simpson's contribution to this collection, on "Manley's Queer Forms: Repetition, Techno-performativity and the Body," makes a similar theoretical point in terms of feminist criticism when she remarks: "The ubiquity of victimhood in Manley's fiction certainly means that the search for explicitly transgressive impulses in her seduction narratives, by which I mean an attempt to radically disrupt or alter the terrain of normative femininity, will likely be a disappointing one" (107). Alternatively, Simpson argues via queer theory that "Manley's formal repetitions have considerable ideological significance in that they recognize, map out, and experiment with the performativity of identity, constituted through repetition, and disrupted by the material." In terms of my analysis, the former model would constitute an *anti-orientalist* stance and the latter a *counter-orientalist* stance.

11. Mary Louise Pratt, *Imperial Eyes: Travel Writing and Transculturation*, 2nd ed. (New York: Routledge, 2008), 8.

12. Ania Loomba, *Colonialism/Postcolonialism* (London: Routledge, 1998), 68.

13. Kathleen Wilson, *The Island Race: Englishness, Empire and Gender in the Eighteenth Century* (New York: Routledge, 2003), Felicity Nussbaum, *Torrid Zones: Maternity, Sexuality, and Empire in Eighteenth-Century English Narratives* (Baltimore: The Johns Hopkins University Press, 1994), and Laura Brown, *Ends of Empire: Women and Ideology in Early Eighteenth-Century English Literature* (Ithaca, NY: Cornell University Press, 1993). For postcolonial approaches, see Daniel D. Carey and Lynn L. Festa, eds., *The Postcolonial Enlightenment: Eighteenth-Century Colonialism and Postcolonial Theory* (Oxford: Oxford University Press, 2009) and Suvir Kaul, *Eighteenth-Century British Literature and Postcolonial Studies* (Edinburgh: Edinburgh University Press, 2009).

14. For the term "proto-imperial," see Robert C. D. Baldwin, "Colonial Cartography under the Tudor and Early Stuart Monarchies, ca. 1480–ca. 1640," in *The History of Cartography: Cartography in the European Renaissance*, ed. J. B. Harley and David Woodward (Chicago: University of Chicago Press, 1987), 1754–80. For the period after 1640, see David Armitage, *The Ideological Origins of the British Empire* (Cambridge: Cambridge University Press, 2000), who stresses that only in the "second quarter of the eighteenth century" does the "concept of the 'British Empire'" emerge "as a political community encompassing England and Wales, Scotland, Protestant Ireland, the British islands of the Caribbean and the mainland colonies of North America" (9, 7). The "second British Empire," extending to India, does not emerge until "the second half of the eighteenth century" (1–2).

15. See Peter Stallybrass, "Marginal England: The View from Aleppo," in *Center or Margin: Revisions of the English Renaissance in Honor of Leeds Barroll*, ed. Lena Cowen Orlin (Cranbury, NJ: Associated University Press, 2006), 27–39.

16. Mita Choudhury, *Interculturalism and Resistance in the London Theater, 1660–1800: Identity, Performance, Empire* (Lewisburg, PA: Bucknell University Press, 2000), 18, citing Homi K. Bhabha, *The Location of Culture* (New York: Routledge, 1994), 56.

17. Choudhury, *Interculturalism and Resistance*, 19; Edward W. Said, *Orientalism* (New York: Vintage, 1979), 1–3. Srinivas Aravamudan productively nuances

Said's definition in *Enlightenment Orientalism: Resisting the Rise of the Novel* (Chicago: University of Chicago Press, 2012), 10–18.

18. Choudhury, *Interculturalism and Resistance*, 109, 111. On "[t]he female wits and the genealogy of feminist orientalism," see Andrea, *Women and Islam*, 78–104.

19. On these gendered binary oppositions, see Said, *Orientalism*, 6, for the modern era, and 20–21, for the classical era.

20. Manley, *The Royal Mischief*, 116; the full quote runs: "Though some are blacker stained than others are,/There's none can say their lives were ever fair." For an analysis, see Andrea, *Women and Islam*, 94–99.

21. On the redeployment of Jason "to lend a mythic aura to the discoverers of America," see Yves Peyré, "Marlowe's Argonauts," in *Travel and Drama in Shakespeare's Time*, ed. Jean-Pierre Maquerlot and Michèle Willems (Cambridge: Cambridge University Press, 1996), 106–23.

22. The Order of the Golden Fleece, founded by Philip the Good, Duke of Burgundy, in 1429, became closely associated with the Spanish Habsburgs who led the colonization of the "New World," on which see Jason Colavito, *Jason and the Argonauts through the Ages* (Jefferson, NC: McFarland and Co., 2014), 206–14.

23. See James J. Clauss and Sarah Iles Johnston, eds., *Medea: Essays on Medea in Myth, Literature, Philosophy, and Art* (Princeton: Princeton University Press, 1997), esp. Marianne McDonald, "Medea as Politician and Diva: Riding the Dragon into the Future," 297–324.

24. Betrand Westphal, *Geocriticism: Real and Fictional Spaces*, trans. Robert T. Tally, Jr. (New York: Palgrave Macmillan, 2011), 114; emphasis in original. For a summary and interrogation of this methodology, see Robert T. Tally, Jr., *Spatiality* (London: Routledge, 2013), 140–45. For a related analysis, see Antoine Eche, "The Shores of Aphrodite's Island: Cyprus and European Travel Memory, 1600–1700," in *Geocritical Explorations: Space, Place, and Mapping in Literary and Cultural Studies*, ed. Robert T. Tally, Jr. (New York: Palgrave Macmillan, 2011), 91–105.

25. Manley, *The Royal Mischief*, 131. Elizabeth Hollis-Berry, "'No Party favour'd, no Designs in view': Female Rakes and Heroes, Politics and Power in Delarivier Manley's Heroic Drama," *Lumen: Selected Proceedings from the Canadian Society for Eighteenth-Century Studies* 19 (2000): 171–86. Hollis-Berry's argument that "the obvious spatial limits placed on Homais" (175), who is immured by her older, jealous husband, means that "Homais may not colonize beyond these walls; her body will be both colonizer and colonized" complements my geocritical analysis of the macro-setting for the play in seventeenth-century Colchis (176).

26. Manley, *The Royal Mischief*, 131.

27. Choudhury, *Interculturalism and Resistance*, 19.

28. Manley, *The Royal Mischief*, 54.

29. Chardin, *Travels*, 53n73; Manley, *The Royal Mischief*, 45.

30. Ibid. 133–34. Other seventeenth-century sources clarify that "Mingrelia is now-a-days the Colchis of old," as in Jonas Moore, *A New Geography with Maps to each country* (London, 1681).

31. Manley, *The Royal Mischief*, 120–21.

32. Lord Kinross [John Patrick Douglas Balfour], *The Ottoman Centuries: The Rise and Fall of the Turkish Empire* (New York: Harper Collins, 1977), 227.

33. Delarivier Manley, *The Adventures of Rivella* (London, 1714), 12.
34. Ibid. 15.
35. Paul Bunyan Anderson, "Mary de la Rivière Manley, a Cavalier's Daughter in Grub Street," unpublished PhD Diss. (Harvard University, 1931), 123–24. Anderson also cites *Letters Writen by Mrs. Manley* (London, 1696), where she remarks, "My study has fallen upon Religion; I am searching into all sorts…" (61, qtd. in Anderson 124n1). Mordechai Feingold, "'The Turkish Alcoran': New Light on the 1649 English Translation of the Koran," *Huntington Library Quarterly* 75.4 (2012): 475–501, has disputed the attribution of this translation to Alexander Ross.
36. Thomas Elyot, *The Dictionary* (London, 1538), XXIv; the second quotation is from "The Addicion of Sir Thomas Eliot Knight vnto his Dictionarye," sig. Ff. Here, and in the subsequent notes, I cite the earliest edition listed in *Early English Books Online*. I retain original spelling in the endnotes, but adjust i/j and u/v pairs when quoting.
37. Samples include *The Cosmographical Glasse* (London, 1559); *The Surueye of the World, or Situation of the Earth* (London, 1572); Walter Ralegh, *The History of the World* (London, 1617); and Peter Heylyn, *A Little Description of the Great World* (Oxford, 1625).
38. Roger Edgeworth, *Sermons very fruitfull, godly, and learned* (London, 1557), Fol. cx.
39. John Hall, *A most excellent and Learned Woorke of Chirurgerie* (London, 1565), 49, 106–7.
40. Colavito, *Jason and the Argonauts*, 3. For more on "Black Sea Voyagers" and "The Real Colchis," see 76–80 and 148–51.
41. William Kerrigan and Gordon Braden, *The Idea of the Renaissance* (Baltimore: The Johns Hopkins University Press, 1989), 5.
42. Richard Eden, comp., *The History of Trauayle in the West and East Indies* (London, 1577). Eden published components of this collection as early as 1553. See also Edward Arber, ed., *The First Three English Books on America* (Birmingham: n. pub., 1885).
43. Charles Anthon, *A Classical Dictionary* (New York: Harper and Brothers, 1872), 807.
44. Martyr qtd. in Eden, *The History of Trauayle*, 93.
45. *OED*, s.v. "cunning, n.1." More nuanced definitions follow, including "[t]he capacity or faculty of knowing; wit, wisdom, intelligence" and "[k]nowledge how to do a thing; ability, skill, expertness, dexterity, cleverness." All are listed as obsolete or archaic.
46. Thomas Minadoi, *The History of the Warres betweene the Turkes and the Persian*, trans. Abraham Hartwell (London, 1595), 53; see also 102–3, 112, 120, 266–67. On the significance of this shift, see Sonja Brentjes, "The Presence of Ancient Secular and Religious Texts in the Unpublished and Printed Writings of Pietro della Valle (1586–1652), in *Travellers from Europe in the Ottoman and Safavid Empires, 16th–17th Centuries* (Farnham: Ashgate, 2010), III. 1–23.
47. Jésus López-Peláez Casellas, "'Race' and the Construction of English National Identity: Spaniards and North Africans in English Seventeenth-Century Drama," *Studies in Philology* 106.1 (2009): 32–51.
48. Mary Floyd-Wilson, *English Ethnicity and Race in Early Modern Drama* (Cambridge: Cambridge University Press, 2003), 25. See also Roxann Wheeler,

The Complexion of Race: Categories of Difference in Eighteenth-Century British Culture (Philadelphia: University of Pennsylvania Press, 2000).

49. Minadoi, *The History of the Warres*, 266.

50. Manley, *The Royal Mischief*, 116; Hélène Cixous, "Sorties," in *Literary Theory: An Anthology*, ed. Julie Rivkin and Michael Ryan (Malden, MA: Blackwell, 1998), 578–84.

51. Richard Knolles, *The Generall Historie of the Turkes* (London, 1603). On Roger Manley's contributions to *The History of the Turkish Empire* (1687), see Andrea, *Women and Islam*, 100, 112.

52. William Lithgow, *A Most Delectable and Trve Discourse* (London, 1616), 45.

53. Fynes Moryson, *An Itinerary* (London, 1617), 267.

54. Westphal, *Geocriticism*, 114.

55. Kerrigan and Braden, *The Idea of the Renaissance*, 5.

56. Bridget Orr, *Empire on the English Stage, 1660–1714* (Cambridge: Cambridge University Press, 2001), influentially describes Homais as "a familiar type from heroic drama, a *femme forte* with generic antecedents in Indian Queens Zempoalla and Nourmahal [from Dryden's plays], as well as the ancient heroines of Greek, Roman and Eastern imperial history" (130–31). More recently, Pilar Cuder-Domínguez, "Gender, Race, and Party Politics in the Tragedies of Behn, Pix, and Manley," in *Teaching British Women Playwrights of the Restoration and Eighteenth Century*, ed. Bonnie Nelson and Catherine Burroughs (New York: MLA, 2010), 263–74, labels Homais "a *femme forte*" (269).

57. Louis Wann, "The Oriental in the English Drama of the Sixteenth and Seventeenth Centuries," unpublished PhD diss. (University of Wisconsin, 1919), 187–90. Margarete Rubik and Eva Mueller-Zettleman in *Eighteenth-Century Women Playwrights*, Vol. 1: *Delarivier Manley and Eliza Haywood* (London: Pickering and Chatto, 2001) similarly remark: "Abca (Abkhazia) was situated in northwest Colchis (Georgia)" (222n37). However, their unqualified equation of Colchis with Georgia is problematic, as Eleni Sideri demonstrates in "'The Land of the Golden Fleece': Conflict and Heritage in Abkhazia," *Journal of Balkan and Near Eastern Studies* 14.2 (2012): 263–78.

58. Andrew J. Newman, *Safavid Iran: Rebirth of a Persian Empire* (London: I. B. Tauris, 2009), 31, 41, 52, 107.

59. Wann, "The Oriental in the English Drama," 188.

60. Ruth Herman, *The Business of a Woman: The Political Writings of Delarivier Manley* (Newark: University of Delaware Press, 2003), 188–89.

61. Cynthia Lowenthal, *Performing Identities on the Restoration Stage* (Carbondale: Southern Illinois University Press, 2003), 30.

62. Pilar Cuder-Domínguez, *Stuart Women Playwrights, 1613–1713* (Farnham: Ashgate, 2011), 86.

63. As Rubik and Mueller-Zettleman point out in *Eighteenth-Century Women Playwrights*, "In the fifteenth century Abca gained its independence from Colchis only to come under the rule of the Ottoman empire shortly afterwards. Therefore, when Osman is in mortal danger [in Act IV], he decides to seek refuge in the Ottoman territories" (222n37).

64. Casellas, "'Race' and the Construction of English National Identity," 39.

65. Floyd-Wilson, *English Ethnicity and Race*, 25, 2.

66. For these terms, see Judith Butler, *Gender Trouble: Feminism and the Subversion of Identity* (New York: Routledge, 1990), ix–xi; 24–5.

Part II

Sex

5 Interrupting Pleasure

Ideology and Affect in Delarivier Manley's *The New Atalantis*

Erin M. Keating

Near the end of Delarivier Manley's play *The Royal Mischief* (1696), she insinuates a necrophilic desire into her virtuous heroine's death scene, having Osman press Bassima to physically complete their love even as she is slowly dying, poisoned by her rival, Homais.[1] Osman's physical lust in his dying mistress's final moments calls attention to the implicit perversity of a dramatic scene that was a commonplace of Restoration pathetic tragedy. For decades, playwrights staged beautiful spectacles of their virtuous heroines dying nobly, creating a pleasure for their audience that, as Jean Marsden argues, "is dependent on the representation of the passive woman's suffering, which is inevitably sexually tinged."[2] Uniting Bassima's death scene with the simultaneous performance of Osman's sexual desire, Manley uses that desire to foreground the physicality of her heroine's dying body. Audiences accustomed to the titillating spectacle of the purely visual, "sexually tinged" tableau usually created by tragic death scenes are forced to encounter Bassima's (and the actress Anne Bracegirdle's) fully material body. By explicitly linking death and desire in her scene, Manley interrupts the pleasure her audience is accustomed to taking from a fully aestheticized pathetic spectacle of Anne Bracegirdle dying yet another virtuous death by reminding them of the physical nature of her dying body. Thus, she introduces the potential for a recoil of revulsion as the purely visual is polluted by the decaying material body.

Manley merely flirts with the interplay of desire and revulsion in *The Royal Mischief*; she returns to this dynamic in much greater detail in her secret history *Secret Memoirs and Manners of Several Persons of Quality of Both Sexes. From the New Atalantis, an Island in the Mediteranean* (1709), a work that has received a great deal of well-deserved scholarly attention in the past decades. Without diminishing the vitality of current discussions of *The New Atalantis* as political satire, secret history, and seduction narrative, I suggest another level of signification for Manley's text, a level that sees it as continuing the work begun in her earlier play.[3] In this chapter, I argue that key incidents in *The New Atalantis* can be understood in conversation with the dominant tropes of late seventeenth-century pathetic tragedy, which as Anne Greenfield has recently argued, presented "tragic rape scenes ... as beautiful components of high art—making this dramatic trope seem elevated and wholesome, rather than obscene and indecent."[4] Working against a literary tradition that figures female suffering as beautiful and erotic, Manley uses a double-pronged strategy: narratively revealing the constructed and performative nature of the eroticized female body in tales such as that of the Duke and Charlot, while, in other parts of her narrative, affectively coupling the aestheticized erotic body featured in the more traditional seduction narratives with that body's fully material counterpart, the female body in labor. Manley completes the critique of this literary trope through the inability of both her fictional society and her frame narrative to provide protection for the text's sole example of triumphant female virtue, Elonora.

From the beginning of *The New Atalantis*, Manley uses her frame characters to link her text with the suffering virtue so popular on the English stage. Manley's portrayal of Virtue, Astrea's unrecognizable mother, draws attention to her "Native Charms" that have been tarnished by neglect, "her *Habit Obsolete* and *Torn*, almost degenerated into Tatters."[5] The beautiful and half-naked Virtue is described as having sunk into a state comparable with her stage votaries of the past decades; Virtue herself is depicted as fallen. Moving from the pathetic stage into the pages of the secret history, Manley's description of Virtue serves as an allegorical reminder of the many female characters destroyed by the conventional plots of Restoration pathetic tragedy, which required their female heroines to fall from virtue through no fault or agency of their own. Readers familiar with the past few decades of London theater would be reminded of the many tragic heroines, like Thomas Otway's Monomia in *The Orphan* (1680) or Elkanah Settle's Cleomira in *Distress'd Innocence: Or, the Princess of Persia* (1691), whose own behavior is virtuous and yet who are ruined and ultimately die through the actions of those around them, both villains and friends.[6] The association with the tragic stage continues in Astrea's description of the trials of her prince's great grandmother, Elizabeth, Queen of Bohemia.[7] Emphasizing that queen's lack of agency in her own sufferings, which were brought about by the "vain Hopes and Pride" of her husband, Astrea describes how her own "Heart melted at the Complainings of this beauteous and upright Princess" who was forced to live a life of continual exile through no fault of her own.[8] Jupiter's response to Astrea's pleas on the princess's behalf combines with the representation of Virtue at the beginning to establish the generic and thematic history in which the text participates. He tells Astrea that the princess "was not punish'd for her proper Crimes, but for her Husband's Ambition, and her Fathers Supineness."[9] In other words, like the heroines of Restoration pathetic tragedy, the princess is forced by the gods themselves to bear the blame for the actions of others and to die alone, in exile. Though Astrea pities the fate of the princess, she does not question "this Sentence of *Jupiter*'s," leaving uncontested the prescription that the virtuous wife must suffer for the sins of the men who surround her.[10]

Manley's many tales of fallen virtue in *The New Atalantis* reference yet problematize the representation of the heroines in the tragedies of the preceding decades and, in the process, reveal the paradoxical and destructive nature of the exemplar of female virtue and the affective relationship that it triggers. Manley began this questioning of the exemplarity of virtue in her representation of Bassima in *The Royal Mischief*, a depiction, as I have argued elsewhere, that can be read as purposely exaggerating the virtuous female exemplar to the point of absurdity, while inviting the audience to relish her destruction and inevitable death.[11] Manley does not turn to satire in her treatment of the virtuous heroines in *The New Atalantis* (that is primarily reserved for the many figures of vice who people the text and for the moralizing frame characters), but rather exposes the society surrounding virtue—the society that has driven Virtue herself to the state in which we first meet her. By highlighting virtue as a social and aesthetic creation, Manley draws attention to the artificiality of eighteenth-century understandings of female virtue and to the role of education and literature in creating and perpetuating that understanding. By drawing attention to the aesthetic thinness of conventional depictions of female virtue in distress, tales like that of the Duke and Charlot lay the groundwork for Manley's re-introduction of a complete female physicality through the tales that feature women in labor.

The Perils of Overeducation; or, the Paradox within Narratives of Virtue and Desire

Manley prepares her reader for the critique of the aesthetic picture of female suffering (and the readers who are seduced by it) in one of the most critically discussed tales in *The New Atalantis*: the tale of Charlot and the Duke. Originally intended by the Duke, her guardian, to be his son's wife, Charlot is brought up in all the virtues appropriate to that role. This changes when the Duke sees her perform Diana to his son's Acteon: "she Acted with so animated a Spirit … that awaken'd the Duke's Attention; and so admirably she varied the Passions, that gave Birth in his Breast, to what he had never felt before."[12] Watching Charlot perform virtue, watching her play the role, arouses the Duke's hitherto dormant desires and links Charlot to the heroines performed in the playhouse. Performance is highlighted here as itself a source of desire; a desire, it must be remembered from the context of the tragic stage tradition, that is ultimately destructive of its object. Enclosing the performance of virtue within the legal and educational relationship of testamentary guardianship that gives the Duke control of Charlot, Manley highlights the way that both the ideology of virtue and the legal structure of guardianship actively "produce … the seeds of [their] own corruption."[13]

After the Duke's decision that he must possess his ward, he introduces Charlot to all of the erotic literature that was once denied her, re-educating her from a virtuous future wife into a willing mistress, thus completing the second of what William B. Warner has called her first and second educations.[14] The process is finished when he surprises her at his country house and rapes her: "neither her prayers, tears, nor strugglings cou'd prevent him, but in her Arms he made himself a full amends for all the pains he had suffered for her."[15] Intelligence's emphasis on the pains suffered by the Duke only serves to highlight Charlot's unwillingness before the encounter that completes her ruin, "provok[ing] in the reader," as Bullard argues in another context, "an alternative judgment" to that promoted by our narrator.[16] In the end, Charlot is impregnated and abandoned by the Duke, who ends up proposing marriage to another woman, the more socially proficient Countess. Charlot dies "a true Landmark: to warn all believing Virgins from shipwracking their Honour upon (the dangerous Coast of Rocks) the Vows and pretended Passion of Mankind."[17] Seemingly a straightforward tale of fallen virtue, Charlot's story is constructed by Manley not only as an exposure of William Bentinck's, and by extension the Whigs', "degeneracy and corruption," but, through her use of narrative irony and her emphasis on education, as an indictment of traditional narratives of blame in the fall of female exemplarity.[18]

As I have argued elsewhere, plays such as Thomas Otway's *The Orphan*, Nicholas Brady's *The Rape* (1692), and Manley's *The Royal Mischief* strip the female exemplar of her agency such that she is destroyed by forces completely beyond her control, whether through mishap (as in *The Orphan*), through force (as in *The Rape*), or through "report" (as in *The Royal Mischief*). Despite this, she is forced to bear the social consequences of her fall from virtue, activating for the audiences an affective relationship of envy as they take pleasure in, pity, and generally are moved by this figure of fallen exemplarity.[19] Intelligence's narrative of Charlot's fall is, on the surface, more akin to the later pathetic tragedies of Nicholas Rowe in that her virtue could easily be read as lost through her own actions and indiscretions, as the result, in Intelligence's concluding summary, of her role as a "believing Virgin ...."[20] However, this reading is strained and ultimately untenable if one takes into account the text's attention to the relationship between Charlot's education and her virtue, as well as the narrative manipulations Intelligence imposes on her tale in order to make it conform to the seduction narrative genre.

Though not nearly so sexy as the erotic education outlined later in the tale, Charlot's first education, into virtue, is equally important to an understanding of the story, in that it emphasizes both the importance of reading for a young woman's education and the natural impulses in Charlot that are stifled by the rather inflexible and thus fragile model of female virtue being created.[21] In his discussion of Charlot's education, Warner notes the paradox that contributes to the fragility of any attempt to teach innocence; in order to warn against worldly temptations, education often informs its subject of "the very desire it would shun" and thus "risks inciting the passion it would ward off."[22] However, the risk in Manley's text is not that Charlot will come to desire but that her excelling through her education will incite the desire of men who view her perfections. Manley constructs female exemplarity as the cause of its own destruction, as in the pathetic tragedies, but the important distinction here is that Manley places the source of that original perfection not in nature but in an education motivated by the ideo-logical construction of female virtue as "desired."[23] That Charlot's virtue is meant to be exemplary is clear in Intelligence's claim that "*Charlot* seem'd to intend herself a Pattern for the Ladies of this degenerate Age."[24] Yet this statement is disingenuous as it places the agency in Charlot's hands, when the previous description of the Duke's method of education makes it clear to whom his future daughter-in-law's exemplarity is of the utmost concern. The "father" is revealed in this tale as both the creator and the destroyer of exemplary virtue, despite Intelligence's attempts to structure the tale along generic lines that would place the blame squarely on Charlot. The exemplar itself is exposed as paradoxical—a gendered virtue constructed by society to incite the desire that leads to its own destruction, while also "accru[ing] all of the guilt" for that destruction.[25]

The Whole Female Body: The Desirable and the Disgusting

Alongside her exposure of the ideologically constructed nature of the model of female virtue provided by the tragic stage, Manley resists a visually based, flat tableau of female suffering by introducing a complete image of the female body into her text, insistently placing messy, leaky, material bodies of women in conjunction with the erotic bodies that are a generic staple of seduction narratives, both in print and on the stage. Using a very Swiftian satirical technique, Manley focuses her use of the grotesque in a distinctly female manner, avoiding Swift's tendencies toward "scatology and misogyny."[26] As Melinda Alliker Rabb argues, Manley "uses the female body's objectification to satirize society rather than to satirize women or women's sexuality per se."[27] While part of Manley's emphasis on the female body is evident in the many erotic scenes of seduction in the narrative, the other side of this erotic body for Manley is the body in labor. Thus, the scenes of eroticism and seduction are balanced in the text with scenes of childbirth. While a number of critics have noted the profusion of painful and grotesque births in *The New Atalantis*, most interpret these moments as contributing to the pathos, or the moral lesson, or the criticism of the Whig gentlemen who abandon women at such critical times.[28] Yet, viewing these depictions through the lens of affective revulsion provides another possible reading of these horrific scenes, which vie with the erotic descriptions in their attention to the motions of the female body. Unlike other heroines of early seduction narratives such as Aphra Behn's Silvia, whose pregnancy is hardly noted and does not stop her from seducing two new lovers and an old one because, as the narrator writes, "she show'd very little of her Condition all the time she went," the heroines in Manley's text undergo often gruesome but at the very least painfully drawn-out labors.[29] And whereas Silvia's child is never mentioned again in the text, even as to whether it lives or dies, the illegitimate children in *The New Atalantis* are clearly present, though often dead at the hands of their distressed mothers.[30]

Manley's introduction of the pains of childbirth into the tales of fallen virtue brazenly avows the part of female physicality ignored by traditional representations. The strategy not only deepens our awareness of the severe consequences that could result for eighteenth-century women who engaged in sex outside of marriage (or in bigamous marriages), but also introduces a response of revulsion on the part of the reader that actually blocks the erotic pleasure a reader takes in a fallen female exemplar. "The active incitement of disgust," as Jonathan Dollimore has argued, "can be an effective strategy of satirical critique and political opposition: a confronting of culture with its constitutive repressions, a provocative violation of cultural boundaries and bodily properties."[31] Like the emphasis on education in the Charlot tale, Manley's use of revulsion brings to the fore elements of the ideology of female virtue ignored by traditional aesthetic narratives and reveals the female body in physical pain beneath the aesthetic spectacle of female suffering. In Restoration pathetic tragedies, the female body, fully present to the audience in the body of the actress upon the stage, remains beautiful and potentially erotic even in her fallen state because her pain is expressed as emotional, pathetic suffering.[32] In contrast, Manley's inclusion of bodies "racked" and "in agonies" interrupts the potential for desire toward the fallen female, thus revealing the aestheticized death scenes of pathetic tragedy as spectacles constructed for audience pleasure and prurience.[33] Shifting the focus of the fallen virtue narrative, Manley complicates the pleasure that can be derived from an affective relationship of envy between the reader and the text. This relationship causes the reader to simultaneously pity and relish the suffering of the fallen female who has been held up as an exemplar, while glossing over the conditions that enable the narrative itself.[34] She effects this shift by introducing scenes of revulsion into her text which, as Sianne Ngai argues in her discussion of disgust, "explicitly [block] the path of sympathy" from reader to character, thus replacing an affective relationship of pathetic and erotic pleasure with one of revulsion.[35]

Manley's destabilization of notions of female nature versus education in stories of fallen virtue combines with her interplay of desire and revulsion with respect to the female body most clearly in the tale of Urania's and Polydore's incestuous love. This particular story exists within multiple narrative frames, creating a proliferation of female bodies in pain surrounding the tale of seduced virtue. Intelligence relates the story of Urania as background information to a scene of childbirth, which the women stumble upon late at night in the woods. The tale serves to expose the hypocritical virtue of Harriat, the woman before them, who has caused the ruin and ultimately the death of her cousins through her revelation of their incestuous affair, yet who now "groans in a terrible manner" and pleads with her seducer to fetch a midwife: "I'm rack'd! I die in Agonies! ... I'm surrounded with Horror, the Rack of Nature is upon me, and no kind assisting Hand to relieve me."[36] Once the midwife, Mrs. Nightwork, has arrived and completed her business, she briefly joins Intelligence and the goddesses and relates a number of stories whose narrative focus is on the preservation of female reputation and the painful lengths women go to in order to hide the recent delivery of a child.

Aggressively inserting the female body and its pain into the narratives of seduction, reputation, and virtue, Manley explicitly entwines desire and pain in her narrative, complicating the potential affective responses of her readers. Despite a critical tendency to see desire and disgust as "dialectically conjoined," Ngai cautions against seeing these feelings as too similar in their affect: "disgust is urgent and specific; desire can be ambivalent and vague."[37] The disgust or revulsion response, as urgent as the pains of childbirth from which it arises, breaks the reader's sympathy with Harriat, a position reinforced by Intelligence's utter lack of compassion for the woman in front of her. In response to Virtue's and Astrea's sympathy, our narrator privileges her own story over Harriat's pain, justifying her insensibility with her knowledge of Harriat's "haughty" spirit and "affectation of Vertue."[38] The affective disconnection between the reader and the female body in pain is reinforced by the language, which directly links observation (rather than feeling or sympathy) with the severity of Harriat's pain: "Let us observe a little; by the extremity of her Pains it can't be long before they are over."[39]

The initial affective recoil created by the Harriat scene is multiplied by the quick succession of female pain stories that follow the encounter in the woods between the frame characters and Mrs. Nightwork. The temporal proximity of the tale of Urania and Polydore to the multiple descriptions of women in pain brings the highly eroticized narrative into direct contact with the torn female bodies that come before it. The traces or "stickiness" left from the revulsion of the frame stories haunt the descriptions of Urania, who is so beautiful she eclipses her wealthy cousins despite her own low fortune: "'twas impossible they should have any Lovers where *Urania* appear'd."[40] Coming after the many references to the "rack of nature," the physical description of Urania, a name with classical, romance, and contemporary theatrical associations, with its emphasis on the erotic side of female nature, is jarring in its juxtaposition of revulsion and desire.[41] Descriptions of her "amorous" complexion and the "perpetual Ferment" of her blood are combined with the revelation that her mother died giving birth to Urania and her twin brother, Polydore.[42] The insistent reminder of childbirth and its pain taints the heroine and keeps suspended the possibility for sympathy and aesthetically created erotic desire.

Manley balances these competing movements of desire and revulsion with a continued attention to the dual discourses of female nature and education. Unlike Charlot, who could be considered overeducated, Urania is described as all nature with no opportunity for education. What is "natural" in the description of Urania, however, sits uneasily beside the natural childbirth pains of the frames, particularly as it is overelaborated and exaggerated by the narrator: "it was but casting your Eyes upon the least Glance of hers, to read the Fever of her Soul; that *Disease* of *Nature*! that enchanting Warmth, which gave her Blood a perpetual Ferment! ... Desire and Disorders in her Air! unintermitting Wishes! delicious Dreams!"[43] The language of the body that permeates Intelligence's highly eroticized description of the heroine connects her to the eroticized female bodies that have come before her in the text, and yet she surpasses all of them in her ability to radiate and to attract sexual desire. This female nature is restrained by nothing, as Urania is not only carelessly educated—"Urania ... had had too heedless an Education"— but also barred from almost all society because her beauty outshines that of her cousins.[44] This isolation from both society and education, as Ellen Pollak has argued, creates the conditions for Urania's incestuous desire and for the expulsion of that desire from the family unit.[45]

Like Charlot's tale, which depicts the fallen woman as equally shaped and destroyed by patriarchal education, Urania's tale plays out the contradictory pressures of female nature and education, actively exploiting ambivalent eighteenth-century attitudes toward incest as "a vice at once profoundly stigmatized and utterly typical" while combining the material body with the heavily eroticized body of her heroine to disturb complacent readings of seduction narratives by introducing an affective recoil of revulsion.[46] Whereas Manley uses the Charlot tale to satirize the narrative of fallen virtue, in the Urania tale she uses techniques of exaggeration and the grotesque to undermine the aestheticized picture of female nature upon which that narrative relies, problematizing a response of desire through her inclusion of the violent scenes of childbirth. Described as an embodiment of desire herself, Urania is seduced by her twin brother Polydore into an incestuous relationship, which is rationalized by that brother as natural: "Nature forbids it not; ... Did we err against her *Eternal Laws*, wou'd not *Instinct* make the *Discovery*?"[47] Although Intelligence wastes no time with a long description of Polydore, as Urania's twin brother he is noted to be as beautiful and seemingly as erotically inclined as she is: "their Faces, their Inclinations were alike, unhappy only in a distinction of the Sex."[48] The "natural" progression of the narrative is fully in place by the time these two children of desire finally consummate their lust for one another, a lust "immediately" followed with equally natural results: "No sooner had they drank of this *delicious Poison*, but *Urania* prov'd the Effects of it! a guilty *Pregnancy* immediately succeeded!"[49]

Although Urania's pregnancy does not interrupt the pleasures of the incestuous pair, they are eventually found out and exposed by their cousin Harriat (the woman whose own clandestine labor prompts the tale), and Urania is sent incognito into the country for her confinement. The scene of her labor is one of the most drawn out of the childbirth scenes in the text, if not quite the most grotesque.[50] Resolute in her desire to die in childbirth, Urania, "when the Mother-Pains came upon hee [sic], forbore to *call*! she forbore to *groan*! ... she drank her Tears, supprest her Cries, groan'd inwardly with strongest Woe."[51] Struggling with her pain, her guilt, and her confusion over the innocence of her child, who also carries the guilt of his incestuous creation, Urania endures a "bitter *Night*" and, finally "having passed that necessary Point of Time wherein the Womens Assistance was absolutely necessary; she fell into strong Convulsions, in which she was so happy as to lose her Understanding."[52] The dreadful scene results in the death of both the child and Urania, who follows her own mother in the manner of her death but blocks the continuation of the narrative by bringing about the death of her child in the process. Manley insistently places before the reader the full picture of female physicality, in contrast to narratives of female virtue that only show the erotic nature of the female body.

The reactions of the frame characters to Urania's tale are instructive. Virtue lays the blame on the Baroness (Urania's aunt and guardian), who neglected her education and failed to properly read her amorous constitution and vigilantly police her interactions with the opposite sex. Astrea sagaciously applauds Virtue's moral gloss on the tale and concludes with her own rhetorical appeal to nature: "O Nature! why are thou so *Potent* and so *Faulty*?"[53] Astrea's statement of the futility of any action against nature is painfully ironic given her role as educator of the future leader; if nature is so powerful as to be unchangeable, what chance does education have to change anything in Atalantis where "Human Nature is universally corrupted?"[54] Manley's ironic portrayal of Astrea, who often acts as a mouthpiece for the ideology of female virtue within the text, combines with her manipulations of narratives of fallen virtue to provide a scathing satirical indictment of the ideological traps created for women living within these narratives. Her satire unites this revelation with the affective distancing of revulsion, thus resisting the erotic, purely visual seductions traditionally created by seduction narratives. Though she is unable to provide a clear way out of the ideological paradox, Manley's exposure of its cracks and her affective challenge to traditional aesthetics open up for her careful readers the possibility of recognizing the perils of these ideologies.

"Where in this bad World shall I find a Protection for my *unwary* Innocence?"

Manley's exposé of the ideological construction of female virtue and its internal contradictions is fully played out by the inability of her own text to find a place for a truly virtuous heroine. Besides Delia, the other heroine who is given the privilege of speaking her own tale in *The New Atalantis* is Elonora, but unlike Delia, she tells her tale directly to Astrea, Virtue, and Intelligence, who have just rescued her from a seemingly scandalous nighttime encounter in the Tuilleries. Although Intelligence immediately construes the situation in its worst possible light—"You *shriek'd*! you call'd for *help*! how comes it that you were so *reduc'd*? How did you agree to so criminal an *Assignation*? It has the Appearance of being *voluntary*!"—Elonora protests her innocence and is allowed by the divinities to relate her own tale.[55] Even Intelligence herself is patient to listen rather than rush off to spread the apparent scandal she has just witnessed, and herself references Truth as a quality she prefers: "My Business is indeed to give Intelligence of all Things; but I take *Truth* with me when I can get her."[56] Frozen into the posture of eager listener by the strange tale promised by the contradictions between the midnight garden setting and "The *Beautiful*, the *Innocent Elonora*," Intelligence embraces Truth once she takes up the position of auditor rather than weaver of tales.[57]

The most frequently noted detail about Elonora is that neither contemporary nor modern scholars have been able to identify an historical counterpart for the character.[58] Ruth Herman argues that since Elonora was not identified by any of the contemporary keys we can "surmise that Elonora's romantic interlude was included without even the pretense of a basis in reality, political or otherwise."[59] Where Herman sees a purely amatory interlude empty of the political significance of the other tales in Manley's text, Toni Bowers calls upon us to "imagine" that "Elonora stands allegorically not for a still untraced individual but for the Tory party of Manley's day" and notes that, while not completely tidy, this allegorical possibility is "available in the text."[60] While these political resonances are available and potentially powerful, I see another role for Elonora's tale that reveals both the bite of the text's satire and the inability of Manley herself to see a way beyond the paradoxes of the social and aesthetic constructions of exemplary virtue. Simply put, the text's treatment of Elonora implies that there is no room for a virtue strong enough to resist seduction in *The New Atalantis* and, by extension, in eighteenth-century society.

Elonora is unique in being the only distressed heroine who retains her virginity. Her tale is a continual struggle against the various men who would take that virtue, and at the moment that the narrators encounter her, she has managed to succeed in her struggles, despite her own inclination toward one of her seducers. The fact that the only virtuous heroine in the text (whose virtue is actually tested) needs to be fictional is a scathing indictment of the society from which Manley is drawing her characters. The text implies that the only heroine who could survive Elonora's struggles must be a figment of the author's imagination.[61]

In Elonora the readers get an example of a woman who acknowledges and understands both the power of desire and the importance of her education for combating that desire. She emphasizes her mother's large jointure, which was used "to educate and provide" for herself and her sister and demonstrates her proper education repeatedly throughout her narrative.[62] Unlike an amatory narrator who would privilege the physical qualities of the loved one, Elonora minutely details Don Antonio's principles and the qualities of his mind, only coming to his physical description at the end in order to allow her listeners to "better judge of him."[63] When her brother discovers her returning from a midnight assignation, she is honest and defers to his authority and judgment—though her deference has fatal consequences, we can assume she acts as she has been educated to act with regard to the male head of her family.

In contrast to this reverence for her honor and virtue, Elonora openly asserts her desire for Don Antonio, acknowledging, "*Inclination* has blinded me; and tho' some of his Faults are *obvious*, yet I have lov'd him with 'em all; incessantly regretting that I cou'd not also *esteem* him."[64] The contrast between her virtuous reason and treasonous desires continues throughout her narrative in statements such as "he spoke to the Passions within me; they all eccho'd back a simpathetick Answer," "We readily believe what we desire," and "I yet lov'd him, tho' I hated him; a *Paradox* that may easily be reconcil'd by those that know our Passions are *involuntary*, and the Opposition of *Reason* and *Inclination*."[65] As Bowers has described her, Elonora becomes "something of a poster figure for a ubiquitous topos: the irrationality and gullibility, even helplessness, of women in love."[66] An important difference between characters like Charlot or Urania and Elonora, however, is that Elonora is clearly aware of her predicament: she both recognizes what is expected from her by her family and by the morals of her society and, more importantly, she recognizes and understands her feelings. Though she cannot conquer them, she is not driven by them.

The piteous exclamation that began this section, "Where in this bad World shall I find a Protection for my *unwary* Innocence?" comes at the end of Elonora's tale as she bemoans her lack of protection against men like the Count and Don Antonio, who would seduce her seemingly at any cost.[67] Although Intelligence is quick to offer the interest of Princess Fame, who would introduce Elonora to the protection of the Empress of Atalantis, this promise must be viewed with a certain degree of skepticism after reading the many tales of fallen virtue told with relish by the narrator. Intelligence's own admission of her narrative preferences when she is asked by Virtue about a particular gentlemen on the Prado furthers this unreliability: "I must take leave to answer your Mightiness, (without power) by a Leer and a malicious Smile, because I am infinitely pleas'd at your Query, it borders so much upon my beloved Diversion, Scandal."[68] Both Intelligence and her Princess Fame thrive on scandal and the loss of virtue and thus provide scant shelter for Elonora.

That the society depicted is unable to protect virtue is made clear in the text's incapacity to incorporate Elonora into the frame narrative. Promised a suspect sort of protection by Intelligence and Fame, Elonora is given temporary shelter by Virtue, who, speaking for both herself and Astrea, declares that "we will not have her leave us till her Establishment."[69] Although Elonora joins the frame narrators at this point, she all but disappears from the narrative, thus demonstrating the text's inability to integrate the particular type of female virtue associated with virginity. As a silent member of the frame narrative, Elonora is referred to only once more near the end of Manley's text as a figure who is blind to the divine presence guarding the family seat of Beaumond (Henry Somerset, second Duke of Beaufort).[70] This sole reference, aptly described by Bowers as "deflating,"[71] not only reminds the reader that she has been present all along despite her silence, but also adds to that silence a description of blindness. Thus, blind and mute, the text's only heroine who has both suffered assaults on her virtue and protected that virtue hovers on the outskirts of even the frame narrative and is, in the end, completely forgotten. As a final irony, Manley's text, which directs the skeptical reader toward the paradox inherent in both her society's and her aesthetic tradition's construction of female virtue, is unable to integrate and thus preserve distressed virtue.

Conclusion

Rebecca Bullard argues convincingly for understanding Manley's brand of secret history as both an appropriation of and an attack on Whig secret history that is based on "an impression of complicity between implied author and implied reader."[72] While Bullard bases her discussion on the frame narrators and their relationship to the secret history genre, the structure of her insight can be extended beyond those specifics. Bringing Manley's text within the tradition of the pathetic tragedy and the ideology of virtue presented in seduction narratives exposes the full extent of Manley's irony, which spares no one and nothing (including her own text). By exposing the hypocrisy that resides at the very center of the definition of female virtue and the aesthetic exploitation of the pathos created by a beautiful, blameless fall from that virtue, Manley subverts the dominant aesthetic tropes of her own generic tradition. Drawing on the full affective potential of the secret history genre, she creates a community of understanding between her authorial persona and her readers built on the affective intimacy of shared knowledge, while simultaneously seducing and repulsing those same readers through her manipulation of the potential erotics of the seduction narrative. This affective manipulation works to expose the paradox within the ideology of female virtue, while unsettling the erotic desire created in narratives of its loss. In the end, however, Manley's own text cannot find a place for a perfect virtue as defined by eighteenth-century society. Despite her education and her control over her desires, Elonora is just as marginalized as Charlot and Urania, exiled from a society within which she has no place. The exclusion of the truly virtuous heroine from both her society and, ultimately, Manley's text presses the reader to question the aesthetic structures of the seduction narrative itself, which does not seem able to accommodate the dominant model of female virtue without also depicting its destruction.

Notes

1. Delarivier Manley, *The Royal Mischief* (London, 1696), 41–45. Early English Books Online.
2. Jean I. Marsden, *Fatal Desire: Women, Sexuality, and the English Stage, 1660–1720* (Ithaca: Cornell UP, 2006), 63.
3. Since John Richetti's and Ros Ballaster's groundbreaking works situating *The New Atalantis* within early seduction narratives, there has been a lot of strong critical discussion focused on the genres drawn upon by Manley's popular secret history. See John J. Richetti, *Popular Fiction before Richardson: Narrative*

Patterns: 1700–1739 (Oxford: Clarendon, 1969) and Ros Ballaster, *Seductive Forms: Women's Amatory Fiction from 1684 to 1740* (Oxford: Clarendon, 1992). See Toni Bowers, *Force or Fraud: British Seduction Stories and the Problems of Resistance, 1660–1760* (New York: Oxford UP, 2011) for a notable continuation of the critical tradition that places the text within the seduction narrative genre. Bowers takes earlier critical discussions further by weaving issues of ideology and political secret history into her discussion of the text. Important work on Manley's satirical strategies can be found in Aaron Santesso, "The New Atalantis and Varronian Satire," *Philological Quarterly* 79, no. 2 (2000): 1–21 and Melinda Alliker Rabb, *Satire and Secrecy in English Literature from 1650 to 1750* (New York: Palgrave Macmillan, 2007). For discussions of Manley's specific satirical targets see chapter seven in Rachel Carnell, *A Political Biography of Delarivier Manley* (London: Pickering & Chatto, 2008), 159–90, Carole Fungaroli Sargent, "Military Scandal and National Debt in Manley's *New Atalantis*," *SEL: Studies in English Literature 1500–1900* 53, no. 3 (2013): 523–40, which links the Elonora tale to a 1708 military pay scandal, and Carole Fungaroli Sargent, "How a Pie Fight Satirizes Whig-Tory Conflict in Delarivier Manley's *The New Atalantis*," *Eighteenth-Century Studies* 44, no. 4 (2011): 515–33, which links the seemingly personal satire of Sarah Fyge Egerton in Manley's narrative with larger political contests between the Tories and the Whigs. For details on the link between *The New Atalantis* and gossip, see Nicola Parsons, *Reading Gossip in Early Eighteenth-Century England* (New York: Palgrave Macmillan, 2009). Finally, for a detailed analysis of the relationship between Manley's secret history and the Whig secret history that came before it, see Rebecca Bullard, *The Politics of Disclosure, 1674–1725: Secret History Narratives* (London: Pickering & Chatto, 2009), 85–101.

4. Anne Greenfield, "The Titillation of Dramatic Rape, 1160–1720," in *Interpreting Sexual Violence, 1660–1800*, ed. Anne Greenfield (London: Pickering & Chatto, 2013), 58.

5. Delarivier Manley, *Secret Memoirs and Manners of Several Persons of Quality, of Both Sexes. From the New Atalantis*, in *The Selected Works of Delarivier Manley*, ed. Rachel Carnell and Ruth Herman, 5 vols (London: Pickering & Chatto, 2005), II, 9. All subsequent references are to this edition. For a fuller discussion of Manley's use of Varronian satire, see Chris Mounsey's essay in this collection.

6. See Erin M. Keating, "Envious Productions: Actresses, Audiences and Affect in the Restoration Playhouse," *Restoration: Studies in English Literary Culture 1660–1700* 37, no. 2 (2013): 37–53 where I argue for the importance of a lack of agency in the female heroines of the early pathetic tragedies.

7. While there is some disagreement among critics and editors of Manley's work as to whether Astrea's prince is supposed to refer to an actual future monarch, those who do see a specific reference tend to follow Ros Ballaster's argument that the prince is meant as the future George II. See Delarivier Manley, *New Atalantis*, ed. Rosalind Ballaster (New York: Penguin, 1992), 270, n.17.

8. Manley, *The New Atalantis*, 11, 12.

9. Ibid., 12.

10. Ibid., 12. The Queen of Bohemia's fate here is quite similar to that of Cleomira in Settle's *Distress'd Innocence*. Both women are punished for the faults of

others and are seen in instrumental ways by their punishers—Cleomira as an instrument to be used to further torment her husband Hormidas and the Queen of Bohemia as a vessel from whose body and sufferings a glorious prince will eventually arise.

11. Keating, "Envious Productions," 46–47.
12. Manley, *The New Atalantis*, 40.
13. Ellen Pollak, *Incest and the English Novel, 1684–1814* (Baltimore: Johns Hopkins UP, 2003), 96. See Pollak, 92–99 for her informative discussion of the origins of testamentary guardianship in England and its importance for Manley's tale of Charlot and the Duke.
14. William B. Warner, *Licensing Entertainment: The Elevation of Novel Reading in Britain, 1684–1750* (Berkeley: U of California P, 1998), 100–109.
15. Manley, *The New Atalantis*, 48.
16. Bullard, *Politics of Disclosure*, 93. Bullard bases her argument for this distancing effect between the text's narrators and the reader on an analysis of Astrea's and Intelligence's commentaries on the inset tales.
17. Manley, *The New Atalantis*, 54.
18. Ballaster, *Seductive Forms*, 130.
19. See Keating, "Envious Productions" 41–42. In my work on the affective structure of pathetic tragedy, I draw on Sianne Ngai's articulation of envy as an affective relationship that reveals ideology. Envy in the Restoration theater is created by the aesthetic suffering of the female heroine, who has been held up as an exemplar and yet who falls despite (and often because of) her perfect virtue; in Ngai's words "envying becomes a way of stripping this 'example' of its exemplarity." Sianne Ngai, *Ugly Feelings* (Cambridge: Harvard UP, 2005), 163.
20. Manley, *The New Atalantis*, 54.
21. Most discussions of Charlot's education have focused on its second stage, her corruption. Though Warner discusses both Charlot's first and second education at the hands of the Duke, he clearly emphasizes the second education or corruption of her virtue, highlighting the initial seduction of Charlot's principles through her reading of the story of Myrrha in Ovid's *Metamorphoses*. Ballaster also pays special attention to this scene of education, arguing that the text is shown as itself an agent of seduction: "it is art that seduces Charlot, rather than the Duke himself." See Ballaster, *Seductive Forms*, 133. Interestingly art also seduces the Duke; though in his case it is an art which he has encouraged and in many ways created in his ward.
22. Warner, *Licensing Entertainment*, 103.
23. Bowers, *Force or Fraud*, 34.
24. Manley, *The New Atalantis*, 39.
25. Bowers, *Force or Fraud*, 35. My argument here draws on Bowers's excellent discussion of the role of ideology and agency in seventeenth-century seduction narratives. However, my focus is on how Manley takes things further through her text's implicit criticism of those very narrative strategies and the ideologies underlying them and perpetuated through them.
26. Melinda Alliker Rabb, "The Manl(e)y Style: Delarivier Manley and Jonathan Swift," in *Pope, Swift, and Women Writers*, ed. Donald C. Mell. (Newark: U of Delaware P, 1996), 140.
27. Ibid., 140.
28. See Paula McDowell, *The Women of Grub Street: Press, Politics, and Gender in the London Literary Marketplace 1678–1730* (Oxford: Clarendon, 1998),

253–54, where she discusses the issue of unwanted pregnancies in *The New Atalantis* through the lens of class, noting how the upper-class women of the Cabal have the power to create for themselves a man-free space whereas many of the lower class women in the text are depicted as unable to escape the "tragic consequences" of illegitimate and unwanted children. Rabb views the scenes of unwanted children as a motif which "nervously connects sex and politics" in its referencing of illegitimate succession and private sexuality: "Thus broken lovers' promises are also broken paternal promises (and broken women's bodies)." See Rabb, *Satire*, 123.

29. Aphra Behn, *Love-Letters Between a Nobleman and his Sister*, in *The Works of Aphra Behn*, ed. Janet Todd, 7 vols (Columbus: Ohio State UP, 1993), II, 365.
30. Kim Simpson also theorizes the pregnant bodies present in Manley's text in another chapter of this collection. Whereas my emphasis is on the affective relationship between text and reader that is created through these scenes and the implications of that affect for Manley's work as a whole, Simpson takes her analysis in a different direction detailing the ways that the material body interrupts and disrupts the performative repetitions enacted on the discursive register of Manley's narrative.
31. Jonathan Dollimore, *Sex, Literature and Censorship* (Cambridge: Polity, 2001), 47. My use of the term revulsion bears strong similarities to Sianne Ngai's and Jonathan Dollimore's use of the concept of disgust. However, revulsion is more specifically appropriate to the late seventeenth and early eighteenth centuries in its medical connotations. The process of bleeding or drawing out the excess humors in order to cure a different part of the body (or the whole) seems particularly apt for Manley's emphasis on the full body and its affective overflow with which she attempts to balance an unbalanced aesthetic tradition and social order between the genders.
32. Recall, for instance, the "spectacle of female sexuality" (Marsden, *Fatal Desire*, 79) displayed through Anne Bracegirdle as Eurione in *The Rape* when "*The Scene draws, and discovers Eurione in an Arbour, gagg'd and bound to a Tree, her hair dishevel'd as newly Ravish'd, a Dagger lying by her.*" See Nicholas Brady, *The Rape: Or, the Innocent Imposters* (1692), 25. Early English Books Online. This spectacle was such an integral part of the audience enjoyment of the play that the tableau is echoed twice more during the course of the play, first by revealing Eurione in her chamber "*discover'd lying on a Couch, her hair dishevel's (as before)*" (29) and again near the end of the play immediately before her suicide where her speech explicitly draws attention to her function as spectacle "I cannot bear their eyes; already see / All turn and gaze, as if they saw a Monster" See Brady, *The Rape*, 29 and 53. Far from a monster, the beautifully erotic spectacle of Anne Bracegirdle's suffering is continually placed before the audience's desiring eyes in Brady's play.
33. Manley, *New Atalantis*, 136.
34. See Keating, "Envious Productions," 41–42, where, drawing on the work of Ngai, I theorize envy for the Restoration period as an affect that is intersubjective (with one subject being the text or performance) and that "expresses an ideological position of the play itself" rather than any subjective state of emotion.
35. Ngai, *Ugly Feelings*, 335.
36. Manley, *The New Atalantis*, 157–58.
37. Ngai, *Ugly Feelings*, 333, 337.

38. Manley, *The New Atalantis*, 158.
39. Ibid., 159.
40. Sara Ahmed, *The Cultural Politics of Emotion* (Edinburgh: Edinburgh UP, 2004, 2014). Manley, *The New Atalantis*, 165. Ahmed's theorization of disgust emphasizes its sticky qualities that cause it to link different ideas or groups into which it has come into contact, allowing the affect to be activated by otherwise innocuous ideas or images: disgust "does not move freely: it sticks to that which is near it; it clings. Furthermore, an object can become disgusting because it resembles another object that is disgusting" (87–88).
41. The name Urania along with its more general romance and classical associations was also the name of the heroine played by Anne Bracegirdle in George Powell's *Alphonso; King of Naples* (1691).
42. Manley, *The New Atalantis*, 164.
43. Ibid., 164.
44. Ibid., 171.
45. "By first confining Urania within its contracted affective space, the baroness's family produces within itself the very desire that it then sustains its self-identity by condemning." Pollak, *Incest and the English Novel*, 106.
46. Ibid., 106. My emphasis on a shared understanding of the genre of seduction narratives both in pathetic tragedies in the theater and in other amatory fiction builds on Bullard's argument for the affective cohesion created by Manley for her readers through her narrative positioning as an author merely relating well-known stories: "If those stories are already well known, the overall effect is of the author signaling to her readers their shared understanding" (95) and my own work on the secret histories about Charles II which created communities of readers based on their understanding of the significations present in the texts. See Bullard, *Politics of Disclosure*, 95 and Erin M. Keating, "In the Bedroom of the King: Affective Politics in the Restoration Secret History," *Journal of Early Modern Cultural Studies* 15, no. 2 (2015): 58–82.
47. Manley, *The New Atalantis*, 166.
48. Ibid., 164.
49. Ibid., 168.
50. That honor belongs to a very short tale in Volume 1 when the frame characters come upon a woman nailed to the gibbet. She came to that fate after secretly giving birth to, then murdering, her illegitimate child. The description of the labor is haunting and grotesque in its vividness of detail: "Pain after pain, Tear after Tear, Cry after Cry. ... after a few more Labour-pains, she is Deliver'd all-alone by her self of a brave Boy. Lest he shou'd cry, she tore out his Bowels in the Birth." Ibid., 96.
51. Ibid., 172–73.
52. Ibid., 173.
53. Ibid., 174.
54. Ibid., 17.
55. Ibid., 187.
56. Ibid., 187.
57. Ibid., 186. Intelligence's desire to listen to Elonora's story is remarkable when contrasted with other instances in which she has to quietly listen to other narrators. For instance in Volume 1, when the goddesses meet a country woman and a count who both briefly inform the frame characters about the scenes

before them, Intelligence is described as quite frustrated with their "usurping upon her Province, and forcing her to a long and painful Silence." See Ibid., 99. Her impatience toward other narrators is also shown in the Mrs. Nightwork episode. As McDowell has pointed out, Intelligence shows a great deal of disdain for the midwife, who is characterized as socially inferior to Lady Intelligence, when Intelligence complains peevishly "I'm afraid you are taking my province from me, and engrossing all the scandal to yourself," Ibid., 138. See McDowell, *Women of Grub Street*, 255.

58. Both Ballaster and Carnell, in the notes to their respective editions of the text, claim that if there is an historical individual implied by this tale, she remains unknown.

59. Ruth Herman, *The Business of a Woman: The Political Writings of Delarivier Manley* (Newark: U of Delaware P, 2003), 69.

60. Bowers, *Force or Fraud*, 188.

61. There are of course many virtuous Tory women mentioned in Manley's text, but the distinction with Elonora is that her virtue has been continually assaulted and tested. Presumably it would have been politically awkward to show the female figures whom Manley was supporting politically in any kind of virtue in distress situation, as merely to be placed in such a position could invite suspicion of their virtue.

62. Manley, *The New Atalantis*, 187.

63. Ibid., 189.

64. Ibid., 189.

65. Ibid., 190, 191, 210.

66. Bowers, *Force or Fraud*, 184.

67. Manley, *The New Atalantis*, 213.

68. Ibid., 113.

69. Ibid., 214.

70. Ibid., 262.

71. Bowers, *Force or Fraud*, 189.

72. Bullard, *Politics of Disclosure*, 93.

6   Manley's Single Ladies

Jennifer Frangos

[T]o be entirely happy one ought never to think of the faithless sex.[1]

The default sexual mode in Delarivier Manley's fiction, especially her scandalous political writings, would seem to be adultery. Sexually active adults almost never confine themselves to one sexual partner, working as they do in a system in which sex is a means to power as well as pleasure. As Toni Bowers has observed, "[i]n *The New Atalantis*, political partisanship becomes a feverishly sexual business, and sexual encounters are always a form of partisan contest."[2] Like Aphra Behn's before her, Manley's writings exhibit a severe critique of the sexual double standard that holds feminine virtue to impossible ideals while excusing and even encouraging male sexual promiscuity.

But what about the few female characters who are set apart from or even opt out of an alloerotic lifestyle?[3] Indeed, there are not many in Manley's fictions, and fewer still who do not die as a consequence of forswearing love and desire, but perhaps that makes them all the more important as characters. A prime example is "the poor, the innocent, the much unhappy Elonora" of *The New Atalantis* (1709), who is traded to a dissipated and sparkish count by her uncle to cover gambling debts and who is given refuge by the traveling party of Astrea, Virtue, and Lady Intelligence until she can be safely recommended to the Princess Fame and the Empress of Atalantis. The title character of *The Adventures of Rivella* (1714), generally accepted as a fictionalized version of Manley herself, also remains staunchly outside of the exploitive heteronormative and adulterous sexuality that permeates that novel: notably, Rivella's early (and regretted) bigamous marriage is not discussed, but rather glossed by a passing reference to Delia's story in *The New Atalantis*, and there is no mention of any subsequent sexual relationships Rivella engages in after she separates from her cousin-husband.

One way to read these characters is as representing an extreme version of feminine modesty, but another, more interesting way is to consider them through the lens of the nascent asexuality movement—a twenty-first century identity movement predicated on the recognition that, for some individuals, it is a *lack* of sexual desire or a *disinterest* in intimate relationships that forms the core of a person's "sexual identity."[4] Recent work establishing the field of asexuality studies has suggested that, as a methodological concept, asexuality allows for new avenues in feminist and queer critique and theory. With this essay, I consider Manley's challenge to a heteronormative sexual economy as manifested through a number of female characters who try to avoid the pitfalls of heterosexual relationships (through martyrdom, capitulation, homoerotic relationships, and singleness), with special attention to the extent to which asexuality serves as a productive lens through which to read Manley's single ladies. My analysis is intended, first, to extend our understanding of Manley's critique of the double standard of sexual behavior by taking seriously the choice to not participate in alloerotic social interactions such as flirtation, physical sexual encounters, and (when economically possible) marriage, and thus, second, to contribute to a collective effort heralded by Susan S. Lanser to "challenge popular culture's widespread investment in a heteronormative eighteenth century."[5]

Manley's fiction depicts an abundance of women who are deceived and exploited by a male-dominated, alloerotic sexual economy. An early story in *The New Atalantis*, and a famous one, concerns the seduction of Charlot by her guardian, the Duke.[6] After the Duke has lost interest in her, Charlot declares that she "was not born to taste the sweets of love and friendship," and removes herself from his villa.[7] Shortly thereafter, she is informed of the marriage of the Duke and her friend the Countess, "which but confirmed her in her resolution of not surviving the loss of his kindness."[8] Lady Intelligence finishes Charlot's story: "The remainder of her life was one continued scene of horror, sorrow and repentance. She died a true landmark to warn all believing virgins from shipwracking their honor upon (that dangerous coast of rocks) the vows and pretended passion of mankind."[9]

Charlot's story is the very stuff of romance novels and, as Ros Ballaster has observed, it is "the story of a landmark and the landmark story in Manley's text, in that it is an exemplary tale of seduction and betrayal to or from which all subsequent stories in the novel correspond or diverge."[10] Charlot's seduction and abandonment by the Duke present a critique of the sexual double standard that holds women responsible for their loss of reputation while allowing their seducers to carry on, and even prosper, untainted by sexual scandal. Her betrayal by her best friend stands as a sharp critique of women who place personal gain above female friendship and alliance. The goddess Astrea, one of the novel's audiences for this narrative, pronounces a pair of morals to this story that are nothing but pragmatic (if a little strange): that women will be taken advantage of by unscrupulous men and that "no woman ought to introduce another to the man by whom she is beloved."[11] And yet, while we are told that Charlot dies a martyr and should serve as an example of the dangers of succumbing to unsanctioned, powerful emotions and desires, it is striking to note that she both removes herself from a heteronormative sexual economy (represented by the Duke's house, scene of their assignations) and renounces "the sweets of love and friendship" as she does so. This is a very small but significant part of the story, and though it is easily subsumed into the sentimental story of seduction and betrayal, it is an element that benefits from further consideration. Charlot does not long survive her heartbreak, but she does suggest that there are alternatives to the exploitive and emotionally vacuous conventions that govern interactions between the sexes in Manley's highly sexualized and politicized depiction of court culture: in this case, remaining single.

There are, of course, other options. One of these is to simply accept the terms upon which marriage and heterosexual interactions are offered. Charlot's best friend, the Countess, advocates for a dispassionate approach to marriage: "the fashionable way of making love," she calls it, "wherein the heart has little or no part."[12] She counsels Charlot that "the first thing a woman ought to consult was her interest and establishment in the world: that love should only be a handle towards it."[13] The Countess takes her own advice and is rewarded with a highly advantageous and respectable—if loveless—marriage to Charlot's beloved, the Duke, who proposes to her in very practical terms: "I have took time to weigh the design. All things plead for you—beauty, merit, sense, and every thing that can render a woman charming. Whilst I pretend nothing to plead for me, but making it your own interest to make me happy."[14] The Countess accepts, despite the fact that his demonstrated inconstancy might prove to be an issue, with the comment that "as the distance was so infinitely great both in their title and other circumstances, she would not pretend to capitulate with him but left all her interest in his, as the best hands, who was so much a friend as to raise her to a rank and fortune she could not, the highest vanity, have expected."[15] The Countess's choice—accepting the terms on which marriages and heterosexual interactions take place—is not presented as an appealing or satisfying alternative to the relationship of mutual attraction and affection imagined by Charlot (though it is almost certainly preferable to dying of a broken heart). Indeed, the Countess appears to enter into a marriage in which the only emotional reward she stands to receive is the prospect of making her husband happy.

When Intelligence tells Charlot's story, Manley implicitly critiques the Countess, both for betraying her female friend and for entering into a marriage for mercenary reasons. The Countess accepts the political dimensions of heterosexual marriage (the awareness that her husband will very likely engage in extramarital affairs, especially if they advance his ambitions and interests in court). She also relinquishes her agency in terms of determining what is in her own best interest. By doing so, she capitulates to the exploitive pressures of heterosexual exchange, even at the expense of a friendship that might alleviate some of her emotional isolation and dependence on her husband.

An alternative to heterosexual marriage comes in the form of the new Cabal, a group of ladies characterized by their near-exclusive homosociality, and perhaps homosexuality.[16] The members of the new Cabal "have wisely excluded that rapacious sex who, making a prey of the honour of ladies, find their greatest satisfaction (some few excepted) in boasting of their good fortune"; instead,

> [t]hey momently exclude men: fortify themselves in the precepts of virtue and chastity against all their detestable undermining arts: ... at the same time lamenting the custom of the world, that has made it convenient (nay, almost indispensable) for all ladies once to marry. To those that have husbands, they have other instructions, in which this is sure to be one: to reserve their heart, their tender amity for their fair friend, an article in this well-bred, wilfully undistinguishing age which the husband seems to be rarely solicitous of.[17]

This same-sex society acknowledges that marriage is, for many women, an economic necessity, but explicitly reserves love and affection, the "tender amity," for the relationships between its members; for the Cabal, then, heterosexual contact is limited to practical necessities while emotional connection and fulfillment is found in same-sex interactions. The Cabal do seem to enjoy their lives: they are introduced as "laugh[ing] loud and incessantly," and Astrea comments that "'Tis certain they have neither the spleen nor the vapours! or, for the present seem to have forgotten them."[18] Lady Intelligence goes to great lengths to proclaim her inability to imagine an erotic or physical sexual component to the Cabal's "mysteries"—though surely by repeatedly calling attention to speculations and accusations about sexual impropriety she invites her listeners and readers to imagine exactly that. These are, therefore—potentially if not actually—homoerotic, *alloerotic* relationships; they are as well open to the censure of public opinion and gossip, which, when it comes to women's virtue and reputations, makes little distinction between potential and actual transgressions. The Cabal is also characterized by secrecy, with its married members particularly enjoined to keep silent, "lest she let her husband into a mystery (however innocent) that may expose and ridicule the community."[19] Members' affectionate and erotic allegiances are strictly policed by the elder members of the Cabal, and anyone whose "foible be found directed to what Nature inspires, [is] unanimously excluded," which further allies the Cabal with the unnatural, the scandalous, and, in the minds of their detractors, "the vices of old Rome revived."[20] Again, preferable to dying of a broken heart, but with certain drawbacks immediately perceivable.

In contrast to these alloerotic sexualities, which are open to condemnation by Intelligence (who represents gossip and scandal), we might identify the figure of the single lady. This is where Charlot's retreat from Atalantis's social circles and her disavowal of "the sweets of love and friendship" come into play. Granted, there are very few women in Manley's scandal fiction who remain single, and fewer still who do not die (like Charlot) as a result of their disappointed expectations and/or broken hearts—but their scarcity may in fact be all the more reason to pay attention to them. In

The New Atalantis, the "unfortunate Elonora" provides an excellent test case: Elonora does indeed survive an exploitive initiation into heterosexual desire, forswears love and marriage in favor of a single life, and is ultimately validated, embraced, protected, and rewarded by the goddesses who arbitrate the narratives and anecdotes of the novel.

The travelers first encounter Elonora when they hear "shrieks like as from a woman in distress" and follow the sounds to find a man making a hasty exit and a woman alone and discomposed on a bench.[21] The woman is invited to tell her story, an opportunity she appreciates because it will give her the chance to tell her own version of events and to counter the "appearance of things ... especially as to that particular of finding me alone with my Lord of ——— at an hour so blameable and a place so suspicious."[22] The story that follows is one of the longest individual narratives in *The New Atalantis* (more than twenty pages in the Penguin edition) and one of the only narratives told in the first person rather than narrated through Intelligence's gossipy perspective.[23] Both of these arguably place it at the moral center of Manley's social and sexual critique.[24]

Elonora's father, the Chevalier de ———, died when she was young. Elonora has a suitor, Don Antonio, who courts her secretly, cajoling and manipulating her into feeling grateful for his professed affection for her; when she asks him why he does not broach the subject of marriage, he anticipates their families' disapproval and paints for her a dismal picture of their lives as a second son and a disinherited heiress. He suggests instead that they marry others for money and implies that they could then carry on an adulterous affair. Antonio's disingenuous intentions are discovered by her brother, who challenges him to a duel and is killed on the spot, the shock of which also kills her mother. Reduced to "a very indifferent" fortune by a miserly younger brother and relegated to the care of a wealthy socialite aunt,[25] Elonora falls into gambling and is introduced to the dissipated (and married) company who frequent her aunt's parties and card tables. Antonio reappears and manages to marry Elonora's aunt, while at the same time renewing his attentions to her; he declares his intentions to "enjoy [her], either by favour, fraud, force, or any other way but money"[26] and contrives the plan to trade Elonora to the Count to cover gambling debts incurred by Elonora (fifty pieces) and himself (four thousand crowns), with the expectation that once she has lost her virtue she will be more receptive to his own advances. The goddesses have arrived at the intended scene of Elonora's ravishing, at just the right moment to prevent the Count from raping her.

Upon finishing her story, Elonora laments, "Ah! what retreat have I? Where in this bad world shall I find a protection for my unwary innocence? ... Don Antonio is implacable and resolute! I will never again return to a place which he dishonours."[27] Like Charlot before her, Elonora rejects the "bad world" dominated by sexually predatory men: Antonio's pursuit of her, and especially his declaration that he will "enjoy" her no matter what, has made Atalantis a place that she cannot stay and remain virtuous. By associating Atalantis with Antonio's pursuit and longing for a "retreat" and "protection" from his efforts to have her raped, Elonora effectively renounces alloerotic sexuality. She throws herself on the mercy of Lady Intelligence and the traveling goddesses, pleading, "Oh advise! assist me! Tell me of a sanctuary! Is there any such receptacle for the poor, the innocent, the unhappy Elonora?"

Intelligence responds:

> I will introduce you with such success to my sovereign Princess Fame, that she shall recommend you to the protection of your graceful Empress, whose noble breast will certainly compassionate your youth, beauty and distress. You want nothing but to be known by her to meet the reward due to suffering virtue. She will receive you into the household, where you shall shine as in your proper sphere, conspicuous by your charms, valued for your conversation, reverenced for goodness and dear to the Empress for a thousand virtues, so much of kindred to her own![28]

Elonora's retreat from the world of love and desire is voluntary and, apparently, final; furthermore, it is to all appearances satisfactory, as she is offered both protection and purpose. She is one of the very few characters in Manley's fiction who escapes disastrous effects of alloerotic entanglements and also one of the few who tells her own tale: Intelligence does not know the story and does not participate in its circulation or interpretation, so Elonora has ostensibly escaped the economy of sexualized scandal and blame that makes up *The New Atalantis*. Though culpable in a number of ways according to the rules defining female virtue in a patriarchal society— for owning an unsanctioned passionate attachment to an unsuitable man, for believing in his protestations of love and his many promises, for racking up gambling debts, for remaining alone in the garden with the lascivious count—she has also, by telling her own story and explaining away the compromising appearances, evaded the label of "fallen woman."[29]

The emerging category of asexuality studies gives us an interesting way to think about Elonora's choice and its implications for the sexual economy of *The New Atalantis* and the larger reading public/social sphere as well. In a 2010 essay entitled "New Orientations: Asexuality and Its Implications for Theory and Practice," Karli June Ceranowski and Megan Milks propose that asexuality offers some useful perspectives to the realm of feminist theory and sexuality studies, especially the chance "to consider how asexuality might critique the rhetoric of liberation in which sex is still steeped within feminism."[30] While not without its benefits, politically and personally, the rhetoric of liberation and its emphasis on freeing female sexuality from the restrictions of patriarchal and heteronormative cultural expectations has the unfortunate effect of pathologizing positions or identities—such as celibacy and asexuality—that do not involve expressions of (alloerotic) sexual desire. Valuing and validating even those forms of sexuality that do not inherently support the sex-positive component of contemporary feminist theory will extend the reach and significance of feminist theoretical critique of oppression along the lines of sex and gender by eliminating the need to define oneself and the measure of one's happiness or success in relation to another person; further, this will allow for a positive reconsideration of female figures like the spinster (and, to a lesser extent, the widow), who are still so easily dismissed as failures or victims of repressed or frustrated sexuality. As well, opening up sexuality studies to include nonalloerotic sexual expressions such as asexuality will diversify our understanding of human sexuality and help to further theorize and critique both heteronormative and queer culture and their tacit reliance on sexual desire directed toward another (or others) as a central component of an individual's identity.

Most narrowly defined, an asexual individual is "a person who does not experience sexual attraction"[31]; the FAQ page of the Asexual Visibility and Education Network (AVEN) website, however, recognizes "a spectrum of sexuality, with sexual and asexual as the endpoints and a gray area in-between," including those who "[do] not normally experience sexual attraction but [do] experience it sometimes; experienc[e] sexual attraction but [have] a low sex drive; experienc[e] sexual attraction and drive but not strongly enough to want to act on them; and/or can enjoy and desire sex but only under very limited and specific circumstances."[32] Hence, my definition of asexuality invoking a lack of sexual desire or a disinterest in intimate, sexual relationships. While it does not seem to be the case that either Charlot or Elonora has *never* experienced sexual desire, insofar as they each had passionate attractions to men who initially (or seemingly) returned those feelings, they both decidedly renounce those past feelings in favor of a single life free from the complications of alloerotic relationships: Charlot forswears "the sweets of love and friendship" while Elonora desires to preserve her "unwary innocence" by removing herself from a social context that has worked only to destroy it. If their experiences have not altogether extinguished their sexual desires, they are at the very least unwilling to act on them for the foreseeable future.[33] While we are told that Charlot has determined not to survive the loss of the Duke's affections, Elonora makes no such fatal prediction or commitment; she does not wish for death, but rather for a life of perpetual and unguarded innocence, meaning one without either temptation or assault. Once she has been taken in by Astrea, Virtue, and Lady Intelligence—under, it is worth mentioning, the specific protection of Virtue—Elonora looks forward to a position in the Empress's household; there will, in other words, be a place for her in the projected future government and social world of Atalantis. This imagined future for an avowedly single lady indeed symbolically outlasts the corrupt, exploitive, and sexualized court of Atalantis and its Whiggish analogues in Queen Anne's government.

Bowers identifies the family tableau of Beaumond, near the end of Volume 2 of *The New Atalantis*, as that of Henry Somerset, second Duke of Beaufort, to whom Manley dedicated her text, and reads the family as the new-Tory hope for the future at the core of Manley's political critique.[34] She also reads the fact that Lady Intelligence and Elonora, the two mortals in the frame narrative's traveling party, are unable to properly understand the family tableau for its political significance as a failure, a "moment of invisibility ... but also of blindness" on Elonora's part.[35] I would counter with the observation that asexuality studies allows us to understand that Elonora, having opted out of heterosexual desire and marriage, may simply not register the manifestations of that sexual economy as represented by the nuclear family. This will not be her future, and she is thus understandably excluded from the appreciation and wonder that Astrea and Virtue (and Manley) bestow on this "epitome of new-tory virtue"[36]; however, we need not characterize Elonora's nonincorporation into this family portrait as a failure or even as an erasure: as I have mentioned, Elonora's story is one of the longest in *The New Atalantis*, which argues for its weight and importance. Elonora is also the only mortal, as Bowers notes, to whom the goddesses make themselves visible and to whom they extend their invisibility and protection.[37] She is therefore favorably singled out by the narrative—and we might even say that she is protected from the type of public visibility, attention, scrutiny, and interpretation that comes with being a representative, public, or allegorical figure. Bowers and others have noted that Elonora is one of the few characters in Manley's scandalous fiction for whom a "real-life" counterpart has not been identified—either in the keys contemporaneous with Manley's novels or in the subsequent scholarship[38]—and this too may be significant. Given the economic pressures on most women of the middling and upper classes to marry in this time period, compounded by the very few means of (respectable) self-support should a woman not wish to marry, the fact that Elonora remains unmarried and yet both virtuous and respectable is admittedly rather fantastic. Perhaps, indeed, such a figure can exist only in the world of fiction. But this speaks to the power of fiction and its ability to imagine alternatives to contemporary realities and to articulate and circulate those alternatives in the cultural imaginary.

The figure of Elonora has connections to both Intelligence and her divine companions as well as to the protagonist of *The Adventures of Rivella*, and thus, fairly directly, to Manley herself: each of these female figures is similarly detached from the heteronormative, politicized court/social scene they observe, which gives each one the ability to comment on the entanglement of sexual expression and politics, power, and government. They all express an interest in morality and acknowledge the sexual double standard at work, so they are not insensible or uninterested in social and sexual dynamics, but none of them betrays any sort of erotic inclination. Lady Intelligence, in particular, is intensely social and well connected but contents herself with relaying and commenting on stories rather than participating in any of the erotic or even flirtatious exchanges. Paula McDowell identifies Lady Intelligence as a stand-in for both Manley herself and the woman writer more generally,[39] a comparison that, for the purposes of my argument, also highlights Manley's own ostensible withdrawal from heterosexual exchange once the bigamous nature of her marriage to her cousin John Manley came to the public's attention and the couple separated in 1693 or '94.

The Adventures of Rivella, published five years after *The New Atalantis* in 1714, is often read as Manley's thinly veiled autobiography.[40] Rivella's story is narrated by an old family friend and admirer, Lovemore, at the prompting of the younger Chevalier d'Aumont, who has read Rivella's writing and wants to know more about the woman who produced the texts he so admires. Like both Charlot and Elonora, Rivella had an early, formative, and devastating experience with heterosexual desire: at the age of twelve, she developed a crush on a young ensign under her father's command, called Lysander in *Rivella* and identified as James Carlisle. "Her eyes were continually fixed upon this young warrior," Lovemore states, "she could neither eat nor sleep; she became hectick, and had all the symptoms of a dangerous indisposition."[41] She steals a handful of guineas from her father to give to Lysander, which she later relates to Lovemore as evidence of "the greatness of her prepossession, being perfectly just by nature, principle, and education, nothing but love, and that in a high degree could have made her otherwise."[42] Through the interventions of her family, Lysander is reassigned and relocated; upon learning this, "poor Rivella fell from one fainting fit into another without the least immodest expression, glance or discovery of what had occasioned her fright."[43] Shortly afterward, Lovemore proposes a secret marriage, which Rivella firmly rejects[44]; he leaves the country for several years, during which time Rivella meets and marries her cousin and has a son by him, only to learn that he has a living wife. The novel and its narrator are cagey about this phase of Rivella's life, referring d'Aumont "to her own story, under the name of Delia, in the *Atalantis*, for the next four miserable years of her life."[45] Devastated by Rivella's "ruin," Lovemore renews his proposals periodically (though significantly he now offers to keep her as a mistress rather than to marry her), and is repeatedly turned down. Between the hysterical result of her early passion for Lysander and the representation of her cousin-husband as duplicitous and abusive, Rivella's disinterest in romantic relationships is perhaps understandable; her resolute singleness is also legible through the lens of asexuality studies as a sexual identity unto itself. Furthermore, despite the evident correspondence between Rivella and Manley herself, there is no allusion in either Delia's or Rivella's stories to the fact that Manley had been in a five-year sexual relationship with one man, John Tilly, with whom she may have had one or more children, and was, at the time she was writing *Rivella*, lodging with, and perhaps sexually involved with, the publisher John Barber.[46] Leaving her sexual relationships out of her autobiographical narratives allows Manley to position herself asexually, as though she were devoid of sexual desires or disinterested in intimate relationships, and to adopt a stance, echoing Elonora's, against participation in the heteronormative, politicized, adulterous social scene depicted in her novels.

Bowers reads the opening scene of *The Adventures of Rivella*, which includes a physical description of Rivella, thus:

> Like a media celebrity today, the female writer constructed in this opening scene offered early eighteenth-century readers a fantasy of sexualized beauty beyond ordinary experience but purporting to be available, however distantly, within that experience. And *Rivella* goes farther. It stirs readers to believe not only in impossible beauty, excitement, and satisfaction, but in the more complicated possibility of finding that beauty in plainness, that excitement in ordinariness; satisfaction and vindication emerge as by-products of the endurance of lifelong unrequited desire (on the narrator's part) or misunderstood virtue (on Rivella's). *Writing* is the sexiest possible activity here.[47]

As with the admittedly fantastic but alluring figure of the single yet virtuous Elonora, it is precisely the power of language, of literature, that evokes and explains Rivella's charms, though she possesses very few of the standard qualities of a literary heroine. Furthermore, although she is figured as the sexualized object of the male fantasies of both Lovemore and d'Aumont—and by extension, of the readers of *Rivella*—it is important to observe that her eroticization is purely one of fantasy and a deferred future. Though the scene of her boudoir is laid out at the very end of the novel and d'Aumont is carefully placed upon a bed and encouraged to imagine that Rivella chooses him as a sexual partner, the scene is never completed: Rivella never appears.[48] Instead, the impatient and impetuous d'Aumont interrupts Lovemore's scene-drawing to go and seek Rivella in person. McDowell writes that "Manley represented her two male narrators as having power over her—celebrating her renunciation of politics and imaginatively placing her in the feminine private sphere of the boudoir,"[49] but I suggest that her absence from that boudoir represents an asexual move on Rivella's part—and by extension, Manley's—away from alloerotic identifications and toward a position beyond the reach of male admirers (well-meaning though they may think themselves), representing the possibility of escape and retreat without judgment or the pathologization of a single life. One can, after all, be the object of others' sexual fantasy without feeling sexual desires of one's own and without those desires dictating one's choices or future.

Like Elonora, Rivella/Manley has something to look forward to in the future: McDowell argues that Manley actually had no genuine intention of giving up party writing when she published *Rivella*. Rather, she was plotting to "go underground," by publicly adopting a more "feminine" authorial persona. She notes that critics have failed to notice that on *precisely the same day* that Manley dated the "Translator's Preface" to *Rivella*, June 3, 1714, she also dated another letter to Robert Harley—offering her services as a propagandist and sketching her plans for another full-length political allegory along the lines of *The New Atalantis*.[50]

I argue that the position of relative power achieved through the deferral of her expected participation in the heterosexual economy is precisely that which will allow for Manley to continue writing. Like Lady Intelligence, she can circulate and gather information and gossip for her reports without becoming intimately involved with either the people she encounters or the messy, politicized, and potentially exploitive sexual exchanges they engage in. The absence of desire on Manley's part makes sense when it becomes clear that, like Charlot and Elonora, she sees no means of achieving happiness or fulfillment through heteronormative, alloerotic sexuality; opting out allows Manley to imagine alternative futures and successes that are dependent on things other than sexual desire directed at and returned by another person.

The perspective offered by the burgeoning asexuality movement and field of asexuality studies allows modern readers to appreciate Manley's single ladies as characters who choose a single life for the benefits it offers, at the same time that it prevents their interpretation as figures of failure, doomed to a life of "horror, sorrow and repentance." A figure like Charlot can still stand as the beacon warning of the dangers of alloerotic sexuality, for those who need such advice (for she certainly suffers as a result of her involvement with and betrayal by the Duke, and is definitely a casualty of the scheming self-interest of the larger court circle, including her false friend the Countess). Asexuality allows for the possibility of a life that is not rooted in the experience and satisfaction of sexual desire, a life that is not deemed successful when a marriage or partnership with another person is realized or declared a failure when it is lived without intimate companionship. In their own ways, Elonora, Lady Intelligence, Delia/Rivella, and Manley herself have things to look forward to despite the apparent absence of sexual feelings for anyone else; in contrast to nearly every other female character in Manley's scandalous fiction, they have avoided exploitation, social censure, heartbreak, and death or martyrdom. My reading of Manley's single ladies also nudges modern feminist theory and queer theory to reconsider their investments in liberatory discourse associated with sexual orientation and sexual practice by illustrating, at least in the literary and cultural imagination, the possibility of a full and satisfying life that is not predicated on alloerotic desire.[51]

Notes

1. Delarivier Manley, *The New Atalantis* [1709], ed. Ros Ballaster (New York: Penguin, 1992), 38.
2. Toni Bowers, *Force or Fraud: British Seduction Stories and the problem of Resistance, 1660–1760* (Oxford: Oxford University Press, 2011), 163.

3. By "alloerotic" I mean a sexual orientation in which one's erotic energies are directed toward another person or persons. Alloerotic is generally contrasted with "auto-erotic," or self-directed sexual energies.

4. The concept of asexuality would therefore complicate the binary between alloerotic and auto-erotic by introducing a third term—perhaps we might call it "anerotic"—that would acknowledge that sometimes a person's sexual energies are absent or so limited as to not be a factor. A closely related concept would be celibacy, which is a decision to ignore or avoid sexual desires; because celibacy acknowledges the presence of sexual energies, however, it is not the same as asexuality; see AVEN Project Team, "The Asexual Visibility & Education Network," *Asexual Visibility & Education Network (AVEN)*, 2012, www.asexuality.org/home/.

5. Susan S. Lanser, "Of Closed Doors and Open Hatches: Heteronormative Plots in Eighteenth-Century (Women's) Studies," in "Essays in Memory of Hans Turley," special issue, ed. Kathryn R. King, *The Eighteenth Century: Theory and Interpretation* 53, no. 3 (Fall 2012): 273–90, 285. My thanks to Lanser for calling attention to the asexuality movement.

6. See Erin M. Keating's essay in this collection for more details of this story.

7. Manley, *New Atalantis*, 43–44.

8. Ibid., 45.

9. Ibid.

10. Ros Ballaster, *Seductive Forms: Women's Amatory Fiction from 1684 to 1740* (Oxford: Clarendon Press, 1992), 132. "The dangerous coast of rocks on which Charlot flounders," she writes, "is amatory fiction itself" (134).

11. Manley, *New Atalantis*, 45. See Rebecca Bullard on the strangeness of these morals; she suggests that the moralizing by Intelligence and Astrea are part of Manley's satire: *The Politics of Disclosure, 1674–1725: Secret History Narratives* (London: Pickering & Chatto, 2009), 93.

12. Manley, *New Atalantis*, 40.

13. Ibid.

14. Ibid., 44.

15. Ibid., 45.

16. On the new Cabal's (homo)sexuality, see my essay, "Manl(e)y Fictions: The Woman in Man's Clothes and the Pleasures of Delarivier Manley's 'new Cabal'" (*Sexual Perversions 1650–1890*, ed. Julie Peakman [London: Palgrave, 2009], 95–116), and Ballaster, 139–42.

17. Manley, *New Atalantis*, 154, 155–56.

18. Ibid., 153.

19. Ibid., 156.

20. Ibid., 156, 154.

21. Ibid., 161.

22. Ibid., 162.

23. The story of Delia's seduction into a bigamous marriage by her cousin, a thinly veiled version of Manley's own bigamous marriage, is another story told in the first person (222–27). Manley's interest in defending her own character against the suggestion of complicity in bigamy would similarly argue for the significance of the first-person narratives in *The New Atalantis*.

24. While Ballaster argues that Charlot's story is a "landmark" tale, meaning the protonarrative of amatory fiction (134), I suggest that Elonora's story figures

quite differently—as the moral center of the novel. As I will discuss, the hope offered at the end of Elonora's tale stands in stark contrast to Charlot's martyrdom and thus demonstrates an alternative outcome to a story of seduction and abandonment, one that recuperates and values the fallen woman.

25. Manley, *New Atalantis*, 174.
26. Ibid., 180.
27. Ibid., 186.
28. Ibid.
29. See also Bowers, who reads Elonora's story as an allegory for the Tory party and finds considerable significance in Elonora's "complicit virtue": 187–88.
30. Karli June Ceranowski and Megan Milks, "New Orientations: Asexuality and Its Implications for Theory and Practice," *Feminist Studies* 36, no. 3 (Fall 2010): 650–64, 657. Ceranowski and Milks have also published an anthology on asexuality studies: *Asexualities: Feminist and Queer Perspectives* (New York: Routledge, 2014). See also Julie Sondra Decker, *The Invisible Orientation: An Introduction to Asexuality* (New York: Skyhorse, 2014) and Anthony F. Bogaert, *Understanding Asexuality* (Lanham, MD: Rowman & Littlefield, 2012).
31. Banner of the Asexuality Visibility and Education Network (AVEN) website, quoted in Ceranowski and Milks, 651.
32. See AVEN's Frequently Asked Questions (FAQ), under "Definitions" for "asexual," "demi-sexual," and "gray-sexual": http://www.asexuality.org/home/general. html#def; the "Experiences" section of the FAQ elaborates on the permutations of "gray-sexual" I have quoted here.
33. AVEN also acknowledges that sexuality is fluid and can change over the course of a person's lifetime, noting for example that "[m]any asexual people were more sexually active during puberty or another period of their lives"; see "Experiences" on the FAQ page.
34. Bowers, 189–90.
35. Ibid., 189.
36. Ibid., 190. Bowers complicates Beaufort's status as a "paragon of statesmanship" on a number of levels; see 190.
37. Ibid., 181, 187.
38. See Bowers, 189, and Ruth Herman, *The Business of a Woman: The Political Writings of Delarivier Manley* (Newark: University of Delaware Press, 2003), 68–69.
39. Paula McDowell, *The Women of Grub Street: Press, Politics, and Gender in the London Literary Marketplace 1678–1730* (Oxford: Clarendon Press, 1998), 235–36, 244. McDowell also observes that "in the carefully distinguished personalities of the three female narrators of the *New Atalantis* Manley's contemporaries would have detected a sophisticated satire on emerging models of 'polite' female authorial self-representation. Manley's female narrators have distinct personalities, personalities that reflect increasingly rigid social divisions of sexual virtue among eighteenth-century women" (235).
40. For a caution on this tendency toward biographical criticism in favor of the allegorical implications of the text, see Bowers: "*Rivella* is less reliable as an autobiography than as a delineation of a new-tory sensibility ... keenly marked by late seventeenth-century old-tory language and assumptions, yet firmly positioned in a new present" (211). See also Rachel Carnell's essay in this collection, which argues that *Rivella* is (more) productively read as a political secret history.

41. Manley, *The Adventures of Rivella* [1714], ed. Katherine Zelinsky (Peterborough: Broadview Press, 1999), 54–55.
42. Ibid., 56.
43. Ibid., 58.
44. Ibid., 59.
45. Ibid., 60.
46. See, for example, Rachel Carnell, *A Political Biography of Delarivier Manley* (London: Pickering & Chatto, 2008), 215, 226. Carnell notes that "[i]n 1705, Manley had reassigned to John Tilly a debt owed for the nursing of children, quite likely hers by Tilly." Melinda Alliker Rabb suggests that Manley's later relationship with Barber was nonsexual (see "The Manl[e]y Style: Delariviere Manley and Jonathan Swift," in *Pope, Swift, and Women Writers*, ed. Donald C. Mell [Newark: University of Delaware Press, 1996], 125–53); if Rabb's speculations are correct, then Manley's (auto)biography may ally her even more strongly with the removal from the alloerotic sexual culture I explore in this essay.
47. Bowers, 194.
48. Manley, *Adventures of Rivella*, 113.
49. McDowell, 283.
50. Ibid., 281–82.
51. I would like to extend my thanks to Aleksondra Hultquist, Elizabeth J. Mathews, Henrietta Rix Wood, Crystal Gorham Doss, and Jennifer Phegley for advice and insight on this essay.

7   Manley's Queer Forms
Repetition, Techno-performativity, and the Body

Kim Simpson

Ah, my dear Lord, I'm racked! I die in Agonies! but Love and Glory be witness for me, my greatest remorse in Death is in leaving you ... O haste and fetch the Midwife. I'm surrounded with Horror, the Rack of Nature is upon me, and no kind assisting Hand to relieve me. Bury me unknown. Oh cou'd you but annihilate me, to preserve my *Fame*!

...

Urania! (resolv'd to meet [death]) when the Mother-Pains came upon hee [*sic*], forbore to *call*! she forbore to *groan*! she trembled for fear of being *assisted*! She dreaded to be relieved; since Life was her greatest *Pain*, *Death* must be her greatest *Ease*! her throws redoubled! so did her *Resolution*! She drank her Tears, supprest her Cries, groan'd inwardly with strongest Woe.

Delarivier Manley, The New Atalantis[1]

In a disturbing inset narrative about incest in *The New Atalantis* (1709), Delarivier Manley goes to great lengths to differentiate cousins Harriat and Urania by situating them within the same oppositional paradigms employed by many contemporary scandal and amatory fictions: reputation versus virtue; worldliness versus naïveté; spoken word versus body. Harriat (probably based on Lady Henrietta Long) is a malicious gossip, who delights in "censuring and exposing the Frailties of others."[2] Her world is a world of constructions, in which she carefully negotiates display and concealment, proliferating rumors about others while masking her own meanness and cruelty. Her cousin, Urania, looks forward to the desiring but passive heroines of sensibility that we find, most obviously, in Samuel Richardson's *Pamela* (1740), but who are also present in the fiction of other amatory writers such as Aphra Behn and, later, Eliza Haywood.[3] In a text populated by Restoration-influenced libertine characters, who mask themselves and manipulate others, Urania is desperately out of place. Her naïveté and transparency are dangerous attributes, and this artlessness, when coupled with an amorous nature whereby Urania has "so bright an *Idea* of the Pleasures of *Love*, that nothing seem'd so great a Misfortune to her, as that they were yet only *Ideas*," eventually proves lethal, when she dies in shame during childbirth after conceiving with her brother.[4] It is Harriat who exposes them, and she eventually gets her comeuppance when she is seduced, a feat her would-be lover achieves through the provision of accounts of women he has ruined. Harriat also falls pregnant: a "strange kind of *Paradox*," Manley notes, "to trust him with her *Honour*, for betraying that of *others*!"[5] Her illicit labor in the countryside, witnessed by the narrator, opens the entire story; the birthing body both initiates and punctuates a story ostensibly about the word.

Both the constructed and the artless versions of femininity that Manley is at pains to distinguish from one another are eventually subordinated in this tale to forms of punishment bound up with the materiality of the birthing body. This peculiar fixation on the destruction wrought upon the transgressing female body informs many of Manley's narratives.[6] Even stories that are sympathetic to their victims and that provide examples of the "martyrdom" that Deborah Ross identifies as a key topos in Manley's fiction manifest a preoccupation with the apparent inevitability of female suffering, which undermines distinctions between artifice and sincerity, or surface and depth.[7] Manley's catalog of female ruin creates, as Janet Todd argues, a "communal fall," which few female characters evade.[8] Her compulsive returns to seduction scenes, her morbid fascination with the destructive effects of passion, and her pathological obsession with punished bodies make these texts seem both formulaic and deeply reactionary, and have prompted criticism whereby Manley is framed as both a misogynist and a bad writer.[9]

In recent years, feminist scholars have recognized and problematized the feminist search for, and privileging of, proto-feminism in early eighteenth-century literature as misguided, in that it limits the scope of the recovery project and excludes worthy subjects of study.[10] The ubiquity of victimhood in Manley's fiction means that the search for explicitly transgressive impulses in her seduction narratives, by which I mean an attempt to radically disrupt or alter the terrain of normative femininity, will likely be a disappointing one. With this point in mind, this essay suggests that a response to formalist criticisms of Manley's work can also yield a response to feminist frustrations with Manley's "communal fall." I argue that Manley's formal repetitions have considerable ideological significance in that they recognize, map out, and experiment with the performativity of identity, constituted through repetition, and disrupted by the material. While Manley's seduction narratives fail to express any stronger proto-feminist sentiments than an awareness of the gendered double standard that informs female victimhood, she is nonetheless using strategies of mimicry and textual play to test the possibilities for both discursive iterations of identity and materializations of the body.[11] I argue that we can bring the insights of queer and materialist feminist theories to bear usefully on Manley's configurations of the relationships between discursive and material structures of being. This reading breaks open formalist and feminist readings that see Manley's work as aesthetically poor or ideologically dissatisfying, opening up new terrains of exploration that these methodologies cannot account for, and providing an approach to Manley's work that identifies her form as a means by which she interrogates the ideological content of her work in deliberate and sophisticated ways. We can, I argue, read Manley's texts as experimentations with the limits of normative identity and with redeployments and reformulations of power, and therefore situate her work as an example of queering as practice in the eighteenth century.

The thread of this essay follows three main ideas, first, examining Manley's construction of discursive identities, and then outlining her experimentation with and disruption of those constructions through both discursive and material means. Manley's deployment of formula in each of her tales works to construct what I will refer to as a techno-performative discursive framework; that is, a tightly structured, internally coherent, and highly restrictive terrain of possibilities for being: a system of representation that produces intelligibility based on conformity. I borrow the term from Caroline Rooney's critique of Judith Butler's notion of gender performativity, to which I return below, but in essence, the framework that Manley creates understands femininity as brought into being through a forcible and continuous repetition of and adherence to certain unchanging narrative paths—seduction, dissimulation, destruction, and so on.[12] I read the "techno" of the term as referring to the inorganic, mechanical nature of these repetitions, which, in Manley's fiction, is often seen as an unthinking use of formula, but also with the term's etymological origins as art, craft, or weaving in mind, as a way of resituating Manley's use of formula as a form of artistry. Although the web of behavioral circularities and similarities that Manley creates for her characters seems monolithic, she is engaged in testing redeployments of power through the repetitions of the same plots with slight differences or mutations. The techno-performative structure that she sets up is put under the most strain by the self-conscious textuality deployed in *The Adventures of Rivella* (1714), which uses mimicry to render the framework visible, and thereby to suggest its limitations. But Manley also recognizes the ways in which punitive discourses seek to put a stop to this sort of mimicry, or to duplicitous nonnormative identities that threaten to proliferate: the masked, desiring, or incestuous body is violently materialized. In Manley's work, there is, in fact, an irony in materialization: in these punitive materializations of the body, which attempt to prevent the framework being altered in any lasting way, another sort of proliferation occurs: the splitting of one body into two in childbirth, and the potential for the creation of new narratives or the further destabilization of established ones. In documenting this proliferation, occurring on a material level as well as a textual one, Manley gestures toward the power of an agential body that can both uphold and disrupt patriarchal and class structures, by being punished or by duplicating, respectively. Her treatments of the way in which the body informs and is informed by language signal the link between the discursive and the material, the torsion of one into the other, as opposed to the inscription of a passive body by culture. The implication is that by interpreting through repetition the ways in which the feminine is defined within the techno-performative, written woman can become writing subject, as we see in *Rivella*, but elsewhere in Manley's fiction there is also, to use Luce Irigaray's phrase, a *"disruptive excess ...* possible on the feminine side."[13]

Strategic Dissimulation: Experimenting with Techno-Performativity

The connections between reputation, appearance, and performativity are most apparent in Manley's treatment of female libertines and hypocrites, for whom dissimulation is crucial to survival. In defining gender performativity, Judith Butler argues that "acts, gestures, and desire produce the effect of an internal core or substance [and are] *performative* in the sense that the essence or identity that they otherwise purport to express are *fabrications* manufactured and sustained through corporeal signs and other discursive means."[14] Because readability is a privileged feminine quality in Manley's texts, dissimulation is prevalent; they are two sides of the same coin, and suggest the lack of internal core or substance that Butler identifies because without performance, Manley's characters are often unable to survive. Her play with surfaces thus situates identity as performative. However, the corporeal signs and discursive means available for characterization are limited. Femininity is figured as either vicious or virtuous, and a failure to perform clearly within these signifying fields can mean extinction. Masquerade or sexual transgression, once detected, are punished. The narrator of *The Husband's Resentment* in Manley's *The Power of Love* (1720) warns erring women to "return again into the Path of Vertue, so as to preserve their Lives from Death, and their Reputation from what is much worse than Death, an infamous Report!"[15] In doing so, she indicates that punishment is enacted through both discursive and corporeal means: the ruin of a reputation is enacted by the spoken word, and bodies are materialized in childbirth, death, or both. Without dissimulation, a woman is cut off from the discursive site of her own existence and left to rely solely on a body that materializes beyond her control. Dissimulation thus provides a way to subtly delay this materialization and, in some places, prevent it altogether. In repeating narratives of female ruin, Manley is mapping out female identity as a series of repeated forms, performative in the sense of Butler's definition: "not as a singular or deliberate 'act,' but, rather, as the reiterative and citational practice by which discourse produces the effects that it names."[16] As such, Manley's texts take part in the establishment and replication of normative femininities, based either around dissimulation or readability, which straddle discourses of libertinism and sensibility, respectively.

In a critique of Butler's notion of gender performativity, Caroline Rooney argues that performativity is not always emancipatory, and it is therefore important to distinguish between two different types of performativity. The first is the mechanical, techno-performativity based in empty citationality, which structures Manley's plots, affords authoritarian power to the word itself, and in Rooney's words, "promotes 'conformativity.'"[17] The second is a more creative, theatrical form of ironic performance that is based in the gap between reality and discursive construction and that gestures toward "a generative capacity outside the order of representation and of iterability."[18] Rooney contends that Butler conflates these two distinct forms of performativity into "an economy of representation as repetition compulsion" and, in doing so, reduces "the potential for transformation to deformative mutations of the norm."[19] Change, in this model, can be effected only by mistakes in the patterns of enforced repetition, which subtly alter future repetitions.

In *The New Atalantis*, we can recognize this theatrical performance in characters such as Harriat, who understands the importance of acting an identity in accordance with patriarchal ideals of feminine behavior. She admits:

> Oh how necessary was Dissimulation! how it bought Opinion! 'Twas like a *Veil* to the *Face*, conceal'd all that one wou'dn't have disclos'd to vulgar Eyes, and intirely at ones own pleasure and discretion, when to wear or when to lay aside.[20]

Harriat's masquerade enables her to manipulate the gap between appearance and being to her own advantage, so that she may continue to proliferate narratives about others, which, in turn, solidify her own claims to virtue in opposition to those she ruins. Her performance of virtue suggests not just Harriat's duplicity, but also that virtue itself is citational in that it is produced by recognizable and easily replicated signs. However, the implication is that her characterization as vicious might also be unstable or derivative; she is situated within a long tradition of vicious women, sourced from misogynistic and amatory predecessors.[21] As such, her dissimulation provides an early example of the parodic strategies Butler locates in drag performance, which work to reveal the impossibility of an origin upon which gender is based. Butler argues that "parodic proliferation deprives hegemonic culture and its critics of the claim to naturalized or essentialist gender identities. Although the gender meanings taken up in these parodic styles are clearly part of hegemonic, misogynist culture, they are nevertheless denaturalized and mobilized through their parodic recontextualization."[22] Although Manley's scandal novels are interested in setting up moral distinctions between women, and thus take part in "hegemonic, misogynist culture," in their adherence to performative models of identity construction they also problematize both positive and negative characterizations of femininity, by suggesting they are nothing more than sets of signs. Despite the ethics of her characterization, Harriat's strategic dissimulation nonetheless dramatizes cultural mechanisms of identity construction and lays bare the ways in which certain feminine behaviors, constituted by surface-level acts, are naturalized.

However, while Harriat has a certain amount of power gleaned through her capacity both to perform and to unpick performance in others, her agency is much more questionable.[23] The limited agency of Manley's characters, and their adherence to specific and stylized forms of behavior with consistently negative results, suggest that her plots are techno-performative in Rooney's sense. In other words, because gaps between appearance and being are ultimately problematized, dissimulation is not an emancipatory act, even if it might be temporarily subversive. Harriat's masquerade is both necessary and punishable, and therefore cannot be said to engender agency. Rather, Manley is establishing a world in which the only option is repetition.

This forcible repetition accounts for the circularities and repeated narratives of *The New Atalantis*: Urania's mother dies in childbirth, just as Urania does; in Charlot and Delia's stories, reading corrupts female innocence by engendering a dangerous mix of desire and unrealistic expectations; nosebleeds, swoons, and fevers signal lovesickness and impending disaster; Harriat appears earlier in the text as a "declining *Coquet*" who loses her lover to a younger woman in a repetition of the female competition that structures many of the inset narratives.[24] Harriat's characterization is also a reflection of Intelligence's. Intelligence justifies her exposure of Harriat by arguing that "the *Libertine* in Practice, the *Devotee* in progression, those that with the Mask of *Hypocrisy* undo the Reputation of Thousands, ought pitilessly, by a sort of retaliation, to be expos'd themselves."[25] But the distinctions between Harriat's and Intelligence's motives are actually rather scanty, boiling down to different political allegiances, their situation within text and narrative frame, respectively, and Harriat's identifiable referent in the real world, although it would not, perhaps, be amiss to align Manley herself with her narrator. Both relish the prospect of rendering clear certain forms of identity as performance, and both displace their own masking onto narratives involving others. Their power lies in the power to tell, to proliferate discourse, and to fracture and multiply discursive sites of identity to defer the fixity of materialization. Elsewhere too, familiar stock characters and romance tropes are repeated: in *The Physician's Stratagem*, the villainous maid, Caton, is seen "treading the Grassy Paths, and pressing the Flow'ry Banks with the young Physician" in a gesture back to pastoral seduction scenes, while ornate bedrooms strewn with flowers on sultry days are also commonplace markers of seductions to follow.[26] These compulsive repetitions signal the situation of Manley's women within an authoritarian machine constituted by set narratives: the techno-performative.

Within this framework, women are writers, masqueraders, or victims. The former two options are, as I have noted, means by which the materialization of the body can be delayed, and Manley's treatments of writing and masking are ways in which she experiments with the edges and limits of the discursive machine. Mutations also play their part here. Following Michel Foucault, Butler argues that "power can neither be withdrawn, nor refused, but only redeployed."[27] There is, for Butler, as for Foucault, no position outside, or prior to, the law itself, for which we might substitute Manley's techno-performative structure. This structure, in its simultaneously generative and prohibitive gestures, constitutes all. Butler writes:

> To enter into the repetitive practices of this terrain of signification is not a choice, for the "I" that might enter is always already inside: there is no possibility of agency or reality outside of the discursive practices that give those terms the intelligibility that they have. The task is not whether to repeat, but how to repeat or, indeed, to repeat and, through a radical proliferation of gender, to *displace* the very gender norms that enable the repetition itself.[28]

Manley plays with variations in her repetitions, testing identities out within different scenarios to stretch out the discursive possibilities for femininity.[29] We see this deployment of repetition with difference most clearly in *Rivella*.

Ros Ballaster argues that Manley's tales "point to their resistance to the imposition of generic norms through the insistent dramatization of the imposition of form upon the body of the woman. ... Invariably, Manley's response is to argue for a resistance to such impositions through the practice of writing itself."[30] But I argue that she is not resisting these impositions explicitly, but rather incorporating them as a defensive and mimetic strategy, which, in Toril Moi's words, mimes "the miming imposed on woman ... to *undo* the effects of phallogocentric discourse simply by *overdoing* them."[31] In compulsively and deliberately repeating certain constructions of identity, Manley renders them visible for what they are: constructions, rather than natural forms. *Rivella* carefully reworks the body/text conflations, exemplified in the question that Chevalier D'Aumont asks Sir Charles Lovemore, as the latter begins his account of Rivella: "Do Her Eyes love as well as Her Pen?"[32] D'Aumont assumes that the passionate text is the product of the passionate body. But this urge to fix identity through embodiment is continually frustrated in the text by situating identity as a product of discourse, rather than the material. Thus Delia's story is reduced to a citation within Rivella's. In stating "I must refer you to her own Story, under the Name of *Delia*, in the *Atalantis*, for the next Four miserable Years of her Life," Lovemore helps Manley to wrap Rivella's characterization in impenetrable textuality.[33] The framing narrative claims that the text is a translation from French, a story passed verbally from Lovemore to D'Aumont, and then to the translator-publisher, situating the tale at least three removes from Rivella herself. As Katherine Zelinsky notes, *Rivella* is "a playful testimony to the uncertainty of origins and the unreliability of sources."[34]

Rivella looks set to repeat the familiar trajectory of the female victim when Lovemore describes her "languishing Melancholy" and the way in which "the white of her Skin, [had] degenerated into a yellowish Hue, occasion'd by her Misfortunes."[35] But these generic norms are ultimately subordinated to the more fundamental norm that structures Manley's texts: citationality.

Rivella rewrites Manley's autobiography as one that ends in the extreme disembodiment entailed by a performativity with no internal core or substance. When Lovemore offers the prospect of "a Bed nicely sheeted and strow'd with *Roses, Jessamins* or *Orange-Flowers*," the techno-performative is rendered most visible.[36] This highly stylized scene is an articulation of Rooney's definition of techno-performativity: "'a form of doing' without 'a form of being.'"[37] It is a scene entirely dictated by the surface conventions of the seduction scene, but entirely lacking in the psychological or physical content that Rivella's presence might provide. The scene is one of overproduced emptiness. Ballaster argues that "*Rivella* and the story of Delia read side by side constitute a resistance to the Madonna/whore opposition imposed on women by masculinist ideologies, subverting them by exposing their status as 'fictions' and insisting on the prerogative of the woman to write her own fictions of the female self."[38] This subversion is effected, and these femininities are shown to be fictitious, but Manley is not producing original fictions of the female self. Rather, the subversion of normative femininities occurs in an overproduction of the techno-performative, in a rendering visible of femininity as a cipher. In Rivella, the techno-performative is followed to its logical conclusion, whereby the woman, refusing the fixity of embodiment, disappears completely beneath a proliferation of different narratives (Delia, Rivella, Manley) and surface signifiers.[39]

Repetitions serve to reiterate and solidify Manley's techno-performative structures of identity, while repetitions with difference experiment with the discursive terrain and the possibilities of rewriting identities by exploiting the implications of that terrain. But what ought we to make of the ultimate subordination of all forms of discursive identities in Manley's work to the material: the naïve and the worldly to childbirth, and even the writing subject to the materiality of the sign on the pages of the book? The next section suggests that Manley's configurations of material bodies can be read as productive as well as punitive, and that the body is sometimes generative beyond the reach of linguistic-discursive performances and control.

The "Rack of Nature": Material Configurations of Punishment and Production

In *Volatile Bodies* (1994), Elizabeth Grosz identifies the "profound somatophobia" that underlies Western philosophical approaches to the body, whereby it is "regarded as a source of interference in, and danger to, the operations of reason ... a betrayal of and a prison for the soul, reason, or mind."[40] As we see in Urania's and Harriat's examples, Manley demonstrates the repressive materialization of the body as a means of preventing further iterations of unacceptable deviations from a feminine norm. The body is produced, then, through the discursive tension between normative repetitions of femininity and mutations. As Grosz argues, "nature may be understood not as an origin or as an invariable template but as materiality in its most general sense, as destination."[41] In Manley's tales, the materialized body is often realized as the end point of a series of acts: Harriat's carefully constructed public persona, for example, is prevented from further reiterations by her labor. But is the "rack of nature" just an end point for the women in Manley's texts? As Karen Barad puts it in a materialist feminist corrective to Butler's constructivism, "there is a sense in which 'the world kicks back.'"[42] Far from ignoring the material, subordinating it to abstracted discursive iterations, or seeing it solely as a product of the discursive, some moments in Manley's work reveal a body in excess of discursive structures, as active, productive, and self-replicating: the body writes. Manley is interested in the possibilities of material bodies to provide sites for readable corporeal signs: languishing eyes and heaving bosoms. But she also recognizes the body as holding the power to disrupt discursive citationality, in both punitive and productive ways. The material can thus provide an alternative source of transformation to the incremental changes wrought on discursive iterations by repetitions with difference. This is not to say that material bodies necessarily have radical potential, but rather more cautiously to posit that the relationships Manley plots between discourse and the body are perhaps not as somatophobic as they might at first appear.[43]

A closer look at Manley's tale *The Physician's Stratagem* will serve to illustrate the capacity of the body to both uphold and disrupt discursive structures. Rachel Carnell has argued that *The Power of Love* ought, because of its lack of key and clear contemporary referents, to be seen as different from her more partisan *roman à clef* texts, and instead as imitative of Haywood's successful amatory novel *Love in Excess* (1719–20).[44] Nevertheless, in rewriting and developing five stories from William Painter's anthology, *The Palace of Pleasure* (1566–67); adding in two, including *The Physician's Stratagem*, from other sources; and deploying similar stylistic features, names, and tropes, *The Power of Love* is clearly indebted to predecessors both within and outside of Manley's oeuvre, including *The New Atalantis* and *Rivella*.[45] Repetition, and repetition with difference remain crucial ways in which Manley continues her experimentation with discursive structures of female identity and gender relations. But because this text is not a direct political intervention, the interactions between discursive and material identities are brought into a sharper focus than in the earlier texts, concerned as they are with fulfilling defamatory or protective functions.

The heroine of the tale, Mariana, is a paradigm of virtue. We hear that "[s]he carried a Sort of Languishment in her Air, that bespoke the Seriousness of her Temper," and that she prefers retirement and reading to fashionable court life.[46] However, Mariana does not possess the naïveté or suggestibility of the women usually chosen to represent corrupted innocence in Manley's fiction. As a result of her studies, she has "a Vogue for Wit and Understanding" and a skill in writing whereby her letters "might justly be thought to proceed from an exalted and refined Genius, and deserved to be made a Rule for the Epistolary way of Writing."[47] Unlike Rivella though, Mariana's skill as a writer is not enough to delay or prevent the materialization of her body. The physician of the title, Fauxgarde, falls in love with Mariana's person and/or fortune and, acting upon a mechanical libertine desire that "left him no longer a free Agent," decides that "he must either possess her or despair."[48] Just as Harriat manipulates herself into positions of power using her knowledge of secrets, Fauxgarde uses his medical knowledge of the body, another secret of sorts, to improve his own position. Having impregnated Mariana's servant Caton, he easily controls her with the promises of an abortion, and then marriage; her body is a bargaining tool. His medical knowledge also wins him access to Mariana and the trust of her family.

With Caton's help, Fauxgarde plans to impregnate Mariana too, without her knowledge, and then offer to marry her to prevent her being exposed and ruined. Mariana's body becomes the site of the entire narrative, and Fauxgarde correctly predicts both the social and the material consequences of his actions, at least in the short term: Mariana gets pregnant; he gets to marry her. In a scene troubling for its euphemistic flippancy, Caton administers a "Soporiferous Powder" to her mistress and Fauxgarde repeatedly rapes Mariana's unconscious body:

> His guilty Design being to make *Mariana* pregnant, he wasted the Night in his Endeavours to render her so; though surely with an imperfect Taste of Happiness to himself, because the Charmer was insensible of his Embrace; but as he had farther Views, he rose from her Bed in a full Belief, that Nature would not be deficient, and he should see the good Effects of his villainous Stratagem.[49]

Mariana is reduced to predictable "Nature" in a repetition with difference of the seduction scene, which strips away social prescriptions for either desire or passive resistance. She is figured solely as the capacity to reproduce. We might read this tale as reflective of seventeenth-century mechanical models of nature, drawn from the atomism of Epicurus, Democritus, and Lucretius. Roy Porter notes that "[t]he new science launched a war on empty words, on reification. ... The body became a *machine carnis*, a machine of the flesh."[50] Mariana's body is, in this model, simply a mechanism for formulaic reproduction; she is Fauxgarde's very own printing press, devoid of creativity or meaning. However, Mariana's pregnancy also proves disruptive, first to class structures and then to Fauxgarde's stratagem itself, demonstrating that in this text, flesh and word are more closely interrelated than conceptions of the body as a passive object, as brute biology, or as an instrument or tool to be owned and occupied allow for.

Mariana's marriage to Fauxgarde demonstrates the capacity of the body to interrupt hierarchical discursive structures and identities in a more profound and lasting way than any performance. We hear that "[s]he gave her Hand to the Doctor, sufficiently mortify'd at the Necessity of so unequal an Alliance," and the class system is altered by the necessity to conceal and legitimize Mariana's pregnant body.[51] The structures that demand female chastity are here subjected to scrutiny; like Manley's earlier martyr tales, this tale explores the possibility that innocence comes in varying forms not necessarily connected to the body, and that failure to recognize this can disrupt the very fabric of society. While Mariana's body elevates Fauxgarde in society, it also proves his undoing. Again like Harriat, he cannot help but disclose. The narrator exclaims: "Contemptible Vanity! abominable Itch of Talking, which rather than not tell, will tell to the Ruin of themselves and their Family."[52] Fauxgarde's drunken boasting reintroduces Mariana back into the discursive world by providing a narrative for, and thus resituating, her inexplicable body. But to some extent the body also remains beyond the discursive structures that seek to explain and mediate it. When Mariana attempts to sue Fauxgarde, we hear that the "Law knew no Name for his Transgression."[53] Discursive measures meant to contain and produce the body prove unable to account for Fauxgarde's crime. Instead, Mariana's former lover, Fonteray, takes measures into his own hands by murdering Fauxgarde. The trauma of Mariana's childbirth is displaced onto Fonteray's brutal murder of Fauxgarde, which leaves him "Breathless, and weltering in [Fauxgarde's] Gore."[54]

At the end of the text, Mariana denies her desire for Fonteray, restricted by "the cruel Laws of Honour."[55] At the close of *The Physician's Stratagem* Mariana "disposed of all her Affairs, and provided with the best Advantage for the Education of her Children; then put her self into the Nunnery of the *Augustin*'s."[56] But this is not full closure. As Margaret Case Croskery has noted, banishment to a nunnery at the end of a tale suggests "not a conclusion, but a sequel," given that many amatory fictions begin in nunneries.[57] Mariana's children remain in the world, potentially to repeat Mariana's narrative, as Urania repeated her mother's. As such, we might read Mariana's body itself as a text, as generative of more text, as informing but also informed by discourse. Pregnancy can thus be read as a structural, or even a grammatical device. It provides closure to the text in a physical form whereby text and body become mutually enabling, mutually productive of more text and more bodies.

In birth, Harriat thinks of reputation as spoken word: "Oh cou'd you but annihilate me, to preserve my *Fame*," while Urania resigns herself to the body: "She drank her Tears, supprest her Cries, groan'd inwardly." Mariana's childbirth, however, is unwritten. It is a productively empty, unwriteable space in the text: the possibility of a disruptive excess, beyond the discursive. While it is, for obvious reasons, extremely problematic to see her materialization as liberatory in any sense, it nonetheless illuminates the way in which Manley is conceiving of a feminine real. In reference to Eliza Haywood's later novel *Fantomina* (1725), Ashley Tauchert argues that

> in birth it is the body-object that speaks forth in a language that accords with Irigaray's "hysteria": a language beyond the confines of masculine discourses and misrepresented by these. Birthing speaks of something beyond the forms of subjectivation and looks back on these as a masking of the body that actively produces form on its own terms.[58]

In childbirth, bodily boundaries are complicated: one becomes two in an act of replication, demonstrating an agential body, but also a destabilizing potential that mirrors the fluidity of identity suggested by repetitions with difference within the techno-performative. So ultimately what treatments of female victimhood in Manley's fiction seem to suggest is that material and discursive identities, while distinct from one another, are characterized by a lack of fixity. While performative identities are prevented from proliferating too far, physical (id)entities are also capable of proliferating both in aid of and in opposition to repressive discursive structures. What this means is that we can read birthing bodies as an admission of the transformative power of the real, which can inform, disrupt, and enable performative iterations of identity in a more profound way than repetitions with difference.

Manley's Queer Forms

The citationality and circularity of Manley's work suggests both that she is searching for a space for maneuver within the techno-performative, and that she is seeking to trouble dominant constructions of female victimhood by overdoing them, to the point at which they become parodic. In this sense, her strategy and her use of form ought to be recognized as proto-queer, as interrogative of the edges and limits of the normative, and as affording an awareness of the presence of those edges and limits. The results of Manley's play with redeployments and reformulations of power, while not engendering agency, are nonetheless rendering visible the workings of the machine of intelligibility. But she is also a materialist, and plots, in some of her texts, the ways in which the body coexists in what Barad has called "an ongoing topological dynamics" with the discursive structures that inform and are informed by it.[59] In 1740, Wetenhall Wilkes wrote:

> There can scarce be a greater Defect in a young Lady than not to express herself well either in speaking or Writing; and yet how many are there, who should have all the good and polite Qualities of the rational World, that cannot tell a Story as they should, that is, join in a continued, coherent Discourse the several parts of it without a Repetition of many bald and poor Phrases to supply the place of Connexion, Propriety and Order.[60]

Manley's discontinuities, incoherencies, and repetitions, however, are crucial to her ideological understandings of the ways in which identities are constituted and maintained through processes of proliferation, repetition with difference, and materialization. The negotiations of oppositional paradigms that inform Manley's characterizations—reputation versus virtue, worldliness versus naïveté, spoken word versus body—are productive of the queer forms of her fiction.

Notes

1. Delarivier Manley, *Secret Memoirs and Manners of Several Persons of Quality, of Both Sexes. From the New Atalantis*, in *The Selected Works of Delarivier Manley*, ed. Rachel Carnell and Ruth Herman, 5 vols (London: Pickering & Chatto, 2005), II, 157–58, 172–73. All subsequent references are to this edition.
2. Ibid., 175.
3. See, for example Behn's eponymous *Agnes de Castro* (1688), or Eliza Haywood's Violetta in *Love in Excess* (1719–20). For the development of both active and passive desiring heroines within the traditions of libertinism and sensibility during this period, see Laura Linker, *Dangerous Women, Libertine Epicures, and the Rise of Sensibility, 1660–1730* (Farnham: Ashgate, 2011).
4. Manley, *The New Atalantis*, 164. See Erin M. Keating's essay in this collection for more details of this story. For a reading of the way in which this story is used to criticize Whig ideology, see Ellen Pollak, *Incest and the English Novel, 1684–1814* (Baltimore: John Hopkins University Press, 2003), 103–09.
5. Manley, *The New Atalantis*, 176.
6. *The New Atalantis* alone documents the ruin of at least nine women at length, including the Duchess de l'Inconstant (Barbara Villiers, Duchess of Cleveland), Charlot (Stuarta Werburge Howard), Louisa (Elizabeth Culling), Zara (Sarah Stout), the Marchioness of Caria (Sarah Churchill), and Delia (Manley herself), and smears many others in passing. See Erin M. Keating's essay in this collection for a reading of the Urania/Polydore/Harriat tale which posits that Manley's situation of the laboring body alongside the eroticized body functions to disrupt the pleasure associated with the spectacle of female suffering.
7. Deborah Ross, *The Excellence of Falsehood: Romance, Realism, and Women's Contribution to the Novel* (Lexington: University Press of Kentucky, 1991), 63. Ross argues that "Manley wishes the reader to feel that Urania has died because she is too good for this world, although she has committed incest, suicide, and murder" (64). For other examples of martyred heroines, see *The Perjur'd Beauty* and *The Physician's Stratagem* in *The Power of Love* (1720).
8. Janet Todd, "Life After Sex: The Fictional Autobiography of Delarivier Manley," *Women's Studies*, 15 (1988): 48.
9. See, for example, Susan Staves, *A Literary History of Women's Writing in Britain, 1660–1789* (Cambridge: Cambridge University Press, 2006), where she argues that most readers have found Manley's scandal chronicles "tedious, dated, badly written, and morally repellent" (148), and that *The New Atalantis*'s acceptance of misogynistic ideas about women did more to reinforce resistance to women's entitlement to write than to advance the cause (149). See also John Richetti, "Popular Narrative in the Early Eighteenth Century: Formats and Formulas," in *The English Novel, Volume 1: 1700 to Fielding*, ed. Richard Kroll (London and New York: Longman, 1998), where he observes that in *The New Atalantis*, "characters and narrator inhabit without embarrassment a stylized world in which the chief attraction is the utterly predictable repetition of character, scene and language" (83).
10. See, for example, Ashley Tauchert, *Against Transgression* (Malden, MA: Blackwell, 2008), in which she claims that seeking transgression in the work of women writers has become a reactionary critical move: "Like the fumes of the automobile and heavy industry which befoul the atmosphere, transgression poisons our critical sensibilities" (2). Cf. Jean Marsden, "Beyond Recovery: Feminism

and the Future of Eighteenth-Century Literary Studies," *Feminist Studies* 28 (2002): 657–62, and Laura J. Rosenthal, "Introduction: Recovering from Recovery," *Eighteenth Century: Theory and Interpretation* 50 (2009): 1–11, along with the other essays in this issue (1), which discuss the future of feminist theory in eighteenth-century studies.

11. For a discussion of Manley's ambivalent treatment of both gender and class hierarchies that reads her treatment of domestic power dynamics in *The Power of Love* as both reactionary and potentially destabilizing, see Earla Wilputte's essay in this collection. Both Keating's and Aleksondra Hultquist's essays also examine the ways in which Manley draws attention to problematic patriarchal structures.

12. See Caroline Rooney, *Decolonising Gender: Literature and a Poetics of the Real* (Abingdon: Routledge, 2007).

13. Luce Irigaray, *This Sex Which Is Not One*, trans. Catherine Porter with Carolyn Burke (Ithaca: Cornell University Press, 1985), 78. Originally published as *Ce sexe qui n'en est pas un* (Paris: Éditions de Minuit, 1977).

14. Judith Butler, *Gender Trouble: Feminism and the Subversion of Identity* (Abingdon: Routledge Classics, 2006), 185.

15. Delarivier Manley, *The Husband's Resentment* in *The Power of Love* in *Selected Works*, ed. Carnell and Herman, IV, 190. All subsequent references are to this edition.

16. Judith Butler, *Bodies That Matter: On the Discursive Limits of "Sex"* (Abingdon: Routledge Classics, 1993), xii.

17. Rooney, 6.

18. Ibid., 29. Rooney writes, "[i]t seems to me that theatrical performativity differs from techno-performativity in that the latter literalises an ideal or pre-given sign whilst the former mimics the real or plays with the gap between image and reality." (56).

19. Ibid., 26.

20. Manley, *The New Atalantis*, 165.

21. See, for example, see Behn's anti-heroine Miranda in *The Fair Jilt* (1688).

22. Butler, *Gender Trouble*, 188.

23. I am differentiating power from agency thus: agency is the ability to act according to one's own volition; power is the situation of a subject above an object and can exist only in relation.

24. Manley, *The New Atalantis*, 114. Also see 343, n. 373.

25. Ibid., 158–59.

26. Manley, *The Physician's Stratagem* in *The Power of Love*, 135.

27. Butler, *Gender Trouble*, 169.

28. Ibid., 202–03.

29. Both Wilputte's and Hultquist's contributions to this collection consider Manley's usage of "palimpsestic" self-conscious repetitions as a means of commenting on the fairness of justice, and on the rhetoric of virtue and love respectively.

30. Ros Ballaster, *Seductive Forms: Women's Amatory Fiction from 1684 to 1740* (Oxford: Clarendon Press, 1992), 152.

31. Toril Moi, *Sexual/Textual Politics: Feminist Literary Theory* (London: Routledge, 1985), 140.

32. Delarivier Manley, *The Adventures of Rivella* in *Selected Works*, ed. by Carnell and Herman, IV, 10. All subsequent references are to this edition.

33. Ibid., 19.
34. Katherine Zelinsky, introduction to *The Adventures of Rivella* by Delarivier Manley (Peterborough, ON: Broadview Press, 1999), 18.
35. Manley, *Rivella*, 19, 20.
36. Ibid., 57–58.
37. Rooney, 29.
38. Ballaster, 151.
39. See Aleksondra Hultquist, "Absent Children and the Emergence of Female Subjectivity in Eliza Haywood's *The British Recluse* and *The City Jilt*," in *Spectacle, Sex, and Property in Eighteenth-Century Literature and Culture*, ed. by Julie A. Chappell and Kamille Stone (New York: AMS, 2015), 15–35, in which she conceptualizes a mutually exclusive balance in Haywood's fiction between motherhood and subjecthood, whereby the maternal body must be denied (children are miscarried, stillborn, or quickly forgotten) for female subjecthood to emerge free from the patriarchal relations that usually define women as mothers or wives. The disembodiment of Rivella is another such method for avoiding reduction to these terms by denying the material; although, as I go on to argue, the material is also productive of its own narratives elsewhere in Manley's fiction.
40. Elizabeth Grosz, *Volatile Bodies: Toward a Corporeal Feminism* (Bloomington: Indiana University Press, 1994), 5.
41. Ibid., 21.
42. Karen Barad, *Meeting the Universe Halfway: Quantum Physics and the Entanglement of Matter and Meaning* (Durham: Duke University Press, 2007), 214–15.
43. See Phyllis Ann Thompson, "Subversive Bodies: Embodiment as Discursive Strategy in Women's Popular Literature in the Long Eighteenth Century" (PhD diss., Louisiana State University, 2003), in which she argues that eighteenth-century women writers were deliberately attempting to author a counter-Cartesian narrative of the relationship between mind and body.
44. Rachel Carnell, *A Political Biography of Delarivier Manley* (London: Pickering and Chatto, 2008), 232–33.
45. See Hultquist's contribution for a consideration of Manley's adaptation of Painter's "Forty-Fifth Nouell" in *The Palace of Pleasure* for her tale *The Fair Hypocrite* (*The Power of Love*).
46. Manley, *The Physician's Stratagem*, 131.
47. Ibid., 133.
48. Ibid., 134.
49. Ibid., 137.
50. Roy Porter, *Flesh in the Age of Reason* (London: Penguin, 2004), 51.
51. Manley, *The Physician's Stratagem*, 141.
52. Ibid., 142.
53. Ibid., 144.
54. Manley, *The Physician's Stratagem*, 144.
55. Ibid., 145. In doing so, she repeats, with difference, a tale from *The New Atalantis*, in which Mme. St. Amant falls in love with her husband's friend but privileges her marriage vows over her desire, promising her husband that she will never marry his friend and remaining constant to her husband even once widowed. In *The Fair Hypocrite*, the first tale in *The Power of Love*, we see another variation on this theme.

56. Ibid., 146.
57. Margaret Case Croskery, "Masquing Desire: The Politics of Passion in Eliza Haywood's *Fantomina*," in *The Passionate Fictions of Eliza Haywood: Essays on Her Life and Work*, ed. Kirsten T. Saxton and Rebecca P. Bocchicchio (Lexington: University Press of Kentucky, 2000), 91–92. Croskery is referring here specifically to Haywood's *Fantomina* (1725).
58. Ashley Tauchert, "Woman in a Maze: *Fantomina*, Masquerade and Female Embodiment," *Women's Writing* 7 (2000): 481.
59. Karen Barad, "Posthumanist Performativity: Toward an Understanding of How Matter Comes to Matter," *Signs: Journal of Women in Culture and Society* 28 (2003): 826.
60. Wetenhall Wilkes, *A Letter of Genteel and Moral Advice to a Young Lady* (Dublin: E Jones, 1740), 101–02.

8 From Pleasure to Power
The Passion of Love in *The Fair Hypocrite*

Aleksondra Hultquist

The Power of Love in Seven Novels (1720) has garnered less attention than Delarivier Manley's other publications. Modern critics of the collection tend to point out its difference from her earlier, politically inspired and thinly veiled love stories such as *The New Atalantis* (1709).[1] As her final work, it is usually read as less politically motivated, less radical, and less tolerant of female-based desire.[2] That *The Power of Love* is an adaptation—all but two of the novels have been recognized as coming from the 1566 continental translated collection *The Palace of Pleasure* by William Painter—may be one reason why critics have generally overlooked it; to modern sensibilities adaptation can imply a lack of originality and a presumed conservatism about the text. But Manley's text demonstrates structural and thematic complexities, as well as original engagements in the eighteenth-century discussion of the passions. In this chapter, I contend that in *The Fair Hypocrite*, the first story in *The Power of Love*, Manley implies that the passions, rather than being destructive, are constructive to individuals as well as political systems as a whole. Comparing the changes that Manley makes to the source text reveals that she sees engagement with the passions as a valuable aspect of political stability and of female subjectivity. While the passion of love is something to avoid in Painter's version, Manley's adaptation converts it into something to understand and to embrace correctly. *The Fair Hypocrite* emphasizes the importance of romantic love in and of itself, not only as metaphor for political conflict but also as a significant passion for the individual. Manley is engaged in the larger discourse of eighteenth-century passion theory; through a comparison of the treatment of the passion of love, and by a close reading of how Manley uses the passion of love, I show how what is only "pleasure" for Painter, becomes a means of "power" for Manley.

Adapting *Pleasure* into *Power*

Manley's collection was working within a tradition of adaptation that valued inventiveness. Seventeenth- and eighteenth-century readers and writers took for granted that creativity and alteration in adaptations and translations were required for the clear communication of ideas, that the text itself, because of cultural as well as linguistic differences, necessitated a form of re-creation.[3]

Eighteenth-century adaptations were contemporarily understood as original artistic endeavors that should be read and evaluated as such; these texts were not only often deeply innovative when compared to the source text, but were also expected to be so, and Manley's introduction demonstrates how she is working within these assumptions. *The Palace of Pleasure* was long known for inspiring great works of literature that have been very deeply valued and evaluated,[4] and as such, was an ideal source text.[5] Manley claims that her idea in writing the tales in *The Power of Love* is "to draw them out of Obscurity,"[6] implying creative adaptation in their modernization. She also explicitly admits to "adding diverse new Incidents ... with the same Design as Mr. *Dryden* had in his Tales from *Boccace* [sic] and *Chaucer*."[7] The comment establishes Manley in a line of important adaptors and translation theorists, connects her to the great English and continental writers of the age (Dryden included), and emphasizes her own new elements, implying that hers is a well-written adaptation according to contemporary standards.[8] She thus calls attention to her textual amendments as an enticement to readers, stressing that her version is fresh, useful, and modern just as much as it is morally valuable and within a prestigious literary tradition, aspects that would have been immediately apparent to her readers.[9]

In situating Manley's text as an adaptation, this essay highlights the cultural context in which it was read as well as what is still present from the originary text, specifically the passion of love and its implications. Linda Hutcheon argues that "the act of adaptation always involves both (re-)interpretation and then (re-)creation"; and that "adaptation is a form of intertextuality: we experience adaptations (*as adaptations*) as palimpsests through our memory of other works that resonate through repetition with variation."[10] In discussing his use of adaptation theory in his film studies classes, Robert Mayer concentrates on how the ideological purposes of an original text differ from those of the adaptation, and is also interested in comparing "what has been retained and what has been discarded."[11] In the case of Painter and Manley's texts, such a comparison helps establish the particular rhetorics of virtue and love that are at stake in both versions. Manley isn't just updating Painter, then, but re-creating and thus reinterpreting the text to reflect what is "modern and useful." Manley's work echoes aspects of Painter's palimpsestic text (whose own adaptation echoes earlier versions), but in her re-creation, there are aspects that come into sharper relief. Those details that have been added or discarded to shape ideology are important points of critical evaluation when discussing Manley's alterations and the principles served by them. Examining the meanings in Manley's overwriting—that is, the details of her re-creation of *The Palace of Pleasure*, what is repeated, what is varied, and what is still visible in the process of overwriting—reveals her text's value of the passion of love. Manley's adaptation serves its own ideology of sexual maturity through desire by adding in extra details about the titular character's history in *The Fair Hypocrite*, thus also managing to make virtue visible. Through her adaptive choices in

The Power of Love, Manley implies that the manipulations of the passion of love, rather than love's existence, cause disruption.

The emphasis of Painter's collection calls for his version of the tale to be read, as past critics have, as one in a set of "romantic tales of the last-minute rescue of falsely accused ladies by their champions."[12] Painter establishes clearly at the beginning of the tale that his story is meant to emphasize the "singular praise and commendation of chaste and honest Ladies" and that love assaults men and creates fevers "which taking [love's] beginning at the harte, desperseth it selfe incurablye, through all the other sensible partes of the bodie."[13] Painter criticizes sexual passion in men and women as well as trusts in the ultimately redeemable qualities of feminine virtue, a characteristic that can be established between men on a jousting field. Love as a passion is bad; virtue and honor are good, thus endeth the lesson. Manley's adaptations belie such pat morals. The collection as a whole focuses on the particular repetition of poor marriage pairings (often in terms of class, although that is not the case in *The Fair Hypocrite*) and how those poor pairings consistently disintegrate into adultery. While the title emphasizes "love," and while clearly the consequences of love unite the tales, the theme of virtue avenged or rewarded also resonates significantly throughout the collection. The prominence of "love" in the title and the repetition of "virtue" in theme point to a necessary relationship between the two concepts: virtue is possible where love exists.

Reading Manley's text through the lens of adaptation therefore makes visible her engagement with the contemporary discussion of the passions, a specific understanding of the emotional system of the individual as well as the social in the eighteenth century. While modern critics often use the terms "passions" and our modern interpretation of "emotions" interchangeably, the eighteenth-century culture of affections understood these terms to be distinct.[14] A more accurate analogy might be the modern term "psychology," which underlies post-twentieth-century knowledge of mental and physical health and public and private responses to stimuli; the term "passions" underlies seventeenth- and eighteenth-century knowledge. In many ways the eighteenth century's vocabulary of emotion was much more sophisticated and delineated than ours. There were clear parameters for words like affect, sentiment, sense, feeling, sympathy, and emotion; and the eighteenth-century theory of the passions encompassed all of these ideas. Like our own terms for emotion and affect, these eighteenth-century terms were contested and contingent upon genre, author, and context. The study of the passions was understood to be of paramount importance by many writers for a variety of reasons: it could aid in religious devotion; it could clarify causes for and cures of human disease; it could provide explanation of certain social and political phenomena. Primarily, the passions were thought to be public, rather than private; they were a social phenomenon that was anchored by a shared morality; sometimes they had their own agency. Most importantly, passionate experience should cultivate judgment and moderation, as the expression and understanding of the passions should be controlled and used for the public good. By the early eighteenth century, philosophers such as John Locke had transformed the seat of the passions from the body to the mind, a distinction that supposedly provided greater control over the passions.[15] This important movement implied that passions, rather than being public phenomena, were becoming private ones, and it is a central shift taking place in the eighteenth-century public culture of feeling. Manley's *Fair Hypocrite* is a significant example of this transition, because it focuses on the passions of one individual (Regina, Duchess of Savoy) and how her private passions influence public occurrences. The passions most in use in *The Fair Hypocrite* are love, curiosity, and revenge, although this chapter focuses predominantly on the language surrounding Regina's experience of the passion of love.

The passion of love was indicative of a state or a response rather than an implication of uncontrolled emotion—eighteenth-century authors do not speak of "passionate love" (specific experiences of intense sexual and emotional attraction) but rather "the passion of love" (that is, a specific idea in an entire system of emotions). Romantic love was understood to encompass a range of feeling, from "longing for association" to "desire for appetite," and ideal love encompasses this entire spectrum (it is both sexually and spiritually fulfilling), with the added notion that it is unchanging.[16] While few male philosophers of the day gave much credence to the passion of love,[17] their contemporary female writers wrote about it constantly. Much of the writing by female authors in the long eighteenth century centers on trying hard to understand what love is, why it differs between males and females, how it creates character (or doesn't), and what its influence might be on the individual. In the poetic, dramatic, and fictional writings of the passion of love, love was not meant to be avoided (to do so was impossible), but negotiated.[18]

Empowering the Passion of Love

My analysis focuses on Manley's first novel, *The Fair Hypocrite*, an adaptation of "The Forty-Fifth Nouell. The Duchesse of Sauoie." *The Fair Hypocrite* is the longest novel in Manley's collection, comprising nearly half of her text.[19] While Painter's version is recognizable in Manley's novel, several details have been changed. The most important change is Manley's inclusion of the duchess's premarital history;[20] Painter's version opens with the duchess already married to the Duke of Sauoie, and the circumstances leading to the marriage are not explicated. Importantly, Manley's textual additions refocus the adaptation from a tale of unvirtuous love to one that emphasizes the political importance of recognizing and negotiating the power that love has over an individual. By adding the Duchess of Savoy's backstory, Manley provides the details of both of her marriages, emphasizing the emotional connections between the duchess and her two husbands.

The comparative affective health of the two marriages becomes noteworthy, which leads to a sub-argument in Manley's adaptation that is not in the original tale: the necessity of reciprocal desire in order for relationships to succeed and kingdoms themselves to remain intact. These textual changes enable Manley to examine the ideology at stake in the system of patriarchal inheritance, and particularly the use of women in such a system. While the overt story of feminine virtue is strongly present, the text can be read more dynamically as a story about the dangers that the very political structure of the land faces when matters of state are dependent upon marriages where women are unequally paired in terms of their passions.

In this backstory, Manley emphasizes the importance of the passions by describing a marriage that, while not forced upon Regina, is clearly a political pairing made prior to her sexual maturity rather than one based on mutual love. Manley's text implies that the lack of equal ardor is a significant problem to be dealt with. In the first few pages, Regina's betrothal causes anxiety for the three major players involved: the King of France, her father; the Duke of Savoy, her fiancé, who is decrepitly old at seventy; and for the princess herself, a mere fifteen. Everyone waits for her to fail in her role as the keystone of a political treaty, as her marriage is to seal an agreement between the king and the duke. Her father laments the match even while he carries it out: "by inevitable Reasons of State, I was constrained to sacrifice thee" to the duke, "who is chill'd, with the Frost of seventy Winters" and who will unhappily "pluck the fair Fruit of Youth."[21] The husband-to-be, the Duke of Savoy, courts her the way a grandfather might woo an estranged grandchild rather than as husband/lover; she is "greatly humored by him, past any Precedent of what she had found in her own Education, grew so fond that if she were separated from him a Moment, she complained,"[22] implying a petulant, childlike devotion, as opposed to a wifely, mature attachment. The night before her wedding, her father implores Regina to keep her virtue once married by avoiding falling in love out of wedlock: "But oh! beware, beware, of ever letting Love for any other Object but your Husband, enter into your Breast! Beware! avoid that Deity as you would a restless, strong, and implacable Enemy: You can be harm'd by no other Passion."[23] He also, "helpfully" explains to her that should she fail in upholding her virtue, she can expect no support at all from her own relatives: "Remember, if once the bare Appearance of your Honour seem to be forfeited, you will appeal in vain to Father, Mother, Brother, or any other of your Kindred or Friends; who tho' they may bewail you in their Hearts secretly, yet for their own Honour they dare not seem to do it, lest they be thought of kindred to your Stain."[24] In this scene, the social structure of her position threatens the very system it is sacrificed to uphold. Not wanting Regina to be given away in so unequal a marriage, the king seems to give her personal advice, but it is the good of the State that this unequal marriage must protect. Regina's sexual maturity is reinterpreted as the irresponsible act of "falling in love" with someone else (it is assumed in the text that the object of her desire will never be her husband due to the age difference). She must remain sexually and emotionally immature to ensure the stability of the kingdom—a fact that even the king knows is bound to backfire. The situation is deeply precarious, and all are wary—excepting maybe the princess herself, as she is depicted as too un-self-aware to do so. Yet, it must go forward. By specifying the details of this marriage, with all of its political and personal implications, Manley critiques the patriarchal structure that creates unreasonable demands on female desires, invests all political interest in them, and then blames them when they fail. This is not just a straightforward issue of an ill-matched pair, but a bridge between female sexuality, the passion of love, and the state itself. Female desire is deeply threatening; the downfall of her father's kingdom is directly aligned with Regina's inevitable sexual maturity and her lack of romantic affection for her husband.

Manley's adaptation highlights the great ironies of patrilineal control when she includes the awkwardness of this match. Although the underlying warning of the dangers of infidelity remain in her version, her overwriting of this unequal love match reshapes the narrative of infidelity, allowing that though adultery will never be acceptable, under certain circumstances the reasons behind it might be understandable. In Painter's text, the duchess's thoughts of infidelity are less excusable because this backstory is absent; Manley, however, creates textual evidence of Regina's early uncritical acceptance of the match, and thus re-creates the moral meaning. The king's warning resonates deeply for Regina, and she educates herself against love by reading all she can about it in an attempt to avoid it. Early on, she is fully aware of the way in which her marriage cheats her of the basics of a happy and honorable marriage, and how she will be "condemned to the withered Arms of the old Duke, where she must never expect to answer the End of her Creation, to be blest with Posterity to know the Delights of mutual Love, or the Pleasures of being a Mother."[25] The absence of even a hope of mutual love resonates throughout these early scenes of Regina's move from princess to duchess; in thinking about marriage she has expected passion and procreation, and both will be impossible. The lack of romantic love for her husband has dire consequences on several levels in the near future: the virtue and therefore honor of the husband and wife destroyed, the marriage ruined, the peace treaty become defunct. Additionally, she recognizes that her life will be purposeless as she expects to remain sexually inactive and therefore barren. Manley's adaptation points out the hypocrisy of this *marriage*—though it confirms patriarchal political relationships, it cannot perpetuate patriarchy itself because the "honorable" end of procreation is impossible. Everyone simultaneously expects and laments her fate; nevertheless, the princess is married, becomes the Dutchess of Savoy, and moves to join her husband's household.

Manley's adaptive choices re-create the duchess's character when the changes show her coming into a sense of selfhood as she becomes sexually mature, thus overwriting a subjectivity that is based on Regina's sexual awareness just as much as it is dependent on her sexual virtue. In effect, Manley reinterprets the ideology of infidelity by linking the ability to be faithful with passion and maturity, rather than through a naïve virtue of inexperience. For many years, it appears that the duke and duchess's marriage will be happy and prosperous. Though she laments that her beauty cannot bring her either the joy of mutual desire or children, i.e. female maturity, she is careful to do her duty to her husband and remains faithful and loving to him. In Painter's tale, the duchess is introduced at this point, already married (the groom's age is unspecified), with the finer points of her character unknown to the readership, so that when she is aroused by seeing a painting of Don Carlos, Duke of Mendoza, illicit passion becomes the moral theme of choice. In Manley's version, the passion is just as sudden and illicit, but more easily connected with the flawed marriage rather than flawed character. Regina craftily invents a near-death illness to facilitate a holy pilgrimage so that she might see Mendoza's face. This pilgrimage, though it does not result in adultery, does cause guilt and punishment—they meet and fall in love, and circumstances, rather than stalwart virtue, prevent them from acting upon their mutual desires. By lying about a fatal sickness, by using a holy pilgrimage to pursue a possible lover, and by desiring that lover over her husband, she consequently becomes the "hypocrite" of the title. Here, Regina's very subjectivity results from the anxieties associated with sexual desire. When Mendoza claims "by the force of Love, that I am vanquished, irrecoverably lost, and know not whom to complain to but your Highness, nor how I shall be redressed,"[26] she likewise admits to the "Fire which burns in my Heart,"[27] and they agree to meet again, for the purposes of continuing and possibly consummating the relationship. Despite her reading knowledge of love, she cannot know herself until she experiences the pain of a mutual desire that is not consummated. She thinks she has herself under control, she thinks she knows her limits, through education and wifely duties. But love's very existence simultaneously disrupts the political events of the kingdom and brings her to knowledge of self; by realizing who she loves, she understands what she wants, who she is, and how those clash. Significantly, this disruption is possible only because her childlike love for her husband is not strong enough to resist attraction to the younger Mendoza; with Savoy, she has esteem, but neither longing for association nor (crucially) desire as appetite. Mendoza, however, can offer her all that her marriage cannot, including the love and children she will always lack while she is married to Savoy. Manley's creation of Regina's first marriage changes the ideology at stake in the story, and the emphasis on virtue becomes more intricate than in Painter's, pointing to circumstance and situation rather than an uncomplicated notion of inviolate sexual virtue. Such a setup makes Regina's profound desire for Mendoza and the actions that she takes to pursue him—her hypocrisy— understandable. Though the value of her virtue is never eradicated from the text, the circumstances of her marriage almost demand an awakening to the passion of love; the necessity of desire is overwritten on the palimpsest of virtue.

Manley's text augments the ironies of the role of women in public marriages because the pure passion of love—that of mutual longing for association, rather than its public construction, marriage—saves her. Soon after this test of desire, Regina's husband joins her on her journey, and though renewed in her affections for her husband (such as they are), she is nevertheless cosmically punished for unholy thinking and action. Sigisbert (her husband's closest advisor and her long-time admirer) becomes angry at his repeatedly rebuffed advances, is jealous of her affection for Mendoza, and spurred by revenge, frames Regina for adultery. Her father is right: once she is framed for adultery, no one will come to her aid: "The King, her Father seemed, by the Grief which Occasioned his Death, to give her up. The Dauphin, his successor ... thought no farther of his sister than sometime to exclaim against the Dishonor she had brought upon their Royal House."[28] Her father's earlier prediction has come true; not only does the rumor of adultery cause her father's death, but also her brother will not help and actually rails against her. She is alone.

Nonetheless, she is not brought down by the passion of love as her father predicts, but by the passion of revenge that Sigisbert feels. Honorable love, in fact, saves her. Seeing she has no other champion, she appeals to Mendoza to defend her honor on their virtuous love: "Love inspired and conducted me [to you]; and it is to [you] that I appeal for my deliverance ... I do not urge your Obligation of Knighthood, I conjure you by a greater Tie, the Debt of Gratitude and Love, of infinite Passion, and incessant Remembrance."[29] Regina notably appeals to their love rather than his duty as a knight, because it is a tie greater than his knightly code of honor. Her appeal to the "infinite Passion," that is, an entire system of love, and his memory of the moments they have shared, is markedly different from a rhetoric of honorable obligation. And that appeal specifically moves Mendoza more than an abstract sense of duty. He is in his castle under siege at the time and doubts her innocence, but arguing with himself he finds that by not immediately going to her aid, "I have neglected my Duty, and refuse'd my Assistance to the chiefest Person of the World, who perhaps may be innocent."[30] Their love for each other, he realizes, is tied up in obligations deeper than public honor. As she "forsook all the World to visit me in her Prosperity, can I do less than attempt to relieve her in her Adversity?"[31] As Regina predicts, public, honorable, appeals are not nearly as powerful as the appeal to the strength of their mutual attractions, the emotions that the passion of love gives rise to. "Pressed and inwardly solicited by this new Desire," he disguises himself, first as a priest, then as a "black" Knight.[32] He champions Regina, wins the joust, causing the death of Sigisbert, and restores her honor, before anonymously disappearing from the scene. Her husband, shamed by his treatment of her, is reduced "to a deep Melancholy, which so far clouded his Faculties, that it disabled him";[33] he dies soon after, and Regina returns home to France.

The palimpsest of virtue and hypocrisy still resonate in Manley's version. Her overwriting of a desire-based subjectivity cannot erase Regina's sinful acts, but her emphasis of Regina's near slip in virtue simultaneously underscores the importance of the passion of love to honorable marriage. There is an odd sense of justice served by Sigisbert's false accusation—Regina may not have sinned in body but certainly did so in thought and intention. Her desire for Mendoza cannot be a politically or personally positive one while it is outside the realm of her legal and holy vows to her husband. These are not the actions of a virtuous woman, and certainly such actions might be seen in certain faiths, such as Catholicism, as just as bad as committing the sin of adultery. Manley has little interest in erasing Regina's mistakes; in emphasizing Regina's hypocrisy, her title underscores the rhetoric of virtue. Nevertheless her adaptation makes the ideological importance of love more resonant than it is in the source text.

The passion of love in Regina's second marriage to Mendoza restructures the meaning of virtue in marriage. The last few pages assure us that this union, because more equal and more affectionate, will be more successful than her first marriage. Painter's description of the new understanding between the lovers stages many discussions of virtue, and virtue nearly missed; they discuss their past indiscretions and make courtly shows of affection, including bowing, kneeling, and public conversations with her brother the king on the second marriage, but after assuring us that the "the mariage [was] solempnized [sic] and consummate[d] with the Duchess,"[34] he ends the tale. Manley's revision of their union begins by emphasizing their physical contact rather than official ceremony: "letting her self fall into the Duke's Arms, she join'd her Mouth to his with such Ardour, as if she would attract his Soul to meet with hers that now seemed to hover on her Lips."[35] Their match, equal in age, rank, and love, elicits not only the physical happiness of being caressed and kissed by him, but also spiritual connection—their souls are accessible to each other through their physical contact of a kiss. There is no need for her brother to do anything other than approve the match. She gets no lectures on having to remain faithful to this husband—the implication is that because their associations and appetites are aligned, they do not need to be warned against sinful behavior. Fidelity is thus linked to love and especially to the desire as appetite end of the spectrum of the passion of love. Thus, Manley emphasizes the appropriateness of this reciprocal love pairing—the text stresses mutual sexual desire, and "no Words can describe the Happiness of the two Lovers, when the close-drawn Curtains left them to whisper to each others Souls their Mutual Desires: Venus bless'd the Bed, and from this beauteous Pair, descended a Race of Heroes, worthy of their Illustrious Extraction."[36] Again, the benefits of mutual sexual attraction are the communion of spirits and the blessing: children.

Manley's explicit connection between the passion of love, self-knowledge, stable politics, and continued patrilineal descent is striking in these final scenes. As a character, Regina develops a clearer understanding of herself through reciprocal love. She is immature in her first marriage, her affections are parental rather than marital; she does not know love and therefore cannot know herself. Despite her reading and self-educating against love, despite her nonsexual tryst, Regina threatens the dukedom because she cannot love her duke. In this reading of the text, virtue doesn't matter as much as emotional sensuality does. Once sexual maturity occurs in physical manifestations of reciprocal desire, the state is no longer dependent on her controlling youthful desires. Her second marriage is almost as important to political alliances as the first, though not as directly. (Her brother is trying to align himself with a house in Spain, to which Mendoza is the ambassadorial representative.) Regina and Mendoza marry because they love each other. Manley includes sexual maturity, signaled through the reciprocal passion of love, as a mark of social stability rather than potential political disruption.

Manley's adaptation is a form of intertextuality, making the reader experience the repetition of virtue through variations of the passion of love. The remaining palimpsest suggests that female desire and sexual maturity are means to both know the self and protect the nation. In Painter's "Duchesse of Savouie," the duchess's virtue is at stake, but in Manley's *The Fair Hypocrite*, unequal love threatens national security and prevents sexual maturity of the heroine. When the passion of love is established, the nation is at peace and Regina emerges as a dynamic character. The overwriting of the importance of mutual desire creates a more complex, more individual character than in the original text. While the object lesson of virtue is still present in the overwriting as knight errantry, her adaptation privileges love in and of itself as well as a metaphor for politics. Read through the lens of overwriting, the text demonstrates important structural and thematic complexities available through a dialogue of the passion of love. *The Fair Hypocrite* demands that love be understood radically as both politically motivated (as in her earlier works) and deeply sympathetic to female-based desire. The "pleasure" elicited by Painter's title alters in Manley's adaptive hands—she emphasizes not the "pleasures" of love and desire, but rather the "power" innate in pure passions.

Notes

1. Ros Ballaster, for instance, has argued that "*The Power of Love* abandoned the complexity of the rediscovered, translated, and reconstructed source commonly employed as a means of simultaneously concealing and signifying political intent in Manley's fiction." Ros Ballaster, *Seductive Forms: Women's Amatory Fiction 1684–1740* (Oxford: Clarendon, 1992), 153. However, it is important to note that rather than pretending to be a rediscovered, translated, and reconstructed source like *The New Atalantis*, *The Power of Love* actually *was* a translated, rediscovered, reconstructed source.

2. Toni Bowers's sustained reading of *The Perjur'd Beauty* in her recent *Force or Fraud* is an exception. Bowers's reading of Manley views *The Power of Love* politically in terms of "new-Tory" writing, emphasizing how broken vows become part of the political context. Toni Bowers, *Force or Fraud: British Seduction Stories and the Problem of Resistance, 1660–1760* (Oxford: Oxford University Press, 2011), Chapter 7. Carnell argues that the novels "bear very little resemblance to Manley's other writings about love, politics or anything else. ... They do not treat the topic of love with anything approaching the tolerant attitude Manley usually conveys," and they are stories that are "violent, rigidly didactic and otherwise uncharacteristic of her work." Rachel Carnell, *A Political Biography of Delarivier Manley* (London: Pickering and Chatto, 2008), 229, 231. Carnell's book focuses especially on Manley's political importance and significantly reads *The Power of Love* as apolitical, 229–234.
3. *Routledge Encyclopedia of Translation Studies*, ed. Mona Baker (London: Routledge, 1997) s.v. "Adaptation."
4. Ernst de Chickera and Elaine Kimmelman note that Elizabethan translations of the "nouelles" inspired some of the great early modern tragedies, such as *Romeo and Juliet* and *The Duchess of Malfi*. Ernst de Chickera "Palaces of Pleasure: The Theme of Revenge in Elizabethan Translations of Novelle," *Review of English Studies*, 11:41 (1960): 1–7. Elaine Kimmelman, "The Palace of Pleasure" in *Boston Public Library Quarterly*, 2 (1950): 231–244.
5. Significantly, Painter himself was a translator and adapter of these tales from Italian and French writers such as Boccaccio, Bandello, and Queen Margaret of Navarre, also available to Manley at that time. Additional versions include Thomas de la Peend's 1565 *The Historie of John Lorde Mandozze* and Thomas Achelley's 1576 *Violenta and Didiaco*. Penelope Aubin adapted a version of *The Wife's Resentment* as "Conjugal Duty Rewarded," an inset narrative to her 1722 *The Life and Amorous Adventures of Lucinda*.
6. Delarivier Manley, *The Power of Love in Seven Novels* (London, 1720), xv.
7. Ibid., xv.
8. She immediately backtracks, apologizing for connecting these writers to herself, claiming her work, is a "far, far unequal Performance! As much as Poetry is more Eloquent than Prose!" Manley, xv–xvi.
9. See also Earla Wilputte's essay in this volume.
10. Linda Hutcheon, *A Theory of Adaptation* (New York: Routledge, 2006), 8. For extended discussions of adaptation theory, see also Deborah Cartmell and Imelda Whelehan, eds. *The Cambridge Companion to Literature on Screen* (Cambridge: CUP, 2007) and *Adaptations: From Text to Screen, from Screen to Text* (New York: Routledge, 1999); Brian McFarlane, *Novel to Film: An Introduction to the Theory of Adaptation* (New York: Oxford University Press, 1996).
11. Robert Mayer, "Introduction: Is There a Text in This Screening Room?" In *Eighteenth-Century Fiction on Screen*, ed. Robert Mayer (Cambridge: Cambridge University Press, 2002), 1–15, 11.
12. Kimmelman 237. Kimmelman also notes that Painter "made few changes in his original texts, beyond omitting some passages and inserting short moral interpretations." Kimmelman 242.
13. William Painter, *The Palace of Pleasure: Beautified, Adorned and well furnished, with Pleasant Histories and Excellent Nouvelles* (London, 1566), 286. http://www.gutenberg.org/files/20241/20241-h/files/volume1.html#authors (Accessed June 6, 2011).

14. For a detailed etymology of the use of the word "emotions," see Thomas Dixon, "'Emotion': The History of a Keyword in Crisis." *Emotion Review* 4 (2012) 338–344. Studies of the passions as an early modern concept include Thomas Dixon, *Passions to Emotions: The Creation of a Secular Psychological Category.* (Cambridge: Cambridge University Press, 2003); Jon Elster, *Alchemies of the Mind: Rationality and the Emotions.* Cambridge: Cambridge UP, 1999; Daniel M. Gross, *The Secret History of Emotion: From Aristotle's "Rhetoric" to Modern Brain Science* (Chicago: University of Chicago Press, 2006); Susan James, *Passion and Action: The Emotions in Seventeenth-Century Philosophy* (Oxford, Clarendon: 1997); David Punter, *Writing the Passions* (London: Longman, 2001).

15. Nancy Armstrong and Leonard Tennenhouse, "A Mind for Passion: Locke and Hutcheson on Desire." In *Politics and the Passions 1500–1850.* Victoria Kahn, Neil Saccamano and Daniela Coli, eds. (Princeton: Princeton UP, 2006), 131–150.

16. William Reddy, *The making of Romantic Love: Longing and Sexuality in Europe, Asia, and Japan 900–1200ce.* (Chicago: U of Chicago P, 2012). See also Niklas Luhman, *Love as Passion: The Codification of Intimacy.* Transl. Jeremy Gaines and Doris L. Jones (Cambridge: Polity Press, 1986); Kenneth S. Pope, "Defining and Studying Romantic Love" in *On Love and Loving.* Ed. Kenneth S. Pope (San Francisco: Jossey-Bass, 1980).

17. While philosophers refer to "love" in their works, such as Francis Bacon's discourse "On Love" (1625), they either remark on its public/political implications, or warn against it. See Rebecca Tierney-Hynes, *Novel Minds: Philosophers and Romance Readers, 1680–1740* (Basingstoke: Palgrave, 2012), for additional examples, Introduction.

18. Examples include Aphra Behn's Libertine plays of the 1670s and her poetry of the 1680s (especially her Pindaric ode "On Desire"). Eliza Haywood dedicated two volumes to the subject in "Reflections of the Various Effects of Love" (1726), though the second volume has yet to be recovered. See Aleksondra Hultquist "Haywood's Progress through the Passions," in *Passions, Sympathy and Print Culture: Public Opinion and Emotional Authenticity in Eighteenth-Century Britain,* edited by Heather Kerr, David Lemmings, and Robert Phiddian. Palgrave Macmillan, 2015, 116–141.

19. *The Power of Love in Seven Novels* contains seven tales: *The Fair Hypocrite, The Physician's Stratagem, The Wife's Resentment, The Husband's Resentment. In Two Examples, The Happy Fugitives,* and *The Purjur'd Beauty.* A source text for *The Physician's Stratagem* has not been identified and may be original. *The Purjur'd Beauty* is a version of the well-known "St. Gregory Legend." See Carnell's *A Political Biography* 229–30 for a more specific source history.

20. Manley often includes backstories for her female characters in *The Power of Love.* See Earla Wilputte's essay in this collection regarding *The Husband's Resentment. In Two Examples.*

21. Manley 11.

22. Ibid., 9.

23. Ibid., 13.

24. Ibid.

25. Ibid., 29.

26. Manley, 66.

27. Manley, 67.

28. Manley, 115.
29. Ibid., 95.
30. Ibid., 103.
31. Ibid., 104.
32. Ibid.
33. Ibid., 128.
34. Painter, 334.
35. Manley 139.
36. Ibid., 140.

Part III
Text

9   Manley's "Sentimental" Deserted Mistress, Women Writers in Literary History, and *The Lost Lover*

Victoria Joule

In the anonymously authored commentary on the theater *The Comparison between the Two Stages* (1702), two of Manley's works are cited as examples of a "Lady's."[1] They incite a misogynistic outburst about women's audacious assumption that they could be writers. When scholars have used this extract, they refer to Manley's *The Nine Muses* (1700) as the cause.[2] However, it is important to observe that it is a play, specifically *The Lost Lover* (1696), which is the original source of provocation:

S[ULLEN]: The lost Lover, or, The jealous Husband
R[AMBLE]: I never heard of that.
S: Oh this is a Lady's!
…
C[RITICK]: What occasion had you to name a Lady in the confounded Work you're about?
R: Here's a Play of hers.
C: The Devil there is: I wonder in my Heart we are so lost to all Sense and Reason: What a Pox have the Women to do with the Muses? I grant you the Poets call the Nine Muses by the Names of Women, but why so? not because the Sex had any thing to do with Poetry, but because in that Sex they're much fitter for prostitution.[3]

Undoubtedly, Manley's edited poetry collection, *The Nine Muses*, to which this rant potentially refers, transgressed contemporary seventeenth-century ideas about poetry, women, and creativity. It made a bold intervention into male literary terrain by revising the concept of the passive muse and was the first known all-female authored poetry collection. Yet, it is still *The Lost Lover* that sparked the rant. In addition to being an example of a work by a female author, what was there in this play that might have provoked particular attention? By all accounts, Manley's second play in this 1695/6 season, *The Royal Mischief* (1696), was the more overtly controversial foray into explicit explorations of female sexuality and power, and it was more popular. *The Lost Lover*'s later critical reception also makes the review's attention surprising, as it has received considerably less scholarly attention and been dismissed as poorly written and underdeveloped.[4] This is a view compounded by Manley's own prefatory remark that it was "the Follies of seven days," as well as its limited audience appeal; it did not run for more than three nights.[5] However, Manley's self-deprecating comments were typical of women writers' strategies of self-representation. Her qualifying claims to be innocent of the theatrical world—"my self so great a Stranger to the Stage"—are unfounded.[6] Moreover, they are undermined at the end of her preface where she proclaims that "I think my Treatment much severer than I deserved; I am satisfied the bare Name of being a Woman's Play damn'd it beyond its own want of Merit."[7] This statement echoes Aphra Behn's railing against gender-biased attacks in *The Luckey Chance* (1686) and gestures toward Manley's allegiance to her influential predecessor, but also reminds us of the interrelated nature of play-texts in this period.[8]

Recognizing the theatrical influences on this play and its place within the context of the theater, or its "intertheatrical" nature, as Jacky Bratton has described, enables a fuller critical account.[9] This approach examines "the mesh of connections between all kinds of theater texts, and between texts and their users."[10] Dismissive comments on *The Lost Lover* often fail to recognize its intertheatrical references, specifically Manley's explicit reworking of Behn's *The Rover; or, The Banish'd Cavaliers* (1677). Significantly, it is mainly theater historians who have identified this instance of appropriation. This essay reclaims the critically neglected *Lost Lover* for its particular stance on and contribution to the "sentimental" in comedies, arguing that Manley played a role in the development of this emerging form, but with a specifically "feminist" approach. In her contribution to the moralizing and sentimentalizing of the stage, Manley paid close attention to the reform of the rake and dramatically revised former representations of the deserted mistress. An intertheatrical reading further reveals Manley's wider concerns with women and women writers in literary history. In addition to reworking Behn's *The Rover*, Manley makes her allegiances clear through her satiric portrait of the "moral" antithesis to Behn: Katherine Philips, whom this essay contends is the real deserted mistress of the play. Through her innovation of models and types in *The Lost Lover*, Manley extended her theatrical characters from purely onstage portrayals to accommodate their offstage counterparts as well as being attuned to the actresses' abilities to portray these figures. In doing so, Manley participated in the formation of the dichotomous model for women writers and asserts her position alongside Behn and the "bad" women by relocating sympathy with her heroic, "sentimental" version of the deserted mistress.

The First Sentimental Comedy

The Lost Lover has been identified as the first sentimental comedy, predating Colley Cibber's *Love's Last Shift, or the Fool in Fashion* (1696), but primary attention is still given to Cibber's work. Of course, the claiming of "firsts" in any generic form is problematic and particularly in the case of sentimental comedy, as a form that is notoriously difficult to define. Nevertheless, Linda Payne, Margrete Rubik, and Eva Mueller-Zettelmann all contend that *The Lost Lover* is the first in its conception.[11] Richard Steele is often associated with defining and writing sentimental comedy, notably detailing the aspects of the sentimental comedy in his literary epilogue to *The Lying Lover* (1704), but the move toward the humane and the moral in plays occurred decades before. Jeremy Collier's well-known *A Short View of the Immorality and Profaneness of the English Stage* (1698) preceded Steele; yet, rather than being responsible for instigating generic change, Collier's text was symptomatic of a wider theatrical move that prevailed in the 1690s.

Moral agendas were made more explicit in this period, but there was no one exemplar; rather, it was a transitional process. Hence, many critical approaches tend toward the descriptive rather than prescriptive.[12] It was not a smooth development, though, as Laura Brown argues, for the merging of social comedy with a clear moral standard often resulted in incoherence and tensions.[13] Cibber's play provides an arguably superficial moral agenda, which glosses over inconsistencies. I argue that Manley's play, however, takes the question of reform much more seriously, adopting a different approach from that of Cibber. Her contribution to sentimental comedy is distinctive because she concentrated on the minor character of the deserted mistress and because she attacked rather than reformed the sexual double-standards of the rake.

Cibber's play is a useful point of comparison, as it is often cited and analyzed for its sentimental attributes, which can highlight Manley's sentimental alternative. In a fairly recent study of sentimental comedy by Frank H. Ellis, Cibber is again cited as the first practitioner of the form. Despite acknowledging problems in attempting a definition—the "sentimental" is "a refractory term with a marked tendency to slump and if anything useful is to be made of it, it must be shaped up"—Ellis insists that the sentimental comedy "may be defined ad hoc as comedy on stage that arouses sentimental reactions."[14] Cibber's play displays the key characteristics of sentimental comedy outlined by Ellis, such as the inclusion of women, the inversion of hierarchies such as parent/child or higher/lower classes, and the subordination of reason to emotion.[15] In addition, Ellis describes "secondary characteristics" that include melancholy conversation, recklessness, self-sacrificing virtue, undeserved distress, and overt moralizing.[16] The play's explicit moral impetus is the return and reformation of the debauched Loveless from his nine-year romp through Europe to his loyal, virtuous, and long-suffering wife of ten years, Amanda. Ultimately, the man/wife hierarchy is subverted when Loveless is reduced to his knees in shame. Emotion reigns and Amanda's self-sacrificing virtue is rewarded as Loveless's last line proclaims: "*And sure the nearest to the Joys above, / Is the chaste Rapture of a virtuous Love.*"[17]

The miraculous and potentially unbelievable transformation from rake to monogamous husband was famously expanded upon by Sir John Vanbrugh in his theatrical riposte, *The Relapse* (1696). It has also troubled critics when examining the generic status of the play as sentimental.[18] However, a performance-based rather than a purely text-based reading provides different information, as Aparna Gollapudi argues.[19] With careful attention to clothing and Cibber's emphasis on these external signs of moral worth, Loveless is revealed to be shabby and pitiable, rather than rakish and successful. The end result was less a rake lost, but more a lost gentleman retrieved, as Gollapudi contends.[20] However, this play and indeed Cibber's other plays tend to rely on this surface value of change, where idealism bypasses problems.[21] For, despite the moralizing visual dimension identified by Gollapudi, the play retains its "hard" element, as the dominant content is sex-comedy or "hard comedy."[22] The marital reunion in *Love's Last Shift*, for example, is devised through the Restoration theatrical trope of the bedroom trick, although instead of the lover supplanting the husband or wife, Amanda is disguised, and thus the wife supplants the mistress. Fidelity is gained by infidelity. Moreover, this central scene also involves a rape. Loveless's re-consummation of his relationship with his "mistress" wife is mirrored in the subplot where Loveless's servant, Snap, rapes Amanda's serving maid. Furthermore, Cibber makes strong counter signals to the reforming or sentimental aspect of the play, as the epilogue reassures the audience that the main character is "*lew'd for above four Acts, Gentlemen!*"[23]

Manley's play shows a much clearer departure from the former "hard" sex comedies than Cibber's. There are no bedroom scenes or explicit references to sex, and there is a stronger emphasis on fidelity in marriage and honorable behavior. Manley's subplot has been identified as the main sentimental dimension.[24] The rake, Wildman, makes repeated attempts to tempt the steadfastly loyal Olivia from her husband, Smyrna. Manley's portrayal of Olivia's obnoxiously jealous husband offers a further comedic dimension, particularly in the extremes he goes to in order to discover or prevent his wife's infidelity. However, this subplot does more to draw upon the sympathy of the audience for women's position in enforced marriage rather than instigating the husband's sentimental reform.

In the main plot, Manley really develops her stance on sentimental comedy. There are recognizable character types, but the centrality and dominance of the deserted mistress, Belira, indicates a notable shift from the norm. Wilmore attempts to secure his fortune through marriage to Marina, but Belira thwarts his plans because she still loves Wilmore. Belira drives the action by organizing two engagements to take Marina away from Wilmore, and push Wilmore back into her arms: Marina with Wilmore's father, the country squire, Sir Rustik Good-Heart, and Wilmore with Marina's mother, the not-so-young Lady Young-Love. However, Belira is fighting a losing battle as Wildman, the other rake, works with Wilmore to unravel her plans. Wildman functions more actively in the subplot as the would-be seducer of Olivia and at times pursues the other female character, Orinda, whose significance shall be examined later. Despite the rakes preventing Belira's success at the end, it is clear that the main plot of this play is coordinated by the typically marginalized figure of the deserted mistress. Moreover, it is her desires rather than the rakes' that take center stage, but crucially Belira's are also given a sentimental value.

Manley's appropriation of *The Rover* builds further sentimental subversions of comedic character types, including the rake. The appropriation is made explicit by the naming of "Wilmore," and on closer examination, Wilmore, Belira, and Marina mirror Behn's characters Willmore, Angellica Bianca, and Hellena. Through her revision of the rake and the deserted mistress, Manley signals a moral concern with male sexuality and relocates sentiment and sympathy with the typically comedic and derisible deserted mistress. Manley recasts her deserted mistress as the heroine, and rather than reforming her rake, she revises the character type and punishes him.

Manley's Revised Rakes and Heroic Deserted Mistress

The defining sentimental feature of Cibber's comedy is his reformation of the rake. Loveless's transformation from lover of debauchery to blissful husband provided Cibber with his moral conclusion. Manley likewise offers newer versions of the rake-plot, but her treatment of this character type differs significantly because instead of demanding repentance from her rake, Manley punishes and exposes him. In this way she not only reflects and contributes to the changing social opinion on male libertinism, but she forms an attack. Manley's rake is also more complex than Cibber's comparatively superficial one. Moreover, there are two rakes in her play: Wilmore and Wildman, both of whom are drawn from a broader theatrical history of rakes as well as, more specifically, Behn's rake, Willmore.[25] For Manley, writing in the 1690s, the serious rakes were being phased out and there was a boom in the *honnête homme*; the male hero who accompanied the rake, such as Wilmore's friend, Belville. Manley also offered two male "heroes," yet the two male protagonists of *The Lost Lover* do not fall into this division as both are clearly identifiable as rakes.

Wildman is an "extravagant" rake, with his name gesturing to his forebears in rakes such as Thomas Shadwell's Wildish (*Bury-Fair*, 1689), yet, as Robert Hume declares, these rakes are often "far wilder in word than in deed."[26] Wildman opens the play plotting his next seduction and conquest as other rakes have done, including Dorimant from *Man of Mode* (1676), but he does not actually manage to conquer any woman in this play. On the other hand, Wilmore is more successful with women and has a forebear in Behn's extravagant rake, Willmore. However, Manley's version of Willmore fits more into a "polite" rake type, as he wishes to maintain his social standing and takes care to assimilate into society. For some critics, such as Nancy Copeland, Wilmore is a softened rake, and as such recognizes a shifting gender ideology at the end of the seventeenth century that "indicates some 'womanly' qualities can be admirable in a man."[27]

I would suggest, however, that Wilmore's character is not inherently "soft," but that he is "softened" by the treatment he receives in the play. By indicating a history of extravagant rakes in his namesake, but then denying his sexual gratification, the play actually implies punishment rather than a shift in character type.

Normally, the rake character type who was punished or humiliated in the 1690s was the foppish one, drawing from earlier rakes such as Sir Fopling Flutter (*The Man of Mode*), who was a model for Manley's Sir Amorous Courtall in *The Lost Lover*. On occasion extravagant rakes have indeed been unmasked—a notable example being Maskwell from William Congreve's *The Double Dealer* (1693)—and not all rakes succeeded in seducing the women they pursued. However, none of these rakes have their power as systematically undermined as Wilmore. Where Behn takes Willmore to the extremes of rakish behavior—"one of the most excessive of his type"—Manley reduces him to the other extreme by feminizing and humiliating him.[28] Manley undermines what would appear to be the pairing of two ostensibly extravagant rakes, indicated to the audience by their names, Wilmore and Wildman. Wilmore functions as a polite rake by assimilating himself into society and demonstrates Manley's concern with double-standards, as his deceit is portrayed as a far worse crime than the overt sexuality of extravagant rakes. Wilmore is reduced from the former glory enjoyed by his predecessor in Behn's play: Behn's Willmore is a "roving" man, a seducer of multiple women, linguistically masterful and financially astute (he even manages not to pay Angellica Bianca). In Manley's revision, however, Wilmore is subjected to a host of degrading situations and is subject to the dictates of his former mistress, Belira.

Wilmore may pursue women and his fortune as others have done— "Marina is the Goddess here; You have doubtless heard her Father left her a Fortune of 1200l"—but ultimately he is subject to women's financial control.[29] He is even compared to a mistress himself when he is effectively bought by Lady Young-Love. Belira observes that Lady Young-Love has "almost purchased him with rich presents, which has more Eloquence in them than all the old Womens [sic] Tongues in England."[30] Manley derives further comic effect from Wilmore's relationship with Lady Young-Love through his attempts to flatter his way into her attention and her purse. Wilmore has to play the modest gentleman in order to limit the physical side of their relationship. He may be given comic double-speak as he flatters his unwitting fiancée—

LADY YOUNG-LOVE: I don't look well to day, Mr. Wilmore. [Looks in her Glass]
WILMORE: Your Ladiship can never look other.[31]

—however, the joke is arguably at Wilmore's expense. Not only is he feminized by the overpowering Lady Young-Love, but he is also denied any other physical relationships. Lady Young-Love describes his excessive modesty with unintentional humor: "he's the Modestest Gentleman; so Civil he never prest for the least Favour, no not for a Kiss" and "he is so bashful, and so modest."[32] Of course, Lady Young-Love is a character designed for comic effect. She has poor taste and a naïve belief in the honesty of her younger lover. However, the familiar theatrical satire of the older woman is softened, as Lady Young-Love acknowledges her mistake at the close of the play and regains her authority and good sense as a mother. She even goes so far as to advise Marina not to accept Wilmore as a husband, saying that "But might I perswade her, it shou'd not be Belira's Lover, he has too many Faults."[33] Significantly, Wilmore's name is erased here, and his identity is determined by a woman. In fact, it is Belira who dictates the main action of the play and manipulates Wilmore into this uncomfortable position as fiancée to Lady Young-Love.

Manley omits the traditional display of masculine authority, often manifested through physical violence, to highlight her different approach to representing the rake in sentimental comedy. This is in stark comparison to *The Rover*, which shows underlying masculine control through physical power, or the threat of it manifested in the sword and thwarted rapes. Although Behn gives women power through language, rhetoric, and cross-dressing, these are typically transitory states and ultimately underwritten by male physical power.[34] The only instance of violence in Manley's play is in the final act, where Belira makes an attempt on Marina's life. This gender inversion contributes to the overall undermining of the rakes' masculine power. Manley revises the traditional comedic plot structure, where the libertine is rewarded and the rake is reformed to a certain extent by marriage to his witty, but virginal, counterpart. This "fantasy" woman is, as Behn's Cornelia describes, "the most mistress-like wife."[35]

These traditional "gay couples," such as Hellena and Willmore, are characterized by their witty banter and sparkling conversation that indicate the woman's sexual promise without compromising her virginity. This is not to say that Behn authorized this type of relationship by dramatizing it, but she did not disrupt the form to the same extent as Manley. Not only does Manley change "the Rover" into a "polite," disempowered, and feminized Wilmore, but she also reworks the heroine. Marina is ostensibly Manley's version of Hellena, Cornelia, and her kin. Although she possesses some wit, Marina severely lacks the charm, ingenuity, and stage presence of her forebears. This may have been in part due to a lack of character development by Manley, yet it was arguably also part of an intentional flattening to give center stage to her main character, Belira. Belira is the deserted mistress, who in traditional theatrical models should be demoted to the comic subplot. Yet here, Manley rewrites the traditional comedic form to supplant the "mistress-like wife" heroine with the mistress.

Manley's characterization of the deserted mistress posed a dramatic challenge to the sustained theatrical representation of this figure as a subject of ridicule.[36] The deserted mistress had an important comedic function, but she was also essential for the assertion of social morals and manners of the period. Her sexual licentiousness provided titillation, added complexity to plot lines, and through her ultimate punishment, restored social order. Pat Gill argues that the sexually active woman functions quite literally as a Freudian obscene joke, because the joke "operates like a power play to confirm the (masculine) tellers as subjects in control and to fix the objects or butts of the jest in a passive (feminine) position."[37] More specifically, the satire works by "opening up the private lives of fallen women to public scrutiny. The threat of exposure, generally posed by the rake-hero, successfully prevents a worldly female adversary from carrying out her plans of independence or revenge."[38]

The comic conclusions for the deserted mistresses are at the expense of their autonomy and independence and, crucially for them, the satisfaction of their desire. However, they are formidable characters with often some of the most vibrant and dramatic speeches and scenes. One of the most recognizable rejected mistresses, Mrs. Loveit from George Etherege *Man of Mode* (1676), is given dramatic scenes where she fluctuates from passionate outrage at the inconstancy of her lover to violent despair and distraction. However, the mistresses' dramatic presence and sexual transgression are ultimately exposed and curtailed. They are never able to sustain any real transgression into the masculine realm of action. This is seen most clearly in their attempts at violence: Mrs. Loveit speaks only of daggers and darts, and her fan is all that suffers at her violent hands. Other rejected mistresses may possess weapons, but are unable to carry out their violent threats. Lady Touchwood in Congreve's *The Double-Dealer* (1694) collapses into tears and is unable to wield the dagger she holds; each of Mrs. Termagent's attempts to murder her rival are prevented in Shadwell's *The Squire of Alsatia* (1688); and Behn's Angellica Bianca similarly falters in her efforts to shoot her former lover.[39]

Manley employs the familiar aspects of this figure as a troublesome burden, but she radically transforms them. Compared with earlier examples, Belira is of a high- rather than lower- or middle-class birth, and rather than being on the outskirts of the plot and society, is fully included in the social scene. She possesses the character traits of the witty, virginal heroine specifically in her scheming and plot manipulation, and with her feisty dialogue with the male lead. Belira appears to be better suited to Wilmore than Marina, and their relationship is set up along similar lines to the traditional pairing of the rake-hero and virginal heroine. Belira thus mirrors Hellena and Cornelia in all but her virginity, which is central to Manley's reassertion of the viability of the mistress as potential wife. Belira assumes the position of heroine through her witty repartee with Wilmore, which sparkles throughout this play. Their dialogue is, for Jacqueline Pearson, a "theatrical masterpiece."[40] In their exchanges, Belira attacks the double-standard that allows men to pursue their desire, but disallows women, and as Angellica Bianca had done before, she rails against broken vows. However, Belira avoids the typical fate of the mistress, exposure; instead, Belira's rake claims to protect her reputation: "No tears Belira, we will always be Friends, your Honour shall be safe, and you my chiefest care."[41] However, Belira's concern is for love, not reputation: "What can pay Love, but Love?"[42]

Belira's words echo Angellica's to Willmore: "The pay I mean, is but thy love for mine."[43] She may parallel Angellica in her desire and concern with love over money and reputation, but she does not suffer "the disease of our sex" in falling for seductive masculine rhetoric like Angellica. In fact, Belira mocks Willmore's romantic flourishes. When Willmore offers Belira his sword for her to take her revenge, she laughs in his face: "Ha, ha, ha, in Love to dying! By all that's good, turn'd Hero: Your Mistress, Sir, is much obliged—Keep your sword."[44] Willmore pleads for her to release her claim upon him, and in dismissing his plea Belira feminizes him further by remarking on "how well [he] canst turn woman."[45]

Both deserted mistresses exist in a tragic, rather than comic vein. Belira's passionate debates with Willmore draw from Angellica Bianca's sympathetic portrayal, in which a deserted mistress is relocated to a more central position. However, Manley's portrayal represents a more extensive revision of the character type. In Behn's plays some women are left on the outside of the social scene; these are most typically those women who are sexually experienced, such as the deserted mistress.[46] The conclusion to *The Lost Lover* similarly renders Belira "outside"—literally, offstage in her case—but she has a much more active role in the exclusion. Belira exits in a dramatic, scene-stealing flourish in the conclusion of the play. Here Manley departs from Behn by rewriting Angellica Bianca's passive response to the treachery of Willmore.

Manley's striking reworking of the deserted mistress's fate is made explicit through comparison with her forebear in Angellica. Both Behn and Manley instill a tragic heroic closing scene for these women, specifically in their final speeches. In *The Rover*, Angellica offer a poignant speech in poetical and tragic blank verse:

ANGELLICA: [To Willmore] But now to show my utmost of contempt,
   I give thee life, which if thou wouldst preserve,
   Live where my eyes may never see thee more;
   Live to undo someone whose soul may prove
   So bravely constant to revenge my love.[47]

Belira is, by contrast, much more explicitly angry and vengeful:

BELIRA: Farewel for ever, both to thy Love and them ... I only live to wish, and hope to see it take your Minion: Love her as long as you are used to Love a Woman, and then let want of Wealth and Liberty pursue you: Be poorly Wretched, and Wretched Poor; ... yet think on me and sigh for such a friend —But may no Friend be found, til scorned at home thou seekest abroad, some Wretched Death unknown.

...

BELIRA: Villain, thou has betray'd me—[to Lady Young-Love] Madam, I warn from that Traytor Wilmore.[48]

The noble Angellica grants Willmore his life, but banishes him from her sight; in contrast, Belira is clearly much more aggressive in her desire for revenge. She places no confidence in Wilmore's intended marriage to Marina; moreover, she foretells and instructs his misery at losing her as his "friend." Her speech does not even end here, as Belira goes on to warn the other characters. Here Manley reuses Angellica's same accusation—"Yes, traitor"—as a final statement and omen.[49] Unlike the comparable scene in *The Rover* where the couple, Willmore and Hellena, has a lively conversation, the close of *The Lost Lover* is overshadowed by Belira's words and actions. Her ominous warning is followed by the report of her attempted murder of Marina. Significantly, this attempt occurs offstage. In previous representations of the deserted mistress type, the violence had occurred onstage for comic effect and was depicted in all its ridiculous ineffectiveness. However, Belira's violent attack is made powerful through its absence. Moreover, there is little dialogue between the remaining characters onstage, and Lady Young-Love even cautions her daughter against marrying Wilmore, echoing Belira's closing warning. The mistress as outsider is subverted in Manley's reworking. She is no longer a character who is the satirical butt of the jokes in the comic subplot; instead she has been redefined as a serious character and the tragic heroine of the play.

Casting Mistresses and Women Writers

Manley's dramatic revision of the fate of the deserted mistress, coupled with her attack on the rake, pushes the boundaries of comedic plot lines of the late-Stuart stage. Her more serious tone would have compared unfavorably with the traditional mood of the sex-comedy, which still appealed to the contemporary audience and which would be evident in the rakish raucousness of *Love's Last Shift*. It would have had an impact on the play's poor running. However, this takes into account only the text, and audience reception depended as much on the performance as it did on the content. Different casting could completely revise the interpretation of a play, including the gender politics. Manley's debut play was performed under distinctive circumstances: the actors' rebellion and the resultant departure of some of the finest actors and actresses to Lincoln's Inn Fields.[50] The loss of acting expertise would have changed the performance, and hence the power and success of Manley's first play.[51]

In her preface to *The Lost Lover*, Manley made explicit reference to the poor acting at Drury Lane, opening with a criticism describing "the little success it [*The Lost Lover*] met with the Acting."[52] Her comment hints at the turbulent competition of stage performance at the time and the importance of securing the right cast. As she moved her subsequent play to the rival house, it also gestures toward the malicious attacks made by the houses on each other as well as suggesting that her rationale for moving houses was the poor acting. As Gilli Bush-Bailey observes, the change of theater company was most likely the spur toward the satire of her in the Drury Lane production *The Female Wits*.[53] The rehearsal scenes in this play, for all their harsh satire, imply a close relationship between playwright and actor/ actress in the direction of the play's performance. As theater historians in particular have clarified, playwrights not only often had hands-on experience of the stage, but also created characters with particular actresses and actors in mind. Manley's play was conceived before the rebellion, and so her characters would have been inspired by the leading players of the theater. Their absence would thus have detrimentally affected its performance. By reading the characters in relation to the actresses, one can begin to imagine how it could have been received.

Elizabeth Barry, the star of the day and instrumental in the actors' rebellion, would have been the intended actress for Belira. Barry had made a name for herself as a successful tragedienne and inspired audience after audience with her evocative performances.[54] The success of Belira's portrayal as a tragic heroine relied upon Barry's skills to kindle audience sympathy. Manley would go on to have *The Royal Mischief* staged at the rival house with Barry starring in the main role as the outrageous royal princess, Homais. Manley noted that in Barry's performance as Homais, "she excelled and made the part of an ill woman, not entertaining, but admirable."[55] This was surely the effect Manley had wished to achieve with Belira, a complexity that could challenge her audience's preconceived impression of the deserted mistress. Moreover, Barry was also a familiar figure in the deserted mistress role.[56] Frances Knight played Belira at Drury Lane, and the comedienne Susanna Verbruggen played Olivia, a direction that may have brought comedy, rather than sympathy, to Olivia's suffering. If the roles had been performed by the leading female figures, the effect would have been rather different. Barry and Anne Bracegirdle were already powerful stage presences and often paired in opposing moral and amoral female parts. They both possessed the ability to capture their audience and transform a play. Bracegirdle would have evoked audience compassion for Olivia's oppressed virtue by bringing to the stage her known history of playing virtuous roles combined with her successful virtuous offstage image, which would have reinforced the moral content of this play. In reading the play as text, we lose the potential for seeing its sentimental intention and portrayal in the expert hands of Barry and Bracegirdle.

Finally, there was the small part of the comedic character Orinda, which was taken by Katherine Cibber in the Drury Lane performances. Although Orinda is ostensibly a minor character, Manley used her as a vehicle to pursue concern with emerging models for women writers. The character of Orinda, and the manner in which she is portrayed, take Manley's play beyond the dramatic confines of plot and cast, and into broader concerns relating to women and literary history. Orinda was Manley's own satirical jab at the renowned author Katherine Philips. A contemporary literary audience would have instantly recognized Philips's poetic pen name, Orinda, and there is an explicit reference in the character list where Orinda is described as "an affected poet." In the context of the play, Orinda is consigned to the subplot, where she is satirized for her pretensions to grandeur and elite literary culture. Her high-minded ways are undermined by her comical country dialect with her exclamations of "Oh Gud," "Lard," and "O Jesu." Philips's involvement in coterie manuscript poetry is viciously mocked as she circulates her verses to an uninterested audience. Orinda is also solipsistic, as Marina comments sarcastically—"I know none so Entertaining as her self"—and her country retreat, again something Philips was well-known for, is also mocked.[57] A portrayal by the renowned comedienne Elizabeth Currer, rather than by Cibber, would have brought this satirical portrait to the forefront of the play.

Paradoxically, I suggest, Orinda is the real "deserted mistress" in this play. She has clearly been having an affair with Wildman, but has been rejected. And, although Wildman seeks her out at the end of the play, his characterization as a "wild rake" does not bode well for Orinda sustaining her affair.[58] The play implies she is likely to suffer the typical conclusion for a deserted mistress. By residing in the play's subplot and providing a source of comedy at her expense, Orinda further conforms to the deserted mistress formula. Moreover, the prologue launches a sordid attack on Orinda, accusing her of performing virtue to the extent that she can enact the appropriate physical effects:

> Our Gallants were undone, show'd you but prove
> Her Apes in Vir[t]ue, as you'r theirs in Love,
> But for our Poetess—Lard no Virgin ever
> Resigned so bashfully her darling Treasure,
> She sweats and reddens, then turns pale for fear[59]

Manley's choice to represent such a well-known and well-respected literary figure in this way should not be underestimated. Both Jane Spencer and Paula Backscheider observe that Manley, as a new woman writer, was treading a perilous path by launching this attack, but it is clear that Manley felt an urgent need to intervene in the way models for women writers were becoming established.[60] Orinda is a relatively minor character, but the satire proves a hostile twist in Manley's revision of literary history where the sexually experienced woman, rather than the virtuous one, takes center stage. Manley's play proves beyond doubt where she stood in literary lineage: her literary appropriation and homage to Behn is set against the reductive and harsh satire on Philips. In an increasingly moral climate for the stage, and for literature more generally, Manley's concern with the deserted mistress was problematic. Not only did this have an impact on the play's reception, coupled with its performance history, but it also shows how Manley prefigured the way women writers would be divided along moral lines. By recognizing the relationship between character types and real women, actress and woman writer, one sees more powerfully how Manley's integration of the poet Katherine Philips as a satiric character in her play made a bold gesture about women writers in history. Manley clearly aligned herself with Aphra Behn by adapting aspects of *The Rover*, and she cast the "moral" Philips as the real deserted mistress.[61]

Thus, more broadly, the "sentimental" in sentimental comedy in Manley's case raised questions about where sympathy should be placed in society. Manley's connected concerns with the relationship between the stage and real life, characters, actresses, and women writers extend throughout her literary career. The stage provided a valuable forum to explore representations of women, women writers, and the way they were constructed along a false division between morality and amorality, something that contemporary feminist literary critics of this period have now also critiqued as staged.[62] Through an intertheatrical reading of Manley's first play, it becomes quite clear what women have "to do with the Muses" to cite again Critick's complaint. Not only was Manley intervening in the development of sentimental comedy with her revisions of existing plays and theatrical types, but her text was engaged in literary history more widely in a bid to place the literary lineage of Aphra Behn in a sympathetic and heroic light.

Notes

1. The full title of the work is *A Comparison between the two stages, with an examen of The generous conqueror; an some critical remarks on The Funeral or Grief alamode, The false friend, Temerlane and other. In dialogue* (London, 1702).
2. See, for example, Anne Kelley, "'What a Pox have Women to do with the Muses?' The Nine Muses (1700): Emulation or Appropriation?" *Women's Writing* 17·1 (2010): 8–29.
3. *A Comparison between the two stages*, 26. The dialogue is between the characters Sullen, Ramble, and Critick.
4. There is very little scholarship on this play compared with Manley's other plays. Most literary scholarship concentrates on the text rather than performance. See, for example, Rachel Carnell, *Political Biography*, 94–95. Candice Brook Katz, "The Deserted Mistress in Mrs. Manley's The Lost Lover, 1696," *Restoration and Eighteenth-Century Theatre Research* 16 (1977): 27–39. The notable exceptions include theater historians who examine this play in the context of other performances, including Gilli Bush-Bailey, *Treading the Bawds: Actresses and Playwrights on the Late-Stuart Stage* (Manchester: Manchester University Press, 2006) and Nancy Copeland, *Staging Gender in Behn and Centlivre: Women's Comedy and the Theatre* (Aldershot: Ashgate, 2004).
5. Preface to *The Lost Lover* in *Eighteenth-century Women Playwrights* Volume 1. General editor Derek Hughes (London: Pickering & Chatto, 2001), 5.
6. Ibid., 5.
7. Ibid., 6.
8. Preface to *The Lucky Chance, or An Alderman's Bargain* in *The Rover and Other Plays*, ed. Jane Spencer (Oxford: Oxford University Press, 1995): 188–191.

9. Jacky Bratton, *New Readings in Theatre History* (Cambridge: Cambridge University Press, 2003).
10. Ibid., 37.
11. See Linda R. Payne, "Delariviere Manley" *Dictionary of Literary Biography* Vol. 80. *Restoration and Eighteenth-Century Dramatists* (1989): 126–130. Margaret Rubik and E. Mueller-Zettelmann, eds. Introduction. *Eighteenth-Century Women Playwrights* (London: Pickering and Chatto, 2001): 31–41, 36. *The Lost Lover* is advertised in the *London Gazette* (April 1696, no. 3166, 20–23), which implies the performance was no later than March.
12. Robert D. Hume describes the 1690s as a period where there is a split between the "hard" and the "humane" comedies, or "old" and "new" respectively, *The Development of English Drama in the Late Seventeenth Century* (Oxford: Clarendon Press, 1976). Laura Brown refers to the emergence of a moral agenda in comedies of this period as "transitional" and "incoherent" because of the merging of "two incompatible modes" of social satire and moral comedy, *English Dramatic Form, 1660–1760: An Essay in Generic History* (London: Yale University Press, 1981), 102–3.
13. Brown, *English Dramatic Form*.
14. Frank H. Ellis, *Sentimental Comedy: Theory and Practice* (Cambridge: Cambridge University Press, 1991), 14.
15. The scale and feature are detailed in Ellis's section, "sentimental comedy," in *Sentimental Comedy: Theory and Practice*, 10–22.
16. Ibid., 19–20.
17. *The Lost Lover*, 5.4: 54–5.
18. For example, it is a key text to demonstrate the problematic and inconsistent results of an attempt to mix the older "hard" comedy with morals as Brown observes, *English Dramatic Form*, 112–117.
19. Aparna Gollapudi, *Moral Reform in Comedy and Culture, 1696–1747* (Cornwall: Ashgate, 2011).
20. ibid., 32.
21. See Helga Drougge, "Colley Cibber's "Genteel Comedy": *Love's Last Shift* and *The Careless Husband*," *Studia Neophilologica* 54 (1982): 62–79.
22. Robert Hume describes the older sex comedies as "hard comedies" and the more humane, sympathetic ones as the "new comedy." Hume, *The Development of English Drama in the Late Seventeenth Century*, 16.
23. *The Lost Lover*, 1: 16.
24. Robert Hume, for example, identifies the Olivia-Smyrna subplot as the "exemplary" story with attention to some of the details and notes Belira as simply showing "the evil effects of yielding," *The Development of English Drama*, 421.
25. R. D. Hume, *The Rakish Stage: Studies in English Drama, 1660–1800* (Carbondale and Edwardsville: Southern Illinois Press, 1983), 154. See also Richard Braverman, "The Rake's Progress Revisited: Politics and Comedy in the Restoration," in *Cultural Readings of Restoration and Eighteenth-Century English Theater*, eds. J. Douglas Canfield and Deborah C. Payne (Athens and London: The University of Georgia Press, 1995), 141–168.
26. Hume, *The Rakish Stage*, 157.
27. Copeland, *Staging Gender in Behn and Centlivre*, 51.
28. Pat Gill, *Interpreting Ladies: Women, Wit, and Morality in the Restoration Comedy of Manners* (Athens: The University of Georgia Press, 1994), 145.

29. *The Lost Lover*, 2.1: 15.
30. Ibid., 1.1: 11.
31. Ibid., 1.i: 11–12.
32. Ibid., 5.ii: 36.
33. Ibid., 5.2: 39.
34. See chapter 5 in Derek Hughes, *The Theatre of Aphra Behn* (Hampshire: Palgrave Macmillan, 2001), 80–115.
35. Aphra Behn, *The Feigned Courtesans*, 5.4.154. In *The Rover and Other Plays*, ed. Jane Spencer (Oxford: Oxford University Press, 1995), 179. On the libertine fantasy of the heroine see Robert Markley, "Behn and the Unstable Traditions of Social Comedy," in *The Cambridge Companion to Aphra Behn*, eds. Derek Hughes and Janet Todd (Cambridge: Cambridge University Press, 2004), 98–117.
36. Katz explores Manley's version of the deserted mistress type in excellent detail in her essay. However, she does not observe the intertheatrical reworking on Behn's *The Rover*. "The Deserted Mistress in Mrs. Manley's *The Lost Lover*, 1696."
37. Gill, *Interpreting Ladies*, 155 and Pat Gill, "Gender, Sexuality and Marriage," in *The Cambridge Companion to Restoration Theatre*, ed. Deborah Payne Fisk (Cambridge: Cambridge University Press, 2000): 191–208, 195.
38. Gill, *Interpreting Ladies*, 14.
39. For further examples, see Katz, "The Deserted Mistress in Mrs. Manley's The Lost Lover, 1696."
40. Jacqueline Pearson, *The Prostituted Muse: Images of Women and Women Dramatists, 1642–1737* (Brighton: Harvester, 1988).
41. *The Lost Lover*, 5.2: 37.
42. Ibid., 5.2: 37.
43. Ibid., 2.2: 52.
44. Ibid., 4.1: 29.
45. Ibid., 4.1: 29.
46. Hughes, *The Theatre of Aphra Behn*, 112.
47. *The Lost Lover*, 5.1: 353–357.
48. Ibid., 5.2: 37.
49. *The Rover*, 5.1. 221.
50. For an account of the split with details of the key documentation involved see Judith Milhous, *Thomas Betterton and the Management of Lincoln's Inn Fields 1695–1708* (Carbondale and Edwardsville: Southern Illinois University Press, 1979). For more recent research on the actress's role in negotiations see Bush-Bailey, *Treading the Bawds*.
51. On the significance of the actors and actresses to the meaning of plays see, for example, Tanya Caldwell, "Meanings of *All for Love*, 1677–1813," *Comparative Drama* 38. 2/3 (Summer 2004): 183–211.
52. Preface, 5.
53. Bush-Bailey, *Treading the Bawds*, 137. Also see Katharine Beutner's contribution to this collection for more specific analysis of this attack on Manley.
54. Barry played Helena in *The Rover* and was often paired with Thomas Betterton in the familiar "gay couple" relationship. However, she became connected with Restoration tragedy, working most notably with Thomas Otway. She was also renowned for playing prostitutes and mistresses with an ability to make them sympathetic. For a detailed examination of her career, see Elizabeth Howe,

The First English Actresses: Women and Drama 1660–1700 (Cambridge: Cambridge University Press, 1992).

55. Preface to *The Royal Mischief*, 49. This concurs with contemporary opinion such as Colley Cibber's comments. He says about Barry, "In the Art of exciting Pity, she had Power beyond all the Actresses I have yet seen, or what your Imagination can conceive." Colley Cibber, *An Apology for the Life of Colley Cibber*, ed. B. R. S. Fone (Ann Arbor: University of Michigan Press, 1968), 92.

56. See Howe, *The First English Actresses*, 136–146.

57. *The Lost Lover*, 2.1: 17.

58. Ibid., 5.1: 40.

59. Epilogue spoken by Miss Cross. *The Lost Lover*, 41.

60. See Chapter 3 and especially p. 71 in Paula Backscheider, *Spectacular Politics: Theatrical Power and Mass Culture in Early Modern England* (Baltimore: Johns Hopkins University, 1993), 71–104; Jane Spencer, *Aphra Behn's Afterlife* (Oxford: Oxford University Press, 2000), 150–51. Also, see Katharine Beutner's essay in this collection, which challenges the limitations of "feminocentric" readings of Manley's work and the need to recognize attacks within the way "women write women." Chris Mounsey's reading of this play as part of Manley's "political strategy" also contributes to more complex understandings of her early work.

61. In her essay, Beutner suggests, along with Paula McDowell, that Orinda probably represents Catharine Trotter. My attention to the overt link made between Orinda and Katherine Philips does not disallow the potential for the character to also be a satiric attack on Trotter. The key point is that Manley uses the flexible boundaries between stage and "real life" to promote the "Behn" literary line.

62. See, for example, Sarah Prescott, *Women, Authorship and Literary Culture, 1660–1740* (Basingstoke: Palgrave Macmillan, 2003).

10 Delarivier Manley Understands the Ladies Better Than You

The Female Wits, Genre, and Feminocentric Satire

Katharine Beutner

The Female Wits, The Nine Muses, and Manley's Personae

It is a truism of literary history that female literary ambition often attracts ridicule and satirical dismissal. Delarivier Manley, herself a tireless producer of dismissive satire, suffered this fate in October 1696, when the Drury Lane theater company produced the satirical play *The Female Wits or, the Triumvirate of Poets at Rehearsal* in response to Manley's having withdrawn *The Royal Mischief* from Drury Lane and taken it to Thomas Betterton's new company at Lincoln's Inn Fields.[1] Purporting to offer a behind-the-scenes glimpse of Manley at work, the play cast her as "Marsilia," an arrogant, flamboyant, and viciously hypocritical woman playwright, and Catharine Trotter and Mary Pix as her hapless colleagues and supposed friends, "Calista" and "Mrs. Wellfed." The anonymously published play follows Marsilia from her boudoir to a rehearsal at the theater, where she holds court over a group of friends, sycophants, and enemies as long-suffering actors rehearse a bombastic tragedy based on *The Royal Mischief*. Modern critics generally assume that *The Female Wits* was thrown together by a group of Drury Lane actors, though Lucyle Hook suggests that the actor and writer Joseph Haynes may have been the group's prime mover.[2] Its title page credits no author. Yet its authors, whoever they may have been, seem to have discerned vital characteristics of Manley's writing and the multifariousness of her public personae. In this essay, I examine the ways that the portrait of Marsilia in *The Female Wits* anticipates Manley's later expressions of bitter disappointment in the trajectory of her literary career and her attacks on other women writers as weak and hypocritical. These attacks, which demand a reading that attends to the variety of genres in which Manley wrote, ought also to complicate our use of the term "feminocentric."

When *The Female Wits* was first performed in 1696, the women it caricatured—Delarivier Manley, Catharine Trotter, and Mary Pix—were friends and colleagues of a sort. They lauded one another in prologues and plotted to annex the masculine province of the stage. Manley vowed in her

first published poem, addressed to Catharine Trotter, that she and her female
cohort would recapture poetic glory for womankind:

> *Orinda*, and the fair *Astrea* gone,
> Not one was found to fill the Vacant Throne.
> Aspiring Man had quite regain'd the Sway,
> Again had Taught us humbly to obey;
> Till you (Natures third start, in favour of our Kind)
> With stronger Arms, their Empire have disjoyn'd,
> And snatch't a Lawrel which they thought their Prize.
> Thus Conqu'ror, with your Wit, as with your Eyes.
> Fired by the bold Example, I would try
> To turn our Sexes weaker Destiny.
> O! How I long in the Poetic Race,
> To loose the Reins, and give their Glory Chase;
> For, thus Encourag'd and thus led by you,
> Methinks we might more Crowns than theirs Subdue.[3]

In 1700, these ambitious women writers produced an elegiac collection
honoring John Dryden, *The Nine Muses*; Manley seems to have served as
its editor and prime mover, and was the only author to include two poems,
written in the personae of "Melpomene" and "Thalia," the tragic and comic
muses.[4] Both poems involve forms of poeticized grief that Manley would
later mock; both invoke the act of mourning with other female companions,
the question of when it is appropriate to demonstrate grief in public, and
the pastoral elegy as a refined expression of loss. Though the anthology
as a whole strikes a solemn and respectful tone, these poems operate on
two levels at once: the muses mourn together for Dryden's death, while the
women writers embodying the muses mourn, too—but mourn by displaying
their skill and their solidarity. Manley's first poem, as Melpomene, begins
the collection by entreating "all my sisters" to "in Consort join" to weep
for the great poet.[5]

Yet by the time *The Female Wits* was printed in 1704, Manley's friendships with Trotter, Pix, and other women writers had soured. In later
works—such as her best-known scandal fiction, 1709's *Secret Memoirs
and Manners of Several Persons of Quality, of Both Sexes. From the New
Atalantis, an Island in the Mediterranean*—Manley viciously satirized her
former friends for what she viewed as their hypocritical behavior and abandonment of their literary ambitions. No longer divine muses, Trotter, Pix,
and Sarah Fyge Egerton appear in *The New Atalantis* and elsewhere as
prudes and liars, while Manley paints herself as a trusting, wounded target
of their spleen. *The Female Wits* portrays her quite differently, as a self-
absorbed hypocrite filled with grandiose theatrical ambitions who mistreats
her female friends. The play's comic action relies on the premise that women
writers must be conniving, hypocritical, and cruel to one another. In effect, it

is feminocentric satire. I propose that the content of this play and its relation to Manley's work should inspire us to attend more carefully to the ways we use the term "feminocentric" when studying the writing lives of early eighteenth-century women. Though Manley's body of work evinces profound concern with women and their suffering, her attacks on other women complicate her self-presentation as a writer who, like Marsilia, "understand[s] the ladies better than you." Yet little attention has been devoted to Manley's willingness to ridicule female colleagues to better her position in the literary marketplace, and few critics have remarked upon the disjunction between the Manley of the 1690s and the Manley who wrote *The New Atalantis* in 1709.[6] As we reconsider Manley's import, I suggest that we include in our studies the text of *The Female Wits*, which offers a contemporary view of a writer who is neither the innocent "Dela Manley" of her early publications nor the savvy "female intelligencer" most critics claim her to be. A study of this play further requires that we consider how the genres in which Manley wrote shaped her self-presentation and her works' reception.

Rachel Carnell's recent political biography describes the Manley we generally accept today: "an intellectually engaged political thinker and a writer who was always fully conscious of the political tides of the publishing world around her."[7] Early feminist attempts at writing Manley's life conjured a similar picture. Fidelis Morgan's *A Woman of No Character: An Autobiography of Mrs Manley*, published in 1986, begins with Morgan's notice to the reader that she has "replaced the romantic names with the generally accepted identifications of the actual people in Manley's life."[8] In other words, Morgan composed Manley's life from pieces of her works, making explicit the process—now regarded with critical suspicion—through which so many early women writers have been reanimated after centuries of neglect. Morgan treats Manley's works as a set of "disguises" under which we can discern the real Manley: a savvy, confident woman author whose works offer proof of her worldliness. Both depictions ascribe to Manley a remarkable level of agency and volition; both critics suggest that Manley chose and even reveled in her status as a hack writer. The final section of this essay demonstrates why such a reading simplifies Manley's experience in the literary marketplace.

In the larger study from which this essay is drawn,[9] I argue that Manley considers her satirical prose and post-1690s occasional poetry touched with "but a faint relish of the muses" and views her own need to write for pay as a betrayal of her early poetic aspirations.[10] The trajectory Manley's career followed—as she first exchanged complimentary poems with friends, then wrote plays with varying success, later turned to print publication, prose writing, and hackwork to support herself, and finally defended herself in print—is echoed in the writing lives of numerous early eighteenth-century women who initially participated in coteries.[11] In order to recognize the repetition of this trajectory, however, we must consider Manley's literary career holistically rather than enforcing an ahistorical separation between works written in different genres. As Betty Schellenberg and Margaret Ezell have shown in their vital historiographical studies of the criticism of women writers, genre fashions among critics occur cyclically. Women have at times been anthologized in verse collections and recognized chiefly for their poetic skills; in other periods, critics have emphasized women's particular talents as novelists, often to the exclusion of their work in other genres.[12] To examine women authors only as poets, playwrights, or prose writers may lead us to construct histories of their literary careers that obscure the nuanced relationships between literary genres, between women and their readers, and between women writers themselves. Different generic forms, which demanded different aesthetic strategies, accumulated and shed historically specific markers of class, economic status, and political sympathy.[13] Approaching women's literary work more holistically can allow us to parse and historicize these fine gradations of signification and appreciate the ways in which the genres women chose were often intertwined and cross-pollinating.

For example, Manley's expressions of bitterness about being forced to abandon her loftier poetic ambitions are inextricably linked to her attacks on female colleagues as hypocrites and literary frauds, and occur in works written in a variety of genres. While she expresses this bitterness in the autobiographical apologia *Rivella* (1714), she also embeds deprecatory self-portraits in her scandal fictions—the same works in which she ridicules disguised versions of other women writers. Furthermore, contemporary depictions of Manley included in texts like *The Female Wits* reveal that even her own colleagues had discerned the link between Manley's mistreatment of other women writers and the grandiosity of the ambitions that drove her in the 1690s—and that they predicted her need to seek "some more profitable Employ" than genteel coterie writing.[14] In other words, the authors of *The Female Wits* seem to have viewed Manley's poetic and dramatic ambition as incompatible with female friendship, even as she and the women she would later attack publicly insisted otherwise. Given the social and literary saturation of satire against women at the turn of the eighteenth century—in the Juvenalian tradition, in British and French *querelle des femmes* texts,[15] in periodicals by Richard Steele, Aaron Hill, and others—it is perhaps unsurprising that Manley's bold pronouncements drew scorn. But their prediction raises the question of how Manley's later drive to annihilate in fiction the writing women she had once befriended was perceived by her colleagues to be linked to these social discourses, and how our contemporary understanding of Manley has been shaped by trends in feminist critical discourse.

Revisiting "Feminocentrism"

Before turning to an examination of the play itself, I want to re-consider the term "feminocentric," frequently used by critics of early eighteenth-century women's writing to denote a state of proto-feminist awareness evident in a text or a particular author's body of work. Several critics, most notably Ros Ballaster and Ruth Herman, have applied this term to Manley's works, and, by extension, to her worldview.[16] The word "feminocentric" was not coined by feminist critics,[17] but it nonetheless resonates with Hélène Cixous's edict, in "The Laugh of the Medusa," that "woman must write woman,"[18] and since it was first broadly popularized around 1980 by Nancy K. Miller and other critics, the term has entered standard feminist critical discourse.

In its most basic sense, this adjective suits Manley's body of work, which is thoroughly concerned with women. But when applied by feminist critics writing since the 1980s, the word "feminocentric" often has a positive overtone, implying that a work centered around women may be more charitable to them than a comparable "androcentric" (or "phallocentric," to use the word Cixous's translators choose) work of the same period. It might be fair for a modern critic to argue that an eighteenth-century woman writer's choice to produce a female-centered work was, itself, feminist or proto-feminist, a stance Cixous would likely approve. Yet the critical unwillingness to acknowledge women writers' satirical attacks on one another calls this assumption of goodwill into question.[19] Some critics have questioned the validity of assuming a larger "feminocentric tradition" in women's writing of the early eighteenth century. In a review essay published in 2000, Kathryn King celebrates many elements of Carol Barash's *English Women's Poetry, 1649–1714*. Yet she notes that Barash's assumption of "a kind of ongoing intertext, a web of interconnections, a shared source of energy, common preoccupations, political tropes and iconic figures—a distinctively female community over time" relies upon several significant misreadings of the poetry she analyzes.[20]

Studies of Manley are not immune to this type of transitive reading. When Ros Ballaster describes "The *New Atalantis* ... [as] the most thoroughly feminocentric of her novels, almost exclusively narrated to women by women and about women," her formulation suggests a kind of proto-feminist agenda to this generic model.[21] Elsewhere, Ballaster notes that "Manley, like Behn, presents her satirical powers as both female and heroic,"[22] emphasizing a positivist stance to female-generated satire against men. Yet Manley employs those satirical powers to create numerous negative portraits of women: of Sarah Churchill, portrayed there and in *Memoirs of Europe* as a hypersexualized witch who will sacrifice nearly anything to accomplish her political ends; of the "new Cabal," a group of crypto-sapphists who are both satirized and celebrated for their independence from men; and of the women writers Manley ridicules.

Ballaster employs the term "feminocentric" as a generic descriptor for Manley's scandal fiction primarily in order to draw connections between her writing and the amatory fiction tradition, but in doing so, she represents both Manley and later writers such as Eliza Haywood as larval proto-feminists. Certainly, *The New Atalantis* laments how commonly men stray from women or betray them, in terms that may well have shaped the amatory fiction model

of heterosexual romantic relations and the sub-genre itself, with its stereotyp-
ically predatory male characters, beautifully suffering ladies, and exclamatory
style. But Haywood's debt to Manley also demonstrates a similarly vexed
practice of "feminocentrism." In her scandal fictions, she adopted Manley's
satirical methods, but did not only attack prominent political figures—she
wrote an entire *roman à clef* novella excoriating Martha Fowke Sansom, a
former literary friend and colleague.[23] Haywood's adoption of Manley's literary strategies produced works centered on women *and* works intended to
destroy women's reputations, and this complicated inheritance demonstrates
why we must also consider applying the term "feminocentric" to their shared
satirical model of "women writing women." Broadening our understanding
of the term will encourage fuller and more accurate readings of the messy
multiplicity of ways in which women writers interacted with one another as
they attempted to move toward professionalization.

Marsilia and Her Friends

The most explicitly feminocentric satire in Manley's literary life is in fact
not to be found in her own work, but in the portrait of her as Marsilia in
The Female Wits. Marsilia's pride and hypocrisy are the central conceits of
the play, which functions as an extended joke about the effects of Manley's
two-faced treatment of Calista and Mrs. Wellfed and her profound misun-
derstanding of the social codes governing women's interactions. Marsilia
believes that she can mock other women in clever asides while maintaining
an appearance of friendship and demanding their praise. She seems to think
that all female friends treat one another in this manner and does not realize that they are perfectly aware of her mistreatment of them. In the play's
opening scene, Marsilia expects Calista and Mrs. Wellfed to visit her before
she goes to the playhouse. Mrs. Wellfed arrives before Calista does, and as
they wait, Marsilia execrates Calista in the following terms:

MAR: Oh! 'Tis the vainest, proudest, senseless Thing, she pretends to Grammar,
      writes in Mood and Figure; does every thing methodically.—Poor
      Creature! She shews me her Works first; I always commend 'em, with
      a Design she shou'd expose 'em, and the Town be so kind to laugh her
      out of her Follies.
MRS. WELLFED: That's hard in a Friend.
MAR: But 'tis very usual.[24]

When Calista arrives, however, Marsilia lauds her as "the charming'st
Nymph of all *Apollo*'s train," leaving Mrs. Wellfed to remark (accurately) to
the audience: "So, I suppose my Reception was preceeded [sic] like this."[25]
    Only a few lines later, Marsilia crows about their collegiality, friendship,
and talent: "Now here's the Female Triumvirate, methinks 'twou'd be but
civil of the Men to lay down their Pens for one Year, and let us divert the

Town; but if we shou'd, they'd certainly be asham'd ever to take 'em up again."[26] This dead-on satirical portrait of Manley as laurel-hungry artist, clearly based on her self-presentation in early 1696, echoes the language of the poems Manley and Trotter wrote to celebrate one another's plays and recalls the dreams of female poetic triumph that Manley trumpeted when she entered the literary marketplace. The previously cited poem written by Manley to preface Trotter's *Agnes de Castro* brims with idealized images and rhetoric of this sort, and poems contributed by Trotter and Pix for the publication of Manley's play *The Royal Mischief*—the very play being mocked in *The Female Wits*—communicate an equally triumphalist spirit. Pix labels Manley "the unequal'd wonder of the Age, / Pride of our Sex, and Glory of the Stage," a poet who "snatch[es] Lawrels with undisputed right, / And Conquer[s] when you but begin to fight; /... / Like *Sappho* Charming, like *Afra* Eloquent, / Like Chast *Orinda*, sweetly Innocent."[27] Trotter invokes Manley as a "greater genius" who will "aid" her in her attempt to "invade" the "Borders of [male poets'] Empire," while an unsigned poem complicates this portrait slightly by describing Manley's eyes and hands as objects of desire, but also the tools of writing and instructing, and boasts: "Quote *Ovid* no more ye amorous Swains; / *Delia*, than *Ovid* has more moving Strains."[28] The bombastic praise of these prefatory poems is typical of the period, but the appearance of collegiality among women writers they create is not.

Given this apparent solidarity, the play's portrait of Manley seems prescient because it demonstrates that Marsilia merely plays at sisterliness. She ridicules Mrs. Wellfed, countering the fop Mr. Aw'dwell's praise of the woman by exclaiming in surprise "That you shou'd wrong your Judgment thus! Don't do it, because you think her my Friend: I profess, I can't forbear saying, her Heroicks want Beautiful Uniformity as much as her Person, and her Comedies are as void of Jests as her Conversation."[29] This attack on Wellfed anticipates Manley's later treatment of Sarah Fyge Egerton, in particular, in its equation of bodily ungainliness with poetic failure. It also characterizes Marsilia as a woman who "can't forbear" transforming friends into targets.

Though Marsilia remains the comic center of the play, Calista draws ire for her youth, beauty, and pedantry, and Mrs. Wellfed for her stolid mediocrity. Both grovel to convince George Powell to produce their plays. Yet the text accords them marginally more respect than it does Manley, who, the preface notes, has "of late discontinued" the "Correspondence with the Muses" for which she was "sufficiently known ... for some more profitable Employ."[30] The preface describes Trotter and Pix as "two Gentlewomen that have made no small Struggle in the World to get into Print; and who are now in such a State of Wedlock to Pen and Ink, that it will be very difficult for them to get out of it."[31] Though Manley is also labeled a gentlewoman, her relationship to print does not resemble "Wedlock." Instead she sacrifices feminine-coded artistic aims for commercial opportunity, as she abandons her "Conference with the Muses" for extra-literary work. Nor, it seems, did the works she produced in 1696 evince an appropriately feminine modesty. Mrs. Wellfed, uninspired but correct, channels the voice of the male and female critics who condemned the sexual content of Manley's plays. When she expresses concern about the "warmth" of a few of Marsilia's favorite lines, Marsilia dismisses her blithely, stating, "Sure, Madam, I understand the ladies better than you."[32] This mistaken confidence in her understanding of female subjectivity and desire represents the heart of the satirical attack on Manley in *The Female Wits*.

Marsilia claims to possess a special ability to craft drama that will involve the emotions of women. In effect, she identifies *The Royal Mischief* as feminocentric. She singles out the female roles in her plays to explain why "there's none like" her dramas in the London theatrical world: "The turns are so surprizing, the Love so passionate, the Lines so strong; 'Gad, I'm afraid there's not a Female Actress in *England* can reach 'em."[33] Manley herself was careful to honor—at least in print—the famous actresses who graced her plays.[34] But Marsilia seems utterly ignorant of the methods of preserving relationships with other women, has no interest in discerning their true feelings, and ascribes little value to those ties. As she declaims later in the play, "I always choose to believe what p[l]eases me best."[35] Marsilia's willful blindness is humorous, of course. But it also suggests that Manley intentionally skews her perception of the world according to the dictates of her own desires and opinions—an excellent quality in a political satirist, perhaps, but a difficult one in a friend.

Eventually, having agreed that Marsilia is "very tedious," Calista and Mrs. Wellfed leave to dine together, breaking the triumvirate.[36] Their reactions unmask Marsilia's deceitful doubleness and demonstrate that her conception of herself as a woman writer knowledgeable about the sentiments of other women is deeply mistaken. Feminocentrism, in the farcical world of *The Female Wits*, means directing one's satirical fire chiefly at women for the purpose of disguising one's own failings. According to this definition, the authors of *The Female Wits* have also produced a feminocentric play, as their satire focuses largely on women. The silly fops who attend Marsilia are props, not targets, and the men of the theater earn only some gentle ribbing for their drinking habits. The play's final dismissal of Manley as "*neither worth*" the "*love or hate*" of those around her relies for dramatic impact upon its depiction of Marsilia as ungrateful and hypocritical in her relationships with women.[37] When Marsilia declares at the work's end that "by this Play, the Town will perceive what a woman can do," the play's immediate satirical targets are the lavish absurdity of her prose and plotting and the hubris of feminine attempts to seize the stage. But her statement seems equally applicable to the play's revelation of her hypocritical treatment of fellow female writers. What a woman can do is attack other women.

Lucyle Hook argues that *The Female Wits* was "merely the distillation" of masculine critical opinion regarding Manley and other contemporary women playwrights.[38] This backlash against female authors was not limited to the stage, nor was it unusual for a powerful woman to be satirized as jealous and conniving—Manley herself would level the same charges at Sarah Churchill. But in 1696, she had barely begun to develop the satirical strategies she would deploy against other women in *The New Atalantis*, its sequel *Memoirs of Europe*, and the autobiographical *Rivella*.[39] This renders the specific satiric thrust of *The Female Wits* and the sharpness with which it targets Manley particularly startling, as it could not simply represent a turning of her own rhetorical tools upon herself. As we seek to study Manley's literary career in a more holistic light, we must try to parse the importance of this play—first a work of performance, and eight years later a work in print—as a contemporary interpretation of Manley's writing and of her persona. What, in 1696, might have inspired this apparently prophetic characterization of Manley as two-faced and willing to ridicule supposed friends to better her own position in the literary marketplace?

If we credit the authors of *The Female Wits* with more subtlety than they display in print, we might theorize that the character of Marsilia is meant to exaggerate the hint of feminine rivalry present in Manley's first play, *The Lost Lover*. In a footnote to her chapter on Manley, Paula McDowell suggests that the character of Orinda, the "Affected Poetess" who takes her name from Katherine Philips's poetic moniker,[40] is meant to satirize Catharine Trotter Cockburn as well as other female writers. McDowell states:

> I read Manley's Orinda as I do her "Astrea" in *The New Atalantis*: as a satirical composite of the contemporary women writers (or rather their self-representations) Manley did not like.[41]

Yet Orinda barely appears in *The Lost Lover*. She speaks one line that evokes *The Female Wits*, declaring that she "finish't a Copy of Verses last night, which I have sent to half a score of my Friends for their approbation."[42] But it is not clear at all why Manley might have wanted to produce a satirical composite character resembling Trotter in 1696, and McDowell does not explain this. She observes elsewhere that "Manley tended to place herself in opposition to didacts ... and she frequently portrayed contemporary moralists as hypocrites."[43] Orinda is not a hypocrite, however—her chief vice is thinking too well of her own poetry. She is "silly," as Susan Staves notes, self-centered, and entirely transparent.[44] Though she probably does represent Trotter, Orinda's presence in *The Lost Lover* does not constitute an attack of the sort Manley would launch against Trotter and other women in *The New Atalantis*.

Conflating these two types of attack contributes to the static reading of Manley and her career that has dominated Manley criticism. I use the term "career" advisedly here, though critics continue to debate whether or not the concept of an intentionally built career can be applied to writers working in the early eighteenth century (and, in particular, to women who supported themselves by writing). Most admit that Alexander Pope viewed himself as an independent professional, despite his ties to the aristocratic wealthy. But the "romance of obscurity," to borrow the phrase Christine Blouch has used to characterize the treatment of Eliza Haywood, has shaded our thinking about the professional lives of women writers.[45] As Margaret Ezell has ably explained, the notion of an "evolutionary model" of feminism and of women's writing has also encouraged the "belief in a uniform female response to life."[46] This identification-driven approach to women's literary history has led critics to "read backward" by interpreting the eighteenth century according to twentieth-century theories of nineteenth-century relationships.[47] By doing so, critics have created a narrative in which deep female friendship, assumed to be an unalterable fact of interaction between women, simply becomes more freely and truly expressed in writing as centuries pass. Yet Manley, like other professional women writers of her time, understood the literary marketplace as a field of competition that required ambitious and intentional self-promotion. Marsilia's actions in *The Female Wits* reveal that her contemporaries observed and despised Manley's methods of self-promotion and of satirical self-defense.

In one sense, Fidelis Morgan is correct to speak of Manley as disguised in her autobiographical writings. Though Manley berated others for wearing public masks, she too adopted different personae: the innocent girl betrayed, the bold authoress, the noble patriot, the retired country woman writing for her own amusement, and the hack. I suggest that we can map these personae and explain the continuities in Manley's self-presentation without defaulting to the assumption that there is an essential Manley to be unearthed beneath the masks. If anything, the strongest continuity in Manley's work is her own use of accusations of masking and hypocrisy as rhetorical tools and the remarkably varied metaphors she employs to portray her enemies as hypocrites.

The simplest explanation for the play's characterization of Manley as Marsilia seems the most convincing. Manley may, in fact, have engaged in this sort of hypocritical behavior in the presence of the Drury Lane actors responsible for *The Female Wits* while they rehearsed *The Lost Lover*. The writers of *The Female Wits* would not likely have chosen to satirize Manley for qualities she did not possess at all. Effective satire depends on the sense of truth it conveys, as Manley herself would argue in her scandal fictions. I want to suggest the possibility that the Manley of *The Female Wits* might represent the real Manley—or *a* real Manley, at least, to the degree to which any person's behavior at a given time can stand in for his or her individual self. *The Female Wits* offers us an early glimpse of a Manley who has not been accounted for by critics, a Manley who is neither the bold and flexible businesswoman of Rachel Carnell's political biography nor the heroic proto-journalist of Paula McDowell's study.

Even if Manley did act hypocritically during the rehearsal of *The Lost Lover*, of course, Marsilia's vices may still reflect the writers' desire to characterize Manley as a symbol of women's failure to achieve parity in the literary marketplace or in the realm of aesthetic achievement. This characterization of Manley as a traitor to other women writers may also have been politically suggestive.[48] But the coterie in-jokiness of the play, in combination with its relative lack of literary sophistication, presents the tantalizing possibility that the Manley on the page might resemble a Manley who truly existed. As we grapple with that possibility, we must keep in mind the darker elements of Manley's works—we must observe both kinds of feminocentrism in her writing, and be careful not to obscure the viciousness, as well as the supportive boldness, of her vision of female literary community.

Writing out of Necessity

As I have argued, developing a more complex portrait of Manley's writing life requires attention to the importance of genre, and the act of shifting between genres, in the trajectory of Manley's literary career. I want to conclude this essay by demonstrating how Manley's self-fashioning relies upon a recognition of generic importance; how she, at times, plays upon contrasts between generic forms to lament the exigencies of her writing life. This is best illustrated by several moments in *The New Atalantis* in which Manley interpolates poems into her prose narrative and engages in her own variety of feminocentric literary criticism, identifying divisions between women writers of the sort that may have motivated the tension observed by the writers of *The Female Wits*.

Manley interpolates into the fabric of her narrative two poems by Anne Finch, Countess of Winchilsea, an ode by Elizabeth Taylor, and two of her own elegies, in which she introduces the character of "Delia," whom her readers later discover to be her own autobiographical persona in *The New Atalantis*. In the sections of narrative surrounding the elegies and "The Progress of Life," in particular, Manley depicts herself as a flatterer who writes for hire, and laments the state of contemporary poetry, implicating herself and other writers as substandard poets and panderers to the public taste. These interpolated poems mark points of tension not only in the narrative itself but in Manley's authorial persona.

In the little-noticed capsule narrative framing Anne Finch's previously unpublished poem entitled "The Progress of Life," Manley establishes a stark and surprisingly poignant opposition between women like Finch who write for "pleasure" and women like herself who write out of "necessity."[49] The speaker in Finch's poem complains of life's disappointing downward course, lamenting, "How promising's the book of fate / Till thro'ly understood!"[50] Though she clearly approves of the poem and its theme, Manley offers a critique of Finch's work in the voice of Astrea, one of the two deities touring Manley's allegorical England, whose name of course recalls Aphra Behn's poetic persona. Astrea suggests an alteration to one stanza of the poem, then concludes, "I presume she's one of the happy few that write out of pleasure and not necessity. By that means it's her own fault, if she publish any thing but what's good, for it's next to impossible to write much and write well."[51] Barred from considering herself one of the "real worthy" among the poets of her age by an awareness of her own artistic compromises, Manley defines herself against the elite tradition of female amateur writing of which Anne Finch was a part.[52] Furthermore, she presents this self-characterization in a section of prose narrative that envelops a poem that had likely been circulated in manuscript form. *The New Atalantis*, though primarily a work of political satire, therefore also functions as a poetic miscellany—and as a vehicle for attacks against rival women writers.

Early in the text of *Atalantis*, Manley engages in an attack of this sort against Mary Pix by way of another frame narrative with inset poems: in this case, her two elegies for Cary Coke, here called Sacharissa, "the richest widow in all Atalantis," and her husband Edward, who died only a few months earlier than she.[53] Manley introduces these elegies by marching the Cokes' opulent funeral parade directly across the paths of Astrea and Virtue, who disapprove of the dishonest "ceremony" of the shrieking mourners. Intelligence, their guide, retorts that the "true grief" Astrea seeks is "none of [the mourners'] business; they are paid for what they do," just as hack writers are.[54] Manley continues to develop a distressingly heartfelt indictment of those who write out of necessity, including herself. An "obscure poet" (Manley) wrote Edward Coke's elegy, Intelligence tells Astrea and Virtue, as a favor for a "lazy" friend whose "genius" had "shrunk" (Mary Pix) and who later mistreated the poet by claiming the elegy as his own.[55] Intelligence's claim to have the second Coke elegy "just warm from the muse, finished but yesterday and newly communicated to me, to be distributed abroad," reinforces the identification of Manley as the wronged poet in question.[56] Manley writes that the poet, "Justly incensed against the treachery of his friend ... resolves to own and print this piece in the next miscellanea."[57] The beginning of the first elegy immediately follows that line, temporarily transforming Manley's scandal fiction itself into "the next miscellanea," as McDowell has noted.[58]

In the first elegy, a stylized, melodramatic tribute to Edward Coke, two nymphs meet to bewail their own romantic losses and to participate in a morbid, unhealthy, and competitive variety of female storytelling and companionship. Joining in them in mourning is Delia, whom first-time readers of the text would not yet recognize as Manley's explicitly autobiographical persona within *The New Atalantis*—her life history appears later in the text.[59] Aminta introduces Delia simply as a heroic poetess, in lines that reveal the aims Manley still seems to have cherished for her poetry in 1709:

> Delia began to sing the hero dead;
> Delia had in Apollo's court been bred.
> Nor Afra, nor Orinda knew so well,
> Scarce Grecian Sappho, Delia to excel.[60]

Manley's references to Behn and Philips recall her 1696 poem to Trotter in celebration of *Agnes de Castro* and Pix's 1696 poem prefacing *The Royal Mischief*, both described earlier in this essay. McDowell suggests that Manley's claim to "excel" both poets here amounts to a rejection of what each woman represented, but this oversimplifies Manley's relationships to her predecessors.[61] Instead, Delia tops Aminta's hierarchy of women poets as a new Sappho for her times, worthy of elegizing the honorable Cokes.

Yet, in the prose narrative following this first elegy, Manley sabotages any promise of poetic truth or preservation offered in the poem and consequently undercuts Delia's role as heroic poetess. Astrea, "used to the genuine elegies of Molpomene … find[s] but a faint relish of the muses in this poem," and asks Intelligence if the poet "drew [Coke] as he was, or as he ought to have been?"[62] In fact, Manley never presents the Cokes as they were, as Intelligence's later satirical recounting of the Cokes' history demonstrates. In the elegies, she lauds them with flattering epithets, while in the main narrative they become satirical targets—and, in the case of Cary Coke, are also reduced to amatory-fiction stereotypes. Most importantly, Astrea's choice to contrast this poem with the "genuine elegies of Molpomene" refers directly to Manley's first poem in *The Nine Muses*, which she published under the name of "Melpomene: *The Tragick Muse*," as noted earlier in this essay.[63] The poignancy of Manley's self-characterization as a hack writer deepens further in the commentary following the second elegy, for Cary Coke, in which the same two nymphs who "live with horror, and [were] formed for pain" rise to a histrionic crescendo of celebration for the Cokes' appearance as constellations in the skies, where "shining gods such happiness approve."[64] In the satirical frame narrative immediately following the poem, Astrea dryly remarks that the shining gods did no such thing on her last visit to the stars, and Intelligence explains that a desire for patronage, not truth, motivates the author of the elegies.

In these two elegies, Manley creates an idealized poetic self-portrait that evokes her 1690s boasts of a heroic literary talent equal to that of Behn or Philips—the boasts mocked so astutely by *The Female Wits*—and the adulatory poems she once received from supportive female friends. Then, through the conjunction of frame narrative and poetic content, she dismisses the elegies and the self-portrait as hackwork produced for purely mercenary reasons. By first suggesting her own authorship of these elegies, then mocking their falseness, she reveals the poems—and, by extension, herself—to be entirely insincere, but "well enough, according to the rate of the present writers."[65] Though she derides the state of contemporary poetry, she also indicts herself as a substandard practitioner who has been forced by financial necessity to produce bombastic verse for pay. These sections of *The New Atalantis* depict a Manley who has returned to the genre in which she began writing not as the triumphant poetic leader prophesied in her dedicatory poem to *Agnes de Castro*, but as a mid-career writer driven, as the writers of *The Female Wits* prophesied, to "seek some more profitable employ."

Manley's distinction between the "happy few" who write for pleasure and the presumably less happy majority who write to support themselves demonstrates that at least one professionally successful woman author writing in the first decade of the eighteenth century considered the growing divides between manuscript and print circulation and between poetry and prose to be formative of a writer's identity. Yet that understanding did not drive her to produce the kind of "feminocentric" writing we might, as feminist critics, hunger to see. The implications of the portrait of Manley as Marsilia in *The Female Wits* justify its inclusion in the canon of Manley studies and argue for a holistic approach to Manley's literary career and to the career trajectories of other eighteenth-century women writers, as well as an expansion of what it means for a work by, for, or about women to be considered "feminocentric." This more capacious understanding of Manley's work and life will illuminate not only the sharpness of her political wit but the poignancy of Marsilia's claim to understand the ladies, Madam, better than you.

Notes

1. Rachel Carnell, *A Political Biography of Delarivier Manley* (London: Pickering & Chatto, 2008), 83. See Carnell's discussion of the date of the play's production and the delay between production and the play's printing in 1704.
2. Lucyle Hook, introduction to *The Female Wits: Or, the Triumvirate of Poets at Rehearsal. A Comedy. As it was Acted Several Days Successively with Great Applause at the Theatre-Royal in Drury- Lane. By Her Majesty's Servants*, by "Mr. W.M." (Los Angeles: William Andrews Clark Memorial Library Augustan Reprint Society Publication no. 124, University of California, 1967), xii. Originally published anonymously (London: William Turner et al., 1704).
3. "To the Author of Agnes de Castro," signed "Dela Manley," was published with Cockburn's play in 1696; see Bibliography. No earlier published works by Manley have been found (McDowell, *Women of Grub Street*, 266).
4. Both of Manley's poems are also signed "Mrs. M——" (*NM* 1, 11). The other contributors to *The Nine Muses* included Sarah Fyge (later Egerton) as Erato, Catharine Trotter as "Calliope: *The Heroick Muse*," Mary Pix as "Clio: *The Historick Muse*," "Mrs. D. E." as "Polimnia: *Of Rhetorick*," "Mrs. L. D." as "Terpsichore: *A Lyrick Muse*," "Mrs. J. E." as "Euterpe: *The Lyrick Muse*," and "the Honourable the Lady P——" (Lady Sarah Piers) as "Urania: *The Divine Muse*." Carnell states that Manley "helped to organize" this anthology, citing an October 1700 letter from Sarah Piers to Catharine Trotter that may refer to Manley's request for a poem (115; qtd. in Carnell 262 n. 49).
5. Manley, *Nine Muses*, 1.
6. Victoria Joule's recent article on the *Nine Muses* notes hints of conflict in that nominally collaborative collection and problematizes the notion of Manley as "literary foremother," and Carole Fungaroli Sargent's essay on the pie fight in *The New Atalantis* performs a valuable close reading of the political nuances of that scene, as well as its meaning for Manley's friendship with Sarah Fyge Egerton.
7. Carnell, *Political Biography*, 4.

8. Fidelis Morgan, *A Woman of No Character: an Autobiography of Mrs. Manley* (Boston: Faber & Faber, 1986), 13. Morgan offers a "Key to Pseudonyms" for the real-life identities of characters in Manley's fiction, and treats these identifications as essentially factual; see p. 165.

9. Katharine Beutner, *Writing for Pleasure or Necessity: Conflict among Literary Women, 1700–1750*. PhD diss, University of Texas, 2011.

10. Delarivier Manley, *New Atalantis*, ed. Rosalind Ballaster (New York: Penguin, 1991), 54. The complete title of the work, as published in 1709, is: *Secret Memoirs and Manners of Several Persons of Quality, of Both Sexes. From the New Atalantis, an Island in the Mediterranean. Written Originally in Italian.*

11. Beutner, *Writing for Pleasure*. The writing lives of Eliza Haywood, Martha Fowke Sansom, and Laetitia Pilkington represent slightly different versions of this trajectory, as I argued in my dissertation. Elizabeth Thomas (1675–1731) offers an especially clear example of this career trajectory. Early in her career, before being financially ruined by family legal problems, she wrote the poetry and genteel letters that formed the germ of *Pylades and Corinna* (1731–32), the volume featuring her work which was posthumously published by Edmund Curll. Her association with Curll began after her financial slide.

12. Ezell addresses this habit of treating women as a "separate category" of writers in *Writing Women's Literary History*, 88; for more recent examples of verse collections, see valuable poetry-focused books by Roger Lonsdale, Paula Backscheider, and Emma Donoghue.

13. Rachel Carnell argues in this volume, for example, that Manley's self-defensive autobiographical text *The Adventures of Rivella* must be read in the generic context of the political secret history, a form that would have been "legible" to her contemporaries (15). Chris Mounsey's essay offers another holistic study, examining *Letters Writen* in conversation with *The Lost Lover* and *The Royal Mischief*, and reading all three as examples of Varronian satire. Finally, Jean McBain's important chapter on Manley's stint as editor of the Tory *Examiner*—briefly replacing Jonathan Swift—contrasts the stylistic features of Manley's periodical writing with her other works.

14. Hook, *Female Wits*, pref. 2.

15. For an excellent summary of the 1680s/1690s *querelles des femmes* texts and how they defined the contemporary cultural discourse on women, see Rae Blanchard, "Richard Steele and the Status of Women," *Studies in Philology* 26.3 (1929): 325–55.

16. Herman refers to the "gyno-centric elements of Manley's work" (Ruth Herman, *The Business of a Woman: the Political Writings of Delarivier Manley* [Cranbury, NJ: Delaware University Press, 2003], 15). See also Ros Ballaster, *Seductive Forms: Women's Amatory Fiction from 1684–1740* (Oxford: Clarendon, 1992), 114–15, 145; and Ballaster's introduction to *The New Atalantis*, xiii. Anne Kelley has also adopted this term in her recent study of Catharine Trotter, which is subtitled "An early modern writer in the vanguard of feminism." William Beatty Warner has criticized Ballaster's use of the term ("Formulating Fiction: Romancing the General Reader in Early Modern Britain," in *Cultural Institutions of the Novel*, ed. Deidre Lynch and William Beatty Warner [Durham and London: Duke University Press, 1996], 279–305), but it otherwise seems to have entered into standard feminist critical discourse with little debate about its precise meaning or usage.

17. The first usage of the term that Google Books turns up is from 1919, in a work by Arthur Wallace Calhoun entitled *A Social History of the American Family from Colonial Times to the Present*, 119. There is no *OED* entry for "feminocentric" or "feminocentrism."

18. Hélène Cixous et al., "The Laugh of the Medusa." *Signs* 1.4 (1976): 877. Cixous's essay, as translated by Keith and Paula Cohen, does not actually use the word "feminocentrism," though it promotes the concept of inscribing femininity. The word "phallocentric" does appear in the essay on page 879.

19. For examples of critics characterizing relationships between eighteenth-century women writers as overwhelmingly positive, see: Paula Backscheider, *Eighteenth-Century Women Poets and Their Poetry: Inventing Agency, Inventing Genre* (2005), 93, 106, 128, 247, 184, 200, 205; Janet Todd, *Women's Friendship in Literature* (1980), 360–61, 379; Emma Donoghue, *Passions Between Women* (1993), 134–37, and *Poems Between Women* (1997), xliv; Paula McDowell, *The Women of Grub Street* (1998), 272; Norma Clarke, *The Rise and Fall of the Woman of Letters* (2004), 119, 123, 125. Backscheider's book epitomizes this stance, claiming that "Incrementally women poets writing between 1660 and 1750 develop a safe space in which women read, write, encourage one another to write, and carry on happy lives in a largely female world" (200). Conflict between literary women also vanishes from studies of individual writers. As an example, Jane Spencer's account of Delarivier Manley's writing life does not mention Manley's satirical attacks on other women writers, and instead presents Manley as a positive model for later female authors (*The Rise of the Woman Novelist* 29, 62). Other studies of Manley that do address relationships between women but neglect to discuss Manley's satires of her fellow female authors include Ros Ballaster, *Seductive Forms: Women's Amatory Fiction from 1684–1740* (1992), and Janet Todd, *Women's Friendship in Literature* (1980).

20. Kathryn R. King, "Female Agency and Feminocentric Romance," *The Eighteenth Century* (41.1: Spring 2000): 59.

21. Ballaster, *Seductive Forms*, 145. Critics have also debated whether or not Manley's (or Haywood's) texts can properly be called "feminocentric": see William B. Warner, "Formulating Fiction: Romancing the Reader in Early Modern Britain," *Cultural Institutions of the Novel*, ed. Deidre Lynch and William B. Warner (Durham: Duke UP, 1996): 282, and Susan Staves, *A Literary History of Women's Writing in Britain, 1660–1789* (Cambridge: Cambridge UP, 2006): 148–49.

22. Ibid., 115.

23. *The Injur'd Husband; Or, the Mistaken Resentment* originally appeared in 1722.

24. *The Female Wits*, 5.

25. Ibid.

26. Ibid.

27. Manley, *The Royal Mischief*, preface 4.

28. Ibid., preface 5.

29. *The Female Wits*, 11.

30. Ibid., preface 2.

31. Ibid., preface 3.

32. Ibid., 4.

33. Ibid., 4. Marsilia later states that "if we Poets did but act, as well as write, the Plays wou'd never miscarry" (ibid., 60).

34. See address "To the Reader" that prefaces *The Royal Mischief*, in which Manley celebrates Mrs. Barry. Victoria Joule's essay in this volume addresses Manley's interactions with Barry in more detail.
35. *The Female Wits*, 57.
36. Ibid., 21.
37. Ibid., 67.
38. Hook, introduction to *The Female Wits*, v.
39. It is difficult to determine why Manley later lashed out at the women who shared her role as satirical target rather than attacking the writer or writers of *The Female Wits* or other male critics who shared an animus against female writers. Manley had already stopped writing by the time the play was performed in October 1696, as the play's preface notes, and did not then feel that she needed to defend herself in print (see preface, 2). It is also possible that she did not know who had authored the play—though, as Hook points out, it hardly mattered which member of the Drury Lane crew actually put pen to paper (Hook, introduction, xii). Given Manley's later insistence on the evils of hypocrisy, however, she might also have been reluctant to draw attention to a portrait of herself as a dishonest, self-obsessed flatterer apparently incapable of real friendship with other women.
40. Delarivier Manley, *The Lost Lover; Or, the Jealous Husband: A Comedy. As It Is Acted at the Theatre Royal by His Majesty's Servants. Written by Mrs. Manley.* (London: R. Bently in Covent-Garden ..., 1696), 13. *Early English Books Online.*
41. Paula McDowell, *The Women of Grub Street: Press, Politics, and Gender in the London Literary Marketplace 1678–1730* (New York: Oxford University Press, 1998), 235 n. 7. Joule's essay in this volume instead identifies Orinda directly as Philips, and identifies Orinda as the "real 'deserted mistress'" in *The Lost Lover* (148).
42. Manley, *Lost Lover*, 13. Marsilia's statement that Calista "shews me her Works first" recalls this line (*FW* 5). Orinda's name also resembles that of "Olinda," the title character in Trotter's *Adventures of a Young Lady* (1693), later retitled *Olinda's Adventures* (1718).
43. McDowell, *Women of Grub Street*, 236.
44. Susan Staves, *A Literary History of Women's Writing in Britain, 1660–1789* (Leiden: Cambridge University Press, 2006), 111. Staves also considers the "Orinda" character evidence that "Manley begins her literary career as a daughter of Behn rather than a daughter of Philips," countering McDowell's assertion that Manley rejected both women writers as unsatisfactory role models (ibid.).
45. Blouch, "Eliza Haywood and the Romance of Obscurity," 535–51.
46. Ezell, *Writing Women's Literary History*, 18, 27.
47. Ibid., 19.
48. Ruth Herman explains that the figure of "Faction" was frequently identified as female, beginning in 1704 (*Business of a Woman*, 52).
49. Manley, *New Atalantis*. 92.
50. Ibid., 90. Manley explains that Finch's poem had "met with abundance of applause," presumably when circulated in manuscript (92). This poem was eventually published in a slightly altered form in Finch's *Miscellany Poems, on Several Occasions* in 1713, printed by John Barber, Manley's business partner and lover (McGovern, *Anne Finch and Her Poetry*, 108). Manley may have obtained copies of Finch's poems via Barber or Jonathan Swift, or may have been acquainted with Finch herself.

51. Ibid., 93.
52. Ibid., 60.
53. Ibid., 47.
54. Ibid.
55. Ibid., 48. Note the masculine pronouns. Both poets in this account are male, but Ros Ballaster and Paul Bunyan Anderson both identify Mary Pix as the "false friend." Though Ballaster notes that "No attribution is given in any of the keys" for the dishonest friend or the poet, she supports this identification by noting that Pix "dedicated her play Queen Catherine (1698) to 'The Honourable Mrs. Coke of Norfolk'" (*NA* 276 n. 111). Considering that Manley also flips the genders of the entire royal court later in the work, coding herself and Pix as male writers is hardly much of a cover for her own authorship, nor is it likely that Manley wanted to obscure her authorial claim to the poems.
56. Manley, *New Atalantis* 54, 54–55. Anderson, who first identified Pix as the friend in question, did not offer any textual support for this assertion ("Delariviere Manley's Prose Fiction" 170). Pix is now known as a playwright, and not a particularly successful one (see Jean I. Marsden's essay discussing her reputation and talents). Though it seems a bit strange for Manley to attack her as a failed poet, the dedication to Cary Coke remains suggestive, and the nature of Manley's attack resonates with her own larger concerns about hierarchies of poetic talent.
57. Manley, *New Atalantis*, 48.
58. *Women of Grub Street*, 239.
59. Though Manley's fictionalized autobiography *The Adventures of Rivella; or, the History of the Author of the Atalantis* was not published until 1714, Manley indicates in that work that the details of her life were well known to the London public long before, and that she intended the publication of *Rivella* as a partial corrective to rumor (and as a means of blocking Edmund Curll's planned biography by Charles Gildon, which would likely have slandered her further). See Rivella's conversation with Lovemore (*Rivella*, 61).
60. Manley, *New Atalantis*, 53.
61. *Women of Grub Street*, 233.
62. Manley, *New Atalantis*, 54.
63. Manley, *Nine Muses*, 1.
64. Manley, *New Atalantis*, 60.
65. Ibid., 60.

11 A Manifesto for a Woman Writer

Letters Writen as Varronian Satire

Chris Mounsey

Introduction

Since my first work in eighteenth-century women's writing, I have always used the forename Chris to hide the fact that I was a mere man meddling in the business of a woman. Therefore, I could have been no more delighted when my name badge at my first British Society for Eighteenth-Century Studies conference at St. John's College, Oxford read "Christine." This act of Valerie Rumbold's led my senior female colleagues loudly to make room for "Christine" on the back row of all the women's writing panels that I attended. In writing this essay, I remain acutely aware that I am still meddling in the business of a woman, and that I am the only man, the token male in the first-ever collection on the work of Delarivier Manley (I am also the token gay male and the token disabled academic). I am also acutely aware that my speculative paper, if taken seriously, rewrites the history of Manley in a way that suggests that earlier academics have missed an important point about her first publication, *Letters Writen by Mrs Manley* (1696)—that it was an early exercise in Varronian satire, tackling two targets, Thomas Tollemache, the Whig war hero, and King William III in the year after the death of his wife, Mary II, to whom he owed his claim to the English throne. All I can do is take refuge behind Catherine Ingrassia's wise words that "[n]arratives ... [about women writers] change as each successive generation of scholars and students refines, revises [and] ... transforms the understanding of the literary period."[1] I cannot apologize for being a male writer, but I can apologize for the format of the piece that follows, which resembles more the notes to a scholarly edition of the letters than an academic paper. The excuse for this is that the reading is so dramatically at odds with the work on *Letters Writen* by Ruth Herman and Rachel Carnell in the *Collected Works of Delarivier Manley* that to make any sense at all, it needs a wholly new set of scholarly machinery.

The first three of Delarivier Manley's known published works—*Letters Writen by Mrs. Manley*, *The Lost Lover*, and *The Royal Mischief*, all of 1696—make strange and uncomfortable bedfellows. Both Ruth Herman[2] and Rachel Carnell[3] argue that the year before their publication Manley was trying out writing in different styles (epistolary fiction and theatrical comedy in prose, and theatrical tragedy in verse) as a way to demonstrate her talent.

Herman and Carnell concur that each was an experiment in technique, which she was practicing while secluded in the West Country, the apparent destination of the journey that *Letters Writen* recounts. But, as this essay will argue, the preface to *Letters Writen* suggests that there was a political strategy that worked across all three of Manley's 1696 publications, though this essay will only give details for *Letters Writen*. I believe that all three have a political subtext since they were advertised together[4] four months after *Letters Writen* was first published and after both runs of the plays.[5] Linking them further was Richard Bentley as publisher.[6] Together, these coincidences seem to suggest the three texts were a carefully planned strategy rather than singular experiments in style, albeit a strategy that failed to lead immediately to fame and fortune. Nevertheless, the existence of a combined political strategy could explain Manley's prominent position in *The Female Wits* of October 1696 (pub. 1704) and its attack on her *Royal Mischief* of May 1696. This would be a more convincing explanation than the play being a theatrical stunt between rival companies, as argued by Lucyle Hook.[7]

Added to this, the eventual success of her writing career as a political satirist suggests that Delarivier Manley might well have had some sort of political intention in her earliest publications. If we agree with Alan Downie and Rachel Carnell that she was not the author of *The Secret History of Queen Zarah* (1705),[8] Manley's turn to political writing looks abrupt. Furthermore, its appearance as fully formed Varronian satire in the hugely successful *Secret Memoirs and Manners of Several Persons of Quality, of Both Sexes. From the New Atalantis* (1709) is unaccountable. Where are the apprentice works? The power of that book, for which she was first arrested, then fêted, then given applause for bringing about the Tory election victory of 1710, suggests a mature political writer. However, if Manley were, as Herman and Carnell argue, exploring her style of writing at the beginning of her career, it would not seem out of the question to argue that at least one of the three publications bore some resemblance to those on which her reputation is based. The style Manley was practicing in *Letters Writen*, this essay will argue, is a disguised Varronian satire. As such, my argument might be read as an addition to Aaron Santesso's magisterial account of Manley's use of Varronian satire in *The New Atalantis*.[9] What is important about the discovery of this style in her early works is, as Carnell points out to us, that Manley "signals her Tory values by claiming in her preface to the second volume [of *The New Atalantis*] that her work is Varronian satire, understood in its day as a 'natural Tory vehicle.'"[10]

The definition of Varronian satire had recently been explored by John Dryden in the dedication to his 1693 translation of Juvenal and Persius, where he tells of the mix of verse and prose that characterized the work of both Varro and Maenippus. However, as he goes on:

> We have nothing remaining of those *Varronian* Satires, excepting some inconsiderable Fragments; and those for the most part are much corrupted. The Titles of many of them are indeed preserv'd, and they

are generally double: From whence, at least, we may understand, how many various Subjects were treated by that Author. *Tully*, in his *Academicks*, introduced *Varro* himself giving us some light concerning the Scope and Design of these Works. Wherein, after he had shown his Reasons why he did not *ex professo* write of Philosophy, he adds what follows. Notwithstanding, *says he*, that those Pieces of mine, wherein I have imitated *Menippus*, though I have not Translated him, are sprinkled with mirth, and gayety: yet many things are there inserted which are drawn from the very intrails of Philosophy, and many things severely argu'd: which I have mingled with Pleasantries on purpose, that they may more easily do down with the Common sort of Unlearn'd Readers.[11]

From Dryden's definition, we can expect what we find: that Manley includes verses amid her prose and that there will be double meanings. From Tully's, that her texts will be funny, but will mask serious arguments dressed up for easier consumption. But Tully goes on (in Dryden's translation): "Thus it appears, that *Varro* was one of those Writers [who was] ..., studious of laughter; and that learned as he was, his business was more to divert his Reader, than to teach him."[12] It is hard to believe that Manley did not know Dryden's account of Varro, particularly since she was one of the Nine Muses who wrote verses on his death.[13] Furthermore, when she proposes to give up writing serious political satire in the semiautobiographical *Rivella*, she uses an echo of the word "business" (referring to writing) from this second quote in the lesson she claims to have learned, voiced through John Tidcomb,[14] "that Politicks is not the Business of a Woman, especially of one that can so well delight and entertain her Readers with more gentle and pleasing Theams."[15]

Manley's political allegiance in her first three publications has been the subject of some debate, which is summed up by Rachel Carnell in her excellent *Political Biography of Delarivier Manley*.[16] The man who introduced her to Sir Thomas Skipwith, who produced her first play, *The Lost Lover*, may have been the Whig Duke of Devonshire.[17] Skipwith himself, though described as being little more than an "engaging roué," was MP briefly for Malmsbury[18] and was recorded as being of the Court Party (a Whig).[19] The politics of Thomas Betterton, who produced her *Royal Mischief* at the breakaway Lincoln's Inn Theatre Company, are not discernible; however, Betterton maintained a close relationship with Charles Sackville, Earl of Dorset, who as Lord Chamberlain ensured him the patent for the new theater company, and Sackville was a staunch Whig and founder of the Kit Kat club.[20] Likewise, John Tidcomb, the possible addressee of *Letters Writen* and narrative voice of *Rivella*, was a Whig and a member of the Kit Kat club.[21]

Albeit surrounded by so many helpful Whigs, Manley maintained in *Rivella* that she was "a perfect Bigot from a long untainted Descent of Loyal Ancestors," that is she was a Tory. Carnell nuances the claim, arguing that we should "probably view this 'autobiographical' detail, one that scholars have hitherto taken as historical fact, as instead an instance of Manley's sophisticated political manoeuvring at a time of dynastic transition."[22] While I agree with Carnell that Manley is carefully repositioning herself, I would suggest that she did it as a known Tory author at the time when the Whigs were likely to remain in power for a long time. In this same scene, her use of the words of Tully's definition of Varronian satire reminds us of the "doubleness" of the style, and appears to indicate to readers that Manley's future productions will be more of the same political scandals. Thus, I would argue that we need not believe that Manley ever wrote in favor of Whig politics, even in her early works, though they were welcomed by Whig sponsors and feature Whig narrators.

It might, of course, be argued that Manley ran with the hare and the hounds, tailoring her texts to fit with the expectations of all members of her potential audience, much as Ellen T. Harris argues for Handel's Academy Operas of the 1720s.[23] In this way, the plot of *Floridante* (1721) concerns a murdered king and a usurping tyrant, which reflected the Jacobite cause, while the king's daughter marrying a foreign prince and returning just rule to the country reflected William and Mary and the Whigs. The power of Harris's argument lies in her assertion that

> the habit of London audiences to read political messages into stage productions meant that there did not need to be an allegory in which individual characters represented specific living persons for a libretto to have political resonance: it sufficed for the libretto to contain situations analogous to current political events.[24]

However, despite the layering of messages, it would seem odd to argue that Handel, a German composer appointed by George I, might be a Jacobite. But then it might seem just as odd to read Manley, who wrote so vehemently against the Whigs in 1709, to be anything other than a Tory. Remembering the doubleness of Varronian satire allows for Whig readers finding things for themselves in her texts, as well as the fun of disguising a Tory message in texts that mocked their Whig sponsors. If this were Manley's strategy—and I shall argue that it was—then the discovery that Sir Thomas Skipwith, the Duke of Devonshire, Thomas Betterton, the Earl of Dorset, and John Tidcomb had all been made fools of might just account for the hiatus in Manley's writing career[25] between 1696 and *Almyna*, which was accompanied by her second epistolary work, *The Unknown Lady's Pacquet of Letters*, in 1707.

The key to the conundrum of Manley's politics, then, lies in the first three of Manley's known published works and in particular in *Letters Writen*, which I will read as an early experiment with Varronian satire. The *Letters* give a series of cleverly voiced stories of lost love met with rational detachment. On one level this is an important statement about gender expectations. Manley appended to *Letters Writen* an imitation of Colonel Pack's letters from an abandoned Portuguese nun, full of histrionics and passion, to show how men thought women ought to behave when abandoned. On the contrary, Manley's own stories demonstrate that women are just as capable of rational detachment as men, and just as capable of cool deception and strategy. However, as would be expected of a Varronian satire, there is another level to *Letters Writen*: an attack on the Whig war hero, Thomas Tollemache, who had just been killed in action in Flanders, which is so subtle that it has not been noticed previously. Likewise there is another attack on William III, written the year after the death of his wife Mary II, to whom he owed his claim to the throne of England. As such, *Letters Writen* might be regarded as a manifesto for Manley's later work in attacking John Churchill and other prominent Whig politicians; in *Letters Writen* Manley begins honing her Varronian satire, the form she would go on to use to such effect in *The New Atalantis*.

Letters Writen—Preface

Carnell has explored in some detail the identity of "J.H.," who wrote the preface and claims to have published the letters without Manley's permission. But while there are a number of candidates who share the initials "J.H."—James Hargreaves, John Hughes, or even John Hervey (later Earl of Bristol)[26]—the addressee of the letters themselves, if different, remains unidentified. He may be a real person, and the original addressee of the letters. He claims to be a friend of her father and believes "Years of Friendship and Veneration" reason enough that he will not lose "the Relish of being esteem'd" by Manley for publishing the letters without her knowledge, although he "has most Warmly oppose'd [her] Design of Writing Plays; and that of Making them Publick." His reason for publishing the letters, he claims, is that they contain "more Sublime and Elevated Thoughts" than the plays, although the fact that he is "stealing [her] from the expecting Rivals"[27] (that is, Skipwith and Betterton, who were about to produce her plays) suggests he may be trying to make money on the back of her success.

However, he may be a realist device, like the narrator of *Rivella*, Sir Charles Lovemore/Sir John Tidcomb, who has a similar view of her skill in letter writing:

> Tho' in her tender Age, she wrote Verses, which considering her Youth were pardonable, since they might be read without Disgust; but there was something surprising in her Letters, so natural, so spirituous, so sprightly, so well turned, that from the first to last I must and will ever maintain, that all her other Productions however successful they have been, come short of her Talent in writing Letters.[28]

In *Rivella*, a quasi-autobiographical piece, we might expect more than this very brief mention of *Letters Writen*. The moreso since the letters published as *Letters Writen* are implied to be the continuation of a correspondence with Lovemore/Tidcomb, who tells us, "I have had a number of them [the letters]; my Servant us'd to wait upon her as if to bring her Books to read, in the Cover of which I had contrived always to send her a Note, which she return'd in the same Manner."[29] The narrator of the preface of *Letters Writen* picks up the same lascivious overtone about Manley's letters and continues:

> Perhaps you may most justly object, These Letters which I expose, were not proper for the Publick; the Droppings of your Pen, fatigu'd with Thought and Travel. But let them who are of that Opinion imagine what Ease and Leisure cou'd produce, when they find them-selves (as they necessarily must) so well entertain'd by these.[30]

However, although we might agree with Carnell, that considering "this publication without Manley's permission, it seems more likely that such a claim was intended as a sales pitch, to suggest that there was something more risqué than there actually was in this brief epistolary collection,"[31] we might look to something other than the sexual as the risqué content. After all, what the preface introduces are relatively dull letters containing conventional love stories, albeit they are published as "entertainment," but this might be expected of the doubleness of Varronian satire.

Thus, toying with lasciviousness could hide a political subtext, since it leaves the suggestion that the narrator, J.H., is a third contender, with "Sir Thomas Skipwith and Mr Betterton, ... as one that honour'd me with your Friendship before you thought of theirs." Manley attempts in the preface to implant in the minds of her readers the idea that the Whigs Skipwith, Betterton, and J.H., and by implication the Duke of Devonshire and the Earl of Dorset, were involved in sexual liaisons with her. However, the fact that she calls attention to these men might have prompted a contemporary reader to look for an insinuation other than the sexual one. In such an instance, politics would appear the real subtext when at the end of the preface, Manley (if indeed writing as J.H.) asks of herself, "Why [have you] thrown your Chance in the Country, who might have adorn'd the Court, and taught a Nation?"[32] An eighteenth-century audience in the "habit of ... read[ing] political messages" might readily understand the references here to "Country" and "Court" as "Tory" and "Whig" respectively. The same audience might pick up on J.H.'s condemnation of her plays as "Trifles" and *Letters Writen* as "more Sublime and Elevated Thoughts,"[33] and take notice of the serious intent behind the stories of the letters. Likewise, it would not seem out of the question to argue that the "courting" Whigs surrounding Manley (pun intended) are all part of the doubleness that defines Tory Varronian satire. It might even be that Manley never spent any time at all in the West Country, and that the journey about which *Letters Writen* sends report was no more than a literary device representing the depth of her feeling for the Country/Tory cause soon after the death of the rightful heir, Mary II, when William III ruled alone with staunchly Whig ministers.

Letters Writen—Letter 1, Egham, June 24, 1694

Nailing her Tory colors to the mast, Manley introduces a quotation in the first letter from an unpublished poem by George Granville, a Jacobite, which repines on his political exile after the Glorious Revolution, asking for "a Life, remote from guilty Court."[34] She, like Granville, feels exiled to the West Country for her Tory beliefs. However, there is more going on in the double-ness of Varronian satire. The quotation of Granville is given in reply to her addressee's misquote of John Donne's *The Will*: "All your Beauty [graces] no more Light [use] will have / Than a Sun-Dial in a Grave."[35] An exchange of verses in the letter is evocative of the end of an impossible love affair,[36] about which Manley complains that her "Constancy is not Proof against the Thoughts[.] I am going to have no Lover but myself for ever ... [whence] ... The green inviting Grass, (upon which I promise to pass many pleasing solitary Hours) seems not at all entertaining."[37] But once again sex leads to politics, since the Donne poem which sets off this reverie also contains the line "My faith I give to Roman Catholics," which may be understood more or less ironically in either context, but here recollects James II's religion and appears to imply allegiance to him, or at least perhaps to his daughter, Anne.

At this point the letter takes a sudden U-turn into comedy, but maintains its political edge. Manley includes a description of a "pert Sir in the Company, that will make himself be taken notice by his Dulness" and "Dinner at Ten-a-Clock, upon a great Leg of Mutton," which meal is alternated with beef, day-in-day-out, and "from which there's no Remedy but Fasting."[38] Giving verisimilitude to her writing a letter, Manley claims to have "left the Limb of the Sheep to the Mercy of my Companions" since the "Coachman [would] ... not stay dressing a Dinner for the King, (God bless him) shou'd he travel in his Coach."[39] However, whether this is another venture into realist writing in epistolary fiction, a disguise for what has gone before, or an example of the miscellaneous nature of Varronian satire is not, at this point, finally clear. The coachman's cheerful "God Bless him" addressed parenthetically to the king does not say which king, William or James, that he will not wait for, but the coach is heading in the direction of Brixham, in Devon, where William had landed in September 1688 to take (usurp?) the throne of England.

Letter 2, Hartley Row, June 22, 1694

The political satire of the book takes its first shot at a living victim in the next letter. Hartley Row is on the road from Bagshot to Basingstoke, and thus the opening line of the second letter, "I am got safe to Hartley Row,"[40] expresses the satisfaction of having avoided the highwaymen who were synonymous with Bagshot Heath, which would later be made famous by John Gay in *The Beggar's Opera*.[41] The letter next introduces the Mayoress of Tatness [Totnes][42] and gives information about the "pert Sir"[43] who tells the first tale with something like a Chaucerian desire for self-revelation.

Manley is pleased neither by his attention to her, nor his desire to tell his tale. However, by resigning herself to hear what he has to recount, when she says, "I had as good consent ... With or without my Leave, I see you are resolv'd upon't,"[44] she sets up ambiguous expectations of the tale teller. He is at once a humorous realist creation who not only overdresses for dinner, but asks her of his waistcoat, "What the brocade was worth a Yard? How many Ounces of Silver Fringe?"[45] However, in his tale, he sets himself up as an amoral gallant, chasing a local "Lady Conquest" for a sexual encounter: "her Honour was my Care, and not Marrying my Design."[46] However he is thwarted in the attempt when his friend Sly, whom he brings along to help him finesse Lady Conquest, tells him "he must enjoy her or die," to which the tale teller expostulates to Manley "*Gad Madam, was this not a very odd Turn? I carried him to speak for me; and he comes to make me the Confident of his Designs?*"[47] The accents of upper-class twit continue, "*Gad! Wou'd you believe, Madam, that Love could make so great an Ass of a Man of my Understanding?*"[48] drawing the tale teller as something of an early-day Bertie Wooster who myopically recounts his story against himself when he hides behind Lady Conquest's bed while she and Sly make love.

If there is a Varronian doubleness underlying the silliness of the tale, it would seem to be Conquest's reasonable explanation for preferring Sly to the tale teller: "*You have no Reason, Sir,* said she, *to complain of me: I could have no Engagements with a Man who never pretended love to me.*"[49] While Conquest makes the point that women can be more rational than men, in 1796 the statement might act less as an assertion of feminism than as a reminder to readers that Anne, a woman capable of rationality, rather than William, should rule England after the death of her sister, Mary. After all, William has no designs on England further than a brief encounter for his own gain ("her Honour was my Care, and not Marrying my Design"), while Anne might expect more, being a princess of the blood.

The party allegiance of the tale teller, being an upper-class twit from Oxford, which was known as a Jacobite university, at once suggests a satire on Tory buffoonery. However, after his tale, Manley tells us, "He concluded it with telling me his Journey to *London,* and short Stay there, only to accoutre, his Design of visiting a Lady-Sister, marry'd into *Devonshire.*"[50] The suggestion that he must dress well to visit Devonshire suggests that his "Lady-sister" might be married to a member of the family of the Duke of Devonshire, thus turning the story back into a satire on the Whigs.

Letter 3, Sutton, June 23, 1694

Continuing the realist account of the tedious journey to the West Country and Manley's abhorrent fellow passengers, the third letter from Sutton dismisses the Mayoress of Totnes, declaring that "now she is acquainted, [she] has all the low, disagreeable Familiarity of People of her Rank."[51] The mayoress tells the next tale, but Manley declares it "a sorry Love-business about her Second Husband; Stuff so impertinent that I remember nothing of it."[52] However, the references to Totnes and Sutton disguise yet another set of political references.

The seat for Totnes was held in the interest of, and sometimes by, Edward Seymour, a Tory anti-Williamite politician, of whom it is recorded

> In the new year ... the death of Queen Mary gave some chance of rallying a specifically Tory following. Early in February 1695 he "gave great offence by letting fall an expression that without doors it was made a question whether the Parliament by the death of the Queen was not dissolved", and queried the propriety of including the word "heirs" in future legislation. He argued that a long-term view was needed because if the King remarried there was a danger that the right of succession would be established in his children, to the exclusion of the more direct claims of Princess Anne; and that even if William had no more children, the word "heirs" still opened the way to his other relations.[53]

As in the former letter, any Whig might read the reference to Totnes, and therefore Seymour, the other way around through the reference to the mayoress. In 1692 Seymour applied to the mayor for his friend and supporter Thomas Coulson to be accepted to the vacant seat for Totnes,[54] Seymour took the seat back after the passing of the triennial act between 1695 and 1698, whence he returned it to his friend. But Manley's reference to Totnes was a reminder that at the time he was soliciting Whig support for his Tory maneuvers. As D. W. Hayton tells us:

> Seymour's identification with the court [in 1692, when he was reappointed to the Privy Council] did not last long, for the rise to power of the whig junto made it necessary for him to rebuild former friendships and to restore his credit both with high-church back-benchers and "country" whigs. The crisis came in 1694 when his critical speeches on naval failures provoked the chancellor of the exchequer, Charles Montagu, to a savage response, which for once rendered Seymour speechless. Soon afterwards Seymour was dismissed from the treasury. In opposition once more, he did not find it easy to re-establish his former position.[55]

In this description of Seymour we have a picture of yet another upper-class twit, this time one who will stick at nothing to cling on to power, and Seymour's political career was destroyed by his *volte faces*. But a reference to Totnes, which brought Seymour to mind, in a work that seems more and more to carry an anti-Williamite message, written soon after the death of Mary, seems too strong simply to dismiss as coincidental. Is it all part of the fun of Varronian satire?

Likewise, the reference to Sutton—and in England there are above a hundred villages to which "Sutton" might refer—adds to the strength of the interpretation. The Sutton at which Manley stayed was almost certainly Sutton Scotney, a tiny village north of Winchester that is off the beaten track of both what is now the A34 and the A303, the ancient routes north-south and east-west. In realist terms the inn at which they stayed was out of the way, and there is still a service station called Sutton Scotney a number of miles away from the actual village. But read as a political metaphor, the member for Hampshire was Charles Powlett, First Marquess of Winchester, a Whig, pro-Williamite, who fought against Seymour about the East India Company, in whose favor Seymour had had Coulson elected with the help of the Mayor of Totnes.[56] Thus Sutton acts as an addition to the attack on Seymour as a foolish Tory who has dallied with the Whigs and helped the pro-Williamites maintain their power.

Letter 4, Salisbury, Saturday night

After some realist information about the sights of Salisbury, the Exeter coach being repaired, and some boorish people who had come into the Inn from it, we hear the second long travelers' tale, from Mrs. Stanhope of Falmouth, one of those who has just arrived on the incoming coach. The tale, which tells of a woman's happy escape from marrying a deceiving sea captain, because she believes her eyes rather than his words, seems to have little to it. However, a passing reference to the "Dutchess of *Grafton*"[57] would alert anti-Williamite readers to the possibility of William providing heirs to follow him to the throne. Isabella Bennet was one of the Hampton Court Beauties whose paintings adorn the state-rooms at the new palace, commissioned by Mary II from Sir Godfrey Kneller. The duchess was grand-daughter of Louis of Nassau-Beverweerd, a close relation (through an illegitimate line) and advisor to William III. She herself was married to Charles II's illegitimate son by Barbara Villers, Henry Fitzroy, Earl of Euston,[58] when she was four and he nine. At the time of the story the duchess was a widow of twenty-two with a seven-year-old son.[59] Mother and son had recently been painted together by Kneller, and the work now hangs at Ickworth, home of John Hervey, Earl of Bristol. It is not out of the question that Manley is going so far as implying that the child was William's. Isabella and he had lived in close proximity at a palace Alexander Pope would soon make synonymous with intrigue.

More important to my argument about the target of satire in the book is the realist information given at the end of the letter, and this is of course a feature of the Varronian satire's miscellaneous nature. Among the banter with her addressee, Manley informs us that "General *Talmash*'s Body was brought in here this Evening: His Secretary I am acquainted with, and have sent to desire the Favour of his Company to Morrow to Dinner, and if any thing in his Relation be Entertaining, you shall not fail of it."[60] Thomas

Tollemache was an ardent supporter of William III, being part of his invading force, for which he was made governor of Portsmouth in January 1689. In 1691, he led a number of daring, if overly optimistic, adventures during William's war in Ireland. These were followed by more daring feats of war in Flanders as William fought to regain Orange from the French. As MP for Chippenham, Tollemache spoke in the House of Commons for an increase in army spending for 1694. Tollemache was then sent to Brest to destroy the French Atlantic fleet, another daring if ill-advised feat, which according to Burnet "the Council and Officers were all against making the attempt; but Talmash had set his heart so much upon it, that he could not be diverted from it,"[61] and he was mortally wounded. Tollemache was remembered in his funeral oration as "one of the noblest of our *English Worthies*,"[62] and was the subject of a number of elegies.[63] By ending with the suggestion that the next letter will be a tell-all about Tollemache in a collection of love stories, Manley whets the appetites of her readers, who are doubtless keen to know more about what he was really like from his secretary. In the event, nothing is forthcoming, and Manley's failure to deliver seems to recollect Tollemache's.

Letter 5, Bridgport, June 26, 1694

Tollemache's support for William and his being a Whig war hero would, with the benefit of hindsight, elicit parallels with John Churchill, whom Manley attacked in *The New Atalantis*. Thus, when we read at the beginning of the next letter that

> The Account of so great a Man's Death as Mr. Talmash (in the middle of all his Enterprises, when Fortune seem'd to promise him much greener Laurels than he had yet gather'd) has so added to my Melancholy, that I will not describe his Misfortune to you, for fear it be contagious; but rather suffer you to expect the public Account; for I am one of those that esteem you more, than to make you unease; as I think none can be otherwise, that hears the Particulars of his Loss.[64]

We might wonder whether, in 1696, when the letter was published, Manley was drawing attention to the disaster Tollemache had led his troops into at Camaret Bay when he tried to smash the French Atlantic fleet.

As in the first letter, Manley makes an abrupt *volte face* in the Varronian style (and thus hiding the significance of the remarks about Tollemache so well that it has not hitherto been noted) after her refusal to recount Tollemache's secretary's story, and tells of Beaux' sexual encounter with another woman who "treated him (in her Chamber) with *Rosa Solis*, and what he calls *Sucket*."[65] She refuses to listen to further details of his conquest, and in mock effrontery "recommend[s] Discretion in Ladies Affairs."[66] The letter concludes with news that "Here's just come into the Inn an Acquaintance of *Beaux*'s, who promises yielding Matter for to Morrow's Letter," before lapsing back into sadness at the news of Tollemache's death. But her refusal to tell the tale of the death of a war hero, which firsthand knowledge one might expect from an intimate letter, becomes less a matter of delicacy than politics when Beaux' acquaintance tells his own story in the next letter.

Letter 6, Exeter, June 26, 1696

The Beaux story allegorizes William's fraught relationship to the country over which he now ruled alone. The teller introduces himself as "a Foreigner. I had the Glory of following the Prince of *Orange*, (now our Auspicious King) in his Expedition into *England*."[67] A little further on we discover he is Swiss, and that he has become the object of the affections of an English woman, with £12,000, who has seen him in Exeter Cathedral. The woman's mother objects to the match, and the pair decide to go to Cornwall to get married, "but for fear her Mother should pursue us, she consented to take me for her Husband before the Parson cou'd be got to make us such."[68] They are happy for three months, but then the Swiss "began to consider a little [his] Affairs, and propos'd to [his] wife my being Naturalised, that I might look after hers." The reaction was not what might be expected from a happily married woman, who "snatch'd a Bayonet of [his], and wounded her self under the Left Breast, but not much."[69] When he asks his wife why she has tried to kill herself, he is told the reason was "The Discovery of Interest in me, when she believ'd Love was the only Motive to our Marriage."[70] The Swiss husband then decides to go to London to be naturalized without his wife knowing, since he wants to be treated "as a Husband, [rather than] … a Lover."[71] But when he tells her that it has been done, she replies, with all the rationality of the jilted women in the book: "*She only knew how to interpret it; but she was out in her Cunning, if I should find an English Wife at my Service, who knew not the true Value and Use of one.*"[72] She will not be ruled by a husband, and wants to maintain her ownership of what is hers by keeping him a lover. True to her words, she hides from her husband, and has a common law process of incapability served upon him.[73] He finishes the story with the vow that he is going to leave England forever, bought off with £1,500. The common law process of making the Swiss husband incapable was a way to forbid him to enter into legal contracts. Thus, the story of a foreigner seeking naturalization with its negative outcome highlights the book's anti-Williamite view: that he no longer held a legitimate claim to rule the country (after the death of his wife, Mary II) and should go back to Orange.

Such views did not appear clearly stated in print until the accession of Anne, when, for example, a person who describes himself as a "High Flyer," that is a High Church Anglican, wrote:

> 'Tis true, K. William Deliver'd us all from Popery and Slavery and was the first King on the English Throne that promoted a Reformation of Manners. But tho' King William signally Retriev'd the Ancient

Honour and Glory of the English Nation; yet his Death made way for a Queen whose Heart is Entirely English and in a most particular manner a morning Mother to the Church of England, we may (with a good Conscience) Rejoice in it, and wish he had died sooner.[74]

Furthermore, the Swiss nationality of the lover in the story reflects the mercenary army that came with William as he swept to power,[75] as well as an English fear that as king he did not trust his subjects, as William Roosen suggests:

> Under Charles II and James II most English diplomats were native Englishmen. After the Glorious Revolution, William often chose Dutchmen, refugee Huguenots, and Swiss Protestants. ... It has been argued that William hesitated to use Englishmen because he could not trust them, and also because he is supposed to have believed "that no Englishman could keep a secret."[76]

Letter 7, July 10, 1694

Returning to the verisimilitude of letter writing, Manley tells of her move into her new house and apologizes for not replying to her correspondent's last three letters. She asks him the favor of sending her chocolate and a few lines of verse, all true to the Varronian miscellaneous style. Adding to the miscellaneous style, two further letters are added dated the following year, which mimic the histrionic style of Colonel Pack's Letters from a Portuguese nun, and the book closes.

Conclusion

Thus, we can see that *Letters Writen* is an early Varronian satire, the same style she employed in *The New Atalantis*, by which, as Carnell argues, "[Manley] signals her Tory values by claiming in her preface to the second volume [of *The New Atalantis*] that her work is Varronian satire, understood in its day as a 'natural Tory vehicle.'"[77] It is miscellaneous, exploring a number of irrelevant topics among others that are political dynamite. It is double in its intentions, with a depth of satire that is so well disguised that it has not been noted hitherto. It hides a serious core within entertaining material.

There is no space in the present essay to explore in detail the other two of Manley's publications of 1696. Carnell helps us with *The Royal Mischief*, which she describes as "in some sense a Tory reworking of Elkannah Settle's Exclusionist (Whig) tragedy *The Female Prelate: Being the History of the Life and Death of Pope Joan* (1680)."[78] This is not to say that the play is a Varronian satire, but it does give weight to the anti-Williamite and pro-Tory readings I have given above. About *The Lost Lover*, Carnell is less clear that Manley is writing a pro-Tory political piece, but where we might agree with Carnell's suggestion that "Manley's Wilmore is sometimes simply unpleasant,"[79] he *is* outwitted by Belira, a calm and rational heroine who, like a *deus ex machina*, sorts out the lovers' problems: rather like the heroines of *Letters Writen*.

I have, therefore, no compunction in reiterating the idea that Manley's first three compositions of 1696 were designed as a tripartite attack written against King William III after the death of his wife Mary II, in whose right lay their legitimate claim to the throne of Britain. If I had yet further space, I would make an argument that the works were meant as a warning to Tories at the rise of the Whig Junto, which would dominate British politics until 1705, and on the edge of which, at its start, was none other than Thomas Tollemache. Thus the political allegories outlined here make a strong case for Manley's apprenticeship in political satire nearly twenty years before the publication of *The New Atalantis*.

Notes

1. Catherine Ingrassia, "Introduction," *Women's Writing in Britain, 1660–1789*, ed. Catherine Ingrassia. (Cambridge: Cambridge University Press, 2015), 1.
2. Ruth Herman, *The Business of a Woman*, (New Haven: Delaware University Press, 2003).
3. Rachel Carnell, *A Political Biography of Delarivier Manley* (London: Pickering and Chatto, 2008).
4. *Post Boy* (1695) (London, England), June 23, 1696—June 25, 1696; Issue 177.
5. An advertisement for *Letters Written by Mrs Manley* appears in the *Post Man and the Historical Account* (London, England), February 20, 1696—February 22, 1696; Issue 123.
6. Bentley published *Letters Writen* alone, and styled himself "R.B." in the earlier advert. Bentley was joined by F. Sanders and J. Knapton for the plays. Carnell notes that *Letters Writen* was listed in *The Term Catalogues* as published by R. Buts, but argues that this is probably incorrect. Carnell, *Political Biography*, 105.
7. Lucyle Hook, Introduction to Anon., *The Female Wits* (1704), The Augustan Reprint Society, (William Andrews Clark Memorial Library/UCLA: Los Angeles, 1967).
8. J. A. Downie, "What if Delarivier Manley Did Not Write *The Secret History of Queen Zarah*?" in *The Library*, Vol. 5, No. 3 (2004), 247–64.
9. Aaron Santesso, "*The New Atalantis* and Varronian Satire," *Philological Quarterly* 79:2 (2000), 177–204.
10. Rachel Carnell, "Slipping from Secret History to Novel," *Eighteenth Century Fiction* 28, no. 1 (fall 2015): 1–24.
11. John Dryden, *The Satires of Decimus Junius Juvenalis. Translated into English Verse. &c.* (London: Jacob Tonson, 1693), xxvii.
12. Ibid., xxvii–xviii.
13. *The Nine Muses, or Poems written by Nine several ladies Upon the Death of the late Famous John Dryden, Esq.*, (London: Richard Bassett, 1700).
14. Named Sir Charles Lovemore, but noted to be Tidcomb in the key attached to the second edition of *Rivella*.

15. Manley, *Rivella*, 117.
16. Carnell, *Political Biography*, 3–93.
17. Ibid., 84.
18. A small town in Wiltshire on the route of the journey described in *Letters Writen*.
19. "Skipwith, Sir Thomas," The History of Parliament, accessed December 14, 2014, http://www.historyofparliamentonline.org/volume/1690-1715/member/skipwith-sir-thomas-1652-1710.
20. A Whig literary club, which met at the Trumpet Tavern, Serle's Place, Lincoln's Inn Fields, London and Water Oakley, Bray, Berkshire.
21. Carnell, *Political Biography,* 13.
22. Ibid., 15.
23. Ellen T. Harris, *George Frideric Handel: A Life among Friends* (London: W.W. Norton, 2014).
24. Ibid., 17.
25. But for the poem to Dryden.
26. Carnell, *Political Biography*, 88.
27. Manley, *Letters Writen*, Preface, unpag.
28. Manley, *Rivella*, 17.
29. Ibid., 17–18.
30. Manley, *Letters Writen*, unpag.
31. Carnell, *Political Biography*, 105.
32. Manley, *Letters Writen*, Preface, unpag.
33. Ibid., Preface, unpag.
34. Ibid., 3.
35. Ibid., 2.
36. Both Manley and her correspondent appear still to be in love, but the decision to be apart is the constant Manley's.
37. Manley, *Letters Writen*, 4.
38. Ibid., 5–6.
39. Ibid.
40. Ibid., 7.
41. I include this point because *Letters Writen* was republished as *A Stage-Coach journey to Exeter*, in 1725, and may have been known to Gay when he refers to Walpole's ministry as Bagshot highwaymen.
42. Manley, *Letters Writen*, 11.
43. Ibid., 5.
44. Ibid., 11.
45. Ibid., 9.
46. Ibid., 12.
47. Ibid., 14–15.
48. Ibid., 15–16.
49. Ibid., 22.
50. Ibid., 22.
51. Ibid., 27.
52. Ibid., 27.
53. "Seymour, Sir Edward," The History of Parliament, accessed December 14, 2014, http://www.historyofparliamentonline.org/volume/1690-1715/member/seymour-sir-edward-1633-1708.

54. In November 1692 Seymour arranged Coulson's election for the vacant seat at Totnes, less than 2 miles from Seymour's country seat at Berry Pomeroy. He informed the mayor [James Buckley] on the 22nd that Coulson was "a considerable merchant of this city who is qualified with very good abilities and integrity" whom he was certain would "not only prove a good patriot to his country, but a benefactor to your town." Seymour's brother Henry Portman, the other Member for Totnes, also commended him as being "very much for the Church of England" and would "always own it as a great obligation ... to be joined with one that is so deserving." "Seymour, Sir Edward," The History of Parliament, accessed December 14, 2014, http://www.historyofparliamentonline.org/volume/1690-1715/member/seymour-sir-edward-1633-1708. The letters were used by William Cavendish, Marquess of Hartington, in 1701, to claim electoral malpractice in that year's election, but Seymour and Coulson were, not surprisingly, exonerated. "Cavendish, William," The History of Parliament, accessed December 14, 2014, http://www.historyofparliamentonline.org/volume/1690-1715/member/cavendish-william-1672-1729.
55. D. W. Hayton, "Seymour, Sir Edward, fourth baronet (1633–1708)," *Oxford Dictionary of National Biography*, Oxford University Press, 2004; online edn, May 2009 [http://www.oxforddnb.com/view/article/25162, accessed December 15, 2014].
56. "Powlett, Charles," The History of Parliament, accessed December 14, 2014, http://www.historyofparliamentonline.org/volume/1690-1715/member/powlett-charles-i-1661-1722.
57. Manley, *Letters Writen*, 37.
58. Henry was killed leading William's forces against Cork in 1690.
59. Charles FitzRoy, who became Lord Lieutenant of Ireland.
60. Manley, *Letters Writen*, 43–44.
61. Piers Wauchope, "Tollemache, Thomas (c. 1651–1694)," *Oxford Dictionary of National Biography*, Oxford University Press, 2004; online edn, January 2008 [http://www.oxforddnb.com/view/article/27500, accessed December 16, 2014].
62. Nicholas Brady, *A Sermon Preached at Helmingham in Suffolk, June 30 1694. At the Funeral of L. Gen. Tolmach* (London: Rich. Parker, 1694).
63. For example: Edward Ward, *On the Death of the Late Lieutenant General Talmach, a Poem* (London: Blackwell, 1694); Edmund Arwaker, *An Elegy on his Excellency Lieutenant General Tolmach* (London: Francis Saunders, 1694).
64. Manley, *Letters Writen*, 44–45.
65. Ibid., 46.
66. Ibid., 46.
67. Ibid., 49.
68. Ibid., 52.
69. Ibid., 53.
70. Ibid., 54.
71. Ibid., 54.
72. Ibid., 55.
73. Ibid., 57.
74. Anon., *A satyr upon King William, being the secret history of his life and reign. Written by a Gentleman that was near his person for many years* (London, 1703), Preface, unpag.

75. William tried to keep up a Swiss mercenary army in Ireland, but in 1689, the Swiss government demanded that their troops act only in a defensive role.
76. William Roosen, *The Age of Louis XIV: The Rise of Modern Democracy* (Cambridge, MA: Schenkman, 1976), 65.
77. Carnell, "Slipping": 1–24.
78. Carnell, *Political Biography*, 103.
79. Ibid., 96.

12 Examined in Manley Style
Epistolary Modes in the Periodical Writings of Delarivier Manley

Jean McBain

> Whilst I was thus reflecting upon this famous *Monitor*, my Printer brought
> me several Letters, but not all of them wrote by my self to the *Examiner*, as
> the Sagacious *Medley* suggests; with his humble Advice, That it would not be
> amiss to Print more frequently those Letters I daily receive ... protesting that
> since the *Roman* Triumph, or what he calls the *Laurel Crown* and *Marcus
> Crassus*, he had not had a greater Call for any particular *Examiner*: The
> Reason seem'd plain, the underhand Endeavours of my Fellow-Writers have
> succeeded; the concurrent Interest of many Authors must be much more pre-
> vailing than that of one; in Consideration of which, I resolved upon that easy
> Method of filling up a Paper.[1]

Delarivier Manley's short spell as editor of the Tory *Examiner* (1710–1714)
has been presented in recent scholarship as the apotheosis of her career as
a party writer. Rachel Carnell opens her 2008 *Political Biography of Delarivier Manley* with this editorship, named before even the infamous *New
Atalantis* (1709).[2] Similarly, Paula McDowell's study of Manley in *The
Women of Grub Street* begins with the *Examiner*, although it presents little
analysis of her writing for the paper thereafter.[3] This "zenith of her career,"
to use Ruth Herman's phrase, was reached in June of 1711, when Manley
took over the weekly paper from Jonathan Swift in the midst of issue 46.[4]
Her tenure continued through the summer of 1711, finishing with issue 52,
of July 19–26. To this small corpus scholars now generally add *Examiner* 7,
from September of 1710, and acknowledge the unknowable extent of her
additional contributions to the paper.

Despite the significance now ascribed to Manley's periodical writings,
their form and style remain largely unexamined. Both Herman and Carnell
discuss the periodical issues in some detail, yet both focus primarily on their
themes. Herman's study has usefully unpacked many of the allegories developed by Manley in her *Examiners*, but the rhetorical tools Manley deploys
are here secondary to the identification of the signified.[5] Carnell's attention
to Manley's periodical form is briefer still, framed as a comparison with
Swift's efforts as editor. Of issue 48, Carnell suggests that "this lacks the bit-
ing authoritative tone that Swift had cultivated and reminds us of Manley's
earlier more miscellaneous epistolary collections and secret histories."[6] In
Carnell's judgment the next issue, which presents "a much more focused

epistolary essay," demonstrates a progression in Manley's periodical form, as it is here that she masters the art of the "taut, focused pamphlet."[7]

This chapter seeks to draw Manley's *Examiners* out of the shadow of both her own canon and the editorship of Swift. The genres of secret history and periodical polemic explore and exploit different tensions, and the formal and stylistic conventions of these genres were consequently divergent.[8] Scholarship on the secret history as a form has come to consider it a genre tailored to the navigation of the boundaries between public and private.[9] In Nicola Parsons's reading, Manley's *New Atalantis* (1709) exposed "seemingly private indiscretions as a way of providing its readership with an index to the public, or political, corruption of those involved."[10] Thus secrecy and publicity are realigned, while the private reader is implicated in the political act of exposition through the necessity to "decode and activate the information that gossip contained."[11] Manley's earlier work *The Lady's Pacquet of Letters, Taken from her by a French Privateer in her Passage to Holland. Suppos'd to be Written by several Men of Quality. Brought over from St. Malo's by an English Officer at the last Exchange of Prisoners* (1707) similarly navigated the question of publicity,[12] but in this case via a tradition of epistolary satire.[13] The *Lady's Pacquet of Letters* reproduced "gossipy anecdotes about somewhat marginal or elusive political figures."[14] This "subtly disruptive" program has led Carnell to frame the work as an epistolary secret history in the manner of Charles Gildon's *The Post-Boy Robb'd of his Mail* (1692), or Vincent de Voiture's *Familiar and Courtly Letters to Persons of Honour and Quality* (1700).[15] Indeed the first publication of the *Lady's Pacquet of Letters* was in a miscellany volume alongside Marie-Catherine Le Jumel de Barneville, Baroness d'Aulnoy's *Memoirs of the Court of England.*[16]

These epistolary secret histories perform discourses of private mail abducted, rent open, and revealed.[17] Yet, as Manley moved into periodical writing after 1710, she began working within another epistolary tradition. In the periodical, epistolarity brought echoes of trade networks, of the public meeting of minds, and of ideals of old English liberty. Editors sought foreign correspondence and invited submissions from readers at home.[18] They presented the pages of their periodicals as a form of public *agora* in which discussion and debate might flourish. In this public literary space it was the boundary between the fictive and factive that was explored by editors seeking rhetorical opportunities. Epistolarity was well suited to this exploration, thanks to its implication of an external correspondent in the content of a periodical. Letters distanced the editor from the content of a paper, complicating questions of authenticity and authority and creating space for contentious material. Such "underhand Endeavours" employed by editors are alluded to by Manley herself in *Examiner* 50, in the passage quoted at the start of this chapter. By recontextualizing Manley's periodical writings within this periodical tradition then, this chapter seeks to provide a deeper account of her style and form in the *Examiner*. Further, a focus on Manley's

epistolarity in the *Examiner* offers an opportunity to attend to the herme-
neutics of letters in periodicals, which remain underexamined in scholarship
of the early eighteenth-century periodical press.[19]

The culture of epistolarity in periodicals stretched back to at least 1691,
when John Dunton built a commercially viable paper upon the basis of
reader submissions with the *Athenian Mercury* (1691–1697).[20] Each issue
of the *Athenian* contained between eight and fifteen questions sent by readers,[21] and answered by the semifictitious Athenian Society, who purported to
be an association of learned gentlemen.[22] The *Athenian*'s lead was followed
widely in the early decades of the eighteenth century. Daniel Defoe printed
numerous reader letters in a subsection to the *Review* (1704–1713) initially
entitled the *Mercure Scandale: Or Advice from the Scandalous Club*. Letters
from readers were equally prominent in the periodicals of Joseph Addison
and Richard Steele. The *Spectator* (1711–1712), which began just a few
months before Manley took over the *Examiner*, made particularly extensive
use of reader contributions. According to Donald F. Bond's count: "about
two out of every three papers with Steele's signature letters are made up of
contributed matter, sometimes with a sentence or two by way of introduction,
at other times with no editorial comment whatever."[23] This was an epistolary culture that continued in almost every essay paper of the early eighteenth century, irrespective of theme and faction. Manley's *Examiners* were
a part of this tradition, emerging as the technique had become established,
but while its possibilities had not been fully exhausted by periodical writers.

In Manley's *Examiners* 48 and 50 she presents sets of epistolary miscellanies. Issue 48, of June 21–28, 1711, opens with an observation on correspondents. Manley, writing in the persona of the Examiner, supposes that
"some Wit, and much Leisure, have made it a Fashion among ingenious
Persons, to send Letters, by way of assistance, to us Weekly Writers."[24] In
recognition of these efforts, she will "do what lies in my Power towards
introducing into the World, the Works of those Anonymous Persons who
are so fond of being Authors."[25] The paper then presents summaries of a
series of letters. The first condemns associations between Christians and
Jews, and especially the Whigs' efforts to "strengthen their *Routed Party*,
by a Reinforcement from the Circumcis'd." The second letter criticizes the
queen's physicians, while the third chastises the Tories for failing to reward
their old supporters who suffered "under the late Junto." The fourth letter
continues a debate with the Whig *Medley* (1710–1712), which was set up in
opposition to the *Examiner* in October of 1710. This letter comments on the
Medley's recent attacks on Abel Roper's *Post-Boy*, occasioned by the latter's
printing of the queen's speech. In the next letter religion is again the topic,
as a "Mr Tol—d" is reported as professing a lack of faith in the Holy Ghost.

Thus far the collection of epistles is certainly miscellaneous, if united in
a broad factional position. The letters attacking Whigs over their Jewish
associates and John Toland, for instance, present a partisan line on religious toleration at both the specific and general levels. The first letter makes

reference to the prominent military contractor Sir Solomon Medina,[26] whose close associations with Marlborough made him the ideal stand-in for Whig corruption on the one hand, and the issue of Jewish naturalization on the other. The reference to Toland further develops this broader critique, as he was a vehement supporter of religious toleration on the basis of common humanity.[27] This was a distinctly party political issue. As Justin Champion has proposed, the naturalization question was "in essence an extension of the Whig/Tory divide over the nature of the relationship between the established Church and civil liberties."[28] Thus, the miscellany collection of issue 48 had a very coherent partisan position, even if the letters appear to present a scatter-shot attack on first reading.

Issue 50 presents a similarly mixed bag of letters, pressing a variety of Whig abuses of position and power.[29] These range from obsequious courtiers, and impropriety among the queen's ladies in waiting, to an account of corruption in the management of Morden College and the sufferings of the late chaplain there on account of his Tory sensibilities.[30] The letters in these issues, united in their disapproval of the Whig faction at every level of public society, serve a rhetorical function for the editor. As Manley's partial *exposé* of the epistolary mode in issue 50 indicates, these letters are supposed to represent a clamor of public agreement with the editorial agenda.[31] As she sees it, "the concurrent Interest of many Authors must be much more prevailing than that of one."[32] This requires a claim of authenticity about the authorship of the letters; a promise that they have truly arrived in the post, sent by external agents. Manley's discussion of "Anonymous Persons" in the introduction to issue 48 makes such a claim of authenticity for the letters. In that introduction she further hints that she is able to oblige only very few of her numerous correspondents by setting their concerns in print. These authenticity claims imply a distance between the editor of the paper and the content printed within it. Responsibility for the content is shifted back to the reading/writing public, creating the impression of public consensus.

This distancing function was a widespread feature of the epistolary mode operating in partisan periodicals in the early eighteenth century. Such a positioning can be seen, for example, in the program of the *London Journal* (1720–1724) in 1720. This was the year of the South Sea Bubble, when stock prices for the South Sea Company rose from around £130 at the start of the year, to over £1,000 in June, before crashing back to around £200 in October.[33] Through the meteoric rise and fall of stock prices, the oppositional Whig *London Journal* launched a series of scathing attacks on the stock-jobbers and corrupt officials who were apparently making huge profits out of the company. Letters from readers were a key part of the journal's editorial strategy. An advertisement for letters to the editor had been printed in the first issue of the paper, noting that these were to be taken in by J. Roberts in Warwick-Lane.[34] Already by late June, "Mr. Journal" was printing letters from readers on the subject of greed and avarice,[35] and through July, August, and September the rate of such letters increased to a steady stream.

Mr. Journal pretends to neutrality in his choice and presentation of letters. In one issue, for instance, he suffixes several letters with a notice "that the World may judge of our impartiality," claiming that "we have inserted these two Letters just as we received them, relating to our South-Sea Gentry."[36] Yet the overwhelmingly negative account of the South Sea Company presented in reader letters and editorial writing alike is clearly more design than coincidence, as were Manley's collections of anti-Whig letters in *Examiners* 48 and 50. Periodical editors had the power to select which letters were printed, and to shape the manner in which they were presented.[37] The editorial decision to print dozens of letters that repeated the same points about a preferred topic should therefore be read as a rhetorical device. By printing these collections of letters, editors created an impression of consensus, and of an overwhelming public outcry.

As suggested above, this impression of public consensus required an assurance from the editor that printed contributions were authentic. They had to convincingly seem genuine in both their authorship and in their capacity to represent the balance of public opinion. Without such assurances a miscellany presentation of letters would not reach its full rhetorical possibility, but this was not the only rhetorical opportunity offered by letters. The epistolary convention offered a singular proposition to factional writers, creating a space for them to write into. For if letters were to be regularly printed, why should the editor not pen some of them? Indeed the historical evidence suggests that while reader participation in the production of content was a real and widespread phenomenon of the early eighteenth-century press, many letters were editorial creations.[38] These "editorial letters" allowed writers to appropriate the distancing effect of an epistolary frame to separate themselves and their publications from segments of their printed content. Further, the epistolary frame created an opportunity to construct a character in the guise of a correspondent. That character could be sympathetic, ridiculous, vile, misguided, or merely exaggerated, whichever possibility served the editorial agenda.

The miscellany of letters attacking Whig corruption and religious toleration presented in *Examiner* 48 is capped off with a sixth and final letter, which makes use of this epistolary opportunity. The letter unites the collection into a comprehensive statement of anti-Whig politics. Its subject is purportedly the extension of an invitation to the Examiner to join with the politically descendant Whigs. Opposition, suggests the author, requires greater talents than government: "Their Business [the Tories'] is done, they have no more occasion for your Pen; you must therefore expect to be neglected and forgotten as your Fellow-Labourers have been."[39] Assuring the Examiner that he will be welcomed by the Whigs, the correspondent writes that "We are so far true Politicians that both our Love and Hatred always give way to our Interest." A modest degree of flattery will achieve the thing, and to that end this Whig ambassador encloses a draft letter, which the Examiner is supposed to use when advertising his defection. This letter within the letter panders to Whig avarice and vanity, assuring them that "Your very Adversaries can't deny but you have more Mony than they, and consequently must give you up the Superiority of Wit."

This caricature of a Whig is transparently a creation of Manley herself, yet superficially at least this letter carries more markers of authenticity than the other contributions in the issue.[40] This piece is deftly prefaced with an assurance that it will be shown "at length, because he [the correspondent] calls himself a *Whig*, and may possibly charge me with unfair Quotation, if I sink any part of what he hath wrote." Significantly, it is the only letter reproduced in full in this issue, and the formal properties of a letter—salutation, subscription, and so forth—are drawn into the show of authenticity. Yet, the *Medley* for one was unconvinced by these assurances. The issue of July 2–9 professed that "It is no Secret that we Weekly Writers very often pretend to Epistolary Commerce ... like some antiquated Beaus, we often write Letters to our selves."[41] He therefore exposes the Examiner as the Whig ambassador, "'tis he himself who is this witty, idle and ingenious Person." For the *Medley* this unmasking removes the sting from the text, as the image of public consensus is dismantled.

I would contend, though, that it is precisely in the combination of probably authentic letters and patently forged ones that Manley reaches the full potential of epistolary journalism. Authenticity is deliberately complicated in this epistolary mode. The editorial letter played upon transparent forgery alongside disingenuous claims of truthfulness. Editorial epistles both required the camouflage of genuine reader correspondence, and drew attention to their own disguise. There is a direct link here to the larger arena of early eighteenth-century satire. The use of epistolary frames for periodical writing works with and alongside allusion, allegory, irony, and other techniques that we associate with the high satire of the period. So, just as any good political allegory drew sufficient attention to its own referential possibilities, the editorial letter made its forgery apparent.

Jonathan Swift's Crassus letter in the *Examiner*—that "Roman triumph" mentioned in the opening excerpt—illustrates the point. This letter was printed in early 1711, well into Swift's program of attack on Marlborough, and a few months before the editorship passed on to Manley. For the issue of February 1–8, 1711, Swift penned a letter supposedly addressed to the Ancient Roman general Marcus Crassus. In case the identification between Crassus and Marlborough had slipped past some inattentive readers, Swift litters the letter with biographical details obviously referring to Marlborough. With the link painstakingly made, the core accusation is landed:

> you are deeply stain'd with that odious and ignoble Vice of Covetousness: 'Tis afirm'd, that you descend even to the meanest and most scandalous Degrees of it; and while you possess so many Millions, while you are daily acquiring so many more, you are solicitous how to save a single Sesterce.

Swift does not stop there, for Marlborough's fame and popularity as a military hero had to be overcome for any criticism of the man to find purchase in the public mind. He therefore goes on to argue that the general's adversaries must reflect on this vice of avarice and be "tempted to talk as if we owed our Success, not to Your Courage or Conduct, but to those Veteran Troops you Command, who are able to Conquer under any General." It is a concise and comprehensive attack, which formed one small part of Swift's greater program to damage Marlborough's reputation in advance of formal corruption charges being laid against the great general.

The full allegorical setting of the Crassus letter is not shared by all examples of editorial letters. Nevertheless, the framing devices, invented correspondents, and plays of authenticity in epistolary journalism serve a very similar rhetorical end to this kind of historical allegory. This epistolary technique was ubiquitous in the early eighteenth-century press, particularly where polemic, or even prohibited, topics were concerned. The Jacobite printer and editor Nathaniel Mist, for instance, repeatedly returned to using an epistolary frame for dangerous content. In 1718, Mist printed a letter from "Sir Andrew Politic" in the *Weekly Journal or Saturday's Post* (1716–1725).[42] The letter questioned the administration's foreign policy, and Mist was arrested and questioned for the libel. The prosecution did not succeed, however, and Mist did not suffer any significant harm from the events.[43] He returned to the technique of framing political commentary in letter form with a series of letters from Persia, printed in *Mist's Weekly Journal* (1725–1728). These included an infamous letter printed on August 24, 1728, and generally credited to the exiled Duke of Wharton. In the words of Jeremy Black, this letter was "an extreme libel on George II."[44] It also offered an extensive praise of the character of the Pretender, James III, all within the frame of "a perfect Relation of the present State of Affairs in Persia" from the correspondent "Amos Dudge."[45]

The *London Journal*, as well as hosting numerous letters from readers, also made use of epistolary frames for editorial material, most famously in Cato's Letters. While these are now generally studied as a collection attributed to Thomas Gordon and John Trenchard, in their original periodical context they were pseudonymous and mixed in among other letters from readers. Indeed Cato's first letter to the *London Journal* appeared in the immediate wake of the bursting of the South Sea Bubble,[46] and the early letters continued the journal's program of attack on the directors of the company.[47] When Gordon began to write illegal parliamentary reports for the *London Magazine* (established 1732) in the 1730s he similarly worked with both allegory and epistolarity.[48] Gordon printed debates and reports from an imaginary club, and enacted charades of receiving letters from anonymous correspondents.[49] His contemporary, Samuel Johnson, provided parliamentary reports to the *Gentleman's Magazine* (established 1731) under the nom-de-plume of Sylvanus Urban in the form of letters reporting on the debates of the Lilliputian parliament.[50]

Such charades were also a feature of Manley's epistolary technique in the *Examiner*. In September of 1710 Manley printed the first of two long letters supposedly authored by "a Swedish Officer at Bender, to his Friend at Stockholm."[51] The second Bender letter appeared in *Examiner* 49.[52] These letters employ the same allegorical referents as Manley's *Memoirs of Europe* (1710), and form an attack on the most prominent Whigs from the Godolphin ministry.[53] In the first letter, the Swedish officer addresses the question of why the King (Anne) has stayed so long among the Turks (the Junto) rather than returning to "His Faithful Subjects" (the Tories). The officer first reproaches his friend for disloyal thoughts, asking "How can you suppose, That a King, whose *Heart is intirely Swedish*, should be content to live so long among *Turks* and *Tartars?*"[54] The friend should rather trust that the King "is heartily weary of His *new Friends* and *Allies*" and that "He intends to set Himself free, as soon as He can." This image of imprisonment, surveillance, and control by the Junto extends through the letter. The Swedish officer represents the Turks as "Spies upon His Conduct, rather than Guards to His Person." Particular reproach is again meted out to Marlborough, in the guise of the rapaciously greedy Commanding Basha.

The allegorical setting of these polemics is one dimension of their design, yet the epistolary features that surround the allegory are also deployed to hermeneutic purpose. In interpreting the letters, for instance, attention to chronology is key. This requires that both the post dates ascribed to the letters and their publication dates be accounted for. So while the first Bender letter was printed in September of 1710, it carries the post date of July 1, 1710. In the period between those two dates Godolphin's ministry had been dismissed, ushering in a period of Tory supremacy. The second Bender letter is introduced with an explicit reference to the earlier piece. Yet while the letter was printed in July of 1711, the text is post dated October 2, 1710. That is, after Harley had won a Tory majority in the September 1710 election, but before this new parliament had met for the first time in November 1710. Thus its allegory must be read in the light of the nine-month interim between the letter's supposed composition and its publication. Given this chronology the second Bender letter reads as a continuation of the program, set out in Manley's *Examiner* number 46, to investigate the vices of the late ministry. For the Tory *Examiner*, this chronological trickery is a celebration of the events of late 1710, alongside a reminder of the ills suffered under the late Whig ministry.

Paratextual elements such as quotation marks and formatting are also used in these issues to contain the allegory within the frame of a letter, and within the voice of the Swedish officer. The first letter carries a full set of formal epistolary elements, which lend an overemphasized air of authenticity to the material. The preface to the letter gives an account of its provenance, while the letter itself runs with the post date and location above a formal opening salutation. The subscription "I am, &c," delimits the end of the letter. Meanwhile each line of the letter text follows a quotation mark, a column of which run down the left side of the text. These same features appear with the sixth letter to the miscellany issue number 48 (featuring the Whig ambassador to the Examiner), and the second Bender letter in issue 49. Through such paratextual devices the text of these letters is separated from the editorial text and voice in material as well as rhetorical ways. Further, quintessential markers of mail such as post dates and salutations contain an implicit suggestion of authenticity. Both of these factors further the distancing function of the epistle.

The context of these letters is also hermeneutically significant, particularly in their publication alongside miscellany collections of reader contributions. The Bender letters are the most extensive examples of Manley utilizing the letter as frame for editorial writing in a periodical. As the discussion above has shown, she was among an extensive company of periodical editors who used such techniques for rhetorical purpose. In the strongest of these cases, Mist's papers and the *London Journal* for instance, the editorial letter sat alongside reader contributions. This setting allowed the editor to claim a clamor of agreement with their program, but also to enact duplicitous claims for authenticity. In Manley's *Examiners* it is essential to read the "focused epistolary essay" of issue 49, to return to Carnell's description, among the miscellanies presented in issues 48 and 50. In the setting of this "epistolary commerce" the second Bender letter gains its rhetorical purchase, as Manley sports with authenticity and epistolarity.

The ultimate expression of this editorial agenda is in Manley's final issue of the *Examiner*, number 52 of July 19–26, 1711. This issue wrapped up her editorship, taking leave of the town while remaining a "conceal'd Pen."[55] In reflecting on the past months in politics and editorial business, Manley admits to some errors of strategy, particularly her lapse into tit-for-tat argument with the *Medley*. Yet she takes a parting shot at that paper in the form of obsequious thanks "for so constantly explaining what he thought my Meaning in any dark Allusions, or Allegories." There is no explicit acquiescence to the *Medley*'s interpretations made here, but the implication is that the Whig paper had served the Examiner's cause in drawing so much attention to the significance of hidden meanings. The pains that the *Medley* took to accuse the Examiner of being in correspondence with himself are thus reframed as assistance to Manley's cause.

In 2009 Nicola Parsons called for a renewed emphasis on the "interactive and fluid relationships between texts, readers, authors, and the state" in the early eighteenth century.[56] I would suggest that epistolary journalism offers an ideal site for such exploration thanks to both the truly participatory dimension of the early eighteenth-century periodical press, and the liberties editors such as Manley took with this epistolary convention. Central to such epistolary journalism is a collapse of the fictive and factive, as editors created characters, drew up allegories, and mocked the powerful, all within an epistolary frame that made explicit claims to authenticity. Studies focused on other genres have recognized this dimension of epistolarity. As Elizabeth Cook has argued, "studies of eighteenth-century epistolarity must begin by rejecting an anachronistic distinction between literatures of fact and fiction."[57] While there are generic differences between different epistolary forms—from the novel, to the secret history or periodical—a central feature delimited through epistolarity is distancing. The implication of an external, often unknown or anonymous, correspondent in the text works alongside a simultaneous positioning of the editor or writer as disinterested intermediary. Truth thus becomes a promise of faithful transmission rather than an assurance that the material itself is accurate or plausible.

Within this epistolary commerce, periodical editors created space for public discussion but also found space for the expression of their own agendas. The letter thus framed an ambiguous terrain in the periodical. Claire Brant has recently proposed that eighteenth-century epistolarity challenges the public/private dichotomy. She states that "Attempts to reconfigure Habermas's model of public and private spheres have led to proposals for a third site, either a zone of overlap between public and private or a realm of more uncertain relations."[58] As Manley's periodical writing demonstrates, epistolary journalism might also demand that we allow for a greater uncertainty in the relations of fictive and factive in remodeling the early eighteenth-century public sphere.

Notes

1. *Examiner* 50, July 5–12, 1711.
2. Rachel Carnell, *A Political Biography of Delarivier Manley* (London: Pickering & Chatto, 2008), 1.
3. Paula McDowell, *The Women of Grub Street: Press, Politics, and Gender in the London Literary Marketplace, 1678–1730* (Oxford: Clarendon Press, 1998), pt. 3.
4. Ruth Herman, *The Business of a Woman: The Political Writings of Delarivier Manley* (Newark: University of Delaware Press, 2003), 14.
5. Ibid., chap. 5.
6. Carnell, *Political Biography*, 203; Nicola Parsons, *Reading Gossip in Early Eighteenth-Century England*, Palgrave Studies in the Enlightenment, Romanticism and Cultures of Print (Basingstoke: Palgrave Macmillan, 2009), 9.
7. Carnell, *Political Biography*, 203.
8. Carnell discusses the potency of the secret history as a polemical form in a chapter for this volume, offering an illuminating reading of Manley's semi-autobiographical *Rivella* as secret history.
9. There is an extensive literature on the genre of the secret history, a review of which is outside the scope of this study. See Michael McKeon, *The Secret History of Domesticity: Public, Private, and the Division of Knowledge* (Baltimore: Johns Hopkins University Press, 2006); Parsons, *Reading Gossip*, Chapter 2 provides a review of recent literature. See also n. 8, p164.
10. Parsons, *Reading Gossip*, 8.
11. Ibid., 152.
12. Carnell, *Political Biography*, 152; Delarivier Manley, *The Selected Works of Delarivier Manley*, ed. Rachel Carnell and Ruth Herman (London: Pickering & Chatto, 2005), vol. 1.

13. Clare Brant, *Eighteenth-Century Letters and British Culture* (Basingstoke: Palgrave Macmillan, 2006), 5, 15.
14. Carnell, *Political Biography*, 154; See also McKeon, *Secret History of Domesticity*, 570.
15. Carnell, *Political Biography*, 154.
16. Translated from the French original *Mémoires de la Cour d'Angleterre* (1695).
17. McKeon, *Secret History of Domesticity*, 570.
18. Michael Harris, *London Newspapers in the Age of Walpole: A Study of the Origins of the Modern English Press* (Rutherford; Madison; Teaneck: Fairleigh Dickinson University Press, 1987), 197.
19. Some work has been done on the use of reader letters in specific periodicals, but as yet the broader questions of editorial uses of reader letters have not been addressed. Some excellent work regarding specific periodicals includes: Helen M. Berry, *Gender, Society and Print Culture in Late-Stuart England: The Cultural World of the Athenian Mercury*, Women and Gender in the Early Modern World (Burlington, VT: Ashgate, 2003); Greg Polly, "A Leviathan of Letters," in *The Spectator: Emerging Discourses*, ed. Donald J Newman (Newark: University of Delaware Press, 2005), 105–28; Eve Bannet, "'Epistolary Commerce' in The Spectator," in *The Spectator: Emerging Discourses*, ed. Donald J. Newman (Newark: University of Delaware Press, 2005), 220–47.
20. The first issue was titled the *Athenian Gazette*, but this was changed with the second issue to the *Athenian Mercury*. The collected volumes were titled the *Athenian Gazette; or Casuistical Mercury*.
21. Berry, *Gender, Society and Print Culture*, 18.
22. Stephen Parks, *John Dunton and the English Book Trade*, Garland Reference Library of the Humanities, vol. 40 (New York: Garland, 1976), 80.
23. Donald F. Bond, "Introduction," in *The Spectator*, ed. Donald F. Bond (Oxford: Clarendon Press, 1965), lix.
24. *Examiner* 48, June 21–28, 1711.
25. *Ibid.*
26. Herman, *Business of a Woman*, 140.
27. Toland's *Reasons for Naturalising the Jews in Great Britain and Ireland* was not published until 1714, but his views on the issue were public before that time. He was similarly outspoken in defense of the naturalization of Protestant refugees from the Palatinate when the issue was debated through 1709–1711. Justin Champion, "Toleration and Citizenship in Enlightenment England: John Toland and the Naturalization of the Jews, 1714–1753," in *Toleration in Enlightenment Europe*, ed. Ole Peter Grell and Roy Porter (Cambridge: Cambridge University Press, 1999), 133–56.
28. Ibid., 141.
29. *Examiner* 50, July 5–12, 1711.
30. Ibid. Morden College was founded in 1695 by Whig MP and merchant Sir John Morden (*bap.* 1623–1708). It housed impoverished pensioners, and by 1710 was run by a panel of trustees drawn from the Levant and East India Companies. The implication of corruption at the College was thus directed at City merchants. For the history of Morden College see Patrick Joyce, *Patronage and Poverty in Merchant Society: The History of Morden College, Blackheath, 1695 to the Present* (London: Gresham Books, 1982).

31. Herman considers this rhetorical function, but does not connect Manley's editorial strategy to that of her peers. See Herman, *Business of a Woman*, 151.
32. *Examiner* 50, July 5–12, 1711.
33. Julian Hoppit, "The Myths of the South Sea Bubble," *Transactions of the Royal Historical Society (Sixth Series)* 12 (2002): 143.
34. Roberts was trade publisher for the *London Journal* in 1720. The printer/ bookseller was in fact John Peele, but Bechdolt Realey's study of the paper suggested that the actual proprietor was Elizée Dobrée. Charles B. Realey, "The London Journal and Its Authors, 1720–1723," *University of Kansas Humanistic Studies 5*, no. 3 (1935): 1–39. For more on Roberts see Giovanni Tarantino, *Republicanism, Sinophilia, and Historical Writing: Thomas Gordon (c.1691–1750) and His "History of England"* (Turnhout: Brepols, 2012), 6, n. 15 and passim. As Carnell's essay in this volume shows, Roberts was also the trade publisher for Manley's *Rivella*.
35. See for example the issue for June 18–25, which contains a letter for a "Humphry Quaery" about greed and the fact that no man will be satisfied that he has enough.
36. *London Journal*, July 30–August 6, 1720.
37. The "structural authority" of editors in their ability to select and filter reader letters has been discussed in Polly, "A Leviathan of Letters," 117.
38. Berry, *Gender, Society and Print Culture*, 35–38; Polly, "A Leviathan of Letters," 105–28.
39. *Examiner* 48, June 21–28, 1711.
40. Manley's experience as a writer of Varronian satire, discussed by Chris Mounsey in a chapter for this volume, is evident here. The many layers of text and meaning built up in the Whig ambassador's letter are typical of the "doubleness" of the Varronian satiric mode.
41. *Medley* 41, July 2–9, 1711.
42. *Weekly Journal or Saturday's Post*, 25 October 1718.
43. Jeremy Black, "An Underrated Journalist: Nathaniel Mist and the Opposition Press During the Whig Ascendency," *Journal for Eighteenth-Century Studies* 10, no. 1 (1987): 37.
44. Ibid., 28.
45. *Mist's Weekly Journal* 175, August 24, 1728.
46. The first Cato Letter appeared in: *London Journal* LXVIII, November 5–12, 1720.
47. John Trenchard and Thomas Gordon, *Cato's Letters, Or, Essays on Liberty, Civil and Religious, and Other Important Subjects*, ed. Ronald Hamowy (Indianapolis: Liberty Classics, 1995); Realey, "London Journal."
48. Realey, "London Journal," 20–21; Thomas Kaminski, *The Early Career of Samuel Johnson* (Oxford: Oxford University Press, 1987).
49. Tarantino, *Republicanism*, 36–37, n 77.
50. Benjamin Beard Hoover, *Samuel Johnson's Parliamentary Reporting* (Berkeley: University of California Press, 1953); Nikki Hessell, *Literary Authors, Parliamentary Reporters: Johnson, Coleridge, Hazlitt, Dickens* (Cambridge; New York: Cambridge University Press, 2012).
51. *Examiner* 7, September 7–14, 1710.
52. *Examiner* 49, June 28–July 5, 1711.

53. Manley, *Selected Works*, vol. 3.
54. The allegory refers to the Battle of Poltava (1709), in which Charles XII of Sweden suffered a decisive loss to Peter I of Russia. After the battle Charles lived for five years in exile in Ottoman-controlled Moldavia. Employed allegorically, these events carried an implication of the decline of an empire against a powerful neighbor. For an account of these events see Robert I. Frost, *The Northern Wars War, State and Society in Northeastern Europe, 1558–1721*, Modern Wars In Perspective (Hoboken: Taylor & Francis, 2014).
55. *Examiner* 52, July 19–26, 1711.
56. Parsons, *Reading Gossip*, 153.
57. Elizabeth H. Cook, *Epistolary Bodies: Gender and Genre in the Eighteenth-Century Republic of Letters* (Stanford, CA: Stanford University Press, 1996), 17.
58. Brant, *Eighteenth-Century Letters*, 5.

13 The Miscellaneous *New Atalantis*

Nicola Parsons

Much like its full title, Delarivier Manley's *Secret Memoirs and Manners of Several Persons of Quality, of Both Sexes. From the New Atalantis, an Island in the Mediterranean* (1709) overflows with character and event. This secret history of England's recent past is a collection of anecdotes, loosely held together by a frame narration in which the Lady Intelligence relates scandalous episodes to two allegorical figures, Virtue and Astrea, as they tour London and its environs. The two volumes that result are peopled with hundreds of characters, occupying a shifting scene that takes in private residences, places of public recreation, and the parliament. The miscellaneous nature of the narrative is extended by its use of various forms, interpolating verse, maxims, dialogues, and fable. Taken together, these episodes build a teeming picture of Whig corruption and vice that is understood as Manley's biggest literary innovation and her greatest political intervention.[1] Although the miscellaneous nature of the text is arguably *The New Atalantis*'s most striking feature, it has not been the focus of existing critical accounts. The important scholarship that rehabilitated *The New Atalantis*, and established its place in literary history, has tended to make its arguments by focusing only on sections of the text, selecting particular passages for discussion as representative of the whole. In demonstrating, for example, that the dynamics of sex and secrecy in *The New Atalantis* are means of engaging complex political issues, the work of Ros Ballaster, Toni Bowers, and others have focused attention on the text's longer episodes of seduction.[2] Concentrating on these scenes establishes important connections between Manley's *roman à clef* and the amatory fiction of the 1720s, but it also downplays the miscellaneity of the text.

In emphasizing and analyzing *The New Atalantis*'s composite form, this essay presents a new perspective on Manley's best-known text. By paying careful attention to the miscellaneous properties of the text and identifying and exploring its fragmentary poetics, rather than focusing on selections from the larger anecdotes, I argue that its digressive nature is not only a means of disrupting a linear narrative and of resisting the teleology of Whig history, as is perhaps appropriate for Manley's genre and politics, but it is also a means of exploring the interstices between conceptualizing alternate worlds and constructing alternate histories.

The title of *The New Atalantis*, together with details of the dedication to the second volume, frames the text by emphasizing its strategic commitment to miscellaneity. In adopting the word "atalantis" for her title, Manley invokes a tradition of utopian political philosophy that refers specifically to England, a genre represented most recently by Francis Bacon's *New Atlantis* (1627).[3] It also indicates an intention to disrupt this tradition: the addition of an extra "a" syncopates the word "atlantis," displacing the original stresses to create an aural dislocation and suggest a fractured vision.[4] This commitment to multiplicity is extended in the dedication to the second volume, in which Manley details the tradition in which she is writing. Drawing from Dryden's essay on the development of satire, Manley describes her text as "Var[r]onian satire," written on "different subjects, tales, stories and characters of invention."[5] In invoking Varro as her model, Manley not only locates herself within contemporary debate on the nature and purpose of satire— Dryden's essay being "the formative statement" for most eighteenth-century satirists[6]—but she also foregrounds the composite and various nature of her own text. Following Dryden, Manley understands Varronian satire as a miscellaneous form, comprising different episodes, various characters, and multiple modes. In fact, like the broader category of Menippean satire in which it stands, Varronian satire is defined by its multiplicity, typically mixing "languages, genres, tones, or cultural and historical periods."[7] Varro's works themselves only survived in fragmentary form and were rarely read.[8] As Howard Weinbrot has recently concluded: "[Varro] is less an author of specific works than a name and authority for the various."[9]

The framework of *The New Atalantis* brings the classical past into contact with England's present and recent past. It opens in a mythological register, recalling the classical past through the introduction of Astrea, the goddess of justice in the Greek pantheon, and her mother Virtue. In describing Astrea's withdrawal from earth and enacting her return, *The New Atalantis* also recalls a literary tradition that extends from Virgil to Dryden wherein the return of Astrea to earth heralds a new golden age. In *The New Atalantis*, however, Astrea has returned to earth only to catalog corruption so that she might better educate her charge, a situation that emphatically forecloses the possibility that England is on the brink of a golden age at the same time as it insists her return is only temporary. The dialogue between the past and present that her temporary return seems to herald is rendered problematic by other aspects of the text. Although her descent to earth and reunion with Virtue are narrated in free indirect discourse, this mode is soon replaced by a dialogue between the two goddesses and their guide Intelligence that centers on their immediate responses to their journey. This dialogue unfolds in the dramatic present tense, rendered typographically on the page through the use of speech tags, as the goddesses try to make sense of what they see and as Intelligence attempts to convey all she knows. The effect of this form becomes apparent as the goddesses set out by sea for Angela, the capital of Atalantis. As the goddesses approach the vessels at anchor, Astrea confesses her wonder at the unfolding scene—"Oh, my dear! can there be a sight more beautiful? they all seem to be in a vast hurry; what are they doing? What use is so much linen, fastened with cords, that trembles in the wind, and is but with struggling made obedient to the hand?"[10]—prompting Virtue to explain the rudiments of sailing and nautical arts. Notably, the journey that follows is not represented: the text moves straight from Virtue's account of the operation of seafaring, delivered on the rural coastline, to Astrea's disgusted assessment of their journey, delivered once they have safely disembarked on the outskirts of Angela. Astrea is so horrified by the "riots and blasphemy"[11] she witnessed in the course of their journey that she declares she will never set foot upon another ship. The fact that the behavior occasioning her ire is referred to but not represented works to privilege the observations of the goddesses, suggesting that their conversation is more important than the dramatic narrative. On other occasions, the insistent focus on present-tense commentary takes place in circumstances designed to foreground the dialogue form at the same time as it raises questions about its efficacy.

The consistent foregrounding of the conversational structure and the consequent insistence on present-tense narration creates a temporality that is oddly static. This is especially apparent in the talkative gentleman's narration of the "chariot races" taking place outside the Atalantic capital. In a crowded paragraph, we witness the competitors conversing with each other, glimpse the race in progress, and hear the results. The gentleman begins with a conversation unfolding between a prince and a marchioness at the side of her coach:

> She has a bottle of ratafia with her. Mark what a pint glass they give. O brave Prince! Twill bring you to the goal indeed. If his head does not swim with this, and the violence of the course, my Lady Marchioness will be much disappointed, but the other prince will be more, who has paid more for it. He loves money above all things, unless it be chastising the domestics. In a word, he is a man of a proud, sullen, yet choleric and avaricious temper. No body will be pleased if the prize falls to him, and yet he cannot possibly fail of it. They are already started and are to have three heats. Charming young hero! The prince himself, by favour of ratafia, has gained it. He is the conqueror for the first time. But see, the second bout his eyes dazzle, he has mistook his ground and runs on the other side of the post. This is the Marchioness's cunning, but she shall not be better for it. The morose Prince has got the prize, as I foretold, and there are very few upon the place that are pleased with his victory.[12]

The staccato movement from commentary to action that has always just concluded suggests the gentleman is so absorbed in pleasurable speculation that he struggles to keep up with events as they unfold. That is to say, he is not able to describe the intrigues of the competitors or the progress of the race because he is too preoccupied with interpretation and forecasting. In this way, the episode highlights the problematic integration of event and interpretation in *The New Atalantis*.

The dialogue between Intelligence, Astrea, and Virtue that unfolds over the course of the text ostensibly mirrors the ideal role of dialogue in humanist education. There, it functioned as a tool enabling the discovery of ideas and the formulation of arguments. Understood as a written representation of a reasoned debate, dialogues both exemplified and inculcated the practice of rational thought: that is, the use of debate to work out ideas and put forward arguments. As a literary form, dialogues present a body of information and represent the process by which that information is transmitted and received.[13] It is, as Chloe Houston has argued, a "textual strategy for embodying dialectical discovery in discourse."[14] The possibilities for mediating different perspectives in pursuit of new understanding implicit in the dialogue form is insistently foreclosed in *The New Atalantis*. In fact, aside from occasions where Astrea or Virtue prompt Intelligence for information about a person they have spotted, the three allegorical figures appear to be in conversation in name only. The speech tags that preface their respective comments are the principal sign they are in conversation: there are very few genuine points of interaction; indeed, the goddesses often talk at cross purposes to each other. Moreover, the impetus for their conversation is not disputation but movement: topics don't arise naturally in the course of discussion, but are prompted instead by the happenstance of their journey. Their conversation is propelled by the advent of a striking scene or a passing figure, such as the rawboned priest, defending himself from his wife's assault with his face smeared with apple pie and butter,[15] or a coach dropping off two passengers in the middle of the night at an otherwise deserted location.[16] These accidental occurrences are sufficient to prompt a story from Intelligence and an assessment from the goddesses. The topic changes with the scene and the transition narrated exclusively through their movement. In the set pieces of each volume—the account of the men and women promenading through St. James Park (the Prado) and the members of parliament gathering in the Divan—neither Intelligence nor the goddesses attempt to make connections between the various scandals that are embodied before them. Instead, another story is elicited each time a new figure draws focus with the shift in narrative attention marked only by grammatical imperatives (such as, "Look!" or "See!") that direct the goddesses' vision and the reader's interest. As a result, scandalous episodes are not brought into meaningful relation. Instead, the text is insistently fractured and miscellaneous, and topics are often violently disconnected from each other.

The opening of the second volume of *The New Atalantis* foregrounds the discrepancies between Intelligence's investments in the scandals she narrates and the perspective shared by Astrea and Virtue. In an implicit response to the corruption uncovered in the previous volume, the goddesses debate whether responsibility for the many failings of the inhabitants of the sublunary world lies with Jupiter, who has created temptations that lead men and women astray, or with humanity's willful disregard of the tenets of religion. Forecasting the consequences of a world in which religion is entirely displaced, Virtue works herself into a state of such agitation that her despair is represented in block capitals: "OH RACE! UNWORTHY OF THE TRUTH! NOW MAY BE SEEN THE BENEFIT OF RELIGION!"[17] At this moment Intelligence breaks her silence, and she does so in terms that draw attention to the incongruity between her interests and those of the goddesses. Noting that Astrea and Virtue have been "declaiming at length beyond my understanding," she seeks their permission to investigate why a hired coach is stopped at midnight at such a remote location. Intelligence poses a series of questions—"[w]hat can a coach of hire do here at this hour of the night?", "what can this adventure mean?"[18]—that impress upon the reader the irregular nature of the scene and convey instantly what might be gained from taking a closer look. The interplay does more than emphasize the discrepancies between the two perspectives presented in the text or possibilities for mediation, as it might when used in political philosophy: it demonstrates a failure to bring scandal, and the narrative interest that accompanies it, into proper conversation with an ethical framework. The dialogue form, in other words, works to showcase different perspectives rather than as a means of mediating between the two and interrogating their differences. It is a means of insisting on disconnection and fragmentation in an inherently episodic text.

The interests of the goddesses and their companion are often comically at odds with each other, a fact of which the three figures themselves are conscious. Having interrupted Intelligence's account of Count Fortunatus's early fortune to reflect on the vice of ingratitude more generally, Astrea recognizes she has different investments in the scandals of Atalantis. She says as much to Intelligence—"but in moralising, I interrupt your story"[19]—casting her commentary as not only other to the story but also as an impediment to it. Following the lengthy story of the unnamed Duke's seduction of his ward, Charlot, his subsequent inconstancy and eventual abandonment of her, Astrea concludes: "no woman ought to introduce another to the man by whom she is beloved. If that had not happened, the Duke had not possibly been false."[20] Many have pointed out the inadequate fit between the knowledge distilled in this maxim and the story of betrayal that has preceded it, but few have noted that early editions of *The New Atalantis* also mark this material as textually other. Rebecca Bullard observes that eighteenth-century editions draw attention to Astrea's reflection with a series of inverted commas in the margins.[21] Combined with the dialogue marker "*Astrea*.]" [sic], which precedes the goddess's reflection, these quotation marks redouble the emphasis on direct speech. But they also act as a type of printed marginalia, or indexical device, suggesting the text they point to is ripe for extraction and repurposing.

In fact, in writing *The New Atalantis*, Manley draws on collections of maxims and on printed commonplace books more frequently than we have realized. Rachel Carnell identifies six instances where adages are drawn directly from *Politeuphuia: Or, Wits Treasury* (1707), the first of a series of "wisdom books" begun in 1597 and in print continuously through-out the seventeenth and eighteenth centuries; I have identified six more commonplaces drawn from the same text.[22] Manley also employs maxims drawn from the fashionable *Réflexions ou Sentences et Maximes Morales* (1706) of La Rochefoucauld (a text she also depicts herself reading in her semiautobiographical text, *The Adventures of Rivella*) alongside sententiae drawn from La Bruyère's *Characters; or the Manners of the Age* (1705).[23] In distilling knowledge of human behavior and principles that govern conduct into pithy formulations, maxims have much in common with the humanist practice of commonplacing. David Allan has recently demonstrated that the commonplace book remained an important cultural form well into the eighteenth century, its popularity propelled in part by its transformation into a printed genre.[24] Commonplaces represent a form of gnomic wisdom that distil general truths without reference to time, sug-gesting that the world operates according to enduring patterns. Printed commonplace books like *Politeuphuia* contain aphorisms derived from multiple longer works by authors including Francis Bacon, Augustine, and Sophocles, organized under thematic headings such as "Concupiscence," "Prudence," and "Fortitude." Its contents represent a kind of decontex-tualized wisdom that points outward to longer arguments. The capacity for aphoristic knowledge to trouble narrative order is exploited fully in La Rochefoucauld's *Réflexions ou Sentences et Maximes Morales*, a best-selling classic in England.[25] Each of Rochefoucauld's numbered maxims is presented as self-sufficient, and all are organized according to the logic of juxtaposition. In fact, the maxims depend on dislocation and variety, as early readers of the texts acknowledged. One of the English translators reflected on the associative structure of the maxims in the preface to his edition, noting that

> As for what regards the order of these reflections, the reader will at first view discover, that as they are all upon different matters, it was in a manner impossible to place them in an exact method: and tho' there are several upon the same subject, it was not judged proper to place them always one after another, for fear of disgusting the reader, who is generally best entertained with an agreeable variety.[26]

This not only suggests that miscellaneity is essential to the maxims them-selves, but also that this variety exactly fits the disposition of readers and is best judged to give them pleasure. What separates the maxim further from other forms of gnomic wisdom like the commonplace is that maxims are not extracted from longer philosophical treatises or literary works. Rather, they are original formulations that are imagined to stand alone without any broader textual context.

Intelligence cites several maxims from *Politeuphuia* in quick succession in describing the education the Duke devises for his ward, Charlot, including "a Friend loves always, a lover but for a time" and "the assaults of love were to be beaten back at the first sight, least they undermine at the second."[27] Here, they seem to highlight the superficial nature of an education in virtue designed by a man who "had a seeming admiration for virtue" but found it "incompatible (in an Age like this) with a Man[']s making his fortune."[28] It is an education that leaves Charlot "fraught with ... precepts"[29] but vulnerable to manipulation. However, the idea that maxims are incorporated in *The New Atalantis* only to emphasize the superficial aspect of this flexible, decontextualized, aphoristic knowledge is belied by the way they are used elsewhere in the text. In describing the overwhelming force of desire on the duke a few pages later, Intelligence again has recourse to a series of maxims, also drawn from *Politeuphuia* on the passion of love. Later, she employs four maxims from the same text to convey the temptations that beset Sereni (identified by eighteenth-century keys and contemporary editors as Lionel Sackville, Duke of Dorset). These instances rupture the text, as they introduce a different temporality by drawing attention away from the specifically located and historically circumscribed scandal that is both the reader and the goddesses' ostensible focus. Rather than being spread out throughout the text, these maxims or adages are often introduced in a rapid sequence that, effectively, presents multiple assessments of the particular instance of human conduct under discussion. These instances represent moments of contact between Intelligence's narrative—that is, the secret, or alternative history of Britain's recent past—and that of Astrea and Virtue, who occupy the classical, or mythological, framework within which that narrative unfolds. Whereas Intelligence describes specific instances of vice and encourages a referential reading that links those portraits to particular biographical individuals, the use of maxims in these portraits suggests these vices have no particular location but exist in the gnomic present tense. Such moments complicate the temporality of the text and suggest the narrative it offers exceeds the remit of the secret history, as it is usually understood.

Indeed, *The New Atalantis* is thick with allusion to classical and contemporary literature. On several occasions, the scandalous scenes Astrea, Virtue, and Intelligence witness prompt recollection of familiar poems that both help them to make sense of contemporary conduct and remind them of the extent of corruption. Virtue and Intelligence, on separate occasions, use lines from Rochester's well-known poem "A Letter from Artemisia in the Town to Chloe in the Country" to illustrate how fashionable love forecloses the ethical and virtuous capacities of passion.[30] Later, in relating Count Biron's history, Intelligence has recourse to four lines from Dryden's poem *Absalom and Achitophel* to illustrate the capricious temper of a people who would rebel against their sovereign in reference to the events of 1688. Poetry is not only incorporated in *The New Atalantis* via selective quotation; entire poems are also interpolated into the text.[31] Unlike the illustrative connections developed between the lines of poetry Virtue, Astrea, and Intelligence recall and the scandalous scenes they witness, these longer poems are only tenuously connected to the surrounding narrative. The introduction of Anne Finch's poem "The Progress of Life," for instance, is prompted by the glimpse Intelligence has of the author in one of the many coaches that crowd the fashionable Prado. She offers it only as a literary text, remarking first on Finch's poetic ability and then on the "abundance of applause" this particular poem has attracted, and not as a component of a longer story.[32] The goddesses respond in kind, commending "the thought that runs thro'" the poem but observing that the second and third stanza need abbreviation. There is even less connection between the second of Finch's poems and the secret history that unfolds over the course of the goddesses' journey. Virtue stumbles across a copy of "The Hymn," part of Finch's longer poem "Upon the Hurricane," as the three leave Count Biron's estate. Intelligence reads it aloud at her direction, but neither the poem nor her performance receive comment.[33] These interpolated poems, then, constitute nonnarrative moments that disrupt the secret history of England's recent past by producing moments of stasis.

The goddesses' journey is specifically located in England's recent past and follows a precise chronology, unfolding over the two days that immediately followed the death of William III in 1702. Significantly, the events Intelligence relates over the course of this journey do not possess a similar temporal logic. They are not ordered by chronology, but circle—seemingly at random—through the events of England's past, present, and future. Far from providing a linear account of recent history, the sequence of events in *The New Atalantis* re-creates that history through analeptic and proleptic shaping. In offering a chronologically disordered account of England's past, the text implicitly invites the reader to impose a meaningful order. But this task is rendered complex by the fact that the text provides more than one account of a single historical event. It is no accident that it is the events of the Revolution of 1688 that Manley returns to, as the revolution was the centerpiece of Whig secret histories.[34] In contrast to those Whig secret histories, which return to the events of 1688 in order to uncover the tyrannical practices of the Stuart monarchs (or their mistresses), *The New Atalantis* reveals the ingratitude and disloyalty of those who claimed to support them. In telling the story twice, however, the text also resists the ideology of Whig history that sought to naturalize the violent break with hereditary kingship the revolution represents and render it "as the natural course of events, part of a national English narrative that seamlessly connected past and present."[35]

In *The New Atalantis*, the events precipitating the revolution and the settlement that followed are narrated for the first time as Intelligence tells the history of John Churchill, under the guise of Count Fortunatus, in Volume

One and then again when she recounts the political career of Sidney, Earl of Godolphin in the figure of Count Biron in Volume Two. Told first as part of the Fortunatus's spectacular rise to power, the events of the revolution are appropriately connected to political and personal history. The events follow their historical sequence, even if their partisan narration gives them a particular color. When they are returned to in the second volume, the expected personal and political connections are absent. They do not unfold in the recent past of Atalantis but are displaced to the neighboring kingdom, known suggestively as utopia (or, literally, "no place"). In effect, this act of naming redoubles the geographical dislocation: the events are not only displaced from English history, but they relocated to the nowhere of utopia. There, the questions of religion and the exercise of monarchical power— questions that underwrote the historical revolution—are rewritten so that they center on gender. James II is represented here as the Princess Ormia, his Catholicism figured as a desire to alter the rules of succession so her son can ascend the throne in place of her daughter. Inverting the gender of the protagonists effectively emphasizes the potentially consequential intersection of politics and gender, as Ros Ballaster and Rebecca Bullard have argued respectively,[36] but together with the geographic dislocation, it also enables an account of the revolution that reaches an alternate conclusion and suggests a potential future for the main actors.

Under Manley's pen, the Princess Olympia (or Queen Anne) dies in childbirth as she was on the verge of succumbing to Robert Harley's persuasions to break with her favorite, Sarah Churchill, the Duchess of Marlborough, and the Lord Treasurer, Sidney Godolphin. Newly cognizant of her errors in judgment, she nominates Abigail Masham to take charge of her daughter's education and appoints Harley to act as regent while she is in her minority. As the episode continues, we learn that Marlborough dies on the battlefield, "covered with honour and wounds"[37] and that Sarah, news of her rapaciousness having spread in the absence of monarchical protection, is besieged by an angry mob, narrowly escaping execution only thanks to the intercession of Masham, who first rescues her and then founds a female monastery so that she can live out the remainder of her days.[38] Taken together, these events project a future that is yet to happen. In the case of Godolphin, the chronology is subject to further dislocation. He falls out of favor under Harley's regency and flees Utopia for a position in Henriquez's (or William of Orange's) court. We are told: "Henriquez, satisfied of his vast abilities and the true taste he had of the interests of Europe, received him into his cabinet, where he has almost as great a share in the management of state affairs as he had in Utopia."[39] As a result, the future consequences of Godolphin's conduct are projected backward, becoming the history of his current position as Lord Treasurer. This produces a complex and uncertain temporality, in which the line between the present and the past cannot be drawn. It further suggests that both the future can still be made and the past invested with new meaning.

Over the course of its two volumes, *The New Atalantis* both engages genres that model fragmentary knowledge, such as the commonplace and the maxim, and selectively engages with classical and contemporary precedent to produce a miscellaneous form. This enables the text to disrupt classical and unifying traditions and to resist the teleology of Whig history, by unsettling its attempts to naturalize the events of the revolution. It opens up temporal disjunctions that dislocate and fragment the narrative, disrupting its rootedness in place and time. As a result, *The New Atalantis* exists both in the "once upon a time" of the narrative opening and in the present political circumstances. In effect, it offers a rhizomatic narrative that allows readers multiple entry points and considerable agency.

Notes

1. Manley frames *The New Atalantis* as a political intervention in a letter to Robert Harley in 1710. She writes many believe she deserves "[r]egard for exposing the enemies of our Constitution for having, with hazard to myself, first circulated their vices and open'd the ey's of the Crow'd, who were then dazzled by the Shine of Power into awe and Reverence of their Persons." 16 [Apr./Jul. 1710], Portland Papers, BL MS 70290, fol. 1. Historians usually judge her intervention to be successful, citing G. M. Trevelyan's assessment that *The New Atalantis* was the piece of writing that did the "most harm" to the Whig ministry in the lead up to the elections. See *England under Queen Anne* (London: Longman, 1934), vol. 3, 62.
2. See, for example, Ros Ballaster *Seductive Forms: Women's Amatory Fiction from 1684–1740* (Oxford: Oxford University Press, 1992) and Toni Bowers, *Force or Fraud: British Seduction Stories and the Problem of Resistance, 1660–1760* (Oxford: Oxford University Press, 2011).
3. Eleanor Shevlin argues a similar point in "The Warwick Lane Network and the Refashioning of 'Atalantis' as a Titular Keyword: Print and Politics in the Age of Queen Anne," in *Producing the Eighteenth-Century Book: Writers and Publishers in England*, ed. Pat Rogers and Laura Runge (Newark: University of Delaware Press), 166.
4. Janet Todd, Ruth Herman, Elizabeth Wahl, and Eve Tavor Bannet suggest the title of Manley's text works to highlight its dystopian aspects. Janet Todd, *The Sign of Angellica: Women, Writing and Fiction, 1660–1800* (New York: Columbia University Press, 1989); Ruth Herman, *The Business of a Woman: The Political Writings of Delarivier Manley* (Newark: University of Delaware Press, 2003); Elizabeth Wahl, *Invisible Relations: Representations of Female Intimacy in the Age of Enlightenment* (Stanford, CA: Stanford University Press, 1999); Eve Tavor Bannet, "'Secret History': Or, Talebearing inside and Outside the Secretoire," *Huntington Library Quarterly* 68, no. 1/2 (2005). I and Melinda Alliker Rabb suggest some of the ways that Manley purposefully engages Bacon's earlier description of an ideal society. Nicola Parsons, *Reading Gossip in Early Eighteenth-Century England* (Basingstoke: Palgrave, 2009) and Melinda Alliker Rabb, *Satire and Secrecy in English Literature from 1650 to 1750* (Basingstoke: Palgrave, 2007).

5. Delarivier Manley, *The New Atalantis*, ed. Ros Ballaster (Harmondsworth: Penguin, 1991), 132. All subsequent references are to this edition.

6. Ros Ballaster, "Manl(e)y Forms: Sex and the Female Satirist," in *Women, Texts & Histories, 1575–1730*, ed. Clare Brant and Diane Purkiss, (London: Routledge, 1992), 221. Ballaster also suggests that Manley's invocation of Varro allows her to sidestep the masculine binary of Juvenal and Horace, although she concludes the reference to his precedent is ultimately "nothing more than an audacious trope" (224).

7. Howard D. Weinbrot, *Menippean Satire Reconsidered: From Antiquity to the Eighteenth Century* (Baltimore, MD: Johns Hopkins University Press, 2005), xi.

8. Only 591 brief fragments, most only 20 words long, survive from works said to number close to 151. Dryden almost certainly did not read Varro before composing his essay, taking his observations instead from André Dacier and Isaac Casaubon, and Manley, in turn, takes her observations from Dryden. See John Dryden, "Discourse Concerning the Original and Progress of Satire," in *The Works of John Dryden*, ed. A. C. Chambers and William Frost (Berkeley, CA: University of California Press, 1974), 28. Weinbrot discusses this chain of influence in *Menippean Satire Reconsidered*, Intro and Chapter 1.

9. Weinbrot, *Menippean Satire Reconsidered*, 37. See also Aaron Santesso, "*The New Atalantis* and Varronian Satire," *Philological Quarterly* 79, no. 2 (2000): 177–204, and P. K. Elkin, *The Augustan Defence of Satire*, (Oxford: Oxford University Press, 1973), 37–39.

10. Manley, 9.

11. Ibid., 10.

12. Ibid., 85.

13. Virginia Cox, *The Renaissance Dialogue Form: Literary Dialogue in Its Social and Political Contexts, Castiglione to Galileo* (Cambridge: Cambridge University Press, 1992), 4–5; Cathy Shrank, "Stammering, Snoring and Other Problems in the Early Modern English Dialogue," in *Writing and Reform in Sixteenth-Century England: Interdisciplinary Essays*, ed. John Blakeley and Mike Pincombe (Lewiston, NY: Edwin Mellen Press, 2008), 101.

14. Chloe Houston, *The Renaissance Utopia: Dialogue, Travel and the Ideal Society* (Farnham: Ashgate, 2014), 19.

15. Manley, 86–89.

16. Ibid., 136ff.

17. Ibid., 136.

18. Ibid.

19. Ibid., 16.

20. Ibid., 45.

21. Rebecca Bullard, *The Politics of Disclosure, 1674–1725*, (London: Pickering and Chatto, 2008), 93. The eighteenth-century editions of *The New Atalantis* I have been able to consult—those published in 1709, 1716, 1718, and 1720—all highlight Astrea's observation in this way.

22. Rachel Carnell tracks Manley's use of *Politeuphuia* in her edition of *The New Atalantis* (London: Pickering & Chatto, 2005), 41, 300, 302, 321n156, 396n365, 374n224. She overlooks the three adages from *Politeuphuia* employed in describing Charlot's education (discussed below), and three employed in drawing Sereni's character.

23. See Manley, 97, 138, 166, 234. I have cited the eighteenth-century translations of La Rochefoucauld and La Bruyère from which Manley quotes.

24. David Allan, *Commonplace Books and Reading in Georgian England*, (New York: Cambridge University Press, 2010).

25. Line Cottegnies provides evidence for the popularity of Rochefoucauld's maxims in England in "Of the Notion of Imitation: The Translations of La Rochefoucauld in England in the Late Seventeenth and Early Eighteenth Centuries," in *"Better in France?": The Circulation of Ideas across the Channel in the Eighteenth Century*, ed. Frederic Ogee, (Lewisburg, PA: Bucknell University Press, 2005), 128–30.

26. "The Translator's Preface," Duc de la Rochefoucauld, *Moral Maxims and Reflections* (London: 1706), v. Another reader noted that "the reason why Montaigne's and the Duke of *Rauchfoucault's* [sic] Manner of Writing pleases a great many is because Men's minds are not more curious than lazy: They had rather pursue for a Spirit some new Game that is started by the Way, than pursue the old one. But this loose manner of writing, as well as negligent style, have had at all times their patrons and admirers." Tamworth Reresby, *A Miscellany of Ingenious Thoughts and Reflections* (London, 1721), 53.

27. Manley, 39.

28. Ibid., 37.

29. Ibid., 39.

30. Ibid., 5, 191.

31. *The New Atalantis* includes "The Progress of Life" and "The Hymn," which formed part of Finch's longer poem *Upon the Hurricane*; both were subsequently printed in *Miscellany Poems, on Several Occasions. Written by the Right Honble Anne, Countess of Winchilsea* (London, 1713). Titled "An Ode" in Manley's text, the poem attributed to Elizabeth Taylor was included in *A Collection of Twenty-Four Songs* (London, 1685) and *The Theater of Music, or, A Choice Collection of the Newest and Best Songs Sung at the Court and Public Theatres* (London, 1685). It was also included in Nahum Tate's play, *A Duke and no Duke*, when it appeared in print in 1693.

32. Manley, 92.

33. Ibid., 211–14.

34. Carnell, *The Political Biography of Delariver Manley*, 176. Rebecca Bullard discusses the centrality of the revolution of 1688 to Whig secret histories in *The Politics of Disclosure*, though she does not make a connection to the multiple revisions of the same event in *The New Atalantis*.

35. Kevin Sharpe, *Reading Revolutions: The Politics of Reading in Early Modern England* (New Haven, CT: Yale University Press, 2000), 6.

36. Bullard, *Politics of Disclosure*, 98–99. Ros Ballaster makes this claim in the textual apparatus of her edition of *The New Atalantis* (296, n.406).

37. Manley, 208.

38. This episode attracted the attention of Arthur Maynwaring, who read *The New Atalantis* on behalf of the Duchess of Marlborough. He did not take episode seriously: rather than being disturbed by the violent near-death imagined for Sarah, he is instead amused at the depiction of Masham's generosity and expresses the hope that "it will make you laugh as it did me." Arthur

Maynwaring, "To the Duchess of Marlborough," [Oct.] 1709, *The Private Correspondence of Sarah, Duchess of Marlborough*. vol. 1 (London: Henry Colburn, 1972), 238. Rachel Carnell astutely argues it is likely this episode that brought *The New Atalantis* to the attention of the Secretary of State and that occasioned a warrant for Manley's arrest. (*The Political Biography of Delarivier Manley*, 180–85). Less noted, Maynwaring—and consequently, Sarah—assume *The New Atalantis* had been written by a man.

39. Manley, 208.

Afterword

Toni Bowers

How heartening it is to see all this work on Manley in one place! And how useful—and overdue—is a single volume where established and emerging scholars talk together, pointing to the astonishing range and influence of Manley's writing and modeling twenty-first-century approaches to it. My first response to this collection is a resounding "Hooray!" It is about time.

Those of us who have been interested in Manley's work for many years have grown accustomed to the tendency of some of our colleagues to dismiss it.[1] We are used to finding it nearly impossible to obtain affordable texts for our students. We have learned to expect difficulty getting space for a Manley-centered panel on academic conference programs, and we long ago gave up holding our breath in anticipation of a volume devoted entirely to Manley's work. And yet, here it is.

New Perspectives on Delarivier Manley and Eighteenth-Century Literature administers a salutary correction to those of us who had perhaps learned too well, over the years, to scale down our expectations.

It also reminds us that a vital community of scholars value and study and teach Manley's work, thinking about that work's roles in literary history in careful, purposeful, and deeply informed ways. Together, the authors whose work is included here take account of existing scholarship on Manley and then build on it, modeling questions and methods for the future. With this interpretive community at work, the future of Manley studies looks bright indeed. And it will be dramatically furthered by this volume.

What might that future look like? One thing this volume suggests is that what we thought we knew is likely to be productively, provocatively reevaluated and revised in coming years. So will the methods according to which Manley's work has so far been considered. A surprisingly broad range of proven and emerging theoretical models is demonstrated here to be of great use when it comes to interpreting Manley's work—geocritical, postcolonial, and affective theory; materialist feminist and queer theory—especially as these models challenge our understandings of power relations, categorization imperatives, hierarchies, and temporalities. Many of the essays in this volume mix up and multiply the objects of analysis, putting Manley's productions into detailed conversation with each other as well as with a range of literary sources, analogues, and archival discoveries. Most reach arresting insights by following the tried-and-true literary critical method that is also the most valuable skill we have to offer our students: critical close reading.

Several authors join in a sophisticated and suggestive conversation about the implications of Manley's practices of adaptation and appropriation. That conversation is especially promising, not only for Manley studies but also for broader considerations of the complicated places inhabited, during the eighteenth century, by "the past." The past, that supposed historical object, is also always an active subject of experience. That purportedly lost world is never *not* present, and its finished, left-behind status is always an interested fiction. In considerations of the place of the past in the multiple presents of the late seventeenth and early eighteenth centuries, Manley studies stands poised to lead the way, thanks to this volume and the larger body of work it represents.

The essays in this volume "thicken up" our understanding of Manley's many important roles in literary history. Readers will gain new understanding of the wide variety of literary traditions in which Manley's work signified—her complex relations to source material and the work of her contemporaries—and of the sophisticated critical conversation that has grown up around her writing over three centuries. As a corporate enunciation, moreover, *New Perspectives on Delarivier Manley* provides answers to the insightful question that Kirsten Saxton asks in the Foreword: "How can we map the critical conversation in new directions without ceding old ground?" We need to think again (and again) about Manley. And while we don't need to reinvent the wheel, state the obvious in ever-more elaborate ways, or repeat ourselves, I agree with Saxton that we *do* need to continue to occupy the places we have already been and the criticism that has already been produced, as well as the problems that still stubbornly remain alive. All these must remain part of any future work on Manley. This collection gives us methods, tools, and inspiration to carry out that complex task.

Much has been gained already, as every inch of this collection shows. But it is still the case that Manley is the least understood, least studied, and least taught of the so-called "fair triumvirate of wit," Behn, Manley, and Haywood. Why is that? And what does *New Perspectives on Delarivier Manley* do to address the problem of Manley's comparative invisibility?

First, this volume illuminates a significant proportion of the remarkable range of genres in which Manley wrote and which she helped to develop. This is important because part of the reason for Manley's relative neglect is the fact that she has traditionally been characterized, primarily at least, as a novelist. Defining Manley as a novelist has for some time now been recognized by many to be problematic; this volume drives the final nails into that coffin. The idea that Manley was primarily a novelist is misleading *even when it comes to her imaginative prose*, which exceeds the (famously fluid and uncertain) boundaries characteristic of other early works that critics tend to label "novels." As a result, Manley's imaginative prose works have been denigrated as bad novels, through a faulty syllogism, rather than recognized as offering something in excess of or different from "the" novel.

The authors whose work is gathered here challenge us to pay much more attention to Manley's extensive work in genres such as periodical writing, partisan writing, a variety of dramatic traditions, poetry, miscellany, and memoir. They offer important single-authored studies of each of these, and together they offer a collective account that will change many people's understandings of what kind of writer Manley was, the audiences she wrote for, and what she accomplished. Just as important, this volume offers a rich bibliography that points readers to even more potential "Manleys." *New Perspectives on Delarivier Manley* demonstrates in one place the significant, and still underestimated, extent to which Manley's was a ubiquitous voice in her time. She seems to have been involved in just about every feature of the literary scene, and to have been just about everywhere in early eighteenth-century metropolitan London. This book helps us to recognize Manley's presence in many textual and cultural places with which readers will be already very familiar; there she is, hidden in plain sight.

New Perspectives on Delarivier Manley also has exciting potential to improve how we teach. The sad truth is that for as long as we critic-teachers have understood Manley mainly as a writer of imaginative prose, we have unwittingly created a pedagogical problem for ourselves. We schedule as the "first stop" for new readers works that are among Manley's most difficult—the extensive, intricate, hypertopical secret histories. Doing so makes sense so long as we think of Manley as a novelist; these are her best-known works of prose fiction (or more accurately perhaps, faction, in both senses of the word). It is difficult, however, to build in *The New Atalantis* or *The Adventures of Rivella* on reading lists designed for uninitiated undergraduates and organized around academic semesters or quarters. The result has been that, too often, Manley drops out entirely from the reading list. This volume provides teachers who may have despaired of including Manley on the survey course with concrete alternatives for our students.

The essays here further suggest that it might be time to scale back the mantralike reiteration of Manley's membership in "the fair triumvirate of wit," unless it is accompanied with a recognition of her embeddedness *elsewhere* as well, in other intellectual and market communities. A practical broadening of Manley's writerly location, as it were, is one of the most valuable contributions this volume stands poised to make. Several of the essays here claim for Manley a wider participation in her own culture than has generally been acknowledged. I hope that in the future that recognition will continue to expand, and with it readers' abilities to better understand so-far neglected texts as well as the more familiar ones, too.

This collection shows how Manley scholarship of the past and the present is *speaking together* at this moment. It will be important, going forward, that new work on Manley not denigrate or attempt to trump what has come before. To do so would be to misunderstand the most basic claims of materialist feminism, poststructuralist theory, and postcolonial theory— all inheritances that, though somewhat long in the tooth, continue to infuse and enable eighteenth-century studies, and to give those studies purchase in the world. This book works because it fashions innovation from established wisdom without leaving that wisdom behind, and does so with both respect and boldness. From that foundation, it demonstrates the energy and vitality that are now driving Manley studies. It will be exciting to see what comes next.

Note

1. See Simpson, 107, 118 n. 9.

Selected Bibliography

Ahmed, Sara. *The Cultural Politics of Emotion*. Edinburgh: Edinburgh UP, 2004.

Allan, David. *Commonplace Books and Reading in Georgian England*. Cambridge: Cambridge University Press, 2010.

Andrea, Bernadette. *English Women Staging Islam, 1696–1707: Delarivier Manley and Mary Pix*. Toronto: Iter/Centre for Reformation and Renaissance Studies, 2012.

———. "Islam, Women, and Western Responses: The Contemporary Relevance of Early Modern Investigations." *Women's Studies: An Interdisciplinary Journal* 38 (2009): 273–92.

———. *Women and Islam in Early Modern English Literature*. Cambridge: Cambridge University Press, 2007.

Aravamudan, Srinivas. *Enlightenment Orientalism: Resisting the Rise of the Novel*. Chicago: University of Chicago Press, 2012.

Arber, Edward, ed. *The First Three English Books on America*. Birmingham, 1885.

Armitage, David. *The Ideological Origins of the British Empire*. Cambridge: Cambridge University Press, 2000.

Armstrong, Nancy and Leonard Tennenhouse. "A Mind for Passion: Locke and Hutcheson on Desire." In *Politics and the Passions 1500–1850*, edited by Victoria Kahn, Neil Saccamano and Daniela Coli. Princeton: Princeton University Press, 2006, 131–50.

Astell, Mary. *Some Reflections on Marriage*. In *A Celebration of Women Writers*, edited by Mary Mark Ockerbloom. http://digital.library.upenn.edu/women/ astell/marriage/marriage.html.

AVEN Project Team. "The Asexual Visibility & Education Network." *Asexual Visibility & Education Network (AVEN)*. 2012. www.asexuality.org.

Backscheider, Paula R. *Spectacular Politics: Theatrical Power and Mass Culture in Early Modern England*. Baltimore and London: The Johns Hopkins University Press, 1993.

Baldwin, Robert C. D. "Colonial Cartography under the Tudor and Early Stuart Monarchies, ca. 1480–ca. 1640." In *The History of Cartography: Cartography in the European Renaissance*, edited by J. B. Harley and David Woodward, 1754–80. Chicago: University of Chicago Press, 1987.

Ballaster, Ros. *Seductive Forms: Women's Amatory Fiction from 1684–1740*. Oxford: Clarendon Press, 1992.

Bannet, Eve Tavor. "'Secret history': Or, Talebearing Inside and Outside the Secretorie." In *The Uses of History in Early Modern England*, edited by Paulina Kewes, 367–88. San Marino: Huntington Library, 2006.

———. "'Secret History': Or, Talebearing inside and Outside the Secretoire." *Huntington Library Quarterly* 68, no. 1/2 (2005): 375–96.

———. "'Epistolary Commerce' in *The Spectator.*" In *The Spectator: Emerging Discourses*, edited by Donald J Newman, 220–47. Newark: University of Delaware Press, 2005.

Barad, Karen. *Meeting the Universe Halfway: Quantum Physics and the Entanglement of Matter and Meaning.* Durham: Duke University Press, 2007.

———. "Posthumanist Performativity: Toward an Understanding of How Matter Comes to Matter." *Signs: Journal of Women in Culture and Society* 28 (2003): 801–31.

Behn, Aphra. *Love-Letters between a Nobleman and His Sister.* In *The Works of Aphra Behn.* Edited by Janet Todd, Vol. 7. Columbus: Ohio State University Press, 1993.

———. *The Lucky Chance, or An Alderman's Bargain.* In *The Rover and Other Plays* edited by Jane Spencer, 183–270. Oxford: Oxford University Press, 1995.

———. *Oroonoko, The Rover and Other Works.* Edited by Janet Todd. Toronto: Penguin, 1992.

Berry, Helen M. *Gender, Society and Print Culture in Late-Stuart England: The Cultural World of the Athenian Mercury.* Women and Gender in the Early Modern World. Burlington, VT: Ashgate, 2003.

Birchwood, Matthew. *Staging Islam in England: Drama and Culture, 1640–1685.* Cambridge: D. S. Brewer, 2007.

Black, Jeremy. "An Underrated Journalist: Nathaniel Mist and the Opposition Press during the Whig Ascendency." *Journal for Eighteenth-Century Studies* 10, no. 1 (1987): 27–41.

Blackstone, Sir William. *Commentaries on the Laws of England (1765–69)*, 4 vols. Chicago: University of Chicago Press, 1979.

Blanchard, Rae. "Richard Steele and the Status of Women." *Studies in Philology* 26, no. 3 (1929): 325–55.

Blouch, Christine. "Eliza Haywood and the Romance of Obscurity." *SEL* 31, no. 3 (1991): 535–51.

Bond, Donald F. "Introduction." In *The Spectator*, edited by Donald F. Bond, xii–cvii. Oxford: Clarendon Press, 1965.

Bowers, Toni. "The Achievement of Scholarly Authority for Women: Trends in the Interpretation of Eighteenth-Century Fiction." *Eighteenth Century: Theory and Interpretation* 50, no. 1 (2009): 51–71.

———. *Force or Fraud: British Seduction Stories and the Problem of Resistance, 1660–1760.* Oxford: Oxford University Press, 2012.

Brady, Nicholas. *The Rape: Or, the Innocent Imposters.* 1692. Early English Books Online.

Brant, Clare. *Eighteenth-Century Letters and British Culture.* Basingstoke: Palgrave Macmillan, 2006.

Bratton, Jacky. *New Readings in Theatre History.* Cambridge: Cambridge University Press, 2003.

Braverman, Richard. "The Rake's Progress Revisited: Politics and Comedy in the Restoration." In *Cultural Readings of Restoration and Eighteenth-Century English Theater*, edited by J. Douglas Canfield and Deborah C. Payne, 141–68. Athens and London: The University of Georgia Press, 1995.

Brentjes, Sonja. "The Presence of Ancient Secular and Religious Texts in the Unpublished and Printed Writings of Pietro della Valle (1586–1652)." In *Travellers from Europe in the Ottoman and Safavid Empires, 16th–17th Centuries.* Farnham: Ashgate, 2010.

Brown, John. *An Account of Barbarossa, The Usurper of Algiers. Being the Story on Which the New Tragedy, Now in Rehearsal at The Theatre Royal in Drury-Lane.* London: W. Reeve, 1755.

Brown, Laura. *Ends of Empire: Women and Ideology in Early Eighteenth-Century English Literature.* Ithaca, NY: Cornell University Press, 1993.

———. *English Dramatic Form, 1660–1760: An Essay in Generic History.* London: Yale University Press, 1981.

La Bruyère, Jean de, *The Moral Characters of Theophrastus.* London, 1705.

Bullard, Rebecca. *The Politics of Disclosure 1674–1725: Secret History Narratives.* London: Pickering & Chatto, 2009.

Bush-Bailey, Gilli. *Treading the Bawds: Actresses and Playwrights on the Late-Stuart Stage.* Manchester: Manchester University Press, 2006.

Butler, Judith. *Gender Trouble: Feminism and the Subversion of Identity.* New York: Routledge, 1990.

———. *Gender Trouble: Feminism and the Subversion of Identity.* Abingdon: Routledge Classics, 2006.

———. *Bodies that Matter: On the Discursive Limits of "Sex".* Abingdon: Routledge Classics, 1993.

Caballero, Yolanda. "Patterns of Female Exploration in Delarivier Manley's Oriental Plays." In *Strangers in Early Modern English Texts.* Anglo American Studies, vol. 41, 227–56. Edited by Jesús López-Peláez. Frankfurt am Main: Peter Lang, 2011.

Caldwell, Tanya. "Meanings of *All for Love*, 1677–1813." *Comparative Drama* 38, no. 2/3 (2004): 183–211.

Carey, Daniel D. and Lynn L. Festa, eds. *The Postcolonial Enlightenment: Eighteenth-Century Colonialism and Postcolonial Theory.* Oxford: Oxford University Press, 2009.

Carnell, Rachel. "Delarivier Manley's Possible Children by John Tilly." *Notes and Queries* 54, no. 4 (2007): 446–48.

———. "More Borrowing from Bellegarde in Delarivier Manley's *Queen Zarah and the Zarazains.*" *Notes and Queries* 51 (2004): 377–79.

———. *A Political Biography of Delarivier Manley.* London: Pickering and Chatto, 2008.

———. "Reading Austen's *Lady Susan* as Tory Secret History." *Lumen* 32 (2013): 1–16.

———. "Slipping from Secret History to Novel." *Eighteenth Century Fiction* 28, no. 1 (fall 2015): 1–24.

Carnell, Rachel and Ruth Herman eds. *Selected Works of Delarivier Manley*, 5 vols. London: Pickering & Chatto, 2005.

Cartmell, Deborah and Imelda Whelehan, eds. *Adaptations: From Text to Screen, from Screen to Text.* New York: Routledge, 1999.

———. *The Cambridge Companion to Literature on Screen.* Cambridge: Cambridge University Press, 2007.

Casellas, Jésus López-Peláez. "'Race' and the Construction of English National Identity: Spaniards and North Africans in English Seventeenth-Century Drama." *Studies in Philology* 106, no. 1 (2009): 32–51.

Castle, Terry, ed. *The Literature of Lesbianism: A Historical Anthology from Ariosto to Stonewall.* New York: Columbia University Press, 2003.

Ceranowski, Karli June and Megan Milks. "New Orientations: Asexuality and Its Implications for Theory and Practice." *Feminist Studies* 36, no. 3 (2010): 650–64.

Champion, Justin. "Toleration and Citizenship in Enlightenment England: John Toland and the Naturalization of the Jews, 1714–1753." In *Toleration in Enlightenment Europe*, edited by Ole Peter Grell and Roy Porter, 133–56. Cambridge: Cambridge University Press, 1999.

Chapman, George. *Revenge for Honour. A Tragedie.* London: Richard Marriot, 1654.

Choudhury, Mita. *Interculturalism and Resistance in the London Theater, 1660–1800: Identity, Performance, Empire.* Lewisburg, PA: Bucknell University Press, 2000.

Chudleigh, Lady Mary. "To the Ladies." Electronic Texts. Edited by Jack Lynch. Accessed Oct. 16, 2014. http://andromeda.rutgers.edu/~jlynch/Texts/ladies.html.

[Churchill, Sarah, the Duchess of Marlborough]. *The Private Correspondence of Sarah, Duchess of Marlborough.* Vol. 1. London: Henry Colburn, 1972.

Cibber, Colley. *An Apology for the Life of Colley Cibber.* Edited by B. R. S. Fone. Ann Arbor: University of Michigan Press, 1968.

Cixous, Hélène "Sorties." In *Literary Theory: An Anthology.* Edited by Julie Rivkin and Michael Ryan, 578–84. Malden, MA: Blackwell, 1998.

Cixous, Hélène, Keith Cohen, and Paula Cohen. "The Laugh of the Medusa." *Signs* 1, no. 4 (1976): 875–93.

Clark, Constance. *Three Augustan Women Playwrights.* New York: P. Lang, 1986.

Clauss, James J. and Sarah Iles Johnston, eds. *Medea: Essays on Medea in Myth, Literature, Philosophy, and Art.* Princeton: Princeton University Press, 1997.

Colavito, Jason. *Jason and the Argonauts through the Ages.* Jefferson, NC: McFarland, 2014.

Conway, Alison. "Accessing Liberal Education." *ABO: Interactive Journal for Women in the Arts, 1640–1830* 2, no. 1 (2012): Open Access. http://scholarcommons.usf.edu/cgi/viewcontent.cgi?article=1033&context=abo.

Cook, Elizabeth H. *Epistolary Bodies: Gender and Genre in the Eighteenth-Century Republic of Letters.* Stanford, CA: Stanford University Press, 1996.

Copeland, Nancy. *Staging Gender in Behn and Centlivre: Women's Comedy and the Theatre.* Aldershot: Ashgate, 2004.

Corporaal, Marguerite. "'Will You to My Discourse Vouchsafe an Eare?': Women Dramatists' Negotiation of Gender and Genre on the Public Stage around 1700," *Journal of English Studies* 4 (2003–2004): 45.

Cottegnies, Line. "Of the Notion of Imitation: The Translations of La Rochefoucauld in England in the Late Seventeenth and Early Eighteenth Centuries." In *"Better in France?": The Circulation of Ideas across the Channel in the Eighteenth Century.* Edited by Frederic Ogee, 128–43. Lewisburg, PA: Bucknell University Press, 2005.

Cox, Virginia. *The Renaissance Dialogue Form: Literary Dialogue in its Social and Political Contexts, Castiglione to Galileo.* Cambridge: Cambridge University Press, 1992.

Croskery, Margaret Case. "Masquing Desire: The Politics of Passion in Eliza Haywood's *Fantomina.*" In *The Passionate Fictions of Eliza Haywood: Essays on Her Life and Work*, edited by Kirsten T. Saxton and Rebecca P. Bocchicchio, 69–94. Lexington: University Press of Kentucky, 2000.

Cuder-Domínguez, Pilar. "Gender, Race, and Party Politics in the Tragedies of Behn, Pix, and Manley." In *Teaching British Women Playwrights of the Restoration and Eighteenth Century.* Edited by Bonnie Nelson and Catherine Burroughs, 263–74. New York: Modern Language Association, 2010.

———. *Stuart Women Playwrights, 1613–1713*. Burlington, VT: Ashgate, 2010.

de Chickera, Ernst. "Palaces of Pleasure: The Theme of Revenge in Elizabethan Translations of Novelle." *Review of English Studies* 11, no. 41 (1960): 1–7.

Dennis, John. *Essay upon the Opera's After the Italian Manner, Which are about to be Establish'd on the English Stage: With some Reflections on the Damage which they may bring to the Publick*. London: John Nutt, 1706.

———. *Liberty Asserted. A Tragedy. As it is acted at the New Theatre in Little Lincoln's-Inn-Fields*. London: George Strahan and Bernard Lintott, 1704.

Dixon, Thomas. "'Emotion': The History of a Keyword in Crisis." *Emotion Review* 4 (2012): 338–44.

———. *Passions to Emotions: The Creation of a Secular Psychological Category*. Cambridge: Cambridge University Press, 2003.

Dollimore, Jonathan. *Sex, Literature and Censorship*. Cambridge: Polity, 2001.

Dryden, John. *The Conquest of Granada by the Spaniards in Two Parts: Acted at the Theatre Royall*, London: Henry Herringman, 1672.

———. "Discourse Concerning the Original and Progress of Satire." In *The Works of John Dryden*, edited by A. C. Chambers and William Frost, 3–90. Berkeley, CA: University of California Press, 1974.

———. "Preface to *Fables Ancient and Modern*." In *Of Dramatic Poesy and Other Critical Essays*, 2 vols. London: Dent, 1962.

———. *The Satires of Decimus Junius Juvenalis. Translated into English Verse. &c.* London: Jacob Tonson, 1693.

Drougge, Helga. "Colley Cibber's "Genteel Comedy": *Love's Last Shift* and *The Careless Husband*," *Studia Neophilologica* 54 (1982): 62–79.

Eche, Antoine. "The Shores of Aphrodite's Island: Cyprus and European Travel Memory, 1600–1700. " In *Geocritical Explorations: Space, Place, and Mapping in Literary and Cultural Studies*. Edited by Robert T. Tally, Jr., 91–105. New York: Palgrave Macmillan, 2011.

Elkin, P. K. *The Augustan Defence of Satire*. Oxford: Oxford University Press, 1973.

Ellis, Frank H. *Sentimental Comedy: Theory and Practice*. Cambridge: Cambridge University Press, 1991.

Elster, Jon. *Alchemies of the Mind: Rationality and the Emotions*. Cambridge: Cambridge University Press, 1999.

Ezell, Margaret J. M. *Writing Women's Literary History*. Baltimore: Johns Hopkins University Press, 1993.

Feingold, Mordechai. "'The Turkish Alcoran': New Light on the 1649 English Translation of the Koran." *Huntington Library Quarterly* 75, no. 4 (2012): 475–501.

Ferguson, Moira, ed. *First Feminists: British Women Writers, 1578–1799*. Bloomington: Indiana University Press, 1985.

Field, Ophelia. *The Favourite: Sarah, Duchess of Marlborough*. London: Hodder and Stoughton, 2012.

Frangos, Jennifer. "Manl(e)y Fictions: The Woman in Man's Clothes and the Pleasures of Delarivier Manley's 'new Cabal.'" In *Sexual Perversions 1650–1890*. Edited by Julie Peakman, 95–116. London: Palgrave, 2009.

Freeman, Lisa. *Character's Theater: Genre and Identity on the Eighteenth-Century English Stage*. Philadelphia: University of Pennsylvania Press, 2002.

Floyd-Wilson, Mary. *English Ethnicity and Race in Early Modern Drama*. Cambridge: Cambridge University Press, 2003.

Frost, Robert I. *The Northern Wars War, State and Society in Northeastern Europe, 1558–1721*. Modern Wars in Perspective. Hoboken: Taylor & Francis, 2014.

Gallagher, Catherine. *Nobody's Story: The Vanishing Acts of Women Writers in the Marketplace, 1670–1820*. Berkeley: University of California Press, 1994.

Gill, Pat. "Gender, Sexuality and Marriage." In *The Cambridge Companion to Restoration Theatre*, edited by Deborah Payne Fisk, 191–208. Cambridge: Cambridge University Press, 2000.

———. *Interpreting Ladies: Women, Wit, and Morality in the Restoration Comedy of Manners*. Athens: The University of Georgia Press, 1994.

Girard, Rene. *Violence and the Sacred*. Trans. Patrick Gregory. Baltimore: Johns Hopkins University Press, 1977.

Gollapudi, Aparna. *Moral Reform in Comedy and Culture, 1696–1747*. Cornwall: Ashgate, 2011.

Gossman, Lionel. "Anecdote and History." In *History and Theory* 42 (May 2003): 143–68.

Gross, Daniel M. *The Secret History of Emotion: From Aristotle's "Rhetoric" to Modern Brain Science*. Chicago: University of Chicago Press, 2006.

Grosz, Elizabeth. *Volatile Bodies: Toward a Corporeal Feminism*. Bloomington: Indiana University Press, 1994.

Green, David. *Queen Anne*. London: Collins, 1970.

Greenfield, Anne. "The Titillation of Dramatic Rape, 1160–1720." In *Interpreting Sexual Violence, 1660–1800*, edited by Anne Greenfield, 57–68. London: Pickering & Chatto, 2013.

Gregg, Edward. *Queen Anne*. London: Routledge & Kegan Paul, 1980.

Harris, Ellen T. *George Frideric Handel: A Life among Friends*. London: Norton, 2014.

Harris, Frances, *A Passion for Government: The Life of Sarah, Duchess of Marlborough*. Oxford: Clarendon Press, 1991.

Harris, Michael. *London Newspapers in the Age of Walpole: A Study of the Origins of the Modern English Press*. Rutherford: Fairleigh Dickinson University Press, 1987.

Hayton, D. W. "Seymour, Sir Edward, fourth baronet (1633–1708)." *Oxford Dictionary of National Biography*. Oxford University Press, 2004. May 2009. http://www.oxforddnb.com/view/article/25162, accessed May 26, 2015.

Heinzelman, Susan Sage. "Teaching Eighteenth-Century Law and Literature: *The Adventures of Rivella*." In *Teaching Law and Literature*, edited by Austin Sarah, Cathrine O. Frank, and Matthew Anderson, 345–53. New York: Modern Language Association, 2011.

Herman, Ruth. *The Business of a Woman: Political Writings of Delarivier Manley*. Newark, DE: University of Delaware Press, 2003.

———. "Enigmatic Gender in Delarivier Manley's *New Atalantis*." In *Presenting. Gender: Changing Sex in Early-modern Culture*, edited by Chris Mounsey. 202–24. Lewisburg, PA: Bucknell University Press, 2001.

———. "An Exercise in Early Modern Branding." *Journal of Marketing Management* 19, no. 7–8 (2003): 709–27.

———. "A New Attribution to Delarivier Manley?" *Notes and Queries* 48 no. 4. (2001): 401–03.

Hessell, Nikki. *Literary Authors, Parliamentary Reporters: Johnson, Coleridge, Hazlitt, Dickens*. Cambridge: Cambridge University Press, 2012.

Heylyn, Peter. *A Little Description of the Great World*. Oxford, 1625.

Hollis-Berry, Elizabeth. "'No Party favour'd, no Designs in view': Female Rakes and Heroes, Politics and Power in Delarivier Manley's Heroic Drama." *Lumen:*

Selected Proceedings from the Canadian Society for Eighteenth-Century Studies 19 (2000): 171–86.

Hook, Lucyle. "Introduction." *The Female Wits: Or, the Triumvirate of Poets at Rehearsal. A Comedy. By "Mr. W. M."* i–xvi. 1704. A facsimile of the first edition. William Andrews Clark Memorial Library Augustan Reprint Society. No. 124. Los Angeles: University of California, 1967.

Hoover, Benjamin Beard. *Samuel Johnson's Parliamentary Reporting.* Berkeley, CA: University of California Press, 1953.

Hoppit, Julian. "The Myths of the South Sea Bubble." *Transactions of the Royal Historical Society, Sixth Series* 12 (2002): 141–65.

Houston, Chloe. *The Renaissance Utopia: Dialogue, Travel and the Ideal Society.* Farnham: Ashgate, 2014.

Howe, Elizabeth. *The First English Actresses: Women and Drama 1660–1700.* Cambridge: Cambridge University Press, 1992.

Hughes, Derek. *The Theatre of Aphra Behn.* Hampshire: Palgrave Macmillan, 2001.

Hultquist, Aleksondra, "Absent Children and the Emergence of Female Subjectivity in Eliza Haywood's *The British Recuse* and *The City Jilt.*" In *Spectacle, Sex and Property in Eighteenth-Century Literature and Culture*, edited by Julie A. Chappell and Kamille Stone. New York: AMS, 2015. 15–35.

Hume, Robert D. *The Development of English Drama in the Late Seventeenth Century.* Oxford: Clarendon Press, 1976.

———. *The Rakish Stage: Studies in English Drama, 1660–1800.* Carbondale: Southern Illinois Press, 1983.

Hutcheon, Linda. *A Theory of Adaptation.* New York: Routledge, 2006.

Hutner, Heidi, Ed. *Rereading Aphra Behn: History, Theory, and Criticism.* Charlottesville: University Press of Virginia, 1993.

Irigaray, Luce. *This Sex Which Is Not One.* Translated by Catherine Porter with Carolyn Burke. Ithaca: Cornell University Press, 1985.

James, Susan. *Passion and Action: The Emotions in Seventeenth-Century Philosophy.* Oxford, Clarendon Press: 1997.

Joule, Victoria. "Feminist Foremother? The Maternal Metaphor Present in Feminist Literary History and Delarivier Manley's *The Nine Muses.*" *Women's Writing* 20, no. 1 (2013): 32–48.

Joyce, Patrick. *Patronage and Poverty in Merchant Society: The History of Morden College, Blackheath, 1695 to the Present.* London: Gresham Books, 1982.

Kaminski, Thomas. *The Early Career of Samuel Johnson.* Oxford: Oxford University Press, 1987.

Katz, Candice Brook. "The Deserted Mistress in Mrs. Manley's *The Lost Lover,* 1696." *Restoration and Eighteenth-Century Theatre Research* 16 (1977): 27–39.

Kaul, Suvir. *Eighteenth-Century British Literature and Postcolonial Studies.* Edinburgh: Edinburgh University Press, 2009.

Keating, Erin. "In the Bedroom of the King: Affective Politics in the Restoration Secret History." *Journal of Early Modern Cultural Studies* 15, no. 2 (2015): 58–82.

———. "Envious Productions: Actresses, Audiences and Affect in the Restoration Playhouse." *Restoration: Studies in English Literary Culture 1660–1700* 37, no. 2 (2013): 37–53.

Kelley, Anne "'What a Pox Have Women to Do with the Muses?' *The Nine Muses* (1700): Emulation or Appropriation?" In *Women's Writing* 17, no. 1 (2010): 8–29.

Kerrigan, John. *On Shakespeare and Early Modern Literature: Essays.* Oxford: Oxford University Press, 2001.

Kerrigan, William and Gordon Braden. *The Idea of the Renaissance*. Baltimore: Johns Hopkins University Press, 1989.

Kimmelman, Elaine. "The Palace of Pleasure" in *Boston Public Library Quarterly* 2 (1950): 231–44.

Lord Kinross [John Patrick Douglas Balfour], *The Ottoman Centuries: The Rise and Fall of the Turkish Empire*. New York: Harper Collins, 1977.

Köster, Patricia. "Humanism, Feminism, Sensationalism: Mrs. Manley vs. Society," *Translations of the Samuel Johnson Society of the Northwest* 4 (1972): 42–53.

———. *The Novels of Mary Delariviere* [sic] *Manley 1705–1714*, 2 vols. Gainesville: Scholars' Facsimiles and Reprints, 1971.

Krueger, Misty. "Revenge in Early Restoration England and Sir William Davenant's *Hamlet*." *New Perspectives on the Eighteenth Century* 8 no. 1 (2011): 31–50.

Kuizenga, Donna. "Villedieu and Manley: Teaching Early Modern Pseudo-Autobiographies." In *Teaching Seventeenth- and Eighteenth-Century French Women Writers*, edited by Faith E. Beasley, 250–57. New York: Modern Language Association, 2011.

Lanser, Susan S. "Of Closed Doors and Open Hatches: Heteronormative Plots in Eighteenth-Century (Women's) Studies." In "Essays in Memory of Hans Turley" (special issue). Edited by Kathryn R. King. *The Eighteenth Century: Theory and Interpretation* 53, no. 3 (2012): 273–90.

Linker, Laura. *Dangerous Women, Libertine Epicures, and the Rise of Sensibility, 1660–1730*. Farnham: Ashgate, 2011.

L[ing], N[icholas]. *Politeuphuia, Wit's Common-Wealth*. London: W. Freeman, 1707.

Loomba, Ania. *Colonialism/Postcolonialism*. London: Routledge, 1998.

Lowenthal, Cynthia. *Performing Identities on the Restoration Stage*. Carbondale: Southern Illinois University Press, 2003.

Luhman, Niklas. *Love as Passion: The Codification of Intimacy*. Translated by Jeremy Gaines and Doris L. Jones. Cambridge: Polity Press, 1986.

Lyons, Paddy. "What Do the Servants Know?" In *Theatre and Culture in Early Modern England, 1650–1737: From Leviathan to Licensing Act*, edited by Catie Gill. 11–32. Surrey: Ashgate, 2010.

M., W. *The Female Wits: Or, the Triumvirate of Poets at Rehearsal. A Comedy. As it was Acted Several Days Successively with Great Applause at the Theatre-Royal in Drury- Lane. By Her Majesty's Servants*. 1704. Edited by Lucyle Hook. Los Angeles: William Andrews Clark Memorial Library Augustan Reprint Society Publication no. 124. University of California, 1967.

Makdisi, Saree and Felicity Nussbaum, eds. *The Arabian Nights in Historical Context Between East and West*. Oxford: Oxford University Press, 2008.

Manley, Delarivier. *The Adventures of Rivella*. Ed. Katherine Zelinsky. Orchard Park, NY: Broadview, 2003.

———. *The Adventures of Rivella; or, the History of the Author of Atalantis*. London, 1714.

———. *The Adventures of Rivella* [1714]. Ed. Katherine Zelinsky. Peterborough: Broadview Press, 1999.

———. *Almyna: or, The Arabian Vow. A Tragedy. As It Is Acted at The Theatre Royal in the Hay-Market, by Her Majesty's Servants*. London: William Turner, 1707.

———. *Letters Writen by Mrs Manley*, London: R[ichard].B[entley]. 1696.

————. *The Lost Lover; Or, the Jealous Husband: A Comedy. As It Is Acted at the Theatre Royal by His Majesty's Servants. Written by Mrs. Manley.* London, 1696. *Early English Books Online.* http://gateway.proquest.com.eres.library.manoa. hawaii.edu/openurl?ctx_ver=Z39.88-2003&res_id=xri:eebo&rft_id=xri:eebo: citation:11967475.

————. *The Lost Lover* in *Eighteenth-century Women Playwrights* Volume 1. Edited by Derek Hughes. London: Pickering & Chatto, 2001.

————. *The New Atalantis.* Edited by Rosalind Ballaster. New York and Harmondsworth: Penguin, 1991.

————. *The New Atalantis.* Edited by Rachel Carnell. Vol. 2. In *The Selected Works of Delarivier Manley.* Edited by Rachel Carnell and Ruth Herman. London: Pickering & Chatto, 2005.

————. *The Power of Love: In Seven Novels.* London: 1720.

————. *The Royal Mischief: A Tragedy. As It Is Acted by His Majesties Servants. By Mrs. Manley.* London, 1696. *Early English Books Online.* http://gateway.proquest. com.eres.library.manoa.hawaii.edu/openurl?ctx_ver=Z39.88-2003&res_id=xri: eebo&rft_id=xri:eebo:citation:11967475.

————. *The Selected Works of Delarivier Manley.* Edited by Rachel Carnell and Ruth Herman. 5 vols. London: Pickering & Chatto, 2005.

————. "To the Author of Agnes de Castro." *Agnes De Castro: A Tragedy. As It Is Acted at the Theatre Royal, by His Majesty's Servants. Written by a Young Lady.* London, 1696. *Early English Books Online.*

Markley, Robert. "Behn and the Unstable Traditions of Social Comedy." In *The Cambridge Companion to Aphra Behn,* edited Derek Hughes and Janet Todd, 98–117. Cambridge: Cambridge University Press, 2004.

Marsden, Jean I. "Beyond Recovery: Feminism and the Future of Eighteenth-Century Literary Studies." *Feminist Studies* 28 (2002): 657–62.

————. *Fatal Desire: Women, Sexuality, and the English Stage, 1660–1720.* Ithaca, NY: Cornell University Press, 2006.

Robert Mayer, "Introduction: Is There a Text in This Screening Room?" In *Eighteenth-Century Fiction on Screen,* edited by Robert Mayer, 1–15. Cambridge: Cambridge University Press, 2002.

McDowell, Paula. *The Women of Grub Street: Press, Politics, and Gender in the London Literary Marketplace.* Oxford: Clarendon Press, 1998.

McFarlane, Brian. *Novel to Film: An Introduction to the Theory of Adaptation.* New York: Oxford University Press, 1996.

McGovern, Barbara. *Anne Finch and Her Poetry: A Critical Biography.* Athens: University of Georgia Press, 1992.

McKeon, Michael. *The Secret History of Domesticity: Public, Private, and the Division of Knowledge.* Baltimore: Johns Hopkins University Press, 2006.

Milhous, Judith. *Thomas Betterton and the Management of Lincoln's Inn Fields 1695–1708.* Carbondale: Southern Illinois University Press, 1979.

Moi, Toril. *Sexual/Textual Politics: Feminist Literary Theory.* London: Routledge, 1985.

Morgan, Fidelis. *The Female Wits: Women Playwrights of the Restoration.* London: Virago, 1981.

————. *A Woman of No Character: An Autobiography of Mrs. Manley.* Boston: Faber & Faber, 1986.

Newman, Andrew J. *Safavid Iran: Rebirth of a Persian Empire.* London: I. B. Tauris, 2009.

Ngai, Sianne. *Ugly Feelings*. Cambridge: Harvard University Press, 2005.

The Nine Muses, Or, Poems Written by Nine Severall Ladies Upon the Death of the Late Famous John Dryden, Esq. London: Richard Basset, 1700. http://gateway.proquest.com.eres.library.manoa.hawaii.edu/openurl?ctx_ver=Z39.88-2003&res_id=xri:eebo&rft_id=xri:eebo:citation:12362030.

Nu, Su Fang. "Delarivere Manley's *Almyna* and Dating the First Edition of the *English Arabian Nights' Entertainments*," *English Language Notes* 40, no. 3 (2003): 19–26.

O'Donnell, Mary Ann. *Aphra Behn: An Annotated Bibliography of Primary and Secondary Sources*. New York: Garland, 1986.

Nussbaum, Felicity. *Torrid Zones: Maternity, Sexuality, and Empire in Eighteenth-Century English Narratives*. Baltimore: Johns Hopkins University Press, 1994.

Orr, Bridget. *Empire on the English Stage, 1660–1714*. Cambridge: Cambridge University Press, 2001.

———. "Galland, Georgian Theatre, and the Creation of Popular Orientalism." In *The Arabian Nights in Historical Context Between East and West*, edited by Saree Makdisi and Felicity Nussbaum, 103–30. Oxford: Oxford University Press, 2008.

Otway, Thomas. *The Orphan*. Edited by Aline MacKenzie Taylor. Lincoln: University of Nebraska Press, 1976.

Peyré, Yves. "Marlowe's Argonauts." In *Travel and Drama in Shakespeare's Time*, edited by Jean-Pierre Maquerlot and Michèle Willems, 106–23. Cambridge: Cambridge University Press, 1996.

Painter, William. *The Palace of Pleasure: Beautified, Adorned and well furnished, with Pleasant Histories and Excellent Nouvelles*. London, 1566.

———. *The Palace of Pleasure*. 1566, 2nd ed., ed. Joseph Jacobs, 3 vols. London: Ballantyne Press, 1890.

Parks, Stephen. *John Dunton and the English Book Trade*. Garland Reference Library of the Humanities, vol. 40. New York: Garland, 1976.

Parsons, Nicola. *Reading Gossip in Early Eighteenth-Century England*. New York: Palgrave Macmillan, 2009.

Patterson, Annabel. *Early Modern Liberalism*. Cambridge: Cambridge University Press, 1997.

Payne, Linda R. "Delariviere Manley." In *Dictionary of Literary Biography* Vol. 80. *Restoration and Eighteenth-Century Dramatists* (1989): 126–130.

Pearson, Jacqueline. *The Prostituted Muse: Images of Women & Women Dramatists 1642–1737*. New York: St. Martin's, 1988.

Peirce, Leslie P. *The Imperial Harem: Women and Sovereignty in the Ottoman Empire*. New York: Oxford University Press, 1993.

Penzer, N. M. *The Harem: An Account of the Institution as it Existed in the Palace of the Turkish Sultans with a History of the Grand Seraglio from its Foundation to the Present Time*. Philadelphia: Lippincott, 1937.

Pollak, Ellen. *Incest and the English Novel, 1684–1814*. Baltimore: Johns Hopkins University Press, 2003.

Polly, Greg. "A Leviathan of Letters." In *The Spectator: Emerging Discourses*, edited by Donald J. Newman, 105–28. Newark: University of Delaware Press, 2005.

Pope, Kenneth S. "Defining and Studying Romantic Love." In *On Love and Loving, edited by* Kenneth S. Pope, 1–24. San Francisco: Jossey-Bass, 1980.

Porter, Roy. *Flesh in the Age of Reason*. London: Penguin, 2004.

Prescott, Sarah. *Women, Authorship and Literary Culture, 1660–1740*. Basingstoke: Palgrave Macmillan, 2003.

Pratt, Mary Louise. *Imperial Eyes: Travel Writing and Transculturation*. New York: Routledge, 2008.

Punter, David. *Writing the Passions*. London: Longman, 2001.

Rabb, Melinda Alliker. *Satire and Secrecy in English Literature from 1650 to 1750*. New York: Palgrave Macmillan, 2007.

———. "The Manl(e)y Style: Delarivier Manley and Jonathan Swift." In *Pope, Swift, and Women Writers*, edited by Donald C. Mell. 125–53. Newark: University of Delaware Press, 1996.

Raleigh, Walter. *The History of the World*. London, 1617.

Realey, Charles B. "The London Journal and Its Authors, 1720–1723." *University of Kansas Humanistic Studies 5*, no. 3 (1935): 1–39.

Reddy, William. *The Making of Romantic Love: Longing and Sexuality in Europe, Asia, and Japan 900–1200ce*. Chicago: University of Chicago Press, 2012.

Reeve, Clara. *The Progress of Romance*. London, 1785.

Reresby, Tamworth. *A Miscellany of Ingenious Thoughts and Reflections. In Verse and Prose; with some Useful Remarks*. London, 1721.

La Rochefoucauld, François, duc de. *Moral Maxims and Reflections. In Four Parts*. London, 1706.

Roosen, William. *The Age of Louis XIV: The Rise of Modern Democracy*. Cambridge MA: Schenkman, 1976.

Ross, Deborah. *The Excellence of Falsehood: Romance, Realism, and Women's Contribution to the Novel*. Lexington: University Press of Kentucky, 1991.

Richetti, John J. *Popular Fiction before Richardson. Narrative Patterns 1700–1739*. Oxford, 1969.

———. "Popular Narrative in the Early Eighteenth Century: Formats and Formulas." In *The English Novel, Volume 1: 1700 to Fielding*, edited by Richard Kroll, 70–106. London and New York: Longman, 1998.

Robinson, David Michael. "'For how can they be guilty?' Lesbian and Bisexual Women in Manley's *New Atalantis*," *Nineteenth-century Contexts* 23 (2001): 187–220.

Rooney, Caroline. *Decolonising Gender: Literature and a Poetics of the Real*. Abingdon: Routledge, 2007.

Rosenthal, Laura J. "Introduction: Recovering from Recovery." *Eighteenth Century: Theory and Interpretation* 50 (2009): 1–11.

Rowe, Nicholas. *The Tragedy of Jane Shore. Written in Imitation of Shakespear's Style*. London: Bernard Lintott, 1714.

Rubik, Margarete. *Early Women Dramatists 1550–1800*. New York: St. Martin's, 1998.

Rubik, Margarete and Eva Mueller-Zettleman. In *Eighteenth-Century Women Playwrights*, Vol 1: *Delarivier Manley and Eliza Haywood*. London: Pickering and Chatto, 2001.

Said, Edward W. *Orientalism*. New York: Vintage, 1979.

Santesso, Aaron. "*The New Atalantis* and Varronian Satire." *Philological Quarterly* 79.2 (2000): 1–21.

Sargent, Carole Fungaroli. "How a Pie Fight Satirizes Whig-Tory Conflict in Delarivier Manley's *The New Atalantis*." *Eighteenth-Century Studies* 44, no. 4 (2011): 515–33.

———. "Military Scandal and National Debt in Manley's *New Atalantis*." *SEL: Studies in English Literature 1500–1900* 53, no. 3 (2013): 523–40.

Saxton, Kirsten T. *Narratives of Women and Murder in England, 1680–1760: Deadly Plots*. Aldershot: Ashgate, 2009.

Saxton, Kirsten T. and Rebecca P. Bocchicchio, Eds. *The Passionate Fictions of Eliza Haywood: Essays on Her Life and Work*. Lexington: University Press of Kentucky, 2000.

Schwartz, Alfred. "An Example of Eighteenth-Century Pathetic Tragedy: Rowe's *Jane Shore*." *Modern Language Quarterly* 22, no. 3 (1961): 236–47.

Settle, Elkanah. *Distress'd Innocence: Or, the Princess of Persia*. London, 1691. Early English Books Online.

Sharpe, Kevin. *Reading Revolutions: The Politics of Reading in Early Modern England*. New Haven: Yale University Press, 2000.

Shevlin, Eleanor F. "The Warwick Lane Network and the Refashioning of 'Atalantis' as Keyword: Print and Politics in the Age of Queen Anne." In *Producing the Eighteenth-Century Book: Writers and Publishers in England*, edited by Pat Rogers and Laura Runge, 163–92. Newark: University of Delaware Press, 2009.

Shrank, Cathy. "Stammering, Snoring and Other Problems in the Early Modern English Dialogue." In *Writing and Reform in Sixteenth-Century England: Interdisciplinary Essays*, edited by John Blakeley and Mike Pincombe, 99–120. Lewiston, NY: Edwin Mellen Press, 2008.

Sideri, Eleni. "'The Land of the Golden Fleece': Conflict and Heritage in Abkhazia." *Journal of Balkan and Near Eastern Studies* 14, no. 2 (2012): 263–78.

Somerset, Anne. *Queen Anne: The Politics of Passion*. New York: Knopf, 2013.

Spencer, Jane. *Aphra Behn's Afterlife*. Oxford: Oxford University Press, 2000.

———. *Rise of the Woman Novelist: From Aphra Behn to Jane Austen*. Oxford and New York: Blackwell, 1986.

Spedding Patrick, *A Bibliography of Eliza Haywood*. London: Pickering and Chatto, 2004.

Stallybrass, Peter. "Marginal England: The View from Aleppo." In *Center or Margin: Revisions of the English Renaissance in Honor of Leeds Barroll*, edited Lena Cowen Orlin, 27–39. Cranbury, NJ: Associated University Press, 2006.

Staves, Susan. *A Literary History of Women's Writing in Britain, 1660–1789*. Cambridge: Cambridge University Press, 2006.

Straub, Kristina. *Domestic Affairs: Intimacy, Eroticism, and Violence between Servants and Masters in Eighteenth-Century Britain*. Baltimore: The Johns Hopkins University Press, 2009.

Swift, Jonathan. *The Examiner and Other Pieces Written in 1710–11*. Edited by Herbert Davis Oxford: Blackwell, 1966.

Tally, Robert T. Jr., "Introduction: The World, the Text, and the Geocritic." In *The Geocritical Legacies of Edward W. Said: Spatiality, Critical Humanism, and Comparative Literature*, edited by Robert T. Tally Jr., 1–16. New York: Palgrave Macmillan, 2015.

———. *Spatiality*. London: Routledge, 2013.

Tarantino, Giovanni. *Republicanism, Sinophilia, and Historical Writing: Thomas Gordon (c.1691–1750) and His "History of England."* Turnhout: Brepols, 2012.

Trenchard, John and Thomas Gordon. *Cato's Letters, Or, Essays on Liberty, Civil and Religious, and Other Important Subjects*. Edited by Ronald Hamowy. Indianapolis: Liberty Classics, 1995.

Tauchert, Ashley. *Against Transgression*. Malden, MA: Blackwell, 2008.

———. "Woman in a Maze: *Fantomina*, Masquerade and Female Embodiment." *Women's Writing* 7 (2000): 469–86.

Tierney-Hynes, Rebecca. *Novel Minds: Philosophers and Romance Readers, 1680–1740.* Basingstoke: Palgrave, 2012.

Temple, Kathryn. "Manley's 'Feigned Scene': The Fictions of Law at Westminster Hall." *Eighteenth-Century Fiction* 22, no. 4 (2010): 573–98.

Todd, Janet. "Life after Sex: The Fictional Autobiography of Delarivier Manley." *Women's Studies* 15 (1988): 43–55.

———. *The Secret Life of Aphra Behn.* New Brunswick, NJ: Rutgers University Press, 1996.

———. *The Sign of Angellica: Women, Writing and Fiction, 1660–1800.* New York: Columbia University Press, 1989.

Trevelyan, G. M. *England under Queen Anne.* 3 vols. London: Longman, 1934.

Trotter, Catharine. *Revolution of Sweden. A Tragedy. As it is acted at the Queens Theatre in the Hay-Market.* London, 1706.

Wahl, Elizabeth. *Invisible Relations: Representations of Female Intimacy in the Age of Enlightenment.* Stanford, CA: Stanford University Press, 1999.

Warner, William B. "Formulating Fiction: Romancing the General Reader in Early Modern Britain." In *Cultural Institutions of the Novel,* edited by Deidre Lynch and William Beatty Warner, 279–305. Durham and London: Duke University Press, 1996.

———. *Licensing Entertainment: The Elevation of Novel Reading in Britain, 1684–1750.* Berkeley: University of California Press, 1998.

Wauchope, Piers. "Tollemache, Thomas (c.1651–1694)." *Oxford Dictionary of National Biography.* Oxford University Press, 2004. Online.

Weinbrot, Howard D. *Menippean Satire Reconsidered: From Antiquity to the Eighteenth Century.* Baltimore, MD: Johns Hopkins University Press, 2005.

Welham, Debbie. "The Political Afterlife of Resentment in Penelope Aubin's *The Life and Amorous Adventures of Lucinda* (1720)," *Women's Writing* 20, no. 2 (2013): 49–63.

Westphal, Betrand. *Geocriticism: Real and Fictional Spaces.* Translated by Robert T. Tally, Jr. New York: Palgrave Macmillan, 2011.

Wheeler, Roxann. *The Complexion of Race: Categories of Difference in Eighteenth-Century British Culture.* Philadelphia: University of Pennsylvania Press, 2000.

Wilkes, Wetenhall. *A Letter of Genteel and Moral Advice to a Young Lady.* Dublin: 1740.

Wilson, Brett D. *A Race of Female Patriots: Women and Public Spirit on the British Stage, 1688–1745.* Lewisburg, PA: Bucknell University Press, 2012.

Wilson, Kathleen. *The Island Race: Englishness, Empire and Gender in the Eighteenth Century.* New York: Routledge, 2003.

Yamanaka, Yuriko and Tetsuo Nishio, eds. *The Arabian Nights and Orientalism: Perspectives from East and West.* New York: Tauris, 2006.

Young, Edward. *The Revenge A Tragedy. As It Is Acted at The Theatre-Royal in Drury-Lane.* London, 1721.

Contributors

Bernadette Andrea is the Celia Jacobs Endowed Professor in British Literature, Department of English at the University of Texas at San Antonio. Her research and teaching interests include Renaissance/early modern studies, women's studies, literary and cultural theory; interactions between Islam and the West in the early modern period, early modern discourses of empire, postcolonial approaches to the early modern; and contemporary women's writing from the Islamic world. Her recent books include *English Women Staging Islam, 1696–1707* (University of Toronto, 2012); *Early Modern England and Islamic Worlds*, with Linda McJannet (Palgrave Macmillan, 2011); and *Women and Islam in Early Modern English Literature* (Cambridge University Press, 2007).

Katharine Beutner is an Assistant Professor of English at the University of Hawai'i at Mānoa, where she teaches literature and creative writing. Her dissertation, *Writing for Pleasure or Necessity: Conflict among Literary Women, 1700–1750*, focused on Delarivier Manley, Eliza Haywood, Martha Fowke Sansom, and Laetitia Pilkington. Her novel *Alcestis* won the 2011 Edmund White Award for Debut Fiction.

Toni Bowers is Professor of English and gender studies at the University of Pennsylvania. She regularly teaches, lectures, and publishes on Manley and is especially interested in the ideological investments that fueled Manley's writing across many genres. Bowers's most recent study of Manley's work may be found in *Force or Fraud: British Seduction Stories and the Problem of Resistance, 1660–1760* (Oxford). She is currently working on a new monograph provisionally entitled *Imagining Union*, on the metaphors writers used, between the ascension of James I in 1603 and the middle of the eighteenth century, to construct Great Britain, an amalgam of two hitherto separate nations, England and Scotland.

Rachel Carnell, Professor of English at Cleveland State University, is the author of *Partisan Politics, Narrative Realism, and the Rise of the British Novel* and of *A Political Biography of Delarivier Manley*. She is the editor (with Ruth Herman) of the five-volume *Selected Works of Delarivier Manley*, and she has published articles on Aphra Behn,

Samuel Richardson, Eliza Haywood, Charlotte Lennox, Jane Austen, and Anne Brontë.

Jennifer Frangos is an Associate Professor of English at the University of Missouri–Kansas City. She has published essays on Aphra Behn, Delarivier Manley, Anne Lister, eighteenth-century ghost stories, and transatlantic pedagogy and is an editor of the academic journal *The Eighteenth Century: Theory and Interpretation* and coeditor of the collection *Teaching the Transatlantic Eighteenth Century*.

Aleksondra Hultquist is an Honorary Researcher at the Centre of Excellence for the History of Emotion, 1100–1800, and a Managing Editor of *ABO: Interactive Journal for Women in the Arts, 1640–1830*. She has published articles on Eliza Haywood and Aphra Behn and is currently finishing her monograph, *The Amatory Mode*.

Victoria Joule is a Lecturer in English literature at the University of Exeter. In her research, she examines women's writing and generic developments, in particular the relationship between life-writing, the novel, and theater. She has published related articles on writers including Delarivier Manley, Mary Davys, and Charlotte Lennox in *Women's Writing*, *Journal for Eighteenth-Century Studies*, and *Rylands Bulletin*, and she is the English literature specialist reviews editor for the *Journal for Eighteenth-Century Studies*.

Erin M. Keating is an Assistant Professor in the Department of English, Film, and Theatre at the University of Manitoba. Her research brings together Restoration theatre, secret history, and affect theory and has been published in *Restoration* and in *The Journal of Popular Culture*. Her latest article focuses on the secret histories written about Charles II and is forthcoming from the *Journal for Early Modern Cultural Studies*.

Misty Krueger is an Assistant Professor of English at the University of Maine at Farmington. She has published essays on Delarivier Manley, Restoration-era adaptations of Shakespearean drama, Jane Austen, and William Blake. Her work addresses revenge, gender, sexuality, adaptation, and pedagogy.

Elizabeth J. Mathews is a PhD candidate at the University of California, Irvine. She has published an essay on Aphra Behn's rhetoric of emotion in *ABO* and is currently working on a study called "Bad Writing: Responses to Early Gothic Fiction and the Cultivation of Emotional Taste."

Jean McBain is a PhD candidate in history at the University of Melbourne, where she is working on a thesis provisionally titled *Liberty, Licence and Libel: Press Freedom and British Periodicals, 1695–1740*. This continues her research program on periodicals, developed in an MA thesis on the participatory dynamic of the early eighteenth-century press. Publications include a forthcoming chapter on Daniel Defoe's *Review*, and McBain's ongoing projects continue to focus on the more obscure periodical writings of canonical authors of the early eighteenth century.

Chris Mounsey is Professor of English at the University of Winchester. He has published widely on sexuality and disability, developing the term "variability" to replace the opposition dis/abled in his latest collection of essays *The Idea of Disability in the Eighteenth Century* (Bucknell, 2014). His work on women writers has centered on the formation of the early English novel.

Nicola Parsons is a Senior Lecturer at the University of Sydney. Her research focuses on the early eighteenth-century novel, in particular novels by women. Her first book, *Reading Gossip in Early Eighteenth Century England,* was published by Palgrave in 2009. She is currently completing a book manuscript, entitled *Form and Matter in the Early Eighteenth-Century Novel,* which focuses on transformations of romance by women novelists including Eliza Haywood, Jane Barker, and Elizabeth Rowe.

Kirsten T. Saxton is Professor of English at Mills College in Oakland, California; she writes on eighteenth-century British literature with a focus on gender, crime, and narrative. Her most recent book is *Deadly Plots: Narratives of Women and Murder in England, 1680–1760.* She is the scholarly editor of *ABO: Interactive Journal for Women in the Arts, 1640–1830* and is currently working on detective fiction by women, female pulp fiction, and a novel.

Kim Simpson is completing her PhD at the University of Kent in Canterbury. Her thesis, entitled "The 'Little Arts' of Amatory Fiction: Identity, Performance, and Process," analyzes the ways in which amatory fiction corresponds to and foreshadows postmodern theories of writing and identity. Simpson's wider research interests include anonymous fiction in the long eighteenth century, performativity, masquerade, the body, lovesickness, as well as feminist and queer theory.

Earla Wilputte is Professor of English at St. Francis Xavier University in Nova Scotia. Her books include *Passions and Language in Eighteenth-Century Literature: The Aesthetic Sublime in the Work of Eliza Haywood, Aaron Hill, and Martha Fowke* (Palgrave, 2014); *The Adventures of Eovaai* (Broadview, 1999); and *Three Novellas by Eliza Haywood* (Michigan State, 1995). She has also published numerous articles on Haywood, Hill, and Fowke as well as on Manley, Henry Fielding, Aphra Behn, and Margaret Cavendish.

Index

adaptation studies 8, 122–4
Addison, Joseph 190
adultery 33, 35, 37, 40, 44, 124,
    127–30 *see also* marriage
affect: and incest 90 n. 45; and negative
    feelings 80–3, 88 n. 19, 89 n. 31, 89
    n. 34; and seduction 75–7, 78, 86; 90
    n. 40; and poetry 148, 161; as a term
    124; *see also* emotion
Ahmed, Sara 90 n. 40
Albemarle, Lord 20–1, 75
Allan, David 206, 212 n. 24
amatory fiction: definition 103 n. 10,
    103 n. 24, 106, 157, 165; and theater
    90 n. 46; as genre 201 *see also*
    seduction narratives
Andrea, Bernadette 53 n. 1, 54 n. 7
Anne, Queen 15–16, 18, 24–6, 29
    n. 44, 47, 177–9, 195, 209; *The
    Arabian Nights' Entertainments*
    44–45, 53 n. 4
Aravamudan, Srinivas 68 n. 17
Armitage, David 68 n. 14
asexuality 92–3, 98–100, 102, 103 n. 4
Astell, Mary 36
Athenian Mercury 190, 198 n. 20

Backscheider, Paula 5, 148
Ballaster, Ros: as feminocentric 157,
    201; "Manl(e)y Forms" 211 n. 6;
    The New Atalantis 87 n. 7, 212
    n. 36; *Seductive Forms* 27 n. 1, 86
    n. 3, 88 n. 21, 93, 103 n. 10, 103
    n. 24, 112–13, 131 n. 1, 167 n. 13
Bannet, Eve Tavor 210 n. 4
Barad, Karen 114, 117
Barash, Carol 157
Barber, John 4, 17, 22–3, 100, 105 n. 46
Barry, Elizabeth 147, 151 n. 54, 152
    n. 55, 169 n. 34
Bath, Lord 21
Bath-Albemarle lawsuit 3, 16, 20–1

Behn, Aphra *Agnes de Castro* 118
    n. 3; *Astrea* 157, 163, 165, 169
    n. 44; *The Fair Jilt* 38–9, 119 n. 21;
    *Love-Letters between a Nobleman
    and his Sister* 79; *The Lucky Chance*
    138; "On Desire" 133 n. 18; *The
    Rover* 141–6, 148–9; *The Younger
    Brother* 57
Bennet, Isabella 180
Bentinck, William 78
Betterton, Thomas 153, 173–4, 176
Bhabha, Homi 59
bigamy 18, 20, 103 n. 23 *see also*
    marriage
Black, Jeremy 194
Blackstone, William 39
Blouch, Christine 162
body: colonized 69 n. 25; disgust 89
    n. 31; disfigured 61; dying 75–6;
    erotic 56 n. 48; female 79–82; 88
    n. 10; passions 120 n. 43,125;
    pregnancy 89 n. 30, 106–9, 120
    n. 39; 112–17, 118 n. 6;
    victimized 68 n. 10
Bond, Donald F. 190
Bowers, Toni: "Achievement" x; *Force
    or Fraud* 184–5, 86–7 n. 3, 88 n. 25,
    92, 99, 101, 104 n. 29 and 40,
    132 n. 2
Bracegirdle, Anne 54 n. 10, 75, 89
    n. 32, 90 n. 41, 147
Braden, Gordon 63
Brady, Nicholas 78, 89 n. 32, 186 n. 62
Brant, Clare 197, 211 n. 6
Bratton, Jacky 138
Brown, Laura x, 59, 139, 150 n. 12
Bullard, Rebecca 15, 28 n. 8, 78, 86, 86
    n. 3, 88 n. 16, 90 n. 46, 103 n. 11,
    205
Bush-Bailey, Gilli 146, 149 n. 4, 151
    n. 50
Butler, Judith x, 108–112, 114

Carlisle, James 100
Carnell, Rachel *The New Atalantis* 58,
   183, 206, *The Adventures of Rivella*
   104 n. 40, 167 n. 13, 197 n. 8, 199
   n. 34, 211 n. 22 *Letters Writen*
   171–4; *Political Biography* 2–4, 32,
   40, 53 n. 1, 54 n. 10, 55 n. 31 and
   32, 87 n. 3, 105 n. 46, 114, 132 n. 2,
   149 n. 4, 155, 162, 166 n. 4, 176,
   184 n. 6, 188–9, 196, 212–13 n. 38;
   "Reading Austen" 29 n. 4
Casellas, Jésus López-Peláez 64, 66
Ceranowski, Karli June 97, 104 n. 30
Champion, Justin 191
Chapman, George 44
Chardin, John 57, 58 f. 4.1, 61, 65–6
Charles II 3, 15, 16, 21, 22, 57, 90
   n. 46, 180, 183
Choudhury, Mita 59–61
Chudleigh, Lady Mary 21, 36
Churchill, John *see* Marlborough,
   Duke of
Churchill, Lady Mary 21
Churchill, Sarah, *see* Marlborough,
   Duchess of
Cibber, Katherine 147, 148
Cibber, Colley 45, 138–141, 146, 152
   n. 55 and 56
Cixous, Hélène 157, 168 n. 18
Clark, Constance 54 n. 10
Coke, Cary 164–5, 170 n. 55
Coke, Sir Edward 66, 164–5
Collier, Jeremy 139; *The Comparison
   between the Two Stages* 137, 149
   n. 1
Congreve, William 142, 144
Conway, Alison x
Cook, Elizabeth 196–7
Copeland, Nancy 141
Corporaal, Marguerite 51
Cottegnies, Line 212 n. 25
Coulson, Thomas 179–180, 186 n. 54
Cowper family 19–20
Croskery, Margaret Case 116
Cuder-Domínguez, Pilar 66, 71 n. 56
Curll, Edmund 17, 21–22, 167 n. 11,
   170 n. 59
Currer, Elizabeth 148

Defoe, Daniel 190
Dennis, John 43, 44–5, 48–9, 52, 53
   n. 3
deserted mistress 137–49, 151 n. 36,
   169 n. 41

desire: female 43, 77–8, 84, 85, 122,
   127, 131, 141, 144–5; lack of 92–3,
   97–102, 98, 102; and love 92, 97;
   performative 109; sexual 78–9, 85,
   86, 90 n. 45, 75, 77, 80–2, 84, 86,
   101, 102, 103 n. 4, 110, 115, 126,
   128, 129, 130, 207; vengeance 45–6,
   48–9, 146
Devonshire, Duke of 173–4, 176, 178
disease 124, 145
Dollimore, Jonathan 80, 89 n. 31
Donne, John 177
Dorset, Duke of (Lionel Sackville) 207
Dorset, Earl of (Charles Sackville)
   173–174
Drury Lane 4, 54 n. 10, 146–7, 153,
   162, 169 n. 39
Dryden, John: *Absalom and Achitophel*
   207; *Aureng-Zebe* 71 n. 56, *The
   Conquest of Granada* 44, 54 n. 12,
   57, *Of Dramatic Poesy* 30; *Nine
   Muses* 54 n. 12, 154, Varronian satire
   172–3, 202
Dunton, John 190

Eden, Richard 63
Edgeworth, Roger 62
Egerton, Sarah Fyge 53 n. 1, 86 n. 3,
   154, 159, 166 n. 6
Ellis, Frank H. 139
emotion 27 n. 3, 30, 80, 89 n. 34, 93–5,
   124–5, 133 n. 14, 139, 160, *see also*
   affect
empire 53 n. 4, 54 n. 7, 59–60, 62–4,
   66–7, 68 n. 14, 71 n. 63, 154, 159,
   200 n. 54
epistolary 25, 29 n. 44, 114, 171, 174,
   176–7, 188–97 *see also* letters
Etherege, George 144
Examiner 18, 26, 29 n. 44, 167 n. 13,
   188–197
Ezell, Margaret 156, 162, 167 n. 12

female friendship 25, 93, 94–5, 98, 154,
   156, 158, 162, 169 n. 39; *The Female
   Wits* 147, 153–156, 158–163, 165–6,
   169 n. 39, 172
feminism 97, 162, 167 n. 16,
   118–19 n. 10, 178, 217
   (proto-feminism 107)
feminist theory ix–xi; 97–8, 102
feminocentric 152 n. 60, 153, 155,
   156–8, 160, 163, 166, 168 n. 17
Field, Ophelia 24

Finch, Anne, Countess of Winchilsea
163–164, 169 n. 50, 208
Floyd-Wilson, Mary 64
Foucault, Michel 111
Freeman, Lisa 52

Gallagher, Catherine 27 n. 1, 31
Gay, John 177, 185 n. 41
Gentleman's Magazine 194
geocriticism 60
George I 22, 30–2, 40, 174
Gildon, Charles 17–18, 20, 22, 170
n. 59, 189
Gill, Pat 144
Girard, Rene 45–7
Gollapudi, Aparna 140
Gordon, Thomas 194
gossip 16, 18, 19, 28 n. 8, 29 n. 44,
86–7 n. 3, 95–6, 102, 106, 189
Granville, George 177 *see also*
Lansdowne
Granville, Mary 30 *see also* Lansdowne
Greenfield, Anne 75
Grosz, Elizabeth 113–14

Hall, John 62–3
Harley, Robert, Earl of Oxford 16,
23–4, 102, 195, 209, 210 n. 1
Hartwell, Abraham 63–4
Haynes, George 19
Haynes, Joseph 153
Hayton, D. W. 179
Haywood, Eliza: amatory writer 106,
157, 216; *Fantomina* 116; *Love in
Excess* 114, 118 n. 3; pregnancy
120 n. 39, professionalism 162, 167
n. 11; *Progress through the Passions*
133 n. 18: and proto-feminism
157–8
Herman, Ruth: *Business of Woman* 11
n. 9 and 12, 55 n. 32, 66, 84, 188,
199 n. 31; feminocentric 157, 167 n.
16; *Letters Writen* 171–2; Manley's
poetry 4; *The New Atalantis* 210
n. 4; *Rivella* 27 n. 2
Hollis-Berry, Elizabeth 61, 69 n. 25
Hook, Lucyle 153, 160–1, 160
n. 39, 172
Houston, Chloe 204
Hultquist, Aleksondra 119 n. 11 and
29, 20 n. 39, 120 n. 45, 133 n. 18
Hume, Robert D. 141, 150 n. 12 and 22
and 24
Hutcheon, Linda 123

ideology: and emotion 88 n. 19, 128;
political secret history 86–7 n. 3;
Whig 15, 118 n. 4, 208; of virtue 75,
77, 83, 86
imaginative prose fiction 216–17
imperial *see* empire
Ingrassia, Catherine 171
Irigaray, Luce 109, 116

Jacobite 30, 32, 47, 174, 177,
178, 194
Johnson, Samuel 194
Joule, Victoria 54 n. 9, 166 n. 6, 169
n. 34 and 41

Katz, Candice Brook 149 n. 4, 151
n. 36
Keating, Erin 87 n. 6, 88 n. 19, 89
n. 34, 90 n. 46, 103 n. 6, 118 n. 4
and 6, 119 n. 11
Kerrigan, John 47, 55 n. 31
Kerrigan, William 63
King, Kathryn 157
Kit Kat Club 173
Knight, Frances 147
Knolles, Richard 64, 66
Köster, Patricia 27 n. 5
Krueger, Misty 41 n. 44, 54 n. 6
Kuizenga, Donna 27 n. 2

Lansdowne, Lady (Mary Granville)
and Baron George *see also* Granville,
George and Granville, Mary 30–32
Lanser, Susan S. 93
letters *see also* epistolary 70 n. 35, 114,
167 n. 11, 175–6, 183, 186 n. 54,
188–96
Lincoln's Inn Fields 146, 153, 173; *see
also* Betterton, Thomas
Linker, Laura 118 n. 3
Lithgow, William 64–5
London Gazette 23, 150 n. 11
London Journal 191, 194, 196, 199
n. 34
London Magazine 194
Loomba, Ania 59
Lowenthal, Cynthia 66
love: incestuous 80; illicit 120 n. 55;
letters 29 n. 44, 181; as a passion
122–31, 144–5, 207; repentance 52;
resistance to 92, 95–8; and revenge
37, 39, 40; subservient 33; and virtue
119 n. 29; women in 85
Lyons, Paddy 34

Manley, Delarivier; *The Adventures of Rivella* 19–26, 92, 100–101, 108, 112–113, 156, 173, 175; *Almyna* 43–53; arrest for libel 3, 23; biography 2–4, 20–1; children 3, 20, 100; *The Fair Hypocrite* 122–31; *History of the Author of the Atalantis* 22; *The Husband's Resentment. In Two Examples* 30–40, 109; *Lady's Pacquet of Letters* 189; *Letters Writen* 171–84; *The Lost Lover* 137–49, 161–2, 171, 183; *Memoirs of Europe* 22, 157; *Memoirs of the Life of Mrs. Manley* 22; *Mrs. Manley's History of Her Own Life and Times* 17, 21–2; *The New Atalantis* 16, 18–19, 22–5, 75–86, 92–9, 106–7, 110–111, 154, 157, 163–5, 172, 183, 189, 201–10; *The Nine Muses* 137, 154; parents 2, 20, 62, 64; *The Physician's Stratagem* 111, 114–16; *The Power of Love* 30, 114, 122–5, 127–8, 130–1; *The Royal Mischief* 43, 57–67, 75, 77–8, 147, 171–2, 183; *The Wife's Resentment* 31, 36
Manley, John 3, 11 n. 6, 18, 20, 53 n. 1, 100
Marlborough, Duke of (John Churchill) 6, 21, 26, 175, 181, 191, 193–5, 208, 209
Marlborough, Duchess of (Sarah Churchill) 6, 16,18, 21, 23–6, 29 n. 44, 118 n. 6, 157, 161, 212 n. 38
marriage: adulterous 80, bigamous 80, 92; and law 35; Manley's to John Manley 3, 11, 18, 20, 53, 100, 103 n. 23; as political metaphor 31, 32; promise of 115; resistance to 93, 94–6, 99, 102; as reward 52, 78, 143, 146; unequal 38, 124–31; vows 120 n. 55 *see also* adultery *and* bigamy
Marsden, Jean I. 49, 56 n. 48, 75, 89 n. 32, 118 n. 10, 170 n. 56
Martyr, Peter 63
Mary II 171, 175, 176, 180, 182, 184
Masham, Abigail 18, 23–5, 38, 209
Masham, Lord 23
Mayer, Robert 123
Maynwaring, Arthur 18, 25, 212–13 n. 38; see also the *Medley*
McDowell, Paula 27 n. 1, 89 n. 28, 91 n. 57, 100–2, 104 n. 39, 152 n. 61, 161–2, 164–5, 169 n. 44, 188
Medina, Sir Solomon 191
Medley 18, 188, 190, 193, 196

miscellany 164, 169 n. 50, 189, 191, 192, 196, 217
Milks, Megan 97, 104 n. 30
Miller, Nancy K. 157
Minadoi, Giovanni Tommaso 63–64
Mist, Nathaniel 194
Moi, Toril 112
Monck, Christopher 21
Montague, Charles 179
Montagu, Elizabeth 55 n. 32
Montagu, Mary Wortley 59
Montagu, Ralph 21
Morgan, Fidelis 53 n. 1, 155, 162, 167 n. 8
Moryson, Fynes 64–65
Mounsey, Chris 3, 53 n. 1, 87 n. 5, 152 n. 60, 167 n. 13, 199 n. 40

new-Tory *see* Tory
Ngai, Sianne 80–1, 88 n. 19, 89 n. 31 and 34; *The Nine Muses* 3, 54 n. 12, 137, 153–4, 165, 166 n. 6, 173
Nu, Su Fang 54–5 n. 13

Orr, Bridget 55 n. 29 and 32, 71 n. 56
Otway, Thomas 76, 78, 151 n. 54

Painter, William 30–1, 34–7, 39, 114, 122–4, 125, 127, 128, 130–1
palimpsest 60, 62, 64, 65–6, 119 n. 29, 123, 129–31
Parsons, Nicola 86–7 n. 3, 189, 196
Payne, Linda R. 139
Pearson, Jacqueline 144
performance 75, 77, 89 n. 34, 109–11, 113, 115, 140, 146–8, 149 n. 4, 150 n. 11
performativity 89 n. 30, 106–13, 115, 119 n. 18
periodical 18, 156, 167 n. 13, 188–97, 198 n. 19
phallocentric 157, 168 n. 18
Philips, Katherine 138, 147–9, 152 n. 61, 161, 165, 169 n. 41 and 44
Pix, Mary 57, 67 n. 7, 153–4, 159, 164–5, 170 n. 55 and 56
pleasure 75, 78, 80, 82, 92, 118 n. 6, 122, 131, 163, 166, 206
poetry 137–8, 155, 157, 161, 163–6
Pollak, Ellen 82, 88 n. 13, 90 n. 45
Porter, Roy 115
Post-Boy 189–90
Powlett, Charles 180
Pratt, Mary Louise 59
pregnancy 78, 79, 82, 115, 116

queer theory 7, 68 n. 10, 93, 98, 102, 107–8, 117

Rabb, Melinda Alliker 79, 89 n. 28, 105 n. 46, 210 n. 4
rake 54 n. 9, 138, 139–44, 148
readership 22, 189
Reeve, Clara 4
reform of character 43, 48, 50, 52, 138–40, 143
Restoration-era drama 43, 57, 66, 75, 76, 80, 88 n. 19, 89 n. 34, 106, 140, 151 n. 54
Richetti, John J. 86 n. 3, 118 n. 9
Roberts, John 22, 191, 199 n. 34
La Rochefoucauld 19, 206, 212 n. 25 and 26
roman à clef, see secret history
Rooney, Caroline 108–11, 113
Roosen, William 183
Roper, Abel 190
Ross, Alexander 62, 70 n. 35
Ross, Deborah 107, 118 n. 7
Rowe, Nicholas 48, 53 n. 3, 78
Rubik, Margarete 71 n. 63, 139

Sacheverell, Henry 26
Sackville, Charles, *see* Dorset, Earl of
Sackville, Lionel, *see* Dorset, Duke of
Said, Edward 60, 68 n. 17, 69 n. 19
Sansom, Martha Fowke 158, 167 n. 11
Santesso, Aaron 86–7 n. 3, 172
Sargent, Carole Fungaroli 86–7 n. 3, 166 n. 6
satire: feminocentric 155, 156, 157, 158, 160, 168 n. 19; literary 31, 77, 83, 84, 153, 162, 189, 193; Menippean 202; political 25, 26, 29 n. 44, 75, 86–7 n. 3, 104 n. 39, 164, 184; theatrical 143, 144, 147, 148, 150 n. 12; Varronian 87 n. 5, 167 n. 13, 171–80, 183, 199 n. 40, 202
Saxton, Kirsten T. 31–2, 216
secret history 15–26, 28 n. 8, 53 n. 1, 75, 76, 86, 86–7 n. 3, 104 n. 40, 167 n. 13, 189, 197, 197 n. 8 and 9, 201, 207, 208
seduction 68 n. 10, 75, 88 n. 21, 93–4, 103 n. 23, 104, 107, 108, 111, 113, 115, 141, 201, 205
seduction narratives 75, 76, 78–9, 82–3, 86, 86–7 n. 3, 88 n. 25, 90 n. 46, 107, *see also* amatory fiction
sentiment/al 48, 94, 124, 137–41, 147, 149
servitude 30–1, 34, 40

sexuality 89 n. 28, 92, 97–8, 102, 127, 137, 141, 142
Seymour, Edward 179–80, 186 n. 54
Shadwell, Thomas 141, 144
Skipwith, Sir Thomas 173–4, 176
Somerset, Henry, Duke of Beaufort 85, 99
Spectator 190
St. John, Henry, Viscount Bolingbroke 23
Staves, Susan 118 n. 9, 161, 169 n. 44
Steele, Richard 23, 53 n. 1, 139, 156, 190 see also *London Gazette* and *Spectator*
Sunderland, Earl of 26
Swift, Jonathan: editor of *Examiner* 18, 26, 29 n. 44, 188–9, 193–4; friend to Manley 105 n. 46; 169 n. 50; Manley replacing as editor 167 n. 13; satire 79; Tory pamphlets 16, see also the *Examiner*

Tauchert, Ashley 116, 118 n. 10
Taylor, Elizabeth 163
Temple, Kathryn 27 n. 3
Thompson, Phyllis Ann 120 n. 43
Tidcomb, John 173–6, 184 n. 14
Tilly, John 3, 18–21, 53 n. 1, 100, 105 n. 46
Todd, Janet 107
Toland, John 190–191, 198 n. 27
toleration 191–2, 198 n. 27
Tollemache, Thomas 171, 175, 180–2, 184
Tory: allegory 84, 104 n. 29; ideology 22, 55 n. 29, 91 n. 61, 183, 191, 195; new-Tory 6, 99, 104 n. 40, 132 n. 2; policies 24–6; propaganda 4, 16, 17, 18, 55 n. 31, 167 n. 13, 172–4, 188; satire 176–80; secret histories 16
tragedy: heroic 43–5, 60–1, satiric 153; civic 48; pathetic 75–6, 80, 86, 88 n. 19
Trenchard, John 194
Trotter, Catharine 48, 57, 152 n. 61, 153–4, 159, 161, 165, 166 n. 4, 167 n. 16, 169 n. 42

Vanbrugh, Sir John 139–140
Verbruggen, Susanna 147
virtue: sexual/female 32, 36, 76–86, 88 n. 19 and 21, 91 n. 61, 92, 95–99, 101, 104 n. 39, 106, 110, 114, 117, 119 n. 29, 123, 124, 126–31, 139, 147–8, 207; heroic 44, 48, 52

vows 43, 45, 52, 93, 120 n. 55, 130, 132 n. 2, 144

Wann, Louis 65
Warner, William B. 77–8, 88 n. 21, 167 n. 16
Weekly Journal or Saturday's Post 194
Weinbrot, Howard 202, 211 n. 8
Whig: ideology 118 n. 4, 208, 210; Junto 179, 184, 190, 195; Manley's relationship to 23, 173–5, 179; and *New Atalantis* 78–9, 98, 201; politics 21–2, 24–26, 171, 173, 180, 190–6; satire 28 n. 8, 171, 174, 176, 183, 199 n. 40; secret histories 15–8, 22, 86, 208

Wilkes, Wetenhall 117
Wilks, Robert 54 n. 10
William III 171, 175, 176, 180–4, 208
Wilson, Brett D. 48, 54 n. 5
women writers: attacks 153–9; models 146–9, 161–4, 168 n. 19, 169 n. 44; strategies 137–8; transgression 118 n. 10; and the passions 120 n. 43
women's studies ix–xi

Young, Edward 52

Zelinsky, Katherine 5, 112